Access Control Management in Cloud Environments

Hua Wang • Jinli Cao • Yanchun Zhang

Access Control Management in Cloud Environments

 Springer

Hua Wang
Victoria University
Melbourne
VIC, Australia

Jinli Cao
Comp Sci & Comp Eng
La Trobe University
Bundoora
VIC, Australia

Yanchun Zhang
Victoria University
Melbourne
VIC, Australia

ISBN 978-3-030-31731-7   ISBN 978-3-030-31729-4   (eBook)
https://doi.org/10.1007/978-3-030-31729-4

This Springer imprint is published by the registered company Springer Nature Switzerland AG
The registered company address is: Gewerbestrasse 11, 6330 Cham, Switzerland

For family members: Lili Sun, Kate Wang, and Dana Zhang

Preface

This book introduces new business concepts on cloud environments such as secure, scalable anonymity and practical payment protocols for the Internet of Things and Blockchain technology. The protocol uses electronic cash for payment transactions. In this new protocol, from the viewpoint of banks, consumers can improve anonymity if they are worried about the disclosure of their identities in the cloud. Currently, there is no such type of book available that reports the techniques covering the protocols with anonymizations and Blockchain technology. Thus, comparing to other published books, this book has included more technology for students and researchers in universities.

This book benefits the researchers by providing new ideas based on access control and Blockchain techniques and how role-based access control methods can be applied to widely distributed and used heterogeneous catalog systems in rapidly increasing cloud environments. The management of relationships among users, roles, and permissions currently requires further development. No similar book is available to help in this way.

This book also gives a new direction for access control management and online business with new challenges within Blockchain technology that may arise in cloud environments. One such challenge is related to the authorization granting process. For example, when a role is granted to a user, this role may conflict with other roles of the user or together with this role; the user may have or derive a high level of authority. Another is related to the authorization revocation. For instance, when a role is revoked from a user, the user may still have the role. The experts tackle these challenges through the developed methodology for authorization granting algorithm and weak revocation and strong revocation algorithms.

Melbourne, VIC, Australia   Hua Wang

Melbourne, VIC, Australia   Yanchun Zhang

Bundoora, VIC, Australia   Jinli Cao
July 2020

Acknowledgements

We express our sincere gratitude and appreciation to Professor Stephen Gray of the Victoria University for his invaluable advice and encouragement during the realization of this research. It is his love for his staff and dedication to research that made them available whenever I needed during all these years. If it was not for him, we may not be getting this book.

We sincerely thank the Institute for Sustainable Industries and Liveable Cities, VU Research, Victoria University for providing the excellent work environment and the financial support. It is a great pleasure to work at the institute.

Finally, our appreciation goes to our family members, Lili Sun, Kate Wang, and Dana Zhang, for their love and affection. We would not be able to complete the book without their encouragement and support.

Contents

Part I
Description

Cloud computing and the Internet of things, including online business, are widely used. The number of world-wide Internet users tripled between 1993 and 1995 to 60 million, and by 2017 there were 3.6 billion users. Online business in cloud environments, especial mobile service system, allows their users to access a large set of traditional and contemporary services without being tethered to one particular physical location. With the increasing use of online service systems for security sensitive application that can be expected in the future, the provision of secure services becomes more important.

This book introduces a bridge between the existing technologies and the online service theory in cloud environments. It aims to provide a foundation for the improvement of technology to aid electronic service application. As a validation, several technologies for online business service have been enhanced and improved in the book.

It is structured in five parts:

Part I: Introduction of E-commerce systems and Untraceable E-cash systems (Chaps. 1–3);
Part II: Tickets for flexible M-services and A self-scalable payment approach with role-based access control (RBAC) model (Chaps. 4–6);
Part III: Role-based access control features with object constraint language and negative authorization (Chaps. 7–8);
Part IV: Using RBAC for ubiquitous computing and social networks (Chaps. 9–10);
Part V: Access control policy model, information sharing and access management with blockchain technology (Chaps. 11–13);

The Part I consists of three Chaps. 1–3. It first introduces motivations, objectives and organization of the book, and also technology issues in e-commerce systems. After a framework for electronic commerce is analysed, an untraceable electronic cash system in the Internet of Things is designed.

Chapter 1
Introduction

This chapter presents the motivation and objectives of this book. There are three sections in the chapter. In the first section, overview and motivation of the book are presented. It consists of Cloud computing, Internet of Things, and access control management. Three technology issues in e-commerce with their unsolved problems are introduced in access control management. The objectives and organization of this book are described in the second and third section respectively.

1.1 Overview and Motivation

1.1.1 Cloud Computing

Cloud computing is the on-demand availability of computational resources, such as data storage and computing power, without direct involvement from users. Cloud computing is generally used to describe data centers available to many users over the Internet. Large clouds, predominant today, often have functions distributed over multiple locations from central servers. Clouds may be limited to a single organization (enterprise clouds), be available to many organizations (public cloud), or a combination of both (hybrid cloud) [19, 76].

Cloud computing, briefly say, is the delivery of computing services including servers, storage, databases, networking, software, analytics and intelligence over the cloud to offer faster innovation, flexible resources and economies of scale as shown in Fig. 1.1. Typically, customers pay for cloud services as they go, helping them lower operating costs, applying infrastructure more efficient https://azure.microsoft.com/.

Cloud computing relies on sharing of resources to achieve aims of business and economies. One benefit of cloud computing is to allow companies to avoid or minimize up-front IT infrastructure costs. Cloud computing also allows enterprises

© Springer Nature Switzerland AG 2020
H. Wang et al., *Access Control Management in Cloud Environments*,
https://doi.org/10.1007/978-3-030-31729-4_1

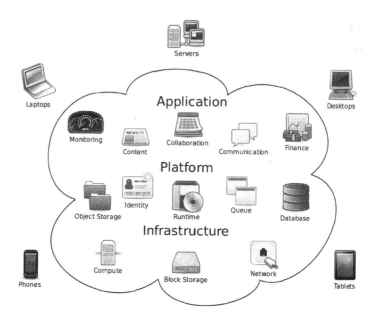

Fig. 1.1 Cloud computing model

to get their applications up and running faster, with improved manageability and less maintenance, and that it enables IT teams to more rapidly adjust resources to meet fluctuating and unpredictable demand [38, 58, 83]. Cloud providers typically use a "pay-as-you-go" model, which can lead to unexpected operating expenses if administrators are not familiarized with cloud-pricing models [22, 85, 91].

Cloud computing has seen a tremendous growth that has reformed the landscape of computing with its storage, elastic resources, easy and fast deployment and reduced costs such that, it instigated many organizations to move their data in the cloud. Even though cloud services provide massive benefits, it still suffers from several security threats. For instance, users are not aware of the massive amount of data stored with the cloud service provider. Due to lack of transparency, it is difficult to be aware of where, how and when the data is processed and therefore makes it difficult to trust the service provider, who in turn can also be a reason for huge data loss. There has been several schemes and developments in the area of cloud security [7, 43, 46, 73].

Data outsourcing is a major component for cloud computing because data owners are able to distribute resources to external services for sharing with users and organizations. A crucial problem for owners is how to secure sensitive information accessed by legitimate users only using the trusted services. The problem was addressed with access control methods to enforce selective access to outsourced data without involving the owner in authorization [34, 69, 73, 88]. The basic idea is to combine cryptography with authorizations, and data owners are assigned to various roles that will enforce access via encryption. A formal access model is designed to analyze a translating authorization policy into an equivalent encryption policy. The paper is also investigated the effect of role hierarchy structure in an authorization process. The role based access management methods are implemented with XACML by using Identity Servers.

The name of "cloud computing" is appeared in recent years, the concept of data as a service, storage as a service, software, platform, and infrastructure as a service has been investigated for a long time. To provide computation as a public utility as water and electricity, new challenges arise for the confidentiality, availability and integrity of the outsourced data in cloud environment. Many research papers have been published on the topics of data management, software as a service and infrastructure as a service, but security research for cloud computing is still in its early stage, especially for access control to outsourced data. The traditional access control management does not fit very well for cloud computing because its highly dynamic and distributed customers and data owners.

Cloud computing has attracted attentions from both academia and industry applications from the beginning. Cloud Security Alliance has recently published a document about secure data storage and management which is an important component of cloud computing (cloudsecurityalliance.org/guidance/csaguide.v3.0. pdf). In the guidance, a secure outsourced data system should be assessed from at least the following aspects: (1) strong encryption and scalable key management; (2) user provisioning, de-provisioning, and information lifecycle management; and (3) system availability and performance [70, 74, 90].

1.1.2 Internet of Things

The Internet of Things (IoT) is the extension of Internet connectivity into physical devices and everyday objects [84]. Embedded with electronics, Internet connectivity, and other forms of hardware (such as sensors), these devices can communicate and interact with others over the Internet, and they can be remotely monitored and controlled as described in Fig. 1.2.

The definition of the Internet of Things has evolved due to the convergence of multiple technologies, real-time analytics, machine learning, commodity sensors, and embedded systems [54, 75, 92]. Traditional fields of embedded systems, wireless sensor networks, control systems, automation (including home and building automation), and others all contribute to enabling the Internet of Things. In the consumer market, IoT technology is most synonymous with products pertaining to the concept of the "smart home", covering devices and appliances (such as lighting fixtures, thermostats, home security systems and cameras, and other home appliances) that support one or more common ecosystems, and can be controlled via devices associated with that ecosystem, such as smartphones and smart speakers.

The Internet is a global system of networks that interconnect computers using the standard Internet protocol suite [18, 37, 39, 57]. It has significant impact on the world as it can serve billions of users worldwide. Millions of private,

Fig. 1.2 The Internet of Things

public, academic, business, and government networks, of local to global scope, all contribute to the formation of the Internet. The traditional Internet has a focus on computers and can be called the Internet of Computers. In contrast, evolving from the Internet of Computers, the Internet of Things (IoT) emphasizes things rather than computers. It aims to connect everyday objects, such as coats, shoes, watches, ovens, washing machines, bikes, cars, even humans, plants, animals, and changing environments, to the Internet to enable communication/interactions between these objects. The ultimate goal of IoT is to enable computers to see, hear and sense the real world. It is predicted by Ericsson that the number of Internet-connected things will reach 50 billion by 2020. Electronic devices and systems exist around us providing different services to the people in different situations: at home, at work, in their office, or driving a car on the street. IoT also enables the close relationship between human and opportunistic connection of smart things [35, 42, 71, 81].

Due to the proliferation of embedded devices in IoT, effective device security mechanisms are essential to the development of IoT technologies and applications. National Intelligence Council argues that, to the extent that everyday objects become information security risks, the IoT could distribute those risks far more widely than the Internet has to date. For example, RFID security presents many challenges [2, 43, 60, 72]. Potential solutions should consider aspects from hardware and wireless protocol security to the management, regulation and sharing of collected RFID data. Moreover, it is argued that there is still no generic framework for deploying and extending traditional security mechanisms over a variety of pervasive systems. Regarding security concerns of the network layer, it is suggested that the Internet can be gradually encrypted and authenticated based on the observations that the recent advances in implementation of cryptographic algorithms have made general purpose processors capable of encrypting packets at high rates. But how to generalize such algorithms to IoT would be challenging as things in IoT normally only maintain low transmission rates and connections are usually intermittent.

IoT Data Taxonomy

The main techniques and state-of-the-art research efforts in IoT from data-centric perspectives are reviewed in paper [57, 83, 86]. It includes data stream processing, data storage models, complex event processing, and searching in IoT. The intrinsic characteristics of IoT data are classified into three categories, including Data Generation, Data Quality, and Data Interoperability.

Data Generation

Velocity In IoT, data can be generated at different rates. For example, for GPS-enabled moving vehicles in road networks, the GPS signal sampling frequency could be every few seconds, every few minutes, or even every half an hour. But some sensors can scan at a rate up to 1,000,000 sensing elements per second. On one hand, it is challenging to handle very high sampling rates, which require efficient processing of the fast generated data. On the other hand, it is also challenging to deal with low sampling rates, due to the fact that some important information may be lost during data processing and decision making.

Scalability Since things are able to continuously generate data together with the foreseeable excessively large number of things, the IoT data is expected to be at an extremely large scale. It is easy to image that, in IoT data processing systems, scalability will be a long standing issue, aligning with the current Big Data trend.

Dynamics There are many dynamic elements within IoT data. Firstly, many things are mobile, which will lead to different locations at different times. Since they will move to different environments, the sensing results of things will also be changing to reflect the real world. Secondly, many things are fragile. This means the generated data will change overtime due to the failure of things. Thirdly, the connections between things could be intermittent. This also creates dynamics in any IoT data processing system.

Heterogeneity There will be many kinds of things potentially connecting to the Internet in the future, ranging from cars, robots, fridges, mobile phones, to shoes, plants, watches, and so on. These kinds of things will generate data in different formats using different vocabularies. In addition, there will be assorted IoT data processing systems, which will also provide data in customized formats to tailor different data needs.

Data Quality

Uncertainty In IoT, uncertainty may come from different sources. In RFID data, the uncertainty can refer to missing readings, readings of non-existing IDs, etc. In wireless sensor networks, uncertainty can refer to sensing precision (the degree of reproducibility of a measurement), or accuracy (the maximum difference that will exist between the actual value and the indicated value), etc.

Redundancy Redundancy can also be easily observable in IoT. For example, in RFID data, the same tags can be read multiple times at the same location (because multiple RFID readers exist at spots or tags are read multiple times at the same spots) or at different locations. In wireless sensor networks, a group of sensors of the same type may also be deployed in a nearby area, which can produce similar sensing results of that area. For the same sensor, due to the possible high sampling rates, redundant sensing data can be produced.

Ambiguity Dealing with a large amount of ambiguity in IoT data is inevitable. The data produced by assorted things can be interpreted in different ways due to different data needs from different things or other data consumers. Such data can also be useful and important to any other kinds of things, which brings about the challenges of proper interpretation of the produced data to different data consumers.

Inconsistency Inconsistency is also prevalent in IoT data. For example, in RFID data, inconsistency can occur due to missing readings of tags at some locations along the supply chain. It is also easy to observe inconsistency in sensing data as when multiple sensors are monitoring the same environment and reporting sensing results. Due to the precision and accuracy of the sensing process and other problems including packet loss during transmission, data inconsistency is also an intrinsic characteristic in sensing data.

Data Interoperability

Incompleteness In order to process IoT data, being able to detect and react to events in real-time, it is important to combine data from different types of data sources to build a big and complete picture of relevant backgrounds of the real world. However, as this process relies on the cooperation of mobile and distributed things who are generating relevant background data, incompleteness is easily observable in IoT data. Suppose there are a large number of available data sources, it is of great importance to determine which data sources can best address the incompleteness of data for a given data processing task.

Semantics To address the challenges posed by the deluge of IoT data, things, or machines acting as the major data consumers should be a promising trend for data processing in the IoT era. Inspired by Semantic Web technologies, in order to enable machines to understand data for human beings, injecting semantics into data could be an initial step. Therefore, semantics within IoT data will play an important role in the process of enabling things/machines to understand and process IoT data by themselves.

1.1.3 Access Control Management

Mobile Service System

E-commerce is revolutionizing the way we work. Its impact is already being felt in consumer goods sales and will be much more widespread in the future. Mobile service systems, as an important subject, extend usages of e-commerce [3, 41, 67, 87]. Mobile commerce is a subset of e-commerce which continues to see phenomenal growth, but so far most e-commerce involves wired infrastructures. Emerging wireless and mobile networks create new opportunities in e-commerce and increased growth. A *mobile service system* (or *M-commerce*) is defined as any type of transaction of an economic value that is conducted through a terminal that uses a wireless telecommunications network for communication with an e-commerce infrastructure.

During the early 1980s, cellular telephone systems experienced rapid growth in Europe, particularly in the United Kingdom and Germany. Each country developed its own system, which was incompatible with everyone else's in equipment and operation. This was undesirable, because not only was a mobile equipment limited to operation within national boundaries, but there was also a very limited market for each type of equipment, so economies of scale and the consequent savings could not be realized [28, 29, 32, 47, 53].

In 1983, a group called the Global System Mobile (GSM) was setup for mobile unified standards. The first version of the GSM specifications were published in 1990. Commercial service was started in mid-1991, and by 1993 there were 36 GSM networks in 22 countries [6, 9, 13, 64]. Over 200 GSM networks are operational in 110 countries around the world. In the beginning of 1994, there were 1.3 million subscribers worldwide [3], which has grown to more than 55 million by October 1997.

Mobile service systems are becoming extremely popular, which makes the provision of services to mobile users an attractive business area [49]. Mobile service can be regarded as a special form of e-commerce, where users buy services instead of products from service providers via the network because services are much wider that products. From a technology perspective, mobile communication systems have been made possible by two factors: advances in wireless communications, and portable devices that are readily available on the market for decreasing costs.

The first has resulted in a number of wireless access network technological telephones, such as, cellular telephone networks and wireless LANs (local area network). Examples of the second are high performance laptop computers, handheld palmtop devices with considerable computing power, and portable sets with increasing functionality. From a business perspective, mobile service systems are possible because mobility is a big attraction for users. Mobile telephones, for instance, have gained more popularity among users than anyone predicted. In Europe, the number of mobile subscribers was 22 million in 1995 and was estimated to reach more than 110 million by 2000 [10]. In Finland and several other countries, the number of mobile subscriptions has already exceeded the figures for fixed telephone lines. The growing success and popularity of mobile communication systems makes the mobile services to be a benefit business area. Therefore, a great number and variety of service providers are expected to appear on the mobile market in the near future.

There are a number of proposals for mobile systems [30, 51, 52], though all of them lack flexibility in security management. The Global system for mobile communications [51], for example, provides mechanisms for user authentication as well as integrity and confidentiality, including protection of information exchanged between the mobile terminal and the fixed network. It provides, however, only limited privacy protection for users by hiding their real identities from eavesdroppers on the radio interface [40, 52, 66]. Another contemporary mobile communication system CDPD [30] provides similar security services, however, there are some other issues and problems in mobile commerce, which need to be addressed:

Global Solution Current solutions only solve particular service problems for mobile users. Users have to change the mobile service systems in order to do other business on the Internet. This is not convenient for users.

Clear Charging Mobile users wish to see a clear and continuously up-dated bill for provided services. Users do not like receiving an account statement only monthly or bi-monthly, but like to be able to check it at anytime.

Trustworthiness In most cases of buying services, we assume that mobile users trust service providers to bill their service usage correctly and not to misuse user and service usage related information. This kind of trust model is not adequate for future mobile communication systems. With the rapidly growing number of service providers, most of which are new on the market and unknown to the users, this assumption is no longer justified. This requires mechanisms that guarantee correct and indisputable billing and ensures anonymous service usage.

Scalability Future mobile communication systems aim at offering access to any service, anywhere, at anytime. The mechanisms of current mobile communication systems are not sufficiently scalable to be able to fulfill this requirement. Traditional solutions for implementing user mobility rely on cross domain authentication and roaming agreements. A user, when visiting a foreign domain and accessing a service there, has to authenticate himself to the foreign service provider with the help of his home domain agent. This may involve a potentially time consuming authentication protocol over long distances. Furthermore, cross domain authentication requires the

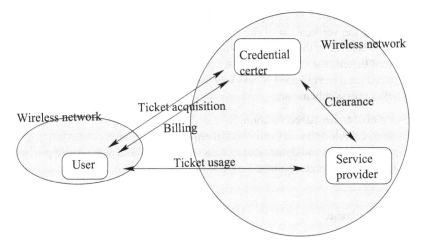

Fig. 1.3 Ticket model

foreign service provider to trust the home domain agent of the user. Today, this trust is based on roaming agreements between various service providers. With the rapidly growing number of service providers, however, roaming agreements are becoming inefficient and no longer feasible. New mechanisms are needed that do not require contact with the home domain of the user when accessing services in a foreign domain, nor business agreements between domains.

In the future, mobile service systems should provide global solutions for all kinds of mobile services and guarantee higher levels of security than current systems. This means that, as well as requiring confidentiality and the protection of the integrity of message exchanged between the user and the service provider, and authentication of the user to the service provider, future systems should also require authentication of the service provider to the user and guarantee the user higher levels of privacy. Furthermore, clear billing has to be ensured.

A new approach is needed to address the above-mentioned problems. This approach is based on the Credential Centre, and a ticket-based mechanism for service access [5, 36, 44, 82]. The main idea is illustrated in Fig. 1.3.

In the first step, the Credential Centre issues tickets for users. In the second step, a ticket-based mechanism is implemented allowing users to remunerate service providers. Tickets can provide a flexible and scalable mechanism for mobile access [4, 8, 25, 26, 33, 61, 80].

There are three participants (User, Service provider, and Credential Centre) and a protocol with several sub protocols (ticket acquisition, ticket usage, clearance, and billing) in the model. Each user is registered with the Credential Centre. The user obtains tickets by running the ticket acquisition protocol with the Credential Centre. These tickets are used to access services anonymously. In the ticket usage protocol, the user presents an appropriate ticket to the service provider, which can verify the validity of the ticket and the legitimacy of the user to use it. While the user's private identity is not revealed in this protocol, the service provider authenticates itself to the user. If the verification of the ticket is successful, then the service provider provides the service to the user according to the conditions on the ticket. Based on the received tickets, the Credential Centre prepares a clear bill for each user.

We introduce a ticket based access scheme in this book. The main contributions of the ticket access scheme are:

1. It is a global ticket-based solution.
2. It is also scalable and users can check their account statement at anytime.
3. It is an anonymous and dynamic system, and new users and new service providers can join the system at anytime.

Electronic Payment

After providing a service, a service provider will ask consumers to pay for the service. There are a number of proposals for electronic payment [14, 24, 27, 31, 63]. David Chaum [14] first proposed an on-line payment system that would guarantee that valid coins are received. This system provides some levels of anonymity against a collaboration of shops and banks. However, users have no flexible anonymity and banks have to keep a very large database for users and coins. Another on-line CyberCoin (http://www.cybercash.com) approach allows clients to make payments by signing fund transfer requests to merchants. The merchants submit the signed requests to the bank for authorization of the payments. The CyberCoin protocol, however, is not fully anonymous since it allows the issuing bank to track every purchase. Furthermore, the scalability of the CyberCoin protocol is questionable since it relies on the availability of a single on-line bank. NetBill [20] extends the above payment mechanism by supporting goods atomicity and certified delivery. The drawbacks of NetBill protocol are the addition of extra messages and the significant increase in the amount of encryption used. In 1995, Chaum [15] proposed blind signatures to provide a fully anonymous coin-based payment system. This system has the disadvantages of centralized management of issuing and checking the double spending of coins. The most sophisticated protocol is the SET protocol [50], which was designed to facilitate credit card transactions over the Internet. SET security comes at a considerable computation and communication cost. SET, unlike other simpler on-line protocols, does not offer full anonymity, non-repudiation, nor certified delivery.

The systems mentioned above are on-line payment systems. The qualifier "on-line" means banks have to connect with service providers for verifications. They need sophisticated cryptographic functions for each coin, and require additional computational resources for the bank to validate the purchases. Forcing the bank to be on-line at payment is a very strict requirement. On-line payment systems protect the merchant and the bank against customer fraud, since every payment needs to be approved by the customer's bank. This increases the computation cost, proportional to the size of the database of spent coins. If a large number of people start using the system, the size of this database could become very large and unmanageable and furthermore keeping a database of every coin ever spent in the system is not a scalable solution [11, 12, 15, 23]. Digicash [15] plans to use multiple banks each minting and managing their own currency with inter-bank clearing to handle the problems of scalability. It seems likely that the host bank machine has an internal scalable structure so that it can be set up not only for a 10,000 user bank, but also for a 1,000,000 user bank. Under these circumstances, the task of maintaining and querying a database of spent coins is probably beyond today's state-of-the-art database systems [16, 21, 48, 77, 78].

In an off-line protocol, the merchant verifies the payment using cryptographic techniques, and commits the payment to the payment authority later in an off-line batch process. Off-line payment systems were designed to lower the cost of transactions due to removing the delay in verifying batch processes. Off-line payment systems, however, suffer from the possibility of double spending, whereby the electronic currency might be duplicated and spent repeatedly.

The first off-line anonymous electronic cash was introduced by Chaum, Fiat and Naor [17]. The security of their scheme relied on some restricted assumptions such as a function $f(x, y)$ is similar to random oracle and g gives a one-to-one map from the second argument onto a special range. There is also no formal proof attempted. Although hardly practical, their system demonstrated how off-line e-cash can be constructed and laid the foundation for more secure and efficient schemes. In 1995, Chan et al. [13] presented a provable secure off-line e-cash scheme that relied only on the security of RSA [59]. This scheme extended the work of Franklin and Yung [28] who aimed to achieve provable security without the use of general computation protocols. The anonymity of consumers is based on the security of RSA and it cannot be changed dynamically after the system is established. NetCents [56] proposed a lightweight, flexible and secure protocol for micropayments of electronic commerce over the Internet. This protocol is designed only to support purchases ranging in value from a fraction of a penny and up. In 2000, Pointcheval [55] presented a payment scheme in which the consumer's identity can be found any time by a certification authority. So the privacy of a consumer cannot be protected.

A new off-line electronic cash scheme is needed, in which the anonymity of consumers is scalable and can be done by consumers themselves. Consumers can get the required anonymity without showing their identities to any third party.

We focus on efficient E-cash systems and consumer anonymity self-scalable payment schemes for the Electronic payment topic.

We have developed a new untraceable electronic cash scheme for transaction [77]. No banks are involved in payment transactions between users and receivers (for example shops). Users withdraw electronic "coins" from banks and use them to pay to receivers. The receivers subsequently deposit the coins back to the bank. In the process users remain anonymous, unless she/he spends a single coin more than once (double spend). The security of the system is based on DLA (Discrete Logarithm Assumption) and the cut-and-choose methodology.

We have designed a consumer anonymity self-scalable payment scheme [79]. This scheme includes two basic processes in system initialization (bank setup and

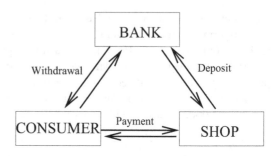

consumer setup) and three main protocols: a new withdrawal protocol with which
a user U withdraws electronic coins from a bank B while his account is debited; a
new payment protocol with which U pays the coin to a shop S; and a new deposit
protocol with which S deposits the coin to B and has his account credited. If a
consumer wants to get a high level of anonymity after she/he has obtained a coin
from the bank (withdrawal), she/he can contact an anonymity provider agent (AP).

Basic Payment Model In the simplest form of a payment model, an e-cash system
consists of three parts (a bank B, a consumer U and a shop S) and three main
procedures as shown in Fig. 1.4 (withdrawal, payment and deposit). In a coin's life-
cycle, the consumer U first performs an account establishment protocol to open an
account with the bank B.

Besides the basic participants, a third party named Anonymity Provider (AP)
agent is involved in our scheme. The AP agent ensures the consumer's required
level of anonymity and is not involved in a purchase process. The AP agent gives a
certificate to the consumer when she/he needs a higher level of anonymity.

The new payment scheme has the following features:

1. Consumers can get a higher level of anonymity by themselves.
2. The identity of a consumer cannot be traced unless the consumer spends the same
   coin twice.
3. It is an off-line scheme with low communication and computation.
4. It can effectively prevent eavesdropping, tampering, impersonation and "perfect
   crime" [68].

Role Based Access Control

To reduce administration cost and complexity and to improve the security of
management, we analyze how to use Role based access control (RBAC) to manage
the new systems. Recently, role based access control (RBAC) has been widely used
in databases system management and operating system products.

RBAC is described in terms of individual users being associated with roles as
well as roles being associated with permissions (each permission is a pair of objects
and operations). As such, a role is associated with users and permissions. A user

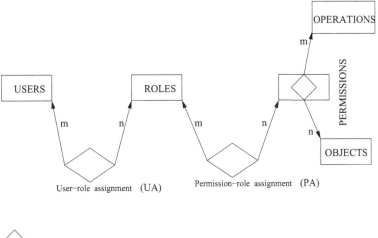

Fig. 1.5 Basic RBAC relationship

in this model is a human being. A role is a job function or job title within the organization associated with its authority and responsibility.

A permission is an approval of a particular operation to be performed on one or more objects. The relationship between roles and permissions is shown in Fig. 1.5, and arrows indicate a many to many relationship (that is, a permission can be associated with one or more roles, and a role can be associated with one or more permissions). The RBAC security model has two components: MC_0 and MC_1. Model component MC_0, called the RBAC authorization database model, defines the RBAC security properties for authorization of static roles. Static properties of a RBAC authorization database include role hierarchy, inheritance, cardinality, and static separation of duty. MC_1, called the RBAC activation model, defines the RBAC security properties for dynamic activation of roles. Dynamic properties include role activation, permission execution, dynamic separation of duties, and object access. In particular, the RBAC model supports the specification of:

1. User/role associations, that is, the constraints specifying user authorizations to perform roles;
2. Role hierarchies, for example, the constraints specifying which role may inherit all of the permissions of another role;
3. Duty separation constraints; these are role/role associations indicating conflicts of interests:

   (a) Static separated duty (SSD); a constraint specifying that a user cannot be authorized for two different roles,
   (b) Dynamic separated duty (DSD); a constraint specifying that a user can be authorized for two different roles but cannot act simultaneously in both.

4. Cardinality; the maximum number of users allowed, that is, how many users can be authorized for any particular role (role cardinality), for example, only one manager in one department.

Properties 1 and 4 depend on how a system is implemented, and can be decided after the system has been designed. However, properties 2 and 3 have to be decided when a system is designed. This is because permissions of different roles may be in conflict compromising the security of the system.

There has been little research done on the usage of RABC in electronic service systems. Methods of using RBAC to manage electronic payment systems is another challenge in management procedures [62]. We have analyzed RBAC and its management for electronic service systems in later chapters.

1.2   Objectives of the Book

With advances in computer networks, in processor speed, and in databases, and with advances in note counterfeiting technology and with both individuals' and businesses' desire for remote and more convenient financial transactions, some forms of electronic cash are likely to become widespread within 5–10 years. Although unconditionally anonymous electronic cash systems have been proposed in the literature, financial institutions are unwilling to be a completely anonymous system. Their reasons for opposing complete untraceability have to do with the containment of user fraud and the desire to restrict new kinds of crime that unrestricted, and spendable electronic cash could facilitate. Because of the necessary concern over crime control, they have previously proposed systems with little or no protection for the users' privacy. On the other hand, consumers, when shopping over the Internet, prefer to have some degree of anonymity so that, for example, they cannot be traced by banks. There are a number of proposals for electronic cash systems [13, 14, 17, 20, 50, 55, 56]. All of these solutions are either too large to manage or lack flexibility in providing anonymity. Therefore, they are not suitable solutions for electronic payment in the future.

Electronic service systems allow users and service providers to be widely distributed and to use heterogeneous catalog systems. It may have conflicts within operations which may cause negative influences with the service systems. The management of these service systems is complex. Whether or not systems are successful depends on the quality of their management.

To investigate these problems, this book will focus on following tasks:

1. Electronic commerce items and related technology
2. Untraceable electronic cash system in the Internet of Things
3. Achieving secure and flexible M-services through tickets
4. A self-scalable anonymity payment approach in cloud environment
5. Using RBAC to secure payment process in cloud
6. Role-based access control constraints and object constraint language

7. Role-based delegation with negative authorization
8. Access control management for ubiquitous computing
9. Trust-based access control management in collaborative open social networks
10. Building access control policy model for privacy preserving and testing policy conflicting problems
11. Effective collaboration with information sharing in virtual universities
12. Distributed access control through Blockchain technology

1.3 Organization of the Book

The book consists of thirteen chapters. Their precedence order is outlined and illustrated in Fig. 1.6.

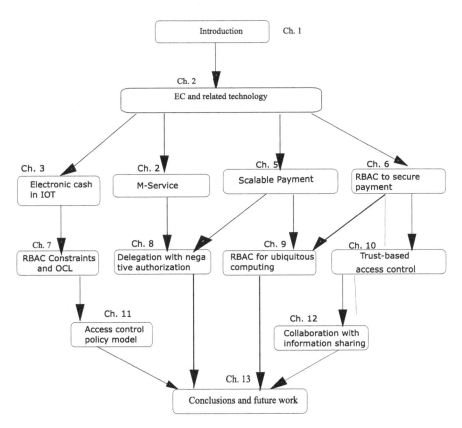

Fig. 1.6 The structure of the book

In Chap. 2, e-commerce issues and a framework for e-commerce are presented. There are three dimensions in the framework: the software technology dimension, the hardware support dimension, and the application dimension. The items include trust and privacy, payment system, management and security and so on. From Chaps. 3 to 12, we focus on the software technology plane. Chapter 3 presents a new scheme for untraceable electronic cash transaction processing, in which the bank involvement in the payment transaction between a user and a receiver is eliminated.

Chapter 4 describes a secure and flexible access control scheme and protocol for M-services based on role based access control (RBAC). The access control architecture involves a Trusted Credential Centre (TCC), a Trusted Authentication and Registration Centre (TARC) and a secure ticket based mechanism for service access. Chapter 5 proposes a secure, anonymity scalable and practical payment protocol for Internet purchases, and analyses its role-based user-role assignment. The protocol uses electronic cash for payment transactions. In this new protocol, from the viewpoint of banks, consumers can improve anonymity if they worried about disclosure of their identities. The next chapter presents basic definitions of role based access control (RBAC) such as user-role assignment, permission-role assignment and role-role assignment and so on. The advantages and significance of RBAC are discussed.

A de facto constraints specification language in software engineering is used to analyze the constraints in user-role assignments and permission-role assignments in Chap. 7. Object Constraints Language (OCL), a part of the Unified Modelling Language (UML) widely used in object-oriented analysis and design is applied to express various constraints in RBAC. Chapter 8 aims to analyse role-based group delegation features that has not studied before, and to provide an approach for the conflicting problem by adopting negative authorization. It presents granting and revocation delegating models first, and then discuss user delegation authorization and the impact of negative authorization on role hierarchies.

Chapter 9 presents a usage control model to protect services and devices in ubiquitous computing environments, which allows the access restrictions directly on services and object documents. The model not only supports complex constraints for pervasive computing, such as services, devices and data types but also provides a mechanism to build rich reuse relationships between models and objects. A trust involved access management framework for supporting privacy preserving access control policies and mechanisms is proposed in Chap. 10. The mechanism enforces access policy to data containing personally identifiable information. The key component of the framework is an access control model that provides full support for expressing highly complex privacy-related policies, taking into account features like purposes and obligations.

Chapter 11 proposes a purpose-based access control model in distributed computing environment for privacy preserving policies and mechanisms, and describes algorithms for policy conflicting problems. The mechanism enforces access policy to data containing personally identifiable information. The key component is purpose involved access control models (PAC) that provide full support for expressing highly complex privacy-related policies, taking into account features like purposes, conditions and obligations. Chapter 12 aims to build a new rule-based framework to identify and address issues of sharing in virtual university environments through role-based access control management (RBAC). The framework includes a role-based group delegation granting model, group delegation revocation model, authorization granting and authorization revocation. Various revocations and the impact of revocations on role hierarchies are analysed. The implementation with XML-based tools demonstrates the feasibility of the framework and authorization methods. Finally, conclusions and future work are indicated in Chap. 13.

1.4 Problems and Exercises

1.4.1 Problems

1. Outsourced data for multi-user accesses can be achieved through encrypted file systems. However, the existing approaches show the shortages for application. For secure and efficient access to outsourced data, both data and metadata must be properly protected from unauthorised users. Miller et al. [93] analysed the basic idea to guarantee information integrity by applying encrypted data, signatures and hash functions. Adya et al. [94] uses symmetric algorithms to encrypt files and public key algorithms to secure the symmetric keys. In [95], encryption is used to both files and directory information and if or not a user can access a file is determined by key verifications. The overhead of key generation is relatively heavy since its procedure depends on power-modular computation. Goh et al. [96] uses another complicated structure that each data file has an encryption key and an access key, and a public/private key pair for each user. The approach continuously signs the metadata tree to guarantee the information update and prevent rollback security attacks. It also generates a new key and reencrypt corresponding data files when a data file is removed.

   Li et al apply hash trees and chains to prevent fork attacks and guarantee the availability of the data file [97]. Kher and Kim presented the advantages and disadvantages of the approaches for outsourced data. A data sharing platform for outsourced information using asymmetric encryption is proposed in [98]. All these approaches adopt asymmetric encryption methods to protect data from unauthorised access, and with a huge key numbers. It makes the key management mechanism to secure data very cumbersome and unrealistic. Therefore, a new approach is needed to protect the safety of the outsourced data. How to design the new approach is a problem in Cloud computing?

2. Privacy protection is a serious challenge in IoT. The development of IoT technologies and applications is merely beginning. Many new challenges and issues have not been addressed, which require substantial efforts from both academia and industry. One of the fundamental problems is the lack of a mechanism to help people expose appropriate amounts of their identity information. Embedded

sensing is becoming more and more prevalent on personal devices such as mobile phones and multi-media players. Since people are typically wearing and carrying devices capable of sensing, details such as activity, location, and environment could become available to other people. Hence, personal sensing can be used to detect their physical activities and bring about privacy concerns [1, 45].

3. Security concern is an obstacle for IOT applications. Due to the proliferation of embedded devices in IoT, effective device security mechanisms are essential to the development of IoT technologies and applications. It argues that, to the extent that everyday objects become information security risks, the IoT could distribute those risks far more widely than the Internet has to date. For example, RFID security presents many challenges. Potential solutions should consider aspects from hardware and wireless protocol security to the management, regulation and sharing of collected RFID data. Besides, there is still no generic framework for deploying and extending traditional security mechanisms over a variety of pervasive systems. Regarding security concerns of the network layer, it is suggested that the Internet can be gradually encrypted and authenticated based on the observations that the recent advances in implementation of cryptographic algorithms have made general purpose processors capable of encrypting packets at high rates [1, 65, 89]. But how to generalize such algorithms to IoT would be challenging as things in IoT normally only maintain low transmission rates and connections are usually intermittent.

1.4.2   Exercises

1. What are concerned for Outsourced data?
2. Symmetric algorithms to encrypt files and public key algorithms to secure the symmetric keys can be used in Outsourced data. Examples for both Symmetric algorithms and public key algorithms are required.
3. What are the privacy concerned in IOT? How to protect your private data in IOT?
4. What are the security concerned in an IOT system? How to secure your own data?
5. How can an outsourced data be protected?

References

1. Alqhatani, A., Lipford, H.: "There is nothing that i need to keep secret": sharing practices and concerns of wearable fitness data. In: Fifteenth Symposium on Usable Privacy and Security (SOUPS 2019), Santa Clara. USENIX Association
2. Andreoli, J., Pacull, F., Pagani, D., Pareschi, R.: Multiparty negotiation of dynamic distributed object services. J. Sci. Comput. Program. **31**, 179–203 (1998)
3. Baggio, A., Ballintijn, G., Steen, M.: Mechanisms for effective caching in the globe location service. In: Proceedings of the 9th Workshop on ACM SIGOPS European Workshop, pp. 55–60. ACM Press, New York (2000)

4. Barkley, J.F., Beznosov, K., Uppal, J.: Supporting relationships in access control using role based access control. In: Third ACM Workshop on Role Based Access Control, pp. 55–65 (1999)

5. Beam, C., Segev, A.: Electronic Catalogs and Negotiations. CITM Working Paper 96-WP-1016, August 1996

6. Bellare, M., Rogaway, P.: Random oracles are practical: a paradigm for designing efficient protocols. In: First ACM Conference on Computer and Communications Security, pp. 62–73. IEEE, Piscataway (1993)

7. Ben-Shaul, I., Gidron, Y., Holder, O. (eds.): A Negotiation Model for Dynamic Composition of Distributed Applications. Institute of Electrical and Electronics Engineers, Piscataway (1998)

8. Bertino, E., Castano, S., Ferrari, E., Mesiti, M.: Specifying and enforcing access control policies for XML document sources. World Wide Web, 3, pp. 139–151 (2000)

9. Boyko, V., Peinado, M., Venkatesan, R.: Speeding up discrete log and factoring based schemes via precomputations. In: Advances in Cryptology—Eurocrypt'98. Lectures Notes in Computer Science, vol. 1807. Springer, Berlin (1998)

10. Buttyan, L., Hubaux, J.: Accountable anonymous access to services in mobile communication systems. In: Symposium on Reliable Distributed Systems, pp. 384–389 (1999). citeseer.nj.nec.com/article/buttyan99accountable.html

11. Canetti, R., Goldreich, O., Halevi, S.: The random oracle methodology. In: Proceedings of the 30th ACM STOC '98, pp. 209–218. IEEE, Piscataway (1998)

12. Canetti, R., Micciancio, D., Reingold, O.: Perfectly one-way probabilistic hash functions. In: Proceedings of the 30th ACM STOC '98. IEEE, Piscataway (1998)

13. Chan, A., Frankel, Y., Tsiounis, Y.: An efficient off-line electronic cash scheme as secure as RSA. Research report NU-CCS-96-03, Northeastern University, Boston (1995)

14. Chaum, D.: Blind signature for untraceable payments. In: Advances in Cryptology—Crypto 82, pp. 199–203. Plenum Press New York (1983)

15. Chaum, D. (ed.): An introduction to e-cash. DigiCash (1995). http://www.digicash.com

16. Chaum, D.: An Introduction to e-cash. DigiCash (1995). http://www.digicash.com

17. Chaum, D., Fiat, A., Naor, M.: Untraceable electronic cash. In: Advances in Cryptology—Crypto 88. Lectures Notes in Computer Science, vol. 403, pp. 319–327. Springer, Berlin (1990)

18. Chen, Z., et al.: Distributed individuals for multiple peaks: a novel differential evolution for multimodal optimization problems. IEEE Trans. Evol. Comput. **24**(4), 708–719 (2020)

19. Chenthara, S., et al.: Security and privacy-preserving challenges of e-health solutions in cloud computing. IEEE Access **7**, 74361–74382 (2019)

20. Cox, B., Tygar, J.D., Sirbu, M.: Netbill security and transaction protocol. In: The First USENIX Workshop on Electronic Commerce. New York (1995)

21. Dogac, A.: Survey of the current state-of-the-art in electronic commerce and research issues in enabling technologies. In: Proceeding of Euro-Med Net 98 Conference, Electronic Commerce Track (1998)

22. Du, J., et al.: Feature selection for helpfulness prediction of online product reviews: an empirical study. PLoS ONE **14**, e0226902 (2019)

23. Eng, T., Okamoto, T.: Single-term divisible electronic coins. In: Advances in Cryptology—Eurocrypt'94. Lectures Notes in Computer Science, vol. 950, pp. 306–319. Springer, Berlin (1995)

24. Feinstein, H.L.: Final report: NIST small business innovative research (SBIR) grant: role based access control: phase 1. Technical report. In: SETA Corporation (1995)

25. Ferraiolo, D.F., Kuhn, D.R.: Role based access control. In: 15th National Computer Security Conference, pp. 554–563 (1992). ferraiolo92rolebased.html

26. Ferraiolo, D.F., Barkley, J.F., Kuhn, D.R.: Role-based access control model and reference implementation within a corporate intranet. In: TISSEC, vol. 2, pp. 34–64 (1999)

27. Ford, W., Baum, M.: Secure electronic commerce: building the Infrastructure for Digital Signatures and Encryption. Prentice Hall PTR (1997)

28. Franklin, M., Yung, M. Secure and efficient off-line digital money. In: Proceedings of the Twentieth International Colloquium on Automata, Languages and Programming. Lectures Notes in Computer Science, vol. 700, pp. 265–276. Springer, Berlin (1993)

29. Frankel, Y., Yiannis, T., Yung, M.: Indirect discourse proofs: achieving fair off-line electronic cash. In: Advances in Cryptology—Asiacrypt'96. Lectures Notes in Computer Science, vol. 1163, pp. 286–300. Springer, Berlin (1996)

30. Frankel, Y., Herzberg, A., Karger, P., Krawczyk, H., Kunzinger, C., Yung, M.: Security issues in a CDPD wireless network. In: IEEE Personal Communications (1995)

31. Garfinkel, S., Spafford, G.: Web Security and Commerce Risks, Technologies, and Strategies. O'Reilly and Associates, Sebastopol (1997)

32. Goldreich, O., Krawczyk, H.: On the composition of zero-knowledge proof systems. SIAM J. Comput. **25**(1), 159–192 (1996)

33. Goldschlag, D., Reed, M., Syverson, P.: Onion routing for anonymous and private Internet connections. Commun. ACM **24**(2), 39–41 (1999)

34. Green, S., et al.: Software Agents: A Review. TCD-CS-1997-06. Trinity College Dublin and Broadcom Eireann Research, Ireland (1997)

35. Guo, B., et al.: Opportunistic IoT: exploring the harmonious interaction between human and the internet of things. J. Netw. Comput. Appl. **36**(6), 1531–1539 (2013)

36. Guttman, R.H., Maes, P.: Cooperative vs. competitive multi-agent negotiations in retail electronic commerce. In: Proceedings of the Second International Workshop on Cooperative Information Agents (CIA'98). Paris (1998)

37. Han, W., et al. DTC: transfer learning for commonsense machine comprehension. Neurocomputing **396**, 102–112 (2019)

38. Hoffman, D.: What-is-cloud-computing (2017). aws.amazon.com

39. Huang, T., et al.: A niching memetic algorithm for multi-solution traveling salesman problem. IEEE Trans. Evol. Comput. **24**(3), 508–522 (2020)

40. Jordi, P., et al.: Distributed access control with blockchain (2019). abs/1901.03568

41. Juels, A., Luby, M., Ostrovsky, R.: Security of blind digital signatures. In: Advances in Cryptology—Crypto 97. Lectures Notes in Computer Science, vol. 1294, pp. 150–164. Springer, Berlin (1997)

42. Kabir, M., et al.: A novel statistical technique for intrusion detection systems. Future Gener. Comput. Syst. **79**, 303–318 (2018)

43. Kabir, E., et al.: Microaggregation sorting framework for k-anonymity statistical disclosure control in cloud computing. IEEE Trans. Cloud Comput. **8**(2), 408–417 (2020)

44. Ketchpel, S.P., Garcia-Molina, H.: Making trust explicit in distributed commerce transactions. In: IEEE Proceedings of the 16th ICDCS, pp. 270–281 (1996)

45. Klasnja, P., et al.: Exploring privacy concerns about personal sensing. In: Pervasive Computing, pp. 176–183. Springer, Berlin (2009)

46. Klusch, M.: Intelligent Information Agents: Agent-Based Information Discovery and Management on the Internet. Springer, Berlin (1998)

47. Lee, C., Hwang, M., Yang, W.: Enhanced privacy and authentication for the global system for mobile communications. Wirel. Netw. **5**(4), 231–243 (1999)

48. Loudon, D., Della, B.: Consumer Behavior: Concepts and Applications, 4th edn. McGraw-Hill, New York (1993)

49. Lynn, B., Xun, Y.: Off-line digital cash schemes providing untraceability, anonymity and change. Electron. Commer. Res. **19**, 81–110 (2019)

50. MastercardVisa: SET 1.0—secure electronic transaction specification (1997). http://www.mastercard.com/set.html

51. Mehrotra, A.: GSM system engineering. In: Artech House Mobile Communications Series, Artech House, Norwood (1997)

52. Mehrotra, A., Golding, L.: Mobility and security management in the GSM system and some proposed future improvements. Proc. IEEE **86**(7), 1480–1497 (1998)

53. Okamoto, T., Ohta, K.: Disposable zero-knowledge authentication and their applications to untraceable electronic cash. In: Advances in Cryptology—Crypto89. Lectures Notes in Computer Science, vol. 435, pp. 481–496. Springer, Berlin (1990)

54. Peng, M., et al.: Pattern filtering attention for distant supervised relation extraction via online clustering. In: Web Information Systems Engineering—WISE 2019, pp. 310–325. Springer, Cham (2019)

55. Pointcheval, D.: Self-scrambling anonymizers. In: Proceedings of Financial Cryptography. Springer, Anguilla (2000)

56. Poutanen, T., Hinton, H., Stumm, M.: Netcents: A lightweight protocol for secure micropayments. In: The Third USENIX Workshop on Electronic Commerce. Boston (1998)

57. Qin, Y., et al.: When things matter: a survey on data-centric internet of things. J. Netw. Comput. Appl. **64**, 137–153 (2016)

58. Rasool, R., et al.: Cyberpulse: a machine learning based link flooding attack mitigation system for software defined networks. IEEE Access **7**, 34885–34899 (2019)

59. Rivest, R.L., Shamir, A., Adleman, L.M.: A method for obtaining digital signatures and public-key cryptosystems. Commun. ACM **21**(2), 120–126 (1978)

60. Rohm, A.W., Pernul, G. COPS: a model and infrastructure for secure and fair electronic markets. In: Proceedings of the 32nd Hawaii International Conference on System Sciences (HICSS-32), Hawaii. IEEE Computer Society Press, Silver Spring (1999)

61. Sandhu, R.: Role activation hierarchies. In: Third ACM Workshop on Role Based Access Control, pp. 33–40. ACM Press (1998)

62. Sandhu, R.: Future directions in role-based access control models. In: MMS, 2001 (2001). http://www.list.gmu.edu/confrnc/misconf/

63. Schnorr, C.P.: Efficient signature generation by smart cards. J. Cryptol. **4**(3), 161–174 (1991)

64. Scourias, J.: An overview of the global system for mobile communications. Technical report, University of Waterloo, Canada (1995)

65. Shenoy, J., et al.: Jive: Spatially-constrained encryption key sharing using visible light communication. In: Proceedings of the 16th EAI International Conference on Mobile and Ubiquitous Systems: Computing, Networking and Services (2019)

66. Shu, J., et al.: Privacy-preserving task recommendation Services for Crowdsourcing. IEEE Trans. Serv. Comput. (2018) https://doi.org/10.1109/TSC.2018.2791601

67. Simon, D.: Anonymous communication and anonymous cash. In: Advances in Cryptology—Crypto'96. Lectures Notes in Computer Science, vol. 1109, pp. 61–73. Springer, Berlin (1997)

68. Solms, S., Naccache, D.: On blind signatures and perfect crimes. Comput. Secur. **11**, 581–583 (1992)

69. Spegel, N., Rogers, B., Buckley, R.: Negotiation Theory and Techniques. Skills Series. Butterworths (1998)

70. Sun, L., Wang, H., Bertino, E.: Role-based access control to outsourced data in cloud computing. In: Proceedings of the Twenty-Fourth Australasian Database Conference, ADC '13, vol. 137, pp. 119–128. Australian Computer Society, Darlinghurst (2013)

71. Vimalachandran, P., et al.: Preserving patient-centred controls in electronic health record systems: a reliance-based model implication. In: 2017 International Conference on Orange Technologies (ICOT), pp. 37–44 (2017)

72. Wang, H., et al.: Privacy preserving on radio frequency identification systems. In: 2009 13th International Conference on Computer Supported Cooperative Work in Design, pp. 674–679 (2009)

73. Wang, H., et al.: Protecting outsourced data in cloud computing through access management. Concurrency Comput. Pract. Exp. **28**(3), 600–615 (2016)

74. Wang, Y., et al.: MTMR: Ensuring mapreduce computation integrity with Merkle tree-based verifications. IEEE Trans. Big Data **4**(3), 418–431 (2018)

75. Wang, G., et al.: Incorporating word embeddings into topic modeling of short text. Knowl. Inf. Syst. **61**(2), 1123–1145 (2019)

76. Wang, H., et al.: Editorial: special issue on security and privacy in network computing. World Wide Web (2019)

77. Wang, H., Zhang, Y.: A protocol for untraceable electronic cash. In: Lu, H., Zhou, A. (ed.) Proceedings of the First International Conference on Web-Age Information Management. Lectures Notes in Computer Science, vol. 1846, pp. 189–197, Shanghai. Springer, Berlin (2000)

78. Wang, H., Zhang, Y.: Untraceable off-line electronic cash flow in e-commerce. In: Proceedings of the 24th Australian Computer Science Conference ACSC2001, pp. 191–198, GoldCoast. IEEE Computer Society, Silver Spring (2001)

79. Wang, H., Cao, J., Kambayashi, Y.: Building a consumer anonymity scalable payment protocol for the internet purchases. In: 12th International Workshop on Research Issues on Data Engineering: Engineering E-Commerce/E-Business Systems, San Jose (2002)

80. Wang, H., Cao, J., Zhang, Y.: Ticket-based service access scheme for mobile users. In: Twenty-Fifth Australasian Computer Science Conference (ACSC2002), Monash University, Melbourne, Victoria, January 28–February 2 (2002)

81. Wang, H., Zhang, Z., Taleb, T.: Editorial: special issue on security and privacy of IoT. World Wide Web **21**(1), 1–6 (2018)

82. Wang, H., Zhang, Y., Cao, J., Kambayahsi, Y.: A global ticket-based access scheme for mobile users. Inf. Syst. Front. **6**(1), 35–46 (2004)

83. Wang, Z., Zhan, Z., Lin, Y., Yu, W., Wang, H., Kwong, S., Zhang, J.: Automatic niching differential evolution with contour prediction approach for multimodal optimization problems. IEEE Trans. Evol. Comput. 24(1), 114—128 (2020)

84. Weiser, M.: Internet of Things (2017). en.wikipedia.org

85. Wray, J.: Where's the rub: cloud computing's hidden costs. Web (2014)

86. Xiao, Y., Jia, Y., Liu, C., Cheng, X., Yu, J., Lv, W.: Edge computing security: state of the art and challenges. Proc. IEEE **107**(8), 1608–1631 (2019)

87. Yacobi, Y.: Efficient electronic money. In: Advances in Cryptology—Asiacrypt'94. Lectures Notes in Computer Science, vol. 917, pp. 153–163. Springer, Berlin (1995)

88. Zhang, Y., Jia, X.: Transaction processing. In: Wiley Encyclopedia of Electrical and Electronics Engineering, vol. 22, pp. 298–311 (1999)

89. Zhang, F., Wang, Y., Wang, H.: Gradient correlation: are ensemble classifiers more robust against evasion attacks in practical settings? In: Web Information Systems Engineering—WISE 2018, pp. 96–110. Springer, Cham (2018)

90. Zhang, Y., Shen, Y., Wang, H., Zhang, Y., Jiang, X.: On secure wireless communications for service oriented computing. IEEE Transact. Services Comput. **11**(2), 318–328 (2018)

91. Zhang, Y., Gong, Y., Gao, Y., Wang, H., Zhang, J.: Parameter-free Voronoi neighborhood for evolutionary multimodal optimization. IEEE Trans. Evol. Comput. **24**(2), 335–349 (2019)

92. Zheng, H., He, J., Huang, G., Zhang, Y., Wang, H.: Dynamic optimisation based fuzzy association rule mining method. Int. J. Mach. Learn. Cybern. **10**(8), 2187–2198 (2019)

93. Miller, E., et al.: Strong security for distributed file systems. In: Proceedings of the 2001 IEEE International Performance, Computing, and Communications, pp. 34–40 (2001)

94. Adya et al.: Farsite: federated, available, and reliable storage for an incompletely trusted environment. SIGOPS Oper. Syst. Rev. **36**, 1–14 (2003)

95. Kallahalla, M., et al.: Plutus: scalable secure file sharing on untrusted storage. In: Proceedings of the 2nd USENIX Conference on File and Storage Technologies, pp. 29–42. USENIX Association (2003)

96. Goh, E., et al.: SiRiUS: securing remote untrusted storage. In: Proceedings of the Internet Society Network and Distributed Systems Security Symposium, pp. 131–145 (2003)

97. Li, J., et al.: Secure untrusted data repository (SUNDR). In: Proceedings of the 6th Symposium on Operating Systems Design and Implementation, pp. 121–136, San Francisco, CA (2004)

98. Kher, V., Kim, Y.: Securing distributed storage: challenges, techniques, and systems. In: Proceedings of the ACM Workshop on Storage Security and Survivability, pp. 9–25 (2005)

Chapter 2
Electronic Commerce Items and Related Technology

This chapter presents e-commerce items including m-commerce, and a framework for e-commerce. The items include trust and privacy, payment system, management and security and so on. The position and the importance of each topic in e-commerce are discussed extensively. Finally, a new framework for e-commerce is proposed. The framework has three-dimensions which are software technology dimension, hardware dimension and e-commerce application dimension. The criteria of a good framework is also indicated. It has been demonstrated that the framework is a natural and efficient framework. Furthermore, all items in e-commerce can fit into the framework very well.

2.1 Introduction

E-commerce can be defined as the buying and selling of information, products, and services via computer network [40, 103]. E-commerce systems can be of significant value as a milestone for new customer access management strategies. This is because e-commerce systems:

1. directly connect buyers and sellers;
2. support fully digital information exchange;
3. have no time and place limits;
4. support interactivity and therefore can dynamically adapt to customer behavior;
5. can be updated in real-time, therefore always up-to-date.

M-commerce The concept of mobile commerce (*M-commerce*) was introduced in the late 1990s. Mobile commerce is a subset of electronic commerce (e-commerce) which continues to see phenomenal growth, but so far most e-commerce involves wired infrastructures. It creates new opportunities in e-commerce and provides new increasing growth when emerging wireless and mobile networks [12, 30]. A mobile

© Springer Nature Switzerland AG 2020
H. Wang et al., *Access Control Management in Cloud Environments*,
https://doi.org/10.1007/978-3-030-31729-4_2

commerce (M-commerce) is defined as any type of transaction of an economic value that is conducted through a terminal that uses a wireless telecommunications network for communication with an e-commerce infrastructure. Mobile devices, involved in M-commerce, are becoming a large market. There were more than 350 million mobile devices in worldwide in 1999 [8], this number may rise to 1 billion in the next few years [16]. There are 40% of consumer-to-business e-commerce will come from smart phones using the wireless application protocol (WAP) [31]. Based on a study by the wireless data and computing service, the annual mobile commerce market may rise to $200 billion by 2004 [65].

However, the mobile commerce industry is still in its infancy, and there are a lot of problems need to be addressed, for example, flexible business to consumer system, secure payments, M-commerce management and interoperability between networks and different devices etc. There is a number of papers review various aspects of mobile e-commerce [52, 80, 82, 84, 85]. Tarasewich et al. [80] introduced different issues related to mobile client, communication infrastructure and mobile commerce application systems. These different issues represent an overview of the social, technical, and practical environment within M-commerce activities in the coming years and provide a foundational analysis research for further within this domain. Varshney and Vetter [84] indicated mobile and wireless networks for novices and explained the difference between mobile and wireless networks, which sometimes occur together. The growth in mobile commerce is illustrated by statistics about increased subscribers, capital investment, and revenues, along with a decrease in monthly billing costs. A brief overview of wireless LANs, wireless local loops, satellites, wireless asynchronous transfer mode (WATM) and mobile IP were mentioned, along with these networks, but no discuss in the text. The authors also discussed middleware and applications, with a focus on wireless application protocol (WAP). Finally, problems of the coexistence of different mobile and wireless networks and of coordinating access were solved. Muller-Veerse [52] published a mobile commerce report with the intention of providing operators, investors, mobile commerce service and equipment vendors, banks and others, with a pragmatic view and analysis of the m-commerce market in Western Europe. It detailed analysis of the mobile commerce space with M-commerce enabling technologies, M-commerce enabling applications, consumer M-commerce Applications, business M-commerce applications etc. The author also indicated how these technologies and markets will evolve to provide growing momentum to the m-commerce applications market, how these applications will shape over time and how the various players will react to such developments by using mobile technologies (GSM, HSCSD, GPRS, EDGE, 3G/UMTS). These papers, however, as well as others cited in the remaining section of this chapter, discussed what exist or is planned but do not discuss the issues of mobile commerce.

There are a few papers that have addressed various mobile commerce issues. Kannan et al. [41] discussed the characteristics of wireless technology and its usage, and viewed how wireless technology's contribution complement the capabilities brought about by the Internet based e-commerce. Based on the characteristics, the authors identified a series of propositions that were related to marketing and marketing research issues of mobile e-commerce. Varshney and Jain [83] presented several issues related to fourth generation wireless networks such as Multimode devices, Overlay network and Common access protocol etc. The differences between the first generation wireless networks, the second generation wireless networks and the third generation were compared. The authors pointed out the possible problems of mobile commerce in the fourth generation wireless networks. Varshney and Vetter [85] envisioned new e-commerce applications that may possible and significantly benefit from emerging wireless and mobile networks. The authors attempted to identify several classes of applications such as mobile financial applications, mobile inventory management, proactive service management, product location and search, and wireless re-engineering and discussed how to successfully define, architect, and implement the necessary hardware/software infrastructure in support of mobile commerce. No paper that I am aware of, however, provides technological details of the issues.

Next, various items within e-commerce are described.

2.2 Items in Electronic Commerce

In this section, some items with technological details on the way to electronic commerce are reviewed. These items are important to understanding e-commerce.

2.2.1 Trust and Privacy

Users are seriously concerned with privacy and trust, which may lead to a backlash against providers using such systems, or customers avoiding the use of these systems [15, 69–71]. Some companies require customers to provide their information on their demographics information, buying patterns or product needs. Unfortunately, this data is critical in many cases since consumers do not know what will be done with their private data. There are two ways of handling these concerns, either customers can be made aware of the benefits of volunteering this data, or material incentives can be offered to customers to attract them.

The concerns with trust can be categorized as follows:

1. Personal data, whether personal data is secure or not during electronic transactions [37, 78, 79];
2. Service processes, whether service processes can be trusted or not during electronic transactions with organizations [48, 74, 102]. The forms of service process involve:

   (a) money paid and received;
   (b) goods and services offered and acquired; and
   (c) assurances that a refund is available for unsatisfactory goods and services;

3. Privacy of personal data, whether data storage of personal data can be trusted or not [38, 39, 91].
4. Subsequent behavior, whether has subsequent behavior with customers data to other companies (that is, sale customers data or share the data with sub companies and so on.) [6, 72, 86, 93]

The concerns with privacy includes:

1. Cookies, websites send cookies (files) to consumers who visit the websites and also get some information of consumers;
2. Internet Privacy: Cyberspace Invades Personal Space [15];
3. Spam, consumers receive a lot of useless messages.

None of consumers like their private data to be reviewed. Electronic services have to protect the privacy of users, and then users trust and be interested in the e-commerce system [45, 67, 68, 88].

2.2.2 Electronic Payment Systems

Electronic business can only be successful if financial exchanges between buyers and sellers can occur in a simple, universally accepted, safe and cheap way [2, 3, 42, 44, 53, 81]. E-commerce assumes that the participants pay for the services they receive. But there has been a marked reluctance among net-users to actually part with their money, particularly for digital goods and services. Various systems have been proposed, some of them based on traditional mechanisms (for example, credit cards accounts) while others rely on new designs, such as electronic money. The key here is to find a few widely accepted mechanisms, which can be used by most participants. Two later chapters address the questions of how to design a secure electronic payment system and how to provide a scalable anonymity payment scheme for consumers.

2.2.3 Mass-Market Adoption

One important issue of mobile commerce is certainly a wide customer adoption of such technologies. There are lots of learnings and benefits to be derived [43, 61, 62, 66], but the technologies of mass-market adoption will take a few more years to come.

The mass-market adoption technology includes three aspects. The first is perceived benefit that is interested for suppliers to invest. For example whether suppliers can have advertising to attract consumers or not. The next one is direct costs and the third one is indirect costs. How much investment needed from suppliers? It is necessary for suppliers to make a decision of whether they have

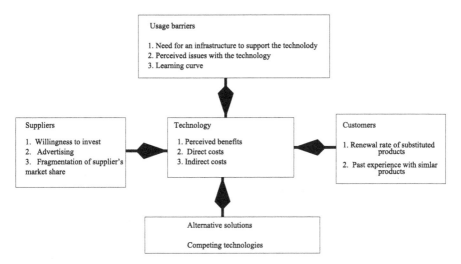

Fig. 2.1   Factors affecting new technology adoption

the ability and it is worth or not? From consumers viewpoint, they have concerns with renewal rate of substituted products and past experience with similar products. Should they still need to train and to pay extra money? There are two important factors that come from the inside of the adoption technology. One is alternative solutions for some unnormal things happened. For instance, when the database of student information does not support Microsoft Explore, whether the Netscape can be used to view? The other one is usage barriers. Figure 2.1 below shows some of the factors linked to adoption technology by consumers [15].

2.2.4   Management and Implementation

This subsection discusses some management and implementation issues. Managerial implicates getting benefits of an electronic commerce system. Indeed, management revolves around the realization that technology alone will not solve issues or create advantages. This technology needs to be integrated by administrators, with the change access operations linked to people involved in a commerce system.

A summarized model of an organization is in Fig. 2.2, and it shows the alignment between these different components as the main issue in establishing a sustained competitive advantage.

The issues of alignment relevant to electronic commerce systems are:

- between strategy and technology
- between technology and the organizational processes
- between technology and people

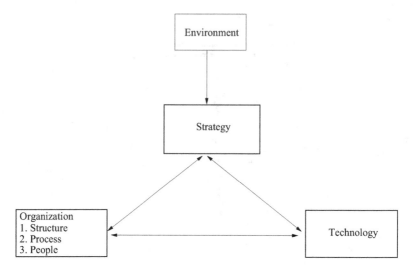

Fig. 2.2 A simplified model of an organization

We do not introduce all above issues but that between technology and the organizational. Basically, technology in itself will not be sufficient to achieve the level of service provided to customers and the relationship that can be established with them. There are two kinds of alignments between technology and the organizational processes. The first is to redefine some processes in an e-commerce system, such that the system becomes fully integrated in the way for business organization. For example, it is necessary to authorize each piece information to be public when a Web system is used to broadcast corporate information. It requires to redefine the process handling corporate communications. The other way of aligning processes and technology is to use the latter to enable a redesign of the processes, thereby reducing the cost, time and number of errors associated with the process, while increasing the service level. This is often the focus of business process reengineering methodologies [7, 17, 18]. The company of amazon.com is a good example that integrated organizations fully relying on information technology both for customer interaction and internal management.

2.2.5 Security

Security is a key enabling factor in e-commerce [36, 47, 73]. With the industry moving toward a consensus on providing service on wireless commerce, the next major challenge for enterprisers and service providers is securing resources from unauthorized access and preventing fraud. As companies allow customers to execute wireless transactions and business partners with wireless access to share information and resources via an Intranet or extranet, security becomes a chief concern. There

Fig. 2.3 Users access service
model

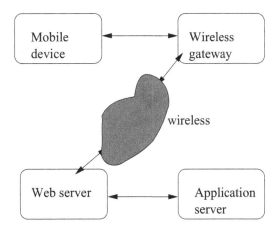

are three levels for e-commerce security [21, 50, 51]. Figure 2.3 illustrates users access services in e-commerce. Three levels are involved in the figure. They are network connection level, management level, and transaction level.

Network Connection Level

In a wired network, firewalls are used to provide the first level of security between the user and the Web server; in the wireless world, mobile gateways manage access to a Web server, provide encryption through the Wireless Transport Layer Security (WTLS) specification and authenticate users to enable a secure connection between the wireless device and the application server. WTLS, which is a version of TLS/SSL for wireless communications, provides secure service such as data integrity, authentication, and denial-of-service protection. Service providers in e-commerce environments must address the same challenges involved in securing wired environments and then users and service providers can trust each other. It means that users are controlled to access both the network and individual resources (applications, content and transactions) [56, 58, 63].

Management Level

When users log in the wireless network, a management system is needed to control which resources users are authorized to access and which transactions they can execute [20, 28, 54]. This management system must also audit a user's actions. This requires an extensible infrastructure that can integrate with complementary security and e-commerce technologies. For example, it should support multiple authentication methods including Personal Identification Numbers (PINs), passwords and Public Key Infrastructure (PKI). A security infrastructure should provide an administration model to support the much higher volume of users associated with wireless applications. Ideally, a wireless access management system should use different roles to protect individual resources and control user access. Systems that use access control lists (ACLs) would require that an administrator manually move the user to a new ACL for every change in status, which is an inefficient and expensive approach. The role based access control (RBAC) provides a new method to easily manage a complex system [1, 90, 94]. We detailed introduce RBAC in later chapters.

Transactions Level

Consumers are all comfortable with conducting transactions face-to-face; there is a physical exchange of goods and payment using a trusted mechanism such as cash, cheque or card [4, 5, 9, 11]. The comfort derives in part from familiarity. Many people are also familiar with, and trust, mail order transactions by post or over the phone, even though there are many opportunities for failure. In an electronic world trust is a more abstract concept:

1. Trust the information in a website?
2. Trust credit card information to the site?
3. Trust goods will be delivered?

These require that sensitive data must be secured throughout the transmission, and all transactions must be confirmed [33, 55, 75]. It is necessary to authenticate a user's identity, authorize the transaction, log the transaction details, and generate a digital receipt. By logging all wireless user activity from accessing portfolio information and applying for loans—organizations can ensure that all transactions are binding and provide customers with detailed transaction reports [19, 29, 49, 64].

With the high progress of wireless technology, M-commerce has been becoming an important subset of e-commerce. The issues mentioned above are also existed in M-commerce.

2.3   A Framework for Electronic Commerce

E-Commerce concerns with using a handheld terminal and mobile terminal such as a mobile phone, connecting with wired and wireless networks, and conducting transactions [92, 98, 101]. Because there are many different kind of e-commerce Services (e-shop, e-bank, M-service, and so on), it is necessary to build a framework to organize them so that some conceptual structures can be discovered and new services may be compared meaningfully with existing ones along some uniform dimensions. In order to build such a framework, this section propose three-dimensions. This integrated three-dimensional framework help users to understand the development status of current e-commerce services and further help designers, developers, and researcher to strategize and effectively implement new e-commerce applications. The three-dimensions are:

1. E-commerce hardware dimension;
2. E-commerce software technology dimension;
3. E-commerce application dimension.

The first dimension of the framework is based on the hardware that is used within e-commerce such as communication server, computer terminal, mobile phone, lap computer, and so on. In the second dimension, we provide various kinds of software technologies in e-commerce such as financial transactions, e-payment, management, and so on. In the third dimension, we categorize different e-commerce applications according to their value added features.

A framework for the field of e-commerce was introduced by Jeffrey F. etc. [34]. There are four infrastructures in the framework; they are Technology, Capital, Media and Public Policy infrastructure. The authors specified the technology infrastructure is the foundation of a system. The hardware backbone of computers, routers, servers, modems, and other network technologies provides half of the technology issues. The other half includes the software and communication standards that run on the hardware, including the core protocol for the web. On the other hand, authors specified a Media infrastructure with communication technology. These two infrastructures are confusing by the communication technology. The main reason of this confused point is because the authors did not analyze the relationship between different infrastructures. Another framework proposed by Varshney and Vetter [85], shows a user plane with four levels and a developer-provider plane with three. The framework has several functional layers. Consumers, providers, designers, and so on can find individual layers in the framework. However, there are some shortcomings in this framework. For instance, there is a tight relationship between the user plane and the developer and provider plane, the authors do not address it well in their framework. Another disadvantage is that the authors put all mobile commerce applications into some classes among the application layer without addressing any relationship among them. Many services involved in this layer have different characteristics and relationships between them.

2.3.1   Criteria for Choosing a Framework

We discuss the criteria for choosing a framework in the context of e-commerce. A framework and its dimensions is a subjective work, there is no exact measure for the quality of a framework along with its dimensions. However, there are some criteria for choosing a framework's dimensions.

One criterion is that a framework should be natural, which means that the framework is easy to understand even to the novice. The next criterion is usefulness, which means that the framework either help customers in e-commerce to strategize e-commerce applications, or provide a model structure for researchers. The third criterion is that the framework should be sufficiently consistent in categorizing e-commerce applications. This means, all existing and possible future e-commerce applications can be included and fit well into the framework.

2.3.2   Framework and Dimensions

The framework proposed in Fig. 2.4 has three-dimensions: software technology dimension; hardware dimension and applications dimension. In this framework, the software technology dimension is faced with an outside layer that supports end-users and other third parties who make use of e-commerce services. These parties are not necessary players in the e-commerce arena. This is because many people such as researchers and technology supporters are not involved in e-commerce.

The hardware dimension is also supported by an outside layer. This layer refers to the hardware environment. Productions, for example, communication servers, mobile computers, gateway, and mobile firewall, act as the cornerstone of e-commerce and are basic requirements to implement an e-commerce.

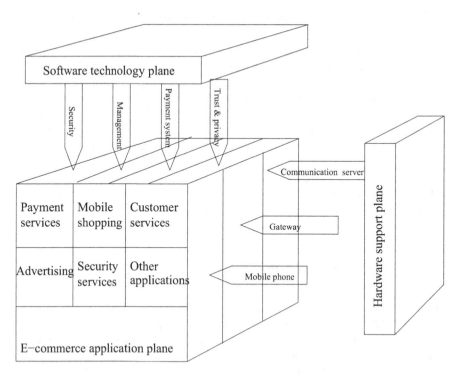

Fig. 2.4 A framework of e-commerce

The e-commerce application dimension can be considered as an application of the first dimension and the second dimension. Therefore we have positioned it on another dimension.

2.3.3   Dimension One: Software Technology in E-Commerce

There are many software technologies in e-commerce and new skills that are still being developed. Consumers and suppliers believe that good technologies can bring them benefit and can be used to build a trusted e-service. Therefore, the software dimension includes the basic and important technology requirements such as payment system, management, and so on in e-commerce. This thesis focus on some topics on this dimension.

Table 2.1 provides some examples of software technologies.

2.3.4   Dimension 2: Hardware Support in E-Commerce

This dimension has several levels from the client side to the server side. We have various hardware productions in e-commerce. For example, mobile phones or handheld computers are used in consumer side while computer servers provide

Table 2.1 Software technology in E-commerce

Software technologies	Description	Examples
Communication	It is used for connection between terminal users and servers	Ray technology, secondary dimension communication
E-service	It provides access for the user on the mobile network, such as billing, helpdesk	Google, Yahoo
Management	It offers how to manage a e-service system and who can access what information in the system	MAC, RBAC
Software platform	Organize a platform to integrate different communications and services for e-commerce	ExpressQ 3.0 by Nettech systems
Financial transaction	Handles the financial transactions	Banks and BEA
Middleware	Middleware is a layer of software that is used by application developers to connect their E-applications with different networks and operating systems without introducing awareness in the applications	Snapshot in Aberdeen

Table 2.2 Hardware in e-commerce

Layers in dimension	Descriptions and example	Example
Terminals	Mobile devices and terminal provides the client side functions in e-commerce applications	Mobile phone, laptops
Computer server	It provides various information of service and users can choose what service they need	Nokia mobile server, SDK 1.0, Yahoo chat service
Gateway	It is used to connect from consumers to servers	InfoSync

Table 2.3 E-commerce application

E-commerce application	Descriptions	Examples
e-shop	e-commerce extends ability to make transactions across time location and creates new, business opportunities	Amazon.com, Yahoo
Financial services	It offers financial transactions and is a key issue in e-commerce environment	ebay, e-pay
Security services	A terminal can function as a security device for gaining access to e-commerce	PKI systems, Wireless PKI systems
Customer services	It can be more economically to provide services	AvantGo, ebay
Advertising	It introduces production for companies and individuals	AdsOnWheel, AvantGo

service context in service provider's side. Gateways, between terminals and servers, are used to connect to each other. Table 2.2 shows some hardware in e-commerce.

2.3.5 Dimension 3: E-Commerce Application

This dimension is based on the unique characteristics of e-commerce that combine the advantages of electronic communications with existing e-commerce services [35, 76, 87]. And these characteristics can also be looked upon as the key drivers for the increasing expanded e-commerce market [12, 100]. Table 2.3 lists these categories and characteristics with examples. This layer can be divided into several minor subsets according to different market segments: C2C, B2B, and B2C layer, and so on.

M-commerce can be defined as mobile variance of e-commerce, most of these categories have their counterpart in a wireless world [23, 24, 46].

From what we have discussed above, we can find that all of these three-dimensions are good in the first criteria. The framework is natural and easy to understand. As to the criteria of consistency and fitness issue, we have shown that it can strategize e-commerce application and all existing and future applications are included in the framework and fit well in these three-dimensions.

2.4 Conclusions

With the accelerating progress of content presentation standards and continuing advances in data transmission speeds, e-commerce is assured by both consumers and business. An overview of e-commerce has been presented in this chapter. Various kinds of e-commerce issues such as mobile devices, e-payment, security and management, and so on are discussed. Finally, a new framework of e-commerce is also presented. Some technology topics in the software dimension such as payment system and management are detail analyzed in the rest of the thesis.

2.5 Problems and Exercises

2.5.1 Problems

Big Data is a hot area in both research and applications of e-commerce. Privacy and security of Big Data is gaining momentum in research community due to emerging technologies like cloud computing, analytics engines, and social networks. There are a number of open problems and future research perspectives related to privacy and security of Big Data [13, 97].

1. Privacy-Preserving Big Data Analytics—Big Data are valuable because they are treasured source of knowledge that is useful for decision making and prediction purposes. It possesses challenging research hurdles, because analytics process huge volumes of Big Data, and hence privacy of target data sets is not preserved yet [14, 27, 89].
2. Privacy-Preserving Social Network Mining—Social network data are the most reliable sources of real-life Big Data, with well known web social networks like Facebook, Twitter and Instagram. Here, data mining is of primary interest, but the need for privacy and security very often limits the real impact of these tasks [25, 57, 77, 96].
3. Privacy-Preserving Electronic Health Data—Electronic health data stores sensitive and confidential patient information in large datasets. Hence, there is a high need to preserve the privacy and security of stored data sets to protect the confidentiality of patient [10, 32, 59, 99].
4. Security Issues of (Big) Outsourced Databases—In cloud infrastructures, databases are often outsourced based on the DaaS (Database as a Service) approach. This elevates more problematic security concern as query-processing procedures may easily access sensitive data sets and determine privacy breaches [22, 26, 60, 95].

2.5.2   Exercises

1. what are the security Issues of Outsourced Databases?
2. List a few privacy issues of Electronic Health Data? One real example is required.
3. What are the privacy challenges in Big data? One example with privacy problem related to Big data in e-commerce environment is required.

References

1. Andreoli, J., Pacull, F., Pagani, D. and Pareschi, R.: Multiparty negotiation of dynamic distributed object services. Sci. Comput. Program. **31**(2–3), 179–203 (1998)
2. Beam, C., Segev, A.: Electronic catalogs and negotiations. CITM working paper 96-WP-1016 (1996)
3. Ben-Shaul, I., Gidron, Y., Holder, O. (eds.): A Negotiation Model for Dynamic Composition of Distributed Applications. Institute of Electrical and Electronics Engineers, Piscataway (1998)
4. Canetti, R., Goldreich, O., Halevi, S.: The random oracle methodology. In: Proceedings of the 30th ACM STOC '98, pp. 209–218. IEEE, Piscataway (1998)
5. Canetti, R., Micciancio, D., Reingold, O.: Perfectly one-way probabilistic hash functions. In: Proceedings of the 30th ACM STOC '98. IEEE, Piscataway (1998)
6. Cao, J., et al.: Towards secure xml document with usage control. In: Web Technologies Research and Development—APWeb 2005, pp. 296–307. Springer, Berlin (2005)
7. Carlson, P.: Information technology and the emergence of a worker-centered organization. ACM J. Comput. Doc. **24**(4), 204–212 (2000)
8. Cellular Telecommunication Industry Association: CTIA's semi-annual wireless industry survey. Wow-company, USA (1999). http://www.wow-com.com/statsury/survey
9. Chaum, D.: Blind signature for untraceable payments. In: Advances in Cryptology—Crypto 82, pp. 199–203. Plenum Press, New York (1983)
10. Chaum, D.: An Introduction to e-cash. DigiCash, (1995). http://www.digicash.com
11. Chaum, D., Fiat, A., Naor, M.: Untraceable electronic cash. In: Advances in Cryptology—Crypto 88. Lectures Notes in Computer Science, vol. 403, pp. 319–327. Springer, Berlin (1990)
12. Chen, Z., Lee, M., Cheung, C.: A framework for mobile commerce. In: Proceedings of the Americas Conference on Information Systems 2001, E-Commerce: Wireless/Mobile. AISeL (2001)
13. Chenthara, S., Wang, H., Ahmed, K.: Security and Privacy in Big Data Environment, pp. 1–9. Springer, Cham (2018)
14. Chenthara, S., et al.: Security and privacy-preserving challenges of e-health solutions in cloud computing. IEEE Access **7**, 74361–74382 (2019)
15. Clarke, R.: Key issues in electronic commerce and electronic publishing. In: Proceedings of the Information Online and on Disc 99, Sydney (1999)
16. ClickServices.com: ClickServices.com unleashes a new web portal for wireless Internet. Wow-company, USA (2000). http://www.wow-com.com/newsline/press_release.cfm?press_id=990
17. O'Leary, D.E., Selfridge, P.: Knowledge management for best practices. Commun. ACM **43**(11es), 11 (2000)
18. Davenport, T.: Process Innovation: Reengineering Work Through Information Technology. Harvard Business School Press, Brighton (1993)

19. Dogac, A.: Survey of the current state-of-the-art in electronic commerce and research issues in enabling technologies. In: Proceeding of Euro-Med Net 98 Conference, Electronic Commerce Track (1998)
20. Eng, T., Okamoto, T.: Single-term divisible electronic coins. In: Advances in Cryptology—Eurocrypt'94. Lectures Notes in Computer Science, vol. 950, pp. 306–319. Springer, Berlin (1995)
21. Eric, O.: Securing m-commerce (2000). ebizQ.net
22. Ford, W., Baum, M.: Secure Electronic Commerce: Building the Infrastructure for Digital Signatures and Encryption. Prentice Hall PTR (1997)
23. Frankel, Y., Yiannis, T., Yung, M.: Indirect discourse proofs: achieving fair off-line electronic cash. In: Advances in cryptology—Asiacrypt'96. Lectures Notes in Computer Science, vol. 1163, pp. 286–300. Springer, Berlin (1996)
24. Franklin, M., Yung, M.: Secure and efficient off-line digital money. In: Proceedings of the Twentieth International Colloquium on Automata, Languages and Programming. Lectures Notes in Computer Science, vol. 700, pp. 265–276. Springer, Berlin (1993)
25. Gabber, E., Silberschatz, A.: Agora: A minimal distributed protocol for electronic commerce. In: The Second USENIX Workshop on Electronic Commerce, Oakland (1996)
26. Garfinkel, S., Spafford, G.: Web Security and Commerce Risks, Technologies, and Strategies. O'Reilly & Associates, Sebastopol (1997)
27. Ge, Y., et al.: A benefit-driven genetic algorithm for balancing privacy and utility in database fragmentation. In: Proceedings of the Genetic and Evolutionary Computation Conference, pp. 771–776. Association for Computing Machinery, New York (2019)
28. Goldreich, O., Krawczyk, H.: On the composition of zero-knowledge proof systems. SIAM J. Comput. 25(1), 159–192 (1996)
29. Green, S., et al.: Software Agents: A review. TCD-CS-1997-06, Trinity College Dublin and Broadcom Eireann Research, Ireland (1997)
30. Guttman, R.H., Maes, P.: Cooperative vs. Competitive Multi-Agent Negotiations in Retail Electronic Commerce. In: Proceedings of the Second International Workshop on Cooperative information Agents (CIA'98), Paris (1998)
31. Haskin, D.: Analysts: smart phones to lead e-commerce explosion. Technical report, AllNet-Devices (1999)
32. Herzberg, A., Yochai, H.: Mini-Pay: Charging per Click on the Web (1996). http://www.ibm. net.il
33. Jansen, W., et al.: Security policy management for handheld devices. In: Proceedings of the 2003 International Conference on Security and Management (SAM'03) (2003)
34. Jeffrey, F., Bernard, J., Jeffrey, R.: E-Commerce. McGraw-Hill/Irwin (2000)
35. Juels, A., Luby, M., Ostrovsky, R.: Security of blind digital signatures. In: Advances in Cryptology—Crypto 97, Lectures Notes in Computer Science, vol. 1294, pp. 150–164. Springer, Berlin (1997)
36. Kabir, E., Wang, H.: Conditional purpose based access control model for privacy protection. In: Proceedings of the Twentieth Australasian Conference on Australasian Database, ADC '09, vol. 92, pp. 135–142. Australian Computer Society, Darlinghurst (2009)
37. Kabir, M., Wang, H., Bertino, E.: A conditional purpose-based access control model with dynamic roles. Expert Syst. Appl. 38(3), 1482–1489 (2011)
38. Kabir, M., Wang, H., Bertino, E.: A conditional role-involved purpose-based access control model. J. Organ. Comput. Electron. Commer. 21, 71–91 (2011)
39. Kabir, M., Wang, H., Bertino, E.: Efficient systematic clustering method for k-anonymization. Acta Inf. 48(1), 51–66 (2011)
40. Kalakota, R., Whinston, A.: Frontiers of Electronic Commerce. Addison-Wesley, Boston (1996)
41. Kannan, P., Chang, A., Whinston, A.: Wireless commerce: Marketing issues and possibilities. In: Proceedings of the 34th Hawaii International Conference on System Sciences. IEEE, Piscataway (2001)

42. Ketchpel, S.P., Garcia-Molina, H.: Making Trust Explicit in Distributed Commerce Transactions. In: IEEE Proceedings of the 16th ICDCS, pp. 270–281 (1996)
43. Khalil, F., Li, J., Wang, H.: Integrating recommendation models for improved web page prediction accuracy. In: Proceedings of the Thirty-First Australasian Conference on Computer Science, ACSC '08, vol. 74, pp. 91–100. Australian Computer Society, Darlinghurst (2008)
44. Klusch, M.: Intelligent Information Agents: Agent-Based Information Discovery and Management on the Internet. Springer, Berlin (1998)
45. Li, M., et al.: Advanced permission-role relationship in role-based access control. In: Information Security and Privacy, pp. 391–403. Springer, Berlin (2008)
46. Li, M., et al.: Optimal privacy-aware path in hippocratic databases. In: Database Systems for Advanced Applications, pp. 441–455. Springer, Berlin (2009)
47. Li, M., Wang, H.: ABDM: an extended flexible delegation model in RBAC. In: 2008 8th IEEE International Conference on Computer and Information Technology, pp. 390–395 (2008)
48. Li, M., Wang, H., Plank, A.: Privacy-aware access control with generalization boundaries. In: Proceedings of the Thirty-Second Australasian Conference on Computer Science, ACSC '09, vol. 91, pp. 105–112. Australian Computer Society, Darlinghurst (2009)
49. Loudon, D., Della, B.: Consumer Behavior: concepts and Applications, 4th edn.. McGraw-Hill (1993)
50. Malloy, A., Varshney, U., Snow, A.: Supporting mobile commerce applications using dependable wireless networks. Mobile Netw. Appl. 7(3), 225–234 (2002)
51. Michael, S., Achim, K.: Mobile commerce for financial services—killer applications or dead end? ACM SIGGROUP Bull. 22(1), 22–25 (2001)
52. Muller-Veerse, F.: M-commerce report. Durlacher Corporation, London (1999)
53. Neubert, R., et al.: Virtual enterprises—challenges from a database perspective. In Proceedings of ADC'01, GoldCoast. IEEE, Piscataway (2001)
54. Okamoto, T., Ohta, K.: Disposable zero-knowledge authentication and their applications to untraceable electronic cash. In: Advances in Cryptology—Crypto89. Lectures Notes in Computer Science, vol. 435, pp. 481–496. Springer, Berlin (1990)
55. Papazoglou, M., Tsalgatidou, A.: Special issue on information systems support for electronic commerce. Inf. Syst. 24(6) (1999)
56. Pfitzmann, B., Waidner, M.: How to break and repair a 'provably secure' untraceable payment system. In: Advances in Cryptology—Crypto'91. Lectures Notes in Computer Science, vol. 576, pp. 338–350. Springer, Berlin (1992)
57. Pointcheval, D., Stern, J.: Security arguments for digital signatures and blind signatures. J. Cryptol. 13(3), 361–396 (2000)
58. Rabin, M.: Digital Signatures, Foundations of Secure Communication. Academic Press, New York (1978)
59. Rasool, R., et al.: Cyberpulse: a machine learning based link flooding attack mitigation system for software defined networks. IEEE Access 7, 34885–34899 (2019)
60. Rohm, A.W., Pernul, G.: COPS: a model and infrastructure for secure and fair electronic markets. In: Proceedings of the 32nd Hawaii International Conference on System Sciences (HICSS-32), Hawaii. IEEE Computer Society Press, Silver Spring (1999)
61. Silicon Image Group: Silicon Image Enters Storage Market with Multi-Rate Serdes Capable of Operating at up to 3.125 Gbps. Silicon (2000). www.siimage.com/press/08_21_00b.asp
62. Silicon Image Group: The Price-Performance Imperative For Mass-Market Adoption Silicon, (2001). www.siimage.com/documents/sii-wp-018-a.pdf
63. Simon, D.: Anonymous communication and anonymous cash. In: Advances in Cryptology—Crypto'96. Lectures Notes in Computer Science, vol. 1109. pp. 61–73. Springer, Berlin (1997)
64. Spegel, N., Rogers, B., Buckley, R.: Negotiation Theory and Techniques. Skills Series. Butterworths (1998)
65. Strategy Analytics: Strategy Analytics forecasts $200 billion mobile commerce market by 2004 Wow-company (2000). http://www.wow-com.com/newsline/press_release.cfm?press$_$id=826

66. Sun, X., et al.: An efficient hash-based algorithm for minimal k-anonymity. In: Proceedings of the Thirty-First Australasian Conference on Computer Science, ACSC '08, vol. 74, pp. 101–107. Australian Computer Society Darlinghurst (2008)

67. Sun, X., et al.: Enhanced p-sensitive k-anonymity models for privacy preserving data publishing. Trans. Data Privacy **1**(2), 53–66 (2008)

68. Sun, X., et al.: (p^+, α)-sensitive k-anonymity: a new enhanced privacy protection model. In: 2008 8th IEEE International Conference on Computer and Information Technology, pp. 59–64 (2008)

69. Sun, X., et al.: Injecting purpose and trust into data anonymisation. Comput. Secur. **30**, 332–345 (2011)

70. Sun, X., et al.: Privacy-aware access control with trust management in web service. World Wide Web **14**(4), 407–430 (2011)

71. Sun, X., et al.: Satisfying privacy requirements before data anonymization. Comput. J. **55**(4), 422–437 (2012)

72. Sun, L., Li, Y., Wang, H.: M-service and its framework. In: 2005 Asia-Pacific Conference on Communications, pp. 837–841 (2005)

73. Sun, X., Wang, H., Li, J.: Priority driven k-anonymisation for privacy protection. In: Proceedings of the 7th Australasian Data Mining Conference, vol. 87, pp. 73–78 (2008)

74. Sun, L., Wang, H., Yong, J.: Authorization algorithms for permission-role assignments. J. UCS **15**, 1782–1798 (2009)

75. Sun, X., Wang, H., Sun, L.: Extended k-anonymity models against attribute disclosure. In: 2009 Third International Conference on Network and System Security, pp. 130–136 (2009)

76. Sun, X., Wang, H., Li, J.: Microdata protection through approximate microaggregation. In: Proceedings of the Thirty-Second Australasian Conference on Computer Science, ACSC '09, vol. 91, pp. 161–168. Australian Computer Society, Darlinghurst (2009)

77. Sun, X., Wang, H., Li, J.: Satisfying privacy requirements: one step before anonymization. In: Advances in Knowledge Discovery and Data Mining, pp. 181–188. Springer, Berlin (2010)

78. Sun, X., Li, M., Wang, H.: A family of enhanced (L, α)-diversity models for privacy preserving data publishing. Future Gener. Comput. Syst. **27**(3), 348–356 (2011)

79. Sun, X., Sun, L., Wang, H.: Extended k-anonymity models against sensitive attribute disclosure. Comput. Commun. **34**(4), 526–535 (2011). Special issue: building secure parallel and distributed networks and systems

80. Tarasewich, P., Nickerson, R., Warkentin, M.: Issues in mobile E-commerce. Commun. Assoc. Inf. Syst. **8**(1), 3 (2002)

81. Timmers, P.: Global and local in electronic commerce. In: Proceedings of EC-Web. Lectures Notes in Computer Science, vol. 1875. Springer, London (2000)

82. Tveit, A.: Peer-to-peer based recommendations for mobile commerce. In: Proceedings of the First International Workshop on Mobile Commerce, pp. 26–29, Rome. ACM, New York (2001)

83. Varshney, U., Jain, R.: Issues in emerging 4G wireless networks. Computer **34**(6), 94–96 (2001)

84. Varshney, U., Vetter, R.: Emerging mobile and wireless networks. Commun. ACM **43**(6), 73–81 (2000)

85. Varshney, U., Vetter, R.: Mobile commerce: framework, applications and networking support. Mobile Netw. Appl. **7**(3), 185–198 (2002)

86. Wang, H., et al.: Authorization algorithms for the mobility of user-role relationship. In: Proceedings of the Twenty-Eighth Australasian Conference on Computer Science, ACSC '05, vol. 38, pp. 69–77. Australian Computer Society, Darlinghurst (2005)

87. Wang, H., et al.: A framework for role-based group deligation in distributed environments. In: Proceedings of the 29th Australasian Computer Science Conference, vol. 48, pp. 321–328 (2006)

88. Wang, H., et al.: Authorization approaches for advanced permission-role assignments. In: 2008 12th International Conference on Computer Supported Cooperative Work in Design, pp. 277–282 (2008)

89. Wang, H., et al. Editorial: Special issue on security and privacy in network computing. World Wide Web **23**, 951–957 (2020)

90. Wang, H., Li, Q.: Secure and efficient information sharing in multi-university e-learning environments. In: Advances in Web Based Learning—ICWL 2007, pp. 542–553. Springer, Berlin (2008)

91. Wang, H., Sun, L.: Trust-involved access control in collaborative open social networks. In: 2010 Fourth International Conference on Network and System Security, pp. 239–246 (2010)

92. Wang, H., Cao, J., Ross, D.: Role-based delegation with negative authorization. In: Frontiers of WWW Research and Development—APWeb 2006, pp. 307–318. Springer, Berlin (2006)

93. Wang, H., Cao, J., Zhang, Y.: A flexible payment scheme and its role-based access control. IEEE Trans. Knowl. Data Eng. **17**(3), 425–436 (2005)

94. Wang, H., Cao, J., Zhang, Y.: Delegating revocations and authorizations in collaborative business environments. Inf. Syst. Front. **11**(3), 293 (2008)

95. Wang, H., Cao, J., Zhang, Y.: Delegating revocations and authorizations in collaborative business environments. Inf. Syst. Front. **11**(3), 293 (2008)

96. Wang, H., Sun, L., Varadharajan, V.: Purpose-based access control policies and conflicting analysis. I: Security and Privacy—Silver Linings in the Cloud, pp. 217–228. Springer, Berlin (2010)

97. Wang, H., Jiang, X., Kambourakis, G.: Special issue on security, privacy and trust in network-based big data. Inf. Sci., **318**(C), 48–50 (2015)

98. Wang, H., Zhang, Y., Cao, J.: Ubiquitous computing environments and its usage access control. In: Proceedings of the First International Conference on Scalable Information Systems, InfoScale '06, New York. ACM, New York (2006)

99. Wang, Z., Zhan, Z., Lin, Y., Yu, W., Wang, H., Kwong, S., Zhang, J.: Automatic niching differential evolution with contour prediction approach for multimodal optimization problems. IEEE Trans. Evol. Comput. **24**(1), 114–128 (2020)

100. Wu, R.: Building a legal framework for e-commerce in Hong Kong. J. Inf. Law Technol. (2000)

101. Yacobi, Y.: Efficient electronic money. In: Advances in Cryptology—Asiacrypt'94. Lectures Notes in Computer Science, vol. 917, pp. 153–163. Springer, Berlin (1995)

102. Zhang, J., et al.: Detecting anomalies from high-dimensional wireless network data streams: a case study. Soft Comput. **15**(6), 1195–1215 (2011)

103. Zhang, Y., Jia, X.: Transaction processing. In: Wiley Encyclopedia of Electrical and Electronics Engineering, vol. 22, pp. 298–311 (1999)

Chapter 3
Untraceable Electronic Cash System in the Internet of Things

Electronic cash payment has been playing an important role in the Internet of things. One of the desirable characteristics is its traceability, which can prevent money laundering and can find the destination of suspicious withdrawals.

In this chapter, a new scheme for untraceable electronic cash transaction processing is developed, in which the bank involvement in the payment transaction between a user and a receiver is eliminated. The user withdraws electronic "coins" from the bank and uses them to pay to a receiver. The receiver subsequently deposits the coins back to the bank. In the process the user remains anonymous, unless s/he spends a single coin more than once (double spend). The security of the system is based on *DLA* (Discrete Logarithm Assumption) and the cut-and-choose methodology.

3.1 Introduction

3.1.1 Electronic Cash and Its Properties

Traditional cash is a bearer instrument that can be used spontaneously and instantaneously, to make payments from one user to another user without the involvement of a bank. It is the preferred method for low and medium value purchases, and transactions. Cash payments also offer privacy protection and they are not normally traceable by a third party [8, 62, 63, 66]. Together these factors account for the wide acceptability of traditional cash.

The Internet of Things (IoT) is the network of physical devices, vehicles, home appliances, and other items embedded with electronics, software, sensors, actuators, and connectivity which enables these things to connect and exchange data, creating opportunities for more direct integration of the physical world into computer-based systems, resulting in efficiency improvements, economic benefits, and reduced human exertions [12, 36, 76, 77].

© Springer Nature Switzerland AG 2020
H. Wang et al., *Access Control Management in Cloud Environments*,
https://doi.org/10.1007/978-3-030-31729-4_3

The number of IoT devices increased 31% year-over-year to 8.4 billion in the year 2017 and it is estimated that there will be 30 billion devices by 2020 [31]. The global market value of IoT is projected to reach $7.1 trillion by 2020 [18].

Traditional cash is playing an important role in IOT but it has some shortcomings [7, 67, 69]. First, cash must be created such that is hard to forge and cash must be transported from one place to another place. Cash must be stored safely. Bank notes can be easily destroyed or forged using sophisticated color copier machines. Cash is annoying to carry. It spreads germs, and people can steal it from other people. Another shortcoming of traditional cash is that of cannot be used for payments over the phone or the Internet.

Cheques and credit cards have reduced cash circulation through out our society, but cheques and credit cards allow people to trace the user's privacy to a degree never imagined before.

Hence, a new "cash" is needed which can allow for authenticated but untraceable messages [2, 58, 68, 70]. For example, Alice can transfer "cash" to Bob. But newspaper reporter Eve does not know Alice's identity. Bob can then deposit that money into his account, and the bank has no idea who Alice is. But if Alice tries to buy cocaine with the same piece of the "cash" she sent to Bob, she will be detected by the bank. And if Bob tries to deposit the same piece of "cash" into two different accounts, he will be detected, but Alice will remain anonymous. It is called Electronic-cash (or E-cash) to differentiate it from digital money with an audit trail, such as cards. Electronic cash can make money laundering more difficult for a coin must run a full cycle from the bank during withdrawal to the same bank for deposit (on Internet). An interesting overview of these issues is available in [15].

Electronic cash (or "e-cash"), can provide stronger anonymity than physical cash, since the latter clearly displays serial numbers which can be recorded to allow further tracing [9, 57–59]. Contrary to their physical counterparts, e-cash has an inherent limitation; it is easy to copy and reuse. To guard against what is traditionally called "double-spending" of electronic coins, Chaum proposed for the bank to keep a list of spent coins and check every deposited coin against this list [1]. Hence the bank has to be on-line during the payment, otherwise the shop will have no guarantee that the coins received are valid. Forcing the bank to be on-line during the payment is a very strict requirement; consider that in the current payment systems the number of payments is at least an order of magnitude larger than the number of deposits, which are performed in batch mode usually at the end of each day. Checking each payment on-line would force banks to migrate to more expensive computers which allow real-time payment verifications. Furthermore, these computers would present a single point of failure for the system since no payments could be conducted off-line.

To bypass the on-line requirement, Chaum et al. [10] proposed a protocol to detect, instead of preventing, double-spending. In their model, called off-line electronic cash, anonymity holds as long as users are legitimate, whereas double-spenders are identified. Off-line electronic cash has since enjoyed considerable attention in the research community, aiming to optimize the originally proposed system for practical applications.

Anonymity is the distinguishing property of e-cash [11, 14, 64, 65]; the user privacy is guaranteed even against collaboration of all other involved parties, i.e., bank and shops. There have been several references in the literature for anonymous-like systems, providing partial privacy under the assumption of no collaboration between involved parties, or assuming the central bank is honest. These are very strong and potentially unjustified assumptions, especially in light of financial benefits from disclosing personal information and efficient ways of collaboration between interested parties, such as bulk transfers of electronic files.

The off-line property is equally significant in e-cash, even in scenarios where shops and bank happen to be the same party (e.g., postal services): on-line systems require constant and real-time involvement of the bank in every payment transaction, resulting in excessive communication and computation costs [35, 54, 71]. In contrast, off-line systems usually operate in dual mode, verifying high-cost transactions on-line (to prevent high-volume fraud, even though the fraudulent party is identified), while the bulk of payments are processed in batch mode by the bank. Several currently employed "electronic cash" (or e-cash) payment systems, such as credit cards, bank and personal checks, operate in this dual-mode operation, showing the viability of the concept.

The ideal electronic cash system should have the following properties:

1. Anonymous [26, 49, 73];
2. Revocation [4, 16, 20, 51];
3. Efficiency [22, 61, 75];
4. Crime prevention [28, 47, 50].

Firstly, electronic-cash should be anonymous for legitimate users [6, 46, 79]. The bank cannot link to the legitimate users, but it will identify the double-spenders. Anonymous is only for legal user, so the revocation of anonymity should be done for illegal user.

E-cash system must be efficient. It means not only should tracing (anonymity revocation) be performed efficiently, but the added burden to the basic system should be minimal for all involved parts—trustees, banks, users and shops [21, 52, 53]. In particular, trustees must be involved only when revocation is required and remain off-line otherwise. At last, a cash system must protect all users for their electronic money, sometimes motivating crimes are more serious than other mistakes.

In an on-line electronic-cash system, the banks have to be on-line during the payment to guarantee that the coins received by shops are valid. But the banks to be on-line during the payment are very strict requirement. In an off-line electronic-cash system, the bank needs not to be involved during the payment proceeding. Of course, the double-spent coins cannot be prevented in the payment but the identity of the double spender can be detected in future.

3.1.2 Off-line Electronic Cash Overview

Off-line anonymous electronic cash was introduced by Chaum et al. [11]. The security of their scheme relied on some arbitrary assumptions. However, no formal proof was attempted. Although hardly practical, their system demonstrated how off-line e-cash can be constructed and laid the foundation for more secure and efficient schemes to follow.

Okamoto and Ohta [33] were the first to attempt an improvement on this system. They modified the model by moving the most complex part of the functionality of the withdrawal protocol, namely the zero-knowledge proof of the user's identity, to the user setup (account establishment) protocol which is executed much less frequently. In the latter the user obtains an untraceable "license" which he uses for withdrawals of coins. Thus, anonymity is established only once, in the form of a pseudonym, instead of being "refreshed" with every withdrawn coin. Hence, a user's coins are linkable and users may be traced with conventional techniques, i.e., using locality, time, type, size, frequency of payments, or by finding a single payment in which the user identified himself. The authors suggested that a compromise between the efficiency and the unlinkability of the system can be found by running the account-establishment protocol more than once. The system relies on more reasonable and clarified assumptions but, it is faster than the work in [11], at least when the account establishment protocol is performed infrequently; otherwise no improvement is claimed.

Pfitzmann and Waidner [34] presented a way to base on-line electronic cash on general two-party computation protocols and zero-knowledge proofs. To combine the security of [34] with the relative efficiency of regular cut-and-choose systems, Franklin and Yung [16] presented a provably secure scheme that was not based on general computation protocols. The security relied on the DLA and on the existence of a mutually trusted party (equivalently, a general computation protocol could substitute the trusted party's functionality). Although a cut-and-choose techniques were used and its efficiency was still not a prime consideration, Franklin and Yung were the first to illustrate how off-line e-cash could be based on the DLA, as well as the first to construct a formal security model; variations of this security model have appeared in subsequent e-cash systems [7, 32].

Chan et al. [7] presented a provably secure off-line e-cash scheme that relied only on the security of RSA. This cut-and-choose based scheme extended the work of Franklin and Yung [16] who aimed to achieve provable security without the use of general computation protocols. T. Yiannis and M. Yung [80] showed that the decision Diffie–Hellman assumption implies the security of the original ElGamal encryption scheme (with messages from a subgroup) without modification and they also showed that the opposite direction holds, i.e., the semantic security of the ElGamal encryption was actually equivalent to the decision Diffie–Hellman problem.

Popescu presented a secure and efficient transaction protocol in 2018 that provides the anonymity and can detect the double spending [13]. The proposed payment system is based on the ElGamal encryption scheme, the ElGamal signature scheme and the ElGamal blind signature protocol. In 2018, Batten and Yi indicated how an off-line e-cash system can solve change-giving problems [29]. The system offers usual expected features of anonymity and unlinkability of the payer, but can reveal the identity of an individual who illegally tries to spend e-cash twice. Siamak and Maria in 2017 proposed a solution for one of the major problems in Bitcoin: selfish mining or block-withholding attack [40]. This attack is conducted by adversarial miners in order to either earn undue rewards or waste the computational power of honest miners.

3.1.3 Outline of the Chapter

In this chapter, we propose an untraceable, off-line electronic cash scheme which achieves provable security without the use of general computation protocols and without the requirement of a trusted third party, or of a costly general computation-based initialization procedure [23, 44, 45, 81]. To illustrate the practicality of schemes that are not based on general computation protocols, and show how to derive an efficient variant based on the random-oracle model; this variant thus achieves provable security based on DLA, cut-and choose technique and the existence of random oracle like hash functions. Further more our untraceable electronic cash scheme is much more simple than [16]. An implication of it is that truly anonymous e-cash can be implemented very efficiently without sacrificing security in comparison to existing account-based or anonymous-like systems.

The chapter is organized as follows: in Sect. 3.2, some basic definitions and the simple examples are reviewed. The basic model of electronic cash is presented in Sect. 3.3. In Sect. 3.4, a new off-line electronic cash scheme is designed and the security analysis of our scheme is given in Sect. 3.5. A simple example is given in Sect. 3.6 and the comparison with other scheme is present in Sect. 3.7. Section 3.8 will be the conclusion.

3.2 Some Basic Definitions

3.2.1 Hash Functions and Random Oracle Model

$h(x)$ is a hash function if and only if given a value x it is computationally hard to find a $y \neq x$ such that $h(x) = h(y)$, i.e., collisions are hard to find.

Hash functions are a major building block for several cryptographic protocols, including pseudorandom generators [2, 3], digital signatures [4], and message authentication.

Hash functions have been used in computer science for a long time [25, 27, 43]. A hash function is a function, mathematical or otherwise, that takes a variable-length input string and converts it to a fixed-length (generally smaller) output string. Regardless of the nature of the function, an adversary can always select values at random from the domain of the function in the hope that they hash on the same value. Counter-intuitively, it can be shown that if the range of a hash function is of size n, a guessing algorithm does not need to perform 2^{n-1} iterations (on average) in order to find a collision, but rather only $O(2^{n/2})$. Currently, a range of 160 bits is considered to be sufficient for most applications.

A random oracle R is a mapping (function) from $\{0, 1\}^* \rightarrow \{0, 1\}^\infty$ chosen by selecting each bit of $R(x)$ uniformly and independently (random and unpredictable), for every x.

Random oracles are very powerful tools, allowing the construction of very efficient signatures.

A system model is called a random oracle model if its operations are under random oracles. In this model, the functions (random oracles) produce a random answer for each new query. Of course, if the same query is asked twice, identical answers are obtained. Random oracle models are commonly used in practice and in electronic cash in particular [1, 5, 17], especially in light of a construction by Bellare and Rogaway [7] showing instantiations of random oracles based on efficient hash function, such as MD5 [38].

For example, suppose $h' : \{0, 1\}^{256} \rightarrow \{0, 1\}^{64}$ is a hash function, $h''(x) = h'(x) \oplus C$, where C is a random chosen 64 bit constant and $\oplus$ denotes bitwise exclusive or. Defining $h_1(x) = h''(x[0])||h''(x[1])||h''(x[2])|| \ldots$, where $|x| = 224$ and $[i]$ is the encoding of i such that $x[i]$ has 256 bits, where $||$ denote concatenation. We define $h : \{0, 1\}^* \rightarrow \{0, 1\}^\infty$ as follows: for any input x, encoding x by x' consisting of x, the bit "1" and "0" to make $|x'|$ a multiple of 224 bits (the "1" and "0" are depended on the encoding). Now let $x' = x'_1|| \ldots ||x'_n$, where $|x'_i| = 224$ and define $h(x) = h_1(x'_1) \oplus \ldots \oplus h_1(x'_n)$. Then $h(x)$ is a random oracle for its output is random and unpredictable.

3.2.2 Cut-and-Choose Technique

Cut-and-Choose technique is a basic method in integer theory. We can use mathematic method to express cut-and-choose technique. Suppose a set $A = \{1, 2, \ldots, 2k\}$.

1. Alice cuts the set A into two parts

$$A_1 = \{j_1, \ldots j_k\}, \ A_2 = A - A_1$$

   the size of A_1 is same as that of A_2.
2. Bob randomly chooses A_1, or A_2.

3. Alice gets the remain part.

The cut-and-choose technique works for no way but Alice can guess which part Bob will choose. Alice has a 50% chance of guessing which party Bob will choose in each round of the protocol, so she has a 50% chance of right guess. Her chance to be right in two rounds is 25%, and the chance of her to be right all n times is 2^{-n}. After 16 rounds, the right rate of Alice'guessing is 1 in 65536. So Alice cannot get anything but guessing. It means Alice gets nothing and it is called zero-knowledge.

Michael Rabin was the first person to use the cut-and-choose technique in cryptography [37].

The first e-cash systems employed a cut-and-choose technique: at withdrawal the user presents $2n$ (where n is the security parameter) "terms"; the bank "cuts-and-chooses" n, for which the user reveals the inner structure. The bank verifies their correctness and blindly signs the remaining n. At payment a similar cut-and-choose technique is employed for the shop to verify a "hint" on the user's identity, such that upon double-spending two hints identify the user. The cut-and-choose technique is a tool for a zero-knowledge proof of correctness of the coin, thus preserving user anonymity. Security is guaranteed with probability overwhelming in n, but a scheme's communication, computation and storage requirements are multiplied by a factor of n.

3.2.3 RSA and DLA

RSA is a public-key cryptosystem that offers both encryption and digital signatures (authentication). Ron Rivest, Adi Shamir, and Leonard Adleman developed RSA in 1977 [39].

RSA works as follows: take two large primes p and q, and compute their product $n = pq$; n is called the modulus. Choose a number e, less than n and relatively prime to $(p-1)(q-1)$, which means e and $(p-1)(q-1)$ have no common factors except 1. Find another number d such that $(ed-1)$ is divisible by $(p-1)(q-1)$. The values e and d are called the public and private exponents, respectively. The public key is the pair (n, e), the private key is d. It is currently difficult to obtain the private key d from the public key (n, e).

The source of DLA is the discrete logarithm problem.

The discrete logarithm problem is as follows: given an element g in a group G of order t, and another element y of G, the problem is to find x, where $0 < x < t - 1$, such that y is the result of composing g with itself x times. In some groups there exist elements that can generate all the elements of G by exponentiation (i.e., applying the group operation repeatedly) with all the integers from 0 to $t - 1$. When this occurs, the element is called a generator and the group is called cyclic. Rivest [38] has analyzed the expected time to solve the discrete logarithm problem both in terms of computing power and cost.

Discrete Logarithm Assumption (DLA) is an assumption that the discrete logarithm problem is believed to be difficult and also to be the hard direction of a one-way function. For this reason, it has been used for the basis of several public-key cryptosystems, including the famous ElGamal system.

3.2.4 Blind Signature

Blind signature schemes, first introduced by Chaum [11] allow a person to get a message signed by another party without revealing any information about the message to the other party.

Suppose Alice has a message m that she wishes to have it signed by Bob, and she does not want Bob to learn anything about m. Let (n, e) be Bob's public key and d be his private key. Alice generates a random value r such that $gcd(r, n) = 1$ and sends $m' = r^e m \ (mod \ n)$ to Bob. The value m' is "blinded" by the random value r, and hence Bob can derive no useful information from it. Bob returns the signed value, $s' = (m')^d = (r^e m)^d \ (mod \ n)$ to Alice. Since $s' = rm^d \ (mod \ n)$, Alice can obtain the true signature s of m by computing $s = s'r^{-1} \ (mod \ n)$.

A probabilistic polynomial time (p.p.t) Turing machine M is a Turing machine which can flip coins as an additional primitive step, and on input string x runs for at most a polynomial in $|x|$ steps. $M(x, y)$ denotes the outcome of M on input x when internal coin tosses are y.

3.3 Basic Model

Electronic cash (in particular off-line untraceable electronic cash) has sparked wide interest among cryptographers ([15, 19, 78], etc.). In its simplest form, an e-cash system consists of three parts (a bank B, a user U and a shop S) and three main procedures as shown in Fig. 3.1 (withdrawal, payment and deposit). In a coin's life-cycle, the user U first performs an account establishment protocol to open an account with the bank B. To obtain a coin U performs a withdrawal protocol with B and during a purchase U spends a coin by participating in a payment protocol with the shop S. To deposit a coin, S performs a deposit protocol with the bank B.

Users and shops maintain an account with the bank, while

1. U withdraws electronic coins from his account, by performing a withdrawal protocol with the bank B over an authenticated channel.
2. U spends a coin by participating in a payment protocol with a shop S over an anonymous channel, and
3. S performs a deposit protocol with the bank B, to deposit the user's coin into his account.

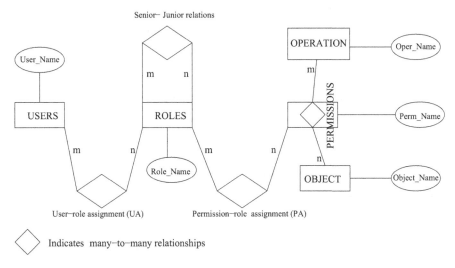

Fig. 3.1 Model of electronic-cash

The system is *off-line* if during payment the shop S does not communicate with the bank B. It is *untraceable* if there is no p.p.t. TM (probabilistic polynomial-time Turing Machine) M access to all bank's views of withdrawal, payment and deposit protocols, can decide a coin's origin. It is *anonymous* if the bank B, in collaboration with the shop S, cannot trace the coin to the user. However, in the absence of tamper-proof hardware, electronic coins can be copied and spent multiple times by the user U. This has been traditionally referred to as double-spending. In anonymous on-line e-cash, double-spending is prevented by having the bank check if the coin has been deposited before. In off-line anonymous e-cash, however, this solution is not possible; instead, as proposed by Chaum et al. [11], the system guarantees that if a coin is double-spent the user's identity is revealed with overwhelming probability.

There are also three additional proceedings such as the bank setup, the shop setup, and the user setup (account opening). They describe the system initialization, namely creation and posting of public keys and opening of bank accounts. Although they are certainly parts of a complete system, these are often omitted as their functionalities can be easily inferred from the description of the three main procedures. For clarity we only describe the bank setup and the user setup (because the shop setup is as similar as user setup) for our new scheme in the next section.

3.4   New Off-line Untraceable Electronic Cash Scheme

In this section, we propose a new off-line untraceable electronic cash scheme.

Our scheme includes two basic processes in system initialization (bank setup and user setup) and three main protocols: a new withdrawal protocol with which

U withdraws electronic coins from B while his account is debited, a new payment protocol with which U pays the coin to S, and a new deposit protocol with which S deposits the coin to B and has his account credited.

3.4.1   System Initialization

We only describe the bank setup and the user setup based on Discrete Logarithm Assumption and random-oracle model here and omit the detail of the shop setup (because the shop setup is similar to the user setup).

Bank's Setup   (Performed once by B)
Primes p and q are chosen such that $|p - 1| = \delta + k$ for a specified constant δ, and $p = \gamma q + 1$, for a specified small integer γ. Then a unique subgroup G_q of prime order q of the multiplicative group Z_p and generators g, g_1, g_2 of G_q are defined. Secret key $x_B \in_R Z_q$ for a denomination is created, where $a \in_R A$ means that the element a is selected randomly from the set A with uniform distribution. Hash function H from a family of collision intractable (or, ideally, according to [15], correlation-free one way) hash function is also defined. B publishes p, q, g, g_1, g_2, H and its public keys $h = g^{x_B} (\bmod\ p), h_1 = g_1^{x_B} (\bmod\ p), h_2 = g_2^{x_B} (\bmod\ p)$.

The secret key x_B is safety under the DLA. The Hash function will be used in withdrawal process.

User's Setup (Account Opening)   (Performed for each user U)
The bank B associates the user U with $I = g_1^{u_1} (\bmod\ p)$ where $u_1 \in G_q$ is generated by U and $g_1^{u_1} g_2 \neq 1 (\bmod\ p)$. U computes $z = h_1^{u_1} h_2 = (I g_2)^{x_B} (\bmod\ p)$.

In system initialization, the communication complexity is $O(l)$ for the user only sends its account I of length l bits to the bank, and the computation complexity is $O(1)$.

After the user's account and the shop's account opening, we can describe the new untraceable electronic cash scheme.

3.4.2   New Untraceable Electronic Cash Scheme

We now describe the new off-line untraceable electronic cash scheme which includes three protocols: withdrawal protocol, payment protocol and deposit protocol.

Withdrawal   (Over an authenticated channel between B and U)
The withdrawal creates a "restrictively blind" signature B_i $(i = 1, \ldots, k)$ of I and using cut-and-choose technology. U will put a signature as $(I g_2)^s$ where s is a random number (chosen by U and kept secret).

1. The user chooses a_i, c_i, $1 \le i \le k$, independently and uniformly at random form the residues (mod p).
2. The user forms and sends to the bank k blinded candidates $B_i =$ $H(x_i, y_i)$ (mod p), $1 \le i \le k$, where

$$x_i = g^{a_i} (mod\ p),\quad y_i = g_1^{a_i \oplus (I||c_i)} (mod\ p).$$

3. The bank chooses a random subset of $k/2$ blinded candidate indices

$$R = \{i_j\},\ 1 \le i_j \le k,\ 1 \le j \le k/2$$

and transmits it to the user.
4. The user transmits $A = (Ig_2)^s (mod\ p)$ and $z' = z^s (mod\ p)$ to bank.
5. The user displays a_i, c_i values for all i in R, and the bank checks them. To simplify notation we assume that $R = \{k/2 + 1, k/2 + 2, \ldots, k\}$.
6. The bank verifies: $A^{xB} = z' (mod\ p)$ and gives the user the electronic coin C,

$$C = \prod_{i \notin R} B_i = \prod_{1 \le i \le k/2} B_i (mod\ p).$$

We use the Hash function in step 2 and the cut-and-choose technique in step 3, steps 5 and 6. The basic safety in withdrawal is protected by Hash function, and the deep safety is kept by the cut-and-choose technique. Indeed, since cut-and-choose technique is zero-knowledge proof, then nothing can be inferred about the coin. At the final step, the output of the coin is random and unpredictable. It is a random oracle model and secure in withdrawal.

In withdrawal process, the communication complexity is $O(k)$ for the user sends B_i, $1 \le i \le k$ to the bank and the bank sends R which length is $k/2$ to the user, the computation complexity is $O(q^{k/2})$, since x_i, y_i, B_i, A, Z', C must be computed. $C = \prod_{1 \le i \le k/2} B_i (mod\ p)$ is the main computation.

Payment (Performed between the user and the shop over an anonymous channel) At payment time the user supplies information to the receiver (which is later forwarded to the bank) so that if a coin is double-spent the user is identified. The detailed payment is as below. (the user and the shop agree on date/time):

1. The user sends C to the shop.
2. The shop chooses a random binary string $z_1, z_2, \ldots, z_{k/2}$, and sends to the user.
3. The user responds as follows, for all $1 \le i \le k/2$:

   (a) If $z_i = 1$, then sends to the shop: a_i, y_i
   (b) If $z_i = 0$, then sends the shop: x_i, $a_i \oplus (I||c_i)$, c_i

4. The shop verifies that C is right since the user's responses can fit C.

The user gives some data to the shop according its random binary string $z_1, z_2, \ldots, z_{k/2}$. The random binary strings from different shops are different with high probability. Two different shops will send to the user complementary binary values for at least one bit z_i for which B_i was of the proper form. The user's account I can be obtained from $a_i, y_i, x_i, a_j \oplus (I||c_j), c_j$ when $i = j$. The different strings will be gotten if the user uses the same coin C twice, then the user has a high probability of being traced.

In payment, the communication complexity is $O(k+l)$ for the shop sends z_i, $1 \leq i \leq k/2$ to the user and the user sends responds $a_i, y_i, x_i, a_i \oplus (I||c_i), c_i$ to the shop. The computation complexity is $O(1)$ for only the shop verifies the form C.

Deposit   (The receiver deposits a coin to a bank)
After some delay for the system is off-line, a shop sends to B a payment transcript, consists of $C, a_i, y_i, x_i, a_j \oplus (I||c_j), c_j$ and the date/ time of the transaction. The bank verifies their correctness and credits in customers' accounts.

In deposit, the communication complexity is $O(k + l)$ for the shop sends user's responds $a_i, y_i, x_i, a_i \oplus (I||c_i), c_i$ to the bank. The computation complexity is $O(1)$, since only the bank verifies whether C was used before or not.

Remark   The receiver (shop) deposits the coin in its account provided by the bank with a transcript of the payment. If the user uses the same coin C twice, then the user has a high probability of being traced: with high probability, two different receivers will send complementary binary values for at least one bit z_i for which B_i was of the proper form. The bank can easily search its records to ensure that C has not been used before. If the user uses C twice, then with high probability, the bank has both $a_i, a_i \oplus (I||c_i)$ and c_i with same i. Thus, the bank can isolate the user and trace the payment to the user's account I.

In our new scheme, the communication complexity is $O(k + l)$ and the computation complexity is $O(q^{k/2})$ where k is the security parameter and l is the size of user's identity I.

The system initialization in Fig. 3.2 includes the security random oracle model and how to get the bank setup and the user setup. It is important for the withdrawal, payment and deposit in our new scheme. The security of our new scheme is also based on the system initialization.

We have shown how to derive an efficient scheme based on the random-oracle model. It achieves provable security based on DLA and the existence of random oracle like hash functions [41, 48, 56]. Based on this system initialization, three new protocols with cut-and-choose methodology are designed. It is much more secure due to the cut-and-choose methodology and random-oracle model.

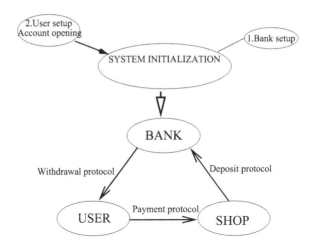

Fig. 3.2 Basic off-line electronic cash system

3.5 Security Analysis

An off-line E-cash scheme is secure [16] if the following requirements are satisfied:

1. *Unreusable*: If any user uses the same coin twice, the identity of the user's can be computed.
2. *Unexpandable*: With n withdrawal proceedings, no p.p.t. (Probabilistic polynomial time) Turing Machine can compute $(n + 1)$th distinct and valid coin.
3. *Unforgeable*: With any numbers of the customer's withdrawal, payment and deposit, no p.p.t. Turing Machine can compute a single valid coin.
4. *Untraceable*: With any numbers of the customer's valid withdrawal, payment and deposit protocols, no p.p.t. Turing Machine can compute a legal user's identity.

We employ Discrete Logarithm methods in our new scheme; these methods have been suggested in many of the recent e-cash schemes to bind identities (an unavoidable issue in off-line e-cash). These methods were started in [34] and continued by others [7, 32] as well as in [79]. The security of our scheme is based on the hardness of Discrete Logarithms [80] and the cut-and-choose technology. The cut-and-choose technology is based on zero-knowledge proof, and the scheme assumes that the hash function used is perfect (i.e., random oracles).

We have analysed the untraceability and unreusebility before. To prevent the cooperation of the bank and some others frame the user as a multiple spender in the scheme, we use digital signature Z^s for s is known only by the user. To prevent unexpanding, we use the Discrete Logarithm methods and cut-and-choose technology.

A possible problem with the scheme is a collusion between a user U and the second shopkeeper. After having user transactions with two receivers which send the same information to the bank, the bank knows that with high probability one of them is lying, and the bank can decide the first purchase is right by the date/time in the payment but cannot trace the coin to the user's account.

To prevent the bank frame the user as a multiple spender in the scheme, we use digital signature Z^s for s is known only by the user. The user is protected against frame-up only computationally, not unconditionally.

3.6 A Simple Example

We give a simple example to explain how our scheme works in this section.

Bank Setup
Suppose $(p, q, \gamma, k) = (47, 23, 2, 4)$, then $G_q = \{0, 1, 2, \ldots, 22\}$ is a subgroup of order 23. $g = 2$, $g_1 = 3$, $g_2 = 5$ are the generators of G_q. Bank's secret key $x_B = 4$ and hash function $H(x, y) = 3^x * 5^y \pmod{47}$. Bank publishes $H(x, y)$ and

$$\{p, q, g, g_1, g_2, h, h_1, h_2\} = \{47, 23, 2, 3, 5, 16, 34, 14\}.$$

User Setup (Opening an Account)
Every user has a secret key. We assume the secret of a user is $u_1 = 7$ and the user sends $I = g_1^{u_1} = 32 \pmod{47}$ to the bank. The user computes

$$z = h_1^{u_1} * h_2 = 18 \pmod{47}.$$

The user will perform the following steps when s/he does shopping.

1. **Withdrawal**
   The user chooses a one-time secret key $s = 3$ and

   (a) Chooses

   $$\{a_1, a_2, a_3, a_4, c_1, c_2, c_3, c_4\} = \{1, 2, 3, 4, 11, 12, 13, 14\}$$

   (b) The user computes (We omit module 47):

   $$\{x_1, x_2, x_3, x_4, y_1, y_2, y_3, y_4\} = \{2, 4, 8, 16, 32, 7, 7, 32\}$$

   and sends B_i to the Bank:

   $$\{B_1, B_2, B_3, B_4\} = \{16, 45, 26, 36\}.$$

   (c) The Bank chooses $R = \{3, 4\}$ (suppose) and sends it to the user.
   (d) The user transmits $A = (Ig_2)^s = 44 \pmod{47}$ and $z' = z^s = 4 \pmod{47}$ to the Bank.

(e) The user displays $(a_3, a_4, c_3, c_4) = (3, 4, 13, 14)$ to the Bank, and The Bank checks the correctness of the B_3, B_4.

(f) The Bank verifies $A^{XB} = 44^4 = 34 = z' \pmod{47}$ and gives the user the coin C:

$$C = B_1 * B_2 = 16 * 45 = 15 \pmod{47}.$$

2. **Payment**

The user can use the coin in shop as follows. If the user uses the coin only once, she is legal. But when she uses the coin twice she will be identified.

(a) The user sends $c = 15$ to a shop (The user needs not to display I).

(b) The shop chooses a random binary string to the user, suppose it is $\{z_1, z_2\} = \{1, 0\}$.

(c) The user responds to the shop $(a_1, y_1) = (1, 32)$ for $z_1 = 1$ and $(x_2, c_2, a_2 \oplus (I || c_2)) = (4, 12, 526)$ for $z_2 = 0$.

(d) The shop sends the responds $(a_1, y_1, x_2, c_2, a_2 \oplus (I || c_2))$ to the bank and the bank checks if the responds are correct with $\{B_1, B_2\} = \{16, 45\}$.

3. **Deposit and Owner Tracing**

The bank will put the money into the shop's account when the checking of the coin C is correct. The shop can also see that the money in his account is added. If the user uses the coin twice, the bank will get $a_i, a_j \oplus (I || c_j)$ and c_j with $i = j$, then the user's identity I can be found.

3.7 Comparisons

In this section, we compare our new scheme with of the proposed approach by M. Franklin and Yung [16]. We will see that the communication complexity and computation complexity of our protocols are better than that in [16].

We first recall the basic main processing stages of M. Franklin and M. Yung [16].

1. $R \rightarrow A : Z_1^* = \rho_1^{e_A} h(z_1) \, mod \, N_A, \ldots, Z_{2k}^* = \rho_{2k}^{e_A} h(z_{2k}) \, mod \, N_A$, where

   (a) $\rho_i \in_R Z_{N_A}^*$ for all $1 \leq i \leq 2k$.
   (b) $z_i = e'(s, r_i)$ for all $1 \leq i \leq 2k$, where each r_i is uniformly random over the appropriate range, and where e' is a public and easily computable function.
   (c) h is a publicly known collision-free hash function.

2. In round two, the following messages are sent:

   (a) $R \rightarrow A : [r_i, \rho_i : i \in S]$.
   (b) $A \rightarrow R : C' = \prod_{j \notin S} (z_j^*)^{d_A} \pmod{N_A}$, assuming that the messages received

   so far are consistent (otherwise A terminates the protocol); i.e.:

   $$z_j^* \rho_j^{-e_A} = h(e'(s, r_j)) \quad j \in S.$$

3. R finds $[r, C]$ where

   (a) $r = [r_j : j \notin S]$

   (b) $C = C' \prod_{j \notin S} \rho_j^{-1} \ (mod \ N_A)$

   (c) The public and easily computable function e is defined to be

$$e(s, r) = [e'(s, r[1]), \ldots, e'(s, r[k])].$$

Where e_A, d_A is A's encryption and decryption key, respectively. e_A is public and d_A is secret key. N_A is public.

In [16], the communication complexity is $O(k^2 l)$ bits where k is a security parameter and l is the size of a signed bit; the computation complexity is $O(n^{k/2})$. In our case, the communication complexity is $O(k + l)$. The computation complexity is $O(q^{k/2})$. As general, $q < n$.

	Communication complexity	Computation complexity
Scheme in [16]	$O(k^2 l)$	$O(n^{k/2})$
New scheme	$O(k + l)$	$O(q^{k/2})$

3.8   Conclusion

In this chapter an untraceable electronic cash scheme is designed which is an off-line scheme and without using of general computation protocols and without the requirement of a trusted party. We have shown how to derive an efficient cash scheme based on the variants in the random-oracle model. The variants thus achieve provable security based on DLA and the existence of random oracle like hash function. The security of the system is based on DLA and the cut-and-choose methodology. We give a simple example to explain our new untraceable scheme. Finally, we compare it with the other scheme used cut-and-choose technique.

3.9   Problems and Exercises

3.9.1   Problems

1. To consumer, E-cash is more than a convenient way of carrying cash, since it also opens avenue for e-commerce to take place [55, 72, 74]. Consumer only needs to have smart card like devices to initiate transaction, either on-line or off-line. For some implementations, E-cash can be stored in a computer for easy

transfer over the Internet for on-line transaction. Anonymity implementation gives consumer a privacy to use E-cash just like the conventional coins and paper notes. Consumers are also able to make transactions without the need of third party verification. E-cash environment enables consumers to purchase small item over the Internet, which is cumbersome in other implementations such as credit cards. For the banks, E-cash implementation does reduce cost in maintaining cash in the bank and therefore increase bank management efficiency. Furthermore with E-cash, banks are now able to provide their services to the world via the Internet more easily. (https://www.giac.org/paper/gsec/1799/overview-e-cash-implementation-security-issues/103204). In e-cash implementation, Banks may ask consumers to accept a few conditions and obligations when using an e-cash system. The problems are how to manage the conditions and obligations, what are the relations between the conditions, obligations and users?

2. One of the disadvantages of E-cash is the existence of counterfeiters who are able to recreate E-cash either stored in smart card or softcopy based [30, 60, 73, 80]. All parties involve, consumers, merchants and banks/issuers, are affected by this counterfeit activity. Liability of the loss E-cash on damage smart card or crashed computer where the E-cash is installed is also in question. Although the number of Internet users is increasing in number, there are many others who do not have the opportunity to own computers and get connected to the Internet. Not to mention that consumer needs to learn new things such as installing software on the computer and understand how E-cash software operates. Furthermore, the numbers of participating companies are still low and it seems companies are not willing to accept e-cash system in order to attract more consumers [24, 32, 39, 42]. This phenomena might relate to the fact that additional fee is incur as processing charges by banks to merchant and consumer. The questions are how to attract potential customers such as aged people? How to support people without Internet connection?

3. Other issue of E-cash is money monitoring by the government. With the conventional coins and paper notes, government can monitor money flow to stabilized economy, but with E-cash, there is no foreseeable way for the government to control the flow of E-cash in and out of a country. Even more mind-boggling is how a government can calculates or collects taxation from untraceable E-cash asset.

3.9.2 Exercises

1. What are conditions and obligations banks may ask customers to accept? Examples are required.
2. What methods or devices may have for aged people to use e-cash system?
3. Can people use e-cash system without the Internet?
4. What are the possible taxations between different countries when e-cash systems are applied in multiple countries?

References

1. Bellare, M., Rogaway, P.: Random oracles are practical: a paradigm for designing efficient protocols. In: First ACM Conference on Computer and Communications Security, pp. 62–73. IEEE, Piscataway (1993)
2. Bellare, M., Goldreich, O., Krawczyk, H.: Stateless evaluation of pseudorandom functions: security beyond the birthday barrier. In: Advances in Cryptology—Crypto 99. Lectures Notes in Computer Science, vol. 1666. Springer, Berlin (1999)
3. Boyko, V., Peinado, M., Venkatesan, R.: Speeding up discrete log and factoring based schemes via precomputations. In: Advances in Cryptology—Eurocrypt'98. Lectures Notes in Computer Science, vol. 1807. Springer, Berlin (1998)
4. Canetti, R., Goldreich, O., Halevi, S.: The random oracle methodology. In: Proceedings of the 30th ACM STOC '98, pp. 209–218. IEEE, Piscataway (1998)
5. Canetti, R., Micciancio, D., Reingold, O.: Perfectly one-way probabilistic hash functions. In: Proceedings of the 30th ACM STOC '98. IEEE, Piscataway (1998)
6. Cao, J., et al.: Towards secure xml document with usage control. In: Web Technologies Research and Development—APWeb 2005, pp. 296–307. Springer, Berlin (2005)
7. Chan, A., Frankel, Y., Tsiounis, Y.: An efficient off-line electronic cash scheme as secure as RSA. Research report NU-CCS-96-03, Northeastern University, Boston (1995)
8. Chaum, D.: Blind signature for untraceable payments. In: Advances in Cryptology—Crypto 82, pp. 199–203. Plenum Press, New York (1983)
9. Chaum, D. (ed.): An introduction to e-cash. DigiCash (1995). http://www.digicash.com
10. Chaum, D., Fiat, A., Naor, M.: Untraceable electronic cash. In: Goldwasser, S. (ed.) Advances in Cryptology—CRYPTO' 88, pp. 319–327. Springer, New York (1990)
11. Chaum, D., Fiat, A., Naor, M.: Untraceable electronic cash. In: Advances in Cryptology—Crypto 88. Lectures Notes in Computer Science, vol. 403, pp. 319–327. Springer, Berlin (1990)
12. Chenthara, S., et al.: Security and privacy-preserving challenges of e-health solutions in cloud computing. IEEE Access **7**, 74361–74382 (2019)
13. Constantin, P.: A secure and efficient payment protocol based on ElGamal cryptographic algorithms. Electron. Commer. Res. **18**(2), 339–358 (2018)
14. Cox, B., Tygar, J.D., Sirbu, M.: Netbill security and transaction protocol. In: The first USENIX Workshop on Electronic Commerce, New York (1995)
15. Frankel, Y., Yiannis, T., Yung, M.: Indirect discourse proofs: achieving fair off-line electronic cash. In: Advances in cryptology—Asiacrypt'96. Lectures Notes in Computer Science, vol. 1163, pp. 286–300. Springer, Berlin (1996)
16. Franklin, M., Yung, M.: Secure and efficient off-line digital money. In: Proceedings of the Twentieth International Colloquium on Automata, Languages and Programming. Lectures Notes in Computer Science, vol. 700, pp. 265–276. Springer, Berlin (1993)
17. Goldreich, O., Krawczyk, H.: On the composition of zero-knowledge proof systems. SIAM J. Comput. **25**(1), 159–192 (1996)
18. Hsu, C., Lin, J.: An empirical examination of consumer adoption of internet of things services: Network externalities and concern for information privacy perspectives. Comput. Hum. Behav. **62**, 516–527 (2016)
19. Huszti, A., Kovács, Z.: Proving anonymity for BILMIX. J. Univ. Comput. Sci. **24**(7), 892–915 (2018)
20. Kabir, E., Wang, H.: Conditional purpose based access control model for privacy protection. In: Proceedings of the Twentieth Australasian Conference on Australasian Database, ADC '09, vol. 92, pp. 135–142. Australian Computer Society, Darlinghurst (2009)
21. Kabir, M., Wang, H., Bertino, E.: A conditional purpose-based access control model with dynamic roles. Expert Syst. Appl. **38**(3), 1482–1489 (2011)
22. Kabir, M., Wang, H., Bertino, E.: A conditional role-involved purpose-based access control model. J. Organ. Comput. Electron Commer. **21**, 71–91 (2011)

23. Kabir, M., Wang, H., Bertino, E.: Efficient systematic clustering method for k-anonymization. Acta Inf. **48**(1), 51–66 (2011)

24. Khalil, F., Li, J., Wang, H.: Integrating recommendation models for improved web page prediction accuracy. In: Proceedings of the Thirty-First Australasian Conference on Computer Science, ACSC '08, vol. 74, pp. 91–100. Australian Computer Society, Darlinghurst (2008)

25. Li, M., et al.: Advanced permission-role relationship in role-based access control. In: Information Security and Privacy, pp. 391–403. Springer, Berlin (2008)

26. Li, M., et al.: Optimal privacy-aware path in hippocratic databases. In: Database Systems for Advanced Applications, pp. 441–455. Springer, Berlin (2009)

27. Li, M., Wang, H.: ABDM: an extended flexible delegation model in RBAC. In: 2008 8th IEEE International Conference on Computer and Information Technology, pp. 390–395 (2008)

28. Li, M., Wang, H., Plank, A.: Privacy-aware access control with generalization boundaries. In: Proceedings of the Thirty-Second Australasian Conference on Computer Science, ACSC '09, vol. 91, pp. 105–112. Australian Computer Society, Darlinghurst (2009)

29. Lynn, B., Xun, Y.: Off-line digital cash schemes providing untraceability, anonymity and change. Electron. Commer. Res. **19**, 81–110 (2019)

30. MastercardVisa: SET 1.0—secure electronic transaction specification (1997). http://www.mastercard.com/set.html

31. Nordrum, A.: Popular Internet of Things Forecast of 50 Billion Devices by 2020 is Outdated. IEEE, Piscataway (2016)

32. Okamoto, T.: An efficient divisible electronic cash scheme. In: Advances in Cryptology—Crypto'95. Lectures Notes in Computer Science, vol. 963, pp. 438–451. Springer, Berlin (1995)

33. Okamoto, T., Ohta, K.: Disposable zero-knowledge authentications and their applications to untraceable electronic cash. In: Advances in Cryptology—CRYPTO' 89 Proceedings, pp. 481–496. Springer, New York (1990)

34. Pfitzmann, B., Waidner, M.: How to break and repair a 'provably secure' untraceable payment system. In: Advances in Cryptology—Crypto'91. Lectures Notes in Computer Science, vol. 576, pp. 338–350. Springer, Berlin (1992)

35. Pointcheval, D.: Self-scrambling anonymizers. In: Proceedings of Financial Cryptography. Springer, Anguilla (2000)

36. Qin, Y., et al., When things matter: a survey on data-centric internet of things. J. Netw. Comput. Appl. **64**, 137–153 (2016)

37. Rabin, M., Digital Signatures, Foundations of secure communication. Academic Press, New York (1978)

38. Rivest, R.T.: The MD5 message digest algorithm. Internet RFC 1321 (1992)

39. Rivest, R.L., Shamir, A., Adleman, L.M.: A method for obtaining digital signatures and public-key cryptosystems. Commun. ACM **21**(2), 120–126 (1978)

40. Siamak, S., Maria, P.: Brief announcement: Zeroblock: timestamp-free prevention of block-withholding attack in bitcoin. In: Spirakis, P., Tsigas, P. (eds.) Stabilization, Safety, and Security of Distributed Systems, pp. 356–360. Springer, Cham (2017)

41. Sun, X., et al.: Enhanced p-sensitive k-anonymity models for privacy preserving data publishing. Trans. Data Privacy **1**(2), 53–66 (2008)

42. Sun, X., et al.: An efficient hash-based algorithm for minimal k-anonymity. In: Proceedings of the Thirty-First Australasian Conference on Computer Science, ACSC '08, vol. 74, pp. 101–107. Australian Computer Society, Darlinghurst (2008)

43. Sun, X., et al.: (p^+, α)-sensitive k-anonymity: a new enhanced privacy protection model. In: 2008 8th IEEE International Conference on Computer and Information Technology, pp. 59–64, (2008)

44. Sun, X., et al.: Injecting purpose and trust into data anonymisation. Comput. Secur. **30**, 332–345s (2011)

45. Sun, X., et al.: Privacy-aware access control with trust management in web service. World Wide Web **14**(4), 407–430 (2011)
46. Sun, L., Li, Y., Wang, H.: M-service and its framework. In: 2005 Asia-Pacific Conference on Communications, pp. 837–841 (2005)
47. Sun, L., Wang, H., Yong, J.: Authorization algorithms for permission-role assignments. J. UCS **15**, 1782–1798 (2009)
48. Sun, X., Wang, H., Li, J.: Priority driven k-anonymisation for privacy protection. In: Proceedings of the 7th Australasian Data Mining Conference, vol. 87, pp. 73–78 (2008)
49. Sun, X., Wang, H., Li, J.: Microdata protection through approximate microaggregation. In: Proceedings of the Thirty-Second Australasian Conference on Computer Science, ACSC '09, vol. 91, pp. 161–168. Australian Computer Society, Darlinghurst (2009)
50. Sun, X., Wang, H., Sun, L.: Extended k-anonymity models against attribute disclosure. In: 2009 Third International Conference on Network and System Security, pp. 130–136 (2009)
51. Sun, X., Wang, H., Li, J.: Satisfying privacy requirements: One step before anonymization. In: Advances in Knowledge Discovery and Data Mining, pp. 181–188. Springer, Berlin (2010)
52. Sun, X., Li, M., Wang, H.: A family of enhanced (L, α)-diversity models for privacy preserving data publishing. Future Gener. Comput. Syst. **27**(3), 348–356 (2011)
53. Sun, X., Sun, L., Wang, H.: Extended k-anonymity models against sensitive attribute disclosure. Comput. Commun. **34**(4), 526–535 (2011). Special issue: building secure parallel and distributed networks and systems
54. Wang, H., et al. Authorization algorithms for the mobility of user-role relationship. In: Proceedings of the Twenty-eighth Australasian Conference on Computer Science, ACSC '05, vol. 38, pp. 69–77. Australian Computer Society, Darlinghurst (2005)
55. Wang, H., et al.: A framework for role-based group deligation in distributed environments. In: Proceedings of the 29th Australasian Computer Science Conference, vol. 48, pp. 321–328 (2006)
56. Wang, H., et al.: Authorization approaches for advanced permission-role assignments. In: 2008 12th International Conference on Computer Supported Cooperative Work in Design, pp. 277–282 (2008)
57. Wang, H., Duan, T.: A signature scheme for security of e-commerce. Comput. Eng. **25**, 79–80 (1999)
58. Wang, H., Zhang, Y.: A protocol for untraceable electronic cash. In: Lu, H., Zhou, A. (eds.) Proceedings of the First International Conference on Web-Age Information Management. Lectures Notes in Computer Science, vol. 1846, pp. 189–197, Shanghai. Springer, Berlin (2000)
59. Wang, H., Zhang, Y.: Untraceable off-line electronic cash flow in e-commerce. In: Proceedings of the 24th Australian Computer Science Conference ACSC2001, pp. 191–198, GoldCoast. IEEE Computer Society, Silver Spring (2001)
60. Wang, H., Li, Q.: Secure and efficient information sharing in multi-university e-learning environments. In: Advances in Web Based Learning—ICWL 2007, pp. 542–553. Springer Berlin (2008)
61. Wang, H., Sun, L.: Trust-involved access control in collaborative open social networks. In: 2010 Fourth International Conference on Network and System Security, pp. 239–246 (2010)
62. Wang, H., Cao, J., Zhang, Y.: A consumer anonymity scalable payment scheme with role based access control. In: Second International Conference on Web Information Systems Engineering (WISE01), pp. 53–62, Kyoto (2001)
63. Wang, H., Cao, J., Kambayashi, Y.: Building a consumer anonymity scalable payment protocol for the internet purchases. In: 12th International Workshop on Research Issues on Data Engineering: Engineering E-Commerce/E-Business Systems, San Jose (2002)
64. Wang, H., Cao, J., Zhang, Y.: A flexible payment scheme and its role-based user-role assignment. In: Proceedings of the Second International Workshop on Cooperative Internet Computing (CIC2002), pp. 58–68, Hong Kong (2002)

65. Wang, H., Cao, J., Zhang, Y.: A flexible payment scheme and its user-role assignment. In: Chan, A. (ed.) Cooperative Internet Computing, pp. 107–128. Kluwer Academic Publisher, Dordrecht (2002)
66. Wang, H., Cao, J., Zhang, Y.: Formal authorization allocation approaches for role-based access control based on relational algebra operations. In: Third International Conference on Web Information Systems Engineering (WISE02), pp. 301–312, Singapore (2002)
67. Wang, H., Cao, J., Zhang, Y.: Ticket-based service access scheme for mobile users. In: Twenty-Fifth Australasian Computer Science Conference (ACSC2002), Monash University, Melbourne, Victoria (2002)
68. Wang, H., Cao, J., Zhang, Y.: A flexible payment scheme and its permission-role assignment. In: Proceedings of the Twenty-Sixth Australasian Computer Science Conference (ACSC2003), pp. 189–198, Adelaide (2003)
69. Wang, H., Cao, J., Zhang, Y.: Formal authorization allocation approaches for permission-role assignments using relational algebra operations. In: Proceedings of the 14th Australian Database Conference ADC2003, Adelaide (2003)
70. Wang, H., Cao, J., Zhang, Y.: An electronic payment scheme and its RBAC management. Concurrent Eng. Res. Appl. **12**(3), 247–275 (2004)
71. Wang, H., Cao, J., Zhang, Y.: A flexible payment scheme and its role-based access control. IEEE Trans. Knowl. Data Eng. **17**(3), 425–436 (2005)
72. Wang, H., Cao, J., Ross, D.: Role-based delegation with negative authorization. In: Frontiers of WWW Research and Development—APWeb 2006, pp. 307–318. Springer, Berlin (2006)
73. Wang, H., Cao, J., Zhang, Y.: Delegating revocations and authorizations in collaborative business environments. Inf. Syst. Front. **11**(3), 293 (2008)
74. Wang, H., Zhang, Y., Cao, J.: Ubiquitous computing environments and its usage access control. In: Proceedings of the First International Conference on Scalable Information Systems, InfoScale '06, New York. ACM, New York (2006)
75. Wang, H., Sun, L., Varadharajan, V.: Purpose-based access control policies and conflicting analysis. In: Security and Privacy—Silver Linings in the Cloud, pp. 217–228. Springer, Berlin (2010)
76. Wang, H., Zhang, Z., Taleb, T.: Editorial: Special issue on security and privacy of IoT. World Wide Web **21**(1), 1–6 (2018)
77. Wang, Z., Zhan, Z., Lin, Y., Yu, W., Wang, H., Kwong, S., Zhang, J.: Automatic niching differential evolution with contour prediction approach for multimodal optimization problems. IEEE Trans. Evol. Comput. **24**(1), 114–128 (2020)
78. Yacobi, Y.: Efficient electronic money. In: Advances in Cryptology—Asiacrypt'94. Lectures Notes in Computer Science, vol. 917, pp. 153–163. Springer, Berlin (1995)
79. Yiannis, T.: Fair off-line cash made easy. In: Advances in Cryptology—Asiacrypt'98. Lectures Notes in Computer Science, vol. 1346, pp. 240–252. Springer, Berlin (1998)
80. Yiannis, T., Yung, M.: On the security of ElGamal-based encryption. In: International Workshop on Practice and Theory in Public Key Cryptography (PKC '98). Lectures Notes in Computer Science, vol. 1346 Yokohama. Springer, Berlin (1998)
81. Zhang, J., et al.: Detecting anomalies from high-dimensional wireless network data streams: a case study. Soft Computing **15**(6), 1195–1215 (2011)

Part II
M-Services and Scalable Payment

The Part II consists of three Chaps. 4–6. Chapter 4 describes the technology for M-service and how to design a secure and flexible access control scheme and protocol for M-services based on role based access control. Chapter 5 proposes a secure, anonymity scalable and practical payment protocol for Internet purchases, and analyses its role-based user-role assignment. The protocol uses electronic cash for payment transactions. In this new protocol, from the viewpoint of banks, consumers can improve anonymity if they worried about disclosure of their identities. Chapter 6 presents basic definitions of role based access control (RBAC) such as user-role assignment, permission-role assignment and role-role assignment and so on. The advantages and significance of RBAC are discussed.

Chapter 4
Achieving Secure and Flexible M-Services Through Tickets

This chapter describes a secure and flexible access control scheme and protocol for M-services based on role based access control (RBAC). The access control architecture involves a Trusted Credential Centre (TCC), a Trusted Authentication and Registration Centre (TARC) and a secure ticket based mechanism for service access. Users and service providers register with the TARC and are authenticated. Based on this, tickets are issued by the TCC to the users. Tickets carry authorization information needed for the requested services. In particular, we are able to specify access control polices based on roles. The protocols between the various entities in the model are protected using appropriate security mechanisms such as signatures, which are used to verify correctness of the requested service as well as to direct billing information to the appropriate user. Our architecture supports efficient authentication of users and service providers over different domains and provides a secure access model for services to users. Our model is also able to support anonymity of users. Only the TCC is able to identify the misbehaving users. In summary, we believe that the proposed architecture forms a good basis for achieving a secure and flexible M-service system.

4.1 Introduction

Web services via wireless technologies (M-services), HTTP and XML have become important for conducting business in the future. W3C XML Protocol Working Group has been developing some common standard techniques such as Web Services Description Language (WSDL), Simple Object Access Protocol (SOAP), and Universal Description Discovery and Integration (UDDI). However, at this stage, there is no standard technique for access control in M-service.

© Springer Nature Switzerland AG 2020
H. Wang et al., *Access Control Management in Cloud Environments*,
https://doi.org/10.1007/978-3-030-31729-4_4

A wireless Web service (M-service) is a Web-based application that accepts requests from different systems on the Internet and can involve a range of wireless and web technologies such as GSM [25], XML [3], SOAP [2] and WSDL [7]. Vendors and customers can provide and obtain services without being limited by the location of an M-service. As a result, the security and privacy issues in M-service systems have become more critical, especially for mobile consumers (e.g. moving from one place to another or using wireless mobile systems) [49, 53, 54]. A static access control is incompatible for such dynamic mobile environments. Consumers may access service across multiple service domains and it is necessary to develop efficient cross-domain authentication and access control that can involve roaming between domains [19, 32, 33]. Cross-domain authentication itself can become complicated authentication activities when the roaming path is long and dynamic. This can limit the future of M-service applications.

Furthermore, there can be different types of M-Services. In some cases, there can be specific binding relationships between the participants whereas in others such as shopping, any user may be able to access a service using say some form of electronic payment. Hence there is a need to develop a secure access control scheme that is flexible enough to capture these specific bindings and take them into account in the decision making. Also, a user may wish to access multiple M-Services over a period of time. This requires that the security management is both efficient and effective when users change from one service to another. There have been several proposals related to M-service systems [10, 25–27]. Probably it is accurate to say that most of them lack the required flexibility in security management. For instance, the Excellent e-service [10]provides service via different channels and manages customer communication via e-mail, text chat, and fax in the same system. However, customers have to trust the system (e.g. with their credit card numbers) and there are not mechanisms for privilege management. Another M-service system Red Hat is designed to provide enterprise-class Linux for enterprise-class servers and applications [27]. It supplies the source codes of some productions and also requires the private information of customers for payment. The Global system for mobile communication [25] provides mechanisms for user authentication as well as integrity and confidentiality, including protection of information exchanged between mobile terminals and fixed networks. It provides only limited privacy protection for users by hiding their real identities from eavesdroppers on the radio interface [26].

There are several security issues that need to be addressed in the design and management of M-Services [57, 58]. In particular, we believe the following are critical to developing a secure and flexible access control architecture.

Trust and Security Model It is essential that there is an explicit representation of trust model in a M-Service system. This is needed to specify the trust relationships between the users and the service providers in the system [6, 11, 47, 57]. The trust model should be supported by security services and mechanisms that can help the participants to make appropriate decisions. For instance, based on the trust model and the security services such as authentication and ticket based credentials, the service provider is able to conclude that the claimed user is who s/he claims to be and that s/he has the privileges to access the requested service. Similarly, based on the trust model and security architecture, the users in the M-Service can reliably identify that a service provider has correctly charged for the service that has been provided. At present, majority of M-Service systems depend entirely on an implicit trust model whereby the users and providers trust each other completely. Such a scheme is not suitable for large scale systems with numerous service providers and users over multi-domains.

Flexibility A basic characteristic of an M-Service is that a service can be provided to a user anywhere and at anytime. This in turn requires an efficient cross-domain authentication and a flexible and effective access control privilege management. Mechanisms present in current M-service systems are not adequate to fulfill these requirements. Current solutions often rely on roaming agreements for cross-domain authentication. A user, when applying services in a foreign domain, authenticates himself to the foreign service provider. This process often assumes that the foreign service provider trusts the home domain agent of the user and is based on roaming agreements between various service providers [14, 30, 45, 56]. With the rapidly growing number of service providers, such schemes may no longer be practical. There will be a need to minimize the number of interactions between the home and foreign domains.

Furthermore, the issue of privilege management across multiple domains poses a number of additional challenges [16, 40, 41]. First, there is a need to represent different types of privileges for different services in different domains. Our access control architecture is able to support a range of access policies including role based access control (RBAC). RBAC has gained much popularity in access control, though the idea of partitioning privileges in terms of specific job functions and roles have been well known over several decades. Second there is a need to verify the correctness and the validity of the privileges at the time of access to a service. This can be done by the service provider itself or some entity that is trusted by the service provider. The security management model should be flexible enough to specify a range of privileges and to evaluate them to make appropriate decisions in an efficient manner.

Efficiency Users are susceptible to being disconnected and loosing data while accessing services in wireless environments [20, 22, 35]. Also a user may need to connect to multiple services and change M-service systems to access different kinds of services on the Internet. The new scheme should provide a scalable solution for different kinds of M-services and use bandwidth efficiently, especially in wireless networks.

In this chapter, we propose a security architecture for M-Services addressing some of the aspects mentioned above. Our architecture involves a Trusted Credential Centre (TCC), a Trusted Authentication and Registration Centre (TARC) (via UDDI) and a secure ticket based mechanism for service access. Users and service providers register with the TARC and are authenticated. Services are described in the Trusted Credential Center and Service Provider by WSDL. Based on authentication, tickets are issued by the TCC to the users. Tickets carry authorization information

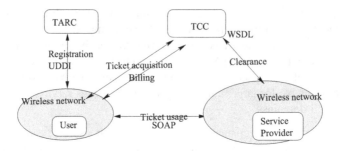

Fig. 4.1 M-service model

needed for the requested services. In particular, we are able to specify access control polices based on roles. Tickets are transferred using SOAP. The protocols between the various entities in the model are protected using appropriate security mechanisms which are used to verify correctness of the requested service, the validity of the privileges, provision of service as well as secure charging users for service usage. Our architecture supports efficient authentication of users and service providers over different domains and provides a secure access model for services to users [21, 23, 36].

The billing information is stored in the TCC for the users to view and access after service provision. There are lots of issues associated with this!

The main stages involved in the architecture are illustrated in Fig. 4.1.

This chapter is organized as follows: in Sect. 4.2, basic definitions and ticket types are introduced. The basic definitions include RSA, multi-signature, and RBAC. There are four different kinds of tickets, they are tickets t_0, t_1, t_2, t_3. A single signature scheme for tickets t_1, t_2 is presented in Sect. 4.3 and the extension of the single signature scheme to a multi-signature scheme for ticket t_3 is discussed in Sect. 4.4. The security of the proposed solution with role based access control as well as its deployment in wireless environments are analyzed in Sect. 4.5. Other related works are discussed and compared in Sect. 4.6. Finally, conclusions are presented in Sect. 4.7.

4.2 Security Primitives in the Proposed Architecture

4.2.1 Basic Definitions

To facilitate discussion, here is a brief review of some well-known primitive cryptographic terminologies that will be used in this chapter.

- **Hash Function**: $h(x)$ is a hash function. For a given Y it is computationally hard to find a x such that $h(x) = Y$, where x might be a vector.

Hash functions have been used in computer science for a long time. They are used in several cryptographic components including pseudo-random generators [1], digital signatures and message authentication [42].

- **RSA**: is a public key cryptosystem that offers both encryption and digital signatures (authentication) [29]. RSA works as follows: taking two large primes p and q, and computing their product $n = pq$; n is called the modulus. Choosing a number e, less than n and relatively prime to $(p - 1)(q - 1)$. Finding another number d such that $(ed - 1)$ is divisible by $(p - 1)(q - 1)$. The public key is the pair (n, e), the private key is d. The factors p and q may be kept with the private key or destroyed.

  It is currently difficult to obtain the private key d from the public key (n, e) for a large n (say some 2048 bit integer). RSA is often used in many different applications such as email, electronic funds transfers and remote access.

- **Multi-Signatures**: imply that several signatures are signed on the same document. There are at least two ways to implement multi-signature. One method is that each person signs separately and is passed on from one person to another. Another scheme is whereby a message is signed simultaneously [31].

- **Role Based Access Control (RBAC)**: in general an RBAC system involves users being associated with roles and the roles being associated with permissions [17, 50, 55]. A permission typically specifies target objects and the operations that can be performed on them. There are many relationships between users and roles, and between roles and permissions as shown in Fig. 8.1. In terms of administration, there is the management of user to role mapping (e.g. assigning users to specific roles) and the management of role to permission mapping (the privileges associated with the roles). In general the authorities that manage these two mappings can be different; furthermore strategies for managing these mappings such as when should elements in these mappings change also vary.

  Typically, an RBAC model has two components: MC_0 and MC_1. Model component MC_0, called the RBAC authorization database model, defines the RBAC security properties for authorization of static roles. Static properties of a RBAC authorization database include role hierarchy, inheritance, cardinality, and static separation of duty. MC_1, called the RBAC activation model, defines the RBAC security properties for dynamic activation of roles. Dynamic properties include role activation, permission execution, dynamic separation of duties, and object access. In particular, the RBAC model supports the specification of [15, 18, 37]:

  (a) User/role associations; the constraints specifying user authorizations to perform roles,
  (b) Role hierarchies; the constraints specifying which role may inherit all of the permissions of another role,
  (c) Duty separation constraints; these are role/role associations indicating conflict of interest:

    (c1) Static separated duty (SSD); a constraint specifying that a user cannot be authorized for two different roles, (c2) Dynamic separated duty (DSD); a constraint specifying that a user can be authorized for two different roles but cannot act simultaneously in both,

(d) Cardinality; the maximum number of users allowed, i.e. how many users can be authorized for any particular role (role cardinality), e.g., only one manager.

A comprehensive administrative model for RBAC must account for all four issues mentioned above [5, 34, 51].

4.2.2 Ticket Types

There are four participants (the user, the service provider, the Trusted Authentication and Registration Centre and the Trusted Credential Centre) and several protocols for ticket acquisition, ticket usage, clearance, and billing in the M-service model [43, 44, 52]. The user obtains tickets by running the ticket acquisition protocol. These tickets are used to access services. The user presents an appropriate ticket to the service provider who can verify the validity of the ticket. If the verification of the ticket is successful, then the service provider provides the service to the user according to the conditions on the ticket. Based on the received tickets, the Trusted Credential Centre prepares a charging bill for each user. The exact forms of the clearance (payment to the service provider) and billing (payment to the Trusted Credential Centre) protocols are not specified in our model. Readers may refer to [48] for details.

There are several advantages in using tickets for accessing services [4]:

User Privacy Tickets can be designed to operate as pure capabilities. In this case, the service provider can make its decision whether to grant a service or not without identifying the real identities of the users.

Scalability If the tickets are designed in such a way that the information in the tickets can be verified without performing cross domain authentication in real time, then this scheme can be made scalable to large systems.

Granularity of Access Control In principle, a ticket can be used to capture a range of access control policies such as role based access and privilege based access. So one can support a fine level of access control in terms of privileges and operations and a coarse level in terms of roles [9, 60].

Delegation In general, it is possible to use the ticket mechanism to transfer privileges to other entities. If the possession of a ticket gives access then delegation can be achieved by controlling the propagation of tickets [38, 39, 54].

However a number of security issues arise such as how to prevent illegal duplication and forgery of tickets [13, 28, 46, 59].

Table 4.1 Ticket types

Types	t_0	t_1	t_2	t_3
User	−	−	+	+
Provider	−	+	−	+

Duplication   There are two types of duplication that need to be considered. The first type is that users either uses or transfers a ticket many times (similar to double spending in electronic cash systems). The second type is an eavesdropper, who listens to someone else acquiring a ticket and makes a copy for himself.

Forgery   Forgery refers to the illegal construction of a valid ticket, which can be used for accessing to resources.

Modification   Users must not modify tickets. This is to prevent users from accessing resources for which the tickets have not permitted, e.g. a ticket that allows travel by a bus, should not be modifiable to allow travel by a plane.

A ticket may bind a given user and a given service provider together. For example, a movie ticket, which usually does not specify who can use it (i.e., the user) or a travel card, which may not restrict the means of transport (i.e., the service). Based on this observation, there are four types of tickets. These are illustrated in Table 4.1, where '+' means that the corresponding entity, user or service provider is bound by the ticket, while '−' means that it is not.

A ticket of type t_0, for instance, does not restrict the service for which it can be used, the service provider who can accept, or the user who can use it. This is very much like "cash" in real life. The other extreme is a ticket of type t_3, which can only be used by a given user with a given service provider. An example of this type is a flight ticket.

As mentioned in Table 4.1, tickets t_1 and t_2 have only one entity bounded and ticket t_3 has two entities bounded. We will design different mechanisms related to each of the tickets. In some cases users may wish to remain anonymous during purchase and no private information of the user should be shown to service providers. Use of a ticket-based system can avoid roaming multiple service domains. A single signature can be used in tickets with only one bound entity (users or service providers). As a signer, the bound entity uses a signature to authenticate a ticket. To cope with the cases of two bound entities, it is extended to $v(v = 2)$ signers (multi-signature). This means that a user can get a service if all v entities agree. The v Signers case can also associate with other services provided by many cooperative providers since the number v is not limited to 2. A Credential_role in the Trusted Credential Centre is set up to issue tickets and control the user's charging bill, and a Trusted_role in the Trusted Centre is also set up to judge conflicts. Each user's statement of account can be seen clearly in the Trusted Credential Centre.

In the remaining sections, we will present schemes for the different types of tickets and discuss how the Trusted Credential Centre issues a continuously updated account statement for users. We will also consider both single and multi-signature schemes. We will not discuss the ticket t_0 further since it does not bind any entities.

4.3   Single Signature Scheme for Tickets t_1 and t_2

In this section, we consider a single signature scheme for tickets t_1 and t_2. There are four roles in the single signature scheme, Signer, Verifier, Credential_role and Trusted_role. Depending on tickets, the Signer can be a user or service provider that signs a ticket. The Verifier might be a user or service provider that verifies the signature of the Signer. The Credential_role in the Credential Centre will issue tickets. It provides information for the Verifier to check the signature. Whether the signature is valid or not depends on the information. The Trusted_role is a judge to solve the conflict between users and service providers. This is because only the Trusted_role has the secret key of the system and can trace users and service providers. Each Signer has a different but fixed identity I, which is validated once the Signer is registered in the Trusted Centre and does not include any private message of the Signer. Ticket t_2, for instance, is bound to a user only. A user can follow this scheme to sign a signature as a ticket, the service provider verifies it and then sends some information to the Credential_role and asks for payment. Tickets t_1 is similar to ticket t_2, the signers are service providers but not users.

The outline of the scheme is shown in Fig. 4.2. In the system initialization, with SOAP methods, the Trusted_role sends the private messages (r, S) to the Signer when the Signer I is set up, where r, S are computed by the Trusted_role, r will be used in the first verification by the Credential_role and S will be used as the first signature key by the Signer. In the second step, the Credential_role verifies if the data (I, r, D) sent by the Signer are valid or not, where D is used in the ticket verification. The data (I, D) will be put on a public directory in the Trusted Credential Centre if the data are valid. At this time, the Signer can do a signing message job.

While the Signer signs a message m, the Signer will send the signed message (t, T, m) as a ticket to the Verifier, and the latter checks if it is true or not, where t and T are computed by the Signer and m may include some service information and conditions etc. The data (I, D) in the Trusted Credential Centre are needed. The

Fig. 4.2 Single signature
scheme for tickets t_1 and t_2

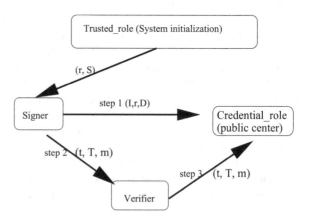

Verifier cannot verify the message when the data (I, D) in the Trusted Credential Centre are not correct. Then the Credential_role can control the usage of the ticket, and even find who the Signer is if it contacts the Trusted_role. In the final step, the Verifier sends a message which includes the ticket to the Trusted Credential Centre while the ticket is true. The latter will update the data (I, D) that is used to issue a charging bill. The data (I, D) is changed while the ticket is used and the ticket is invalid if the verifier cannot get the correct data (I, D). Thus, the ticket cannot be used twice and the user can see a clear statement.

4.3.1   System Initialization

There are two elements in a signature scheme: one is the Signer represented by consumers (users) or service providers; the other is the Verifier. As a ticket, a signature is valid only if its verification is correct.

The Trusted_role computes a public composite modulus $n = pq$ where factors are strong primes. The Trusted_role chooses also prime exponents e and d such that:

$$e * d = 1 \ (mod \ \phi(n)).$$

Where $\phi(n) = (p - 1)(q - 1)$. The pair (n, e) are made public, and d is kept secret by the Trusted Centre as the system key. The Trusted_role computes when the Signer with identity I signs up:

$$r = k^e \ (mod \ n), \quad S = k * I \ (mod \ n)$$

where $k \in_R Z_n$ ($a \in_R A$ means that the element a is selected randomly from the set A with uniform distribution). Then

$$S^e = r * I^e \ (mod \ n).$$

Let $D = S^e \ (mod \ n)$. The Trusted_role secretly sends (r, S) to the Signer whose public identity is I. S will be used as the first signature key to issue a ticket. Obviously, it is hard to compute S from D without system key d under the RSA assumption.

The Signer with the public key I sends (I, r, D) to the Credential_role, and the latter verifies the following equation:

$$D = r * I^e \ (mod \ n).$$

The data (I, r, D) are valid when the equation is successful, in which r and D are computed by the Trusted_role; otherwise the (I, r, D) are invalid. The Credential_role publishes in a public directory the pair (I, D) for the Signer with the public key I. The initialization processes of the system are shown in Fig. 4.3.

Fig. 4.3 Initialization for group_1

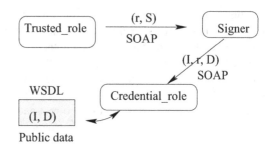

4.3.2 The Single Signature Scheme

The Verifier can access the public values n, e and the public pair (I, D) registered in the Trusted Credential Centre (TCC). The data D in the TCC must be right; otherwise the signed message (the ticket) cannot be verified by the Verifier.

To express the general process of the single signature scheme, it is assumed that the messages $m_1, m_2, \ldots, m_{l-1}$ $(l \geq 1)$ have already been signed by the Signer I. The messages $m_1, m_2, \ldots, m_{l-1}$ $(l \geq 1)$ can indicate different service requirements that are included in tickets. A user can get a valid ticket if the signature is right. The corresponding public key (I, D_{l-1}) $(D_0 = D)$ of the Signer is now registered in the public directory of the Credential Centre. The message m_l for the next service will be signed by the Signer using the secret key $S_{l-1} (S_0 = S)$. The Signer and the Verifier perform the following steps.

Input (I, D_{l-1}, e, n),

Signer
1. Picks $r_{l-1} \in_R Z_n$ and computes: $T_{l-1} = r_{l-1}^e (mod\ n)$.
2. Computes: $S_l = S_{l-1} * m_l\ (mod\ n)$, S_l will be used as the secret key by the Signer I in the next signing operation.
3. Computes the Hashing value $d_{l-1} = h(T_{l-1}, m_l)\ (mod\ n)$.
4. Computes the final witness $t_{l-1} = r_{l-1} * (S_{l-1} * m_l)^{-d_{l-1}}\ (mod\ n)$.

Note A ticket is the signature (t_{l-1}, T_{l-1}, m_l). The ticket will be recorded at the TCC; the user will send the ticket to a service provider when s/he needs the service.

Credential_role
The Credential_role computes D_l for the ticket, where

$$D_l = D_{l-1} * m_l^e\ (mod\ n) = S_l^e\ (mod\ n).$$

D_l is published in the TCC. It will be used to verify the ticket by the Verifier and used to issue another ticket.

Verifier
5. The Verifier gets (t_{l-1}, T_{l-1}, m_l) and knows (I, D_{l-1}), then checks that:

$$d_{l-1} = h(t_{l-1}^e * D_{l-1}^{d_{l-1}} * m_l^{ed_{l-1}} \ (mod \ n), m_l) \ (mod \ n).$$

It is easy to see that if the Signer follows the protocol, the equation will be valid. Indeed:

$$d_{l-1} = h(T_{l-1}, m_l) \ (mod \ n).$$
$$T_{l-1} = r_{l-1}^e \ (mod \ n)$$
$$= (t_{l-1} * (S_{l-1} * m_l)^{d_{l-1}})^e \ (mod \ n)$$
$$= (t_{l-1}^e * D_{l-1}^{d_{l-1}} * m_l^{ed_{l-1}}) \ (mod \ n).$$

Using this protocol the Verifier is convinced with overwhelming probability that the Signer knows the secret key S_{l-1}. This S_{l-1} is used but not revealed at the end of the protocol.

6. The Verifier sends the ticket to the Credential_role. The latter updates (I, D_{l-1}) in the public director and takes a record. The ticket (t_{l-1}, T_{l-1}, m_l) cannot be used twice since it has been marked by the Credential_role. ◇

Remark The Verifier must use the public data D_{l-1} in the TCC when it checks whether the signed message is true or not. The signed message will be unavailable if the data D_{l-1} are changed, then the Credential_role can revoke the anonymity of the Signer.

However, this scheme only suits the tickets t_1 and t_2. The problem of ticket t_3 cannot be solved in the scheme of this section. A multi-signature scheme to solve the problem is explained in the next section.

4.4 Multi-Signature Scheme for Ticket t_3

We will extend the scheme to a multi-signature scheme for tickets of type t_3. Now the number of signers is not limited to two, instead we have v signers. This means that the scheme can also be used when services are provided by many cooperative providers.

Now, instead of the public key I of a signer (in the last section), we use ID_i ($i = 1, 2, \ldots v$) as a public keys for signers U_i since there are more than one signers in a multi-signature. At the beginning of the multi-signature scheme, the Trusted_role computes and secretly sends the messages (r_i, S_i) to signers U_i in the group when the Signers are set up. This step is same as the first step in the last section. In the second step, the Credential_role verifies if the data (ID_i, r_i, D_i) sent by the Signers are valid or not. A vector $(ID_1, ID_2, \ldots, ID_v, g_1)$, as the group public key, will be put in the TCC, where g_1 is computed by the Credential_role and will be used in the first ticket verification, then the group can sign.

In the signature process, the Credential_role gets v pairs of data (t_{il}, T_{il}) from the Signers with identity $ID_i (1 <= i <= v)$ when a message m is signed, where (t_{il}, T_{il}) are computed by the Signer ID_i. In the next step, the Credential_role sends

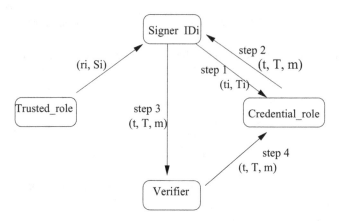

Fig. 4.4 Multi-signature scheme for ticket t_3, using SOAP to transfer data

the signed message $(t_l = \prod_{il=1}^{v} t_{il} \ (mod \ n), T_l = \prod_{il=1}^{v} T_{il} \ (mod \ n), m)$ to the Signer
as a ticket, where n is a public integer defined in the system initialization. The ticket
will be sent to the Verifier and the Verifier checks if it is true or not. The Verifier may
not verify if the data g_1 in the TCC is not correct, and the signed message is invalid.
Therefore the TCC can revoke the anonymity of the Signers. In the final step, the
Verifier sends the ticket to the TCC and then the Credential_role can make a record
for the ticket. This process is shown in Fig. 4.4.

4.4.1   Scheme Initialization

Similar to the previous section, the pair (n, e) are made public, and d is kept secret
by the TCC as the system key. The Signer U_i of the system has a public key ID_i
which is produced by the TCC when the signer joins the system. The Trusted_role
computes:

$$r_i = k_i^e \ (mod \ n), \quad S_i = k_i * ID_i \ (mod \ n)$$

$k_i \in_R Z_n$, then $S_i^e = r_i * ID_i^e \ (mod \ n)$. Let $D_i = S_i^e \ (mod \ n)$, the Trusted_role
secretly sends (r_i, S_i) to the Signer with the public key ID_i. S_i will be used by U_i
as the first signature key. It is hard to compute S_i from ID_i without the system key
d under the RSA assumption.

The Signer U_i sends (ID_i, r_i, D_i) to the Credential_role, and the latter verifies
the following equation:

$$D_i = r_i * ID_i^e \ (mod \ n) \tag{4.1}$$

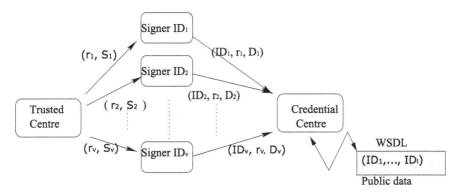

Fig. 4.5 Initialization of multi-signature scheme, SOAP technologies can be used in data transmission

The data (ID_i, r_i, D_i) are valid if Eq. (4.1) is successful, which means all v Signers agree to issue a ticket. Otherwise the data (ID_i, r_i, D_i) are invalid. While the equation is successful for $i = 1, 2, \ldots, v$, the Credential_role computes a system public key:

$$g_1 = \prod_{i=1}^{v} D_i \ (mod \ n) = \prod_{i=1}^{v} S_i^e \ (mod \ n).$$

The Credential_role registers in a public directory a vector $(ID_1, ID_2, \ldots, ID_v, g_1)$ for Signers $U_1, U_2, \ldots, U_v$. The data g_1 will be used and changed when a valid signature is done. The processes are shown in Fig. 4.5.

4.4.2   The Multi-Signature Scheme

When the Verifier accesses the system public key n, e and the public vector $(ID_1, ID_2, \ldots, ID_v, g_1)$ in the Credential Centre, the data g_1 must be correct, otherwise the signature is unavailable since the Verifier cannot verify the signed message.

Assuming that a message $m_l (l = 1, 2, 3, \ldots)$ including service information and users requirements will be signed by the Signers $U_1, U_2, \ldots, U_v$. $S_{i\,l-1}$, the secret key of Signer U_i is changed when the message m_l has been signed $((i = 1, 2, \ldots, v)$ and $S_{i0} = S_i$). This means $S_{i\,l-1}$ is a once-a-time secret key and it will improve the security of the system. z is a public prime number which is known to v Signers and it will be used in the new multi-signature scheme. The processes of the multi-signature scheme are below.

Input (ID_i, D_i, e, n),

Signer U_i:

Step 1
1.1 Picks $r_{il} \in_R Z_n$ and computes: $T_{il} = r_{il}^e (mod\ n)$.
1.2 Computes: $S_{il} = S_{i\,l-1} * m_l\ (mod\ n)$.
   S_{il} will be used as the secret key by U_i in the next signing operation.

1.3 Computes: $t_{il} = r_{il} * (S_{i\,l-1} * m_l)^z\ (mod\ n)$.
1.4 Sends the pair (t_{il}, T_{il}) to the Credential_role.

The Credential_role can now produce a ticket but it is not able to get the secret key $S_{i\,l-1}$ from the data (t_{il}, T_{il}).

Credential_role

Step 2 The Credential_role computes:

$$g_{l+1} = g_l * m_l^{ve}\ (mod\ n).$$

and

$$t_l = \prod_{il=1}^{v} t_{il}\ (mod\ n), \quad T_l = \prod_{il=1}^{v} T_{il}\ (mod\ n)$$

g_{l+1} is published in the public directory, it will be required to issue another ticket. (t_l, T_l, m_l) is a ticket which will be used for asking services.

It should be noted, for instance a ticket t_6, both the user and the service provider are Signers, however, the ticket (t_l, T_l, m_l) is only sent by the Credential_role to the user. The user will send the ticket to a service provider to ask for a purchase. The service provider, as a verifier, will verify the ticket. The verifier will follow the next steps when the ticket is received.

Verifier

Step 3 The Verifier knows the public data $(ID_1, ID_2, \ldots, ID_v, g_l)$ in the TCC and data (t_l, T_l, m_l), checks that:

$$T_l = t_l^e * g_l^{-z} * m_l^{-zve}\ (mod\ n) \tag{4.2}$$

It is easy to see that if the Signer and the Credential_role follow the steps, Eq. (4.2) will be valid. Indeed,

$$
\begin{aligned}
T_l &= \prod_{il=1}^{v} T_{il}\ (mod\ n) \\
&= \prod_{il=1}^{v} t_{il}^e * (S_{i\,l-1} * m_l)^{-ze}\ (mod\ n) \\
&= t_1^e * g_1^{-z} * m_l^{-zve}\ (mod\ n).
\end{aligned}
$$

Step 4 The Verifier sends the ticket to the TCC. The latter will update the data g_l and prepare a charging bill for the user.

Remark The signed message in the multi-signature scheme will be invalid if the data g_l is changed. Then the Credential_role can revoke the ability to sign messages of the Signers.

4.5 System Security

4.5.1 Threat Analysis

First we can analyze the threats to the system, including threats from outsiders and consider how to address the security problems of duplication, forgery and modification. Recall that there are four roles in the scheme. They are the Signer, the Verifier, the Credential_role and the Trusted_role.

- *Outsider threat*: an outsider knows the public data (I, D_l) and $(ID_1, \ldots, ID_v, g_l)$. It is hard to compute the secret key S_l from D and S_{il} from g_l without system key d under the RSA assumption.
- *Verifier*: knows (I, D_l) and ticket (t_{l-1}, T_{l-1}, m_l) in the first sub-scheme and $(ID_1, \ldots, ID_v, g_l)$ and ticket (t_l, T_l, m_l) in the second sub-scheme. But no useful message can be obtained from these public data. The Verifier knows no more information about the key than the outside.
- *Credential_role*: can revoke the anonymity of the users since it can control the ability to sign messages by the Signers. It knows only as much as the outside does and hence it cannot get the secret key either.
- *Signer*: knows the secret key S_l of tickets t_1, t_2, but cannot use the secret key S_l and the ticket twice. Using the secret key S_l a second time, to produce another ticket, requires a second verification. If the previous verifier was honest, the public data in the TCC would be updated and the second ticket would be rejected. There are similar cases for the Signers in the second sub-scheme.
- *Trusted_role*: knows the system key d, and can get the signer's key S_l. So the TCC must be trusted. Here the Trusted_role can be a judge.

The secret keys S_l and S_{il} are not revealed at the end of the process and no secret information is revealed during the running of the system. They are only dependent on the Trusted_role, and does not depend on the Credential_role. The security is also improved since the secret keys are changed once a message is signed.

Duplication is prevented since using a ticket twice requires that the ticket be verified twice, and the second verification cannot succeed as the data in TCC are changed after the first verification. In the multi-signature scheme, for instance, the TCC issues tickets and sends them to users. The other four, even the Trusted_role, cannot forge a ticket because the messages of (t_{il}, T_{il}) are only sent to the TCC which is not able to get the secret key S_{il-1} from the data. To protect from eavesdropping or sending the ticket to other users, SOAP technology can be used between users and the TCC. The user cannot modify the service information since it is needed in the ticket verification.

There is no limitation on the service providers with our approach. Hence this scheme can be used by wireless service providers. The PKI technologies [12]could be used in the processing of the scheme. For example, in the initialization of the system for the tickets t_1, t_2, the Trusted_role may use PKI approach to secretly send (r, S) to a Signer.

The data transferred in current wireless environments is prone to loss. The ticket scheme can preserve the integrity of exchanged data in the lossy wireless environments. This means either the system can find the lost data or users cannot obtain services. For instance, tickets t_1, t_2 need to be sent to the TCC and the Verifier. Tickets are invalid if data is lost in these two processes. When this occurs, users have to send tickets again until they are received. The Verifier will send tickets to the Credential_role. The system can find the lost data when they are missing, and users can still get services since tickets are valid through verifications. Users may use tickets twice since the data (I, D_{l-1}) in the Credential Centre are not updated in time. However, the system will double charge the users because it receives the same ticket twice.

4.5.2 Analysis of Ticket Usage

First let us consider the tickets t_1 and t_2. Since the signature of t_1 and t_2 are similar, we will only consider ticket t_2.

Let us suppose that users, service providers are registered by UDDI in the TCC. A ticket will be obtained by a user who requests the service in the ticket. When requiring a service, the user goes to the TCC for a ticket. The Credential_role will use SOAP to send a message m_l including the service information, current time and user's requirements to the user. As a Signer, the user signs the message and makes a ticket (t_{l-1}, T_{l-1}, m_l). The ticket (t_{l-1}, T_{l-1}, m_l) is acceptable to the service provider. As a Verifier, the service provider verifies if the ticket is valid or not, using the data (I, D_{l-1}) in the TCC. Neither the service provider nor the Credential_role knows who the user is. Only the Trusted_role can trace the user from the public key I. When the ticket (t_{l-1}, T_{l-1}, m_l) is used the Credential_role will make a record for the data D_{l-1}. The record will be used to prevent the ticket from being duplicated and to issue a charging bill. Then users can see the bill at any time. Finally, the Credential_role can send a bill to the user.

In the mechanism presented here, a user can issue many tickets which can be used at any time, because a ticket's validity depends only on the data in the TCC. The data $D_0, D_1, \ldots, D_{l-1}, D_l, \ldots$ are published in the public directory. Thus there is no order of tickets. The user can also lend the ticket (t_{l-1}, T_{l-1}, m_l) to others. This is very convenient for users. Furthermore, most computing in this scheme is done by the terminal side (the user or the service provider); this can reduce the resources needed for the M-service system.

Let us now consider t_3. Ticket t_3 binds a user and service providers and it should be an agreement between the user and the service providers.

When a user requires a ticket t_3 from the TCC, the Credential_role will send the user's requirement to the service providers. The Credential_role will issue a public key for the user and the service providers if the service providers agree to provide the service. The Credential_role sends a message including the service information, current time, requirement and agreements of the service providers to the user and the service providers. As Signers, the user and the service providers use their secret key to sign this message, and then return the data (t_{il}, T_{il}) to the TCC. The Credential_role makes a ticket (t_l, T_l, m_l) and sends it to the user. The ticket (t_l, T_l, m_l) can be used by the service provider. As a Verifier, the service provider uses the public data $(ID_1, \ldots, ID_v, g_l)$ in the TCC to verify if the ticket is valid or not. Neither the service provider nor the Credential_role knows who the user is. Only the TCC can trace the user's identity from the public key ID_i. After the data g_l is updated, the user can see a clear charging bill in the TCC. Finally, the Credential_role can send a bill to the user. This can be shown in Fig. 4.6.

As the tickets t_1, t_2, and t_3 have no fixed order, this means no ticket must be used earlier or later. This is because the data for a ticket verification are $g_1, \ldots, g_l, g_{l+1}$ in the public directory. In addition, the datum g_l is changed and marked while the ticket (t_l, T_l, m_l) is used. Therefore, a ticket cannot be used twice.

Based on the two sub-schemes, the overall solution has the following features:

1. It is anonymous for the user.
2. The ticket can be transferred to others.
3. The security of the system is improved since the secret keys S_l and S_{il} are used only once.

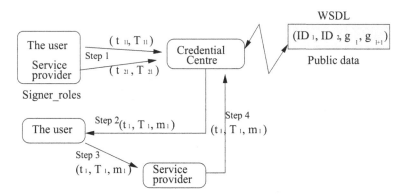

Fig. 4.6 Usage of ticket t_3, SOAP is used in data transmission

4.6   Comparisons

Related work has been done on secure billing for E-services [24], securing XML Web services [8] and accountable anonymous access to services [4].

A secure billing scheme for M-service has been proposed in [24]. It demonstrates how a micro payment scheme can be integrated into a pre-paid charging protocol and users obtain tickets from the Universal Mobile Telecommunication Systems (UMTS) service providers, who act as brokers. When requiring services from service providers, the tickets are then sent by the users to the service providers. The settlements between the service providers and the brokers are then accomplished off-line. The UMTS service providers will collect the billing information from all the service providers accessed by given users and integrate them in a single bill addressed to the users. The proposal is different from ours in two aspects. First, it focusses on authentication between users and service providers to billing by using smart card technology and elliptic curve cryptography. Therefore, there is no discussion for various services and no protocols for different kinds of tickets. By contrast, our work provides a rich variety of options that can deal with all documents of services. Second, users in the secure billing scheme have to send their identities to service providers. The identities are encrypted on the way to the service providers and are protected from eavesdroppers. However, the service providers know the identities. Hence, it has the weakness of not providing anonymity for the users with respect to service providers. In our scheme, users are anonymous with respect to service providers since tickets sent by the users to the service providers include all required information for services.

Securing XML Web services is described by Damiani, Vimercati and Samarati in 2002 [8]. Two experiments are discussed. One is that restricting access to a XML Web service to authorized users. Another one is that protecting the integrity and confidentiality of XML message exchanged in a Web service environment. The authors introduce SOAP highlights, how to use SOAP headers for credential transfer and access control. The main difference between our scheme and the work in [8] is that we focus on a trusted model for users and service providers in wireless environment and consider a solution for different kinds of M-services, whereas the latter is a discussion of providing a secure infrastructure to XML Web services.

Finally, an anonymous access to services in mobile environments is presented in [4]. It has illustrated a ticket based mechanism for service access and proposed how agencies and tickets work together by a ticket based protocol between users, customer care agencies and service providers. The protocol accomplishes authentication of service providers to mobile users, establishment of a shared session key between users and service providers, and correct and undeniable charging. However, our work substantially differs from that proposal. Differences arise in the following three aspects. First, their protocol does not provide an overall solution for various services but only a special mobile service of type t_2. By comparison, we have analyzed the characteristics of various services and presented a detailed scheme for different kinds of services. Second, the protocol addresses the problems of lack of trust and scalability in mobile systems. We have discussed in addition a possible charging scheme for M-services. Finally, the tickets in their work have to follow some specific models such as the Outlet model, the Kiosk model or the Agency model. Therefore, the main processing in the protocol is authentication between users, service providers and customer care agencies. By contrast, users in our scheme obtain the required tickets and use them when a service is required; we have also provided authentication between users, trusted authorities and the service providers.

4.7   Conclusions

M-service systems are becoming increasingly popular in business. They can be regarded as a special form of electronic commerce, where users buy services instead of products from service providers over the network. In this chapter, a secure and flexible scheme for accessing M-services is proposed. In our secure M-service system, the Trusted Credential Centre issues tickets for the users. The ticket can specify a range of access control policies for different types of services. The user presents the ticket to the service provider who can then verify its validity. Based on the privileges in the ticket the access to the service is provided to the user. The scheme is scalable to large systems involving multiple domains. It is also able to support anonymity and user privacy if required. We have considered a possible approach to charging the users for the service provided.

4.8   Problems and Exercises

4.8.1   Problems

1. Tickets can be used in e-commerce systems. There are eight types of tickets according users, providers and services. The basic technologies include single signature scheme and multi-signature scheme. What single signature and multi-signature schemes should be applied for tickets is a problem in e-commerce applications.
2. Hash function is another important process in M-service. Which hash function is more efficient for tickets in e-commerce is a challenge.
3. RSA algorithms are also significant in the system design of M-service. How to set up an RSA algorithm? and how to select prime numbers p and q is a challenge.

4.8.2 Exercises

1. How hash function works in an M-service system? An example of Hash function is required.
2. Design a single signature scheme and multi-signature scheme.
3. Select two prime numbers p and q, build an RSA algorithm for M-service.
4. Implementation of M-service with Mobile message. SMS is a service available on most digital mobile phones that permits the sending of short messages between mobile phones, other handheld devices and even landline telephones. RS232 (https://en.wikipedia.org/wiki/RS-232) is a standard for serial binary data interconnection between a data terminal equipment and a data communication equipment, and it is commonly used in computer serial ports. The standard defines the electrical characteristics and timing of signals, the meaning of signals, and the physical size and pinout of connectors. This exercise asks the implementation of the mobile service system with SMS and RS232.

References

1. Bellare, M., Canetti, R., Krawczyk, H.: Pseudorandom functions revisited: the cascade construction and its concrete security. extended abstract. In: 37th Annual Symposium on the Foundations of Computer Science. IEEE, Piscataway (1996)
2. Box, D.: Simple Object Access Protocol (SOAP) 1.1. World Wide Web Consortium (W3C), Cambridge (2000)
3. Bray, T., Paoli, J., Sperberg, M., Maler, E.: Extensible Markup Language (XML) 1.1, 2nd edn. World Wide Web Consortium (W3C), Cambridge (2000)
4. Buttyan, L., Hubaux, J.: Accountable anonymous access to services in mobile communication systems. In: Symposium on Reliable Distributed Systems, pp. 384–389 (1999). citeseer.nj.nec. com/article/buttyan99accountable.html
5. Cao, J., et al.: Towards secure xml document with usage control. In: Web Technologies Research and Development—APWeb 2005, pp. 296–307. Springer, Berlin (2005)
6. Chenthara, S., et al.: Security and privacy-preserving challenges of e-health solutions in cloud computing. IEEE Access **7**, 74361–74382 (2019)
7. Chinnici, R., Gudgin, M., Moreau, J., Weerawarana, S.: Web Services Description Language (WSDL) 1.2. World Wide Web Consortium (W3C), Cambridge (2002)
8. Damiani, E., et al.: Towards securing xml web services. In: Proceedings of the 2002 ACM Workshop on XML Security, pp. 90–96. Association for Computing Machinery, New York (2002)
9. Du, J., et al.: Feature selection for helpfulness prediction of online product reviews: an empirical study. PLoS ONE **14**, e0226902 (2019)
10. Excellent E-Service: Excellent E-service (2002). http://www.excellenteservice.com/
11. Ge, Y., et al.: A benefit-driven genetic algorithm for balancing privacy and utility in database fragmentation. In: Proceedings of the Genetic and Evolutionary Computation Conference, pp. 771–776. Association for Computing Machinery, New York (2019)
12. Housley, R., Ford, W., Polk, W., Solo, D.: Internet x.509 public key infrastructure certificate and CRL profile. In: Internet X.509 Public Key Infrastructure Certificate and CRL Profile (1999). http://www.ietf.org/rfc/rfc2459.txt

13. Kabir, M., et al.: A novel statistical technique for intrusion detection systems. Future Gener. Comput. Syst. **79**, 303–318 (2018)
14. Kabir, E., et al.: Microaggregation sorting framework for k-anonymity statistical disclosure control in cloud computing. IEEE Trans. Cloud Comput. **8**(2), 408–417 (2020)
15. Kabir, E., Wang, H.: Conditional purpose based access control model for privacy protection. In: Proceedings of the Twentieth Australasian Conference on Australasian Database, ADC '09, vol. 92, pp. 135–142. Australian Computer Society, Darlinghurst (2009)
16. Kabir, M., Wang, H., Bertino, E.: A conditional purpose-based access control model with dynamic roles. Expert Syst. Appl. **38**(3), 1482–1489 (2011)
17. Kabir, M., Wang, H., Bertino, E.: A conditional role-involved purpose-based access control model. J. Organ. Comput. Electron. Commer. **21**, 71–91 (2011)
18. Kabir, M., Wang, H., Bertino, E.: Efficient systematic clustering method for k-anonymization. Acta Inf. **48**(1), 51–66 (2011)
19. Khalil, F., Li, J., Wang, H.: Integrating recommendation models for improved web page prediction accuracy. In: Proceedings of the Thirty-First Australasian Conference on Computer Science, ACSC '08, vol. 74, pp. 91–100. Australian Computer Society, Darlinghurst (2008)
20. Li, M., et al.: Advanced permission-role relationship in role-based access control. In: Information Security and Privacy, pp. 391–403. Springer, Berlin (2008)
21. Li, M., et al.: Optimal privacy-aware path in hippocratic databases. In: Database Systems for Advanced Applications, pp. 441–455. Springer, Berlin (2009)
22. Li, M., Wang, H.: ABDM: an extended flexible delegation model in RBAC. In: 2008 8th IEEE International Conference on Computer and Information Technology, pp. 390–395 (2008)
23. Li, M., Wang, H., Plank, A.: Privacy-aware access control with generalization boundaries. In: Proceedings of the Thirty-Second Australasian Conference on Computer Science, ACSC '09, vol. 91, pp. 105–112. Australian Computer Society, Darlinghurst (2009)
24. Martin, K., Preneel, B., Mitchell, C., Hitz, H., Poliakova, A., Howard, P.: Secure billing for mobile information services in UMTS. In: International Conference on Intelligence in Services and Networks. Springer, Berlin (1998)
25. Mehrotra, A.: GSM system engineering. In: Artech House Mobile Communications Series. Norwood, Artech House (1997)
26. Mehrotra, A., Golding, L.: Mobility and security management in the GSM system and some proposed future improvements. Proc. IEEE **86**(7), 1480–1497 (1998)
27. Paul, C.: Migrate with red hat Linux advanced server. Redhat (2002). http://www.redhat.com/solutions
28. Pratel, B., Crowcroft, J.: Ticket based service access for the mobile user. In: In Proceedings of MobiCom: International Conference on Mobile Computing and Networking, pp. 223–232, Budapest, 1997
29. Rivest, R.L., Shamir, A., Adleman, L.M.: A method for obtaining digital signatures and public-key cryptosystems. Commun. ACM **21**(2), 120–126 (1978)
30. Shu, J., et al.: Privacy-preserving task recommendation Services for Crowdsourcing. IEEE Trans. Serv. Comput. (2018) https://doi.org/10.1109/TSC.2018.2791601
31. Stinson, D.R.: Cryptography: Theory and practice. CRC Press, Boca Raton (1995)
32. Sun, X., et al.: An efficient hash-based algorithm for minimal k-anonymity. In: Proceedings of the Thirty-First Australasian Conference on Computer Science, ACSC '08, vol. 74, pp. 101–107. Australian Computer Society, Darlinghurst (2008)
33. Sun, X., et al.: Enhanced p-sensitive k-anonymity models for privacy preserving data publishing. Trans. Data Privacy **1**(2), 53–66 (2008)
34. Sun, L., Li, Y., Wang, H.: M-service and its framework. In: 2005 Asia-Pacific Conference on Communications, pp. 837–841 (2005)
35. Sun, X., Wang, H., Li, J.: Priority driven k-anonymisation for privacy protection. In: Proceedings of the 7th Australasian Data Mining Conference, vol. 87, pp. 73–78 (2008)
36. Sun, X., Wang, H., Li, J.: Microdata protection through approximate microaggregation. In: Proceedings of the Thirty-Second Australasian Conference on Computer Science , ACSC '09, vol. 91, pp. 161–168. Australian Computer Society, Darlinghurst (2009)

37. Sun, L., Wang, H., Yong, J.: Authorization algorithms for permission-role assignments. J. UCS **15**, 1782–1798 (2009)
38. Sun, X., Wang, H., Sun, L.: Extended k-anonymity models against attribute disclosure. In: 2009 Third International Conference on Network and System Security, pp. 130–136 (2009)
39. Sun, X., Wang, H., Li, J.: Satisfying privacy requirements: one step before anonymization. In: Advances in Knowledge Discovery and Data Mining, pp. 181–188. Springer, Berlin (2010)
40. Sun, X., Sun, L., Wang, H.: Extended k-anonymity models against sensitive attribute disclosure. Comput. Commun. **34**(4), 526–535 (2011). Special issue: building secure parallel and distributed networks and systems
41. Sun, X., Li, M., Wang, H.: A family of enhanced (L, α)-diversity models for privacy preserving data publishing. Future Gener. Comput. Syst. **27**(3), 348–356 (2011)
42. Waleffe, D.D., Quisquater, J. J.: Better login protocols for computer networks. In: ESORICS'90, pp. 163–172 (1990)
43. Wang, H., et al.: Authorization algorithms for the mobility of user-role relationship. In: Proceedings of the Twenty-Eighth Australasian Conference on Computer Science , ACSC '05, vol. 38, pp. 69–77. Australian Computer Society, Darlinghurst (2005)
44. Wang, H., et al.: A framework for role-based group deligation in distributed environments. In: Proceedings of the 29th Australasian Computer Science Conference, vol. 48, pp. 321–328 (2006)
45. Wang, H., et al.: Protecting outsourced data in cloud computing through access management. Concurrency Comput. Pract. Exp. **28**(3), 600–615 (2016)
46. Wang, Y., et al.: MTMR: Ensuring mapreduce computation integrity with Merkle tree-based verifications. IEEE Trans. Big Data **4**(3), 418–431 (2018)
47. Wang, H., et al.: Editorial: special issue on security and privacy in network computing. World Wide Web **23**, 951–957 (2020)
48. Wang, H., Zhang, Y.: Untraceable off-line electronic cash flow in e-commerce. In: Proceedings of the 24th Australian Computer Science Conference ACSC2001, pp. 191–198, GoldCoast. IEEE Computer Society, Silver Spring (2001)
49. Wang, H., Li, Q.: Secure and efficient information sharing in multi-university e-learning environments. In: Advances in Web Based Learning—ICWL 2007, pp. 542–553. Springer, Berlin (2008)
50. Wang, H., Sun, L.: Trust-involved access control in collaborative open social networks. In: 2010 Fourth International Conference on Network and System Security, pp. 239–246 (2010)
51. Wang, H., Cao, J., Zhang, Y.: A flexible payment scheme and its role-based access control. IEEE Trans. Knowl. Data Eng. **17**(3), 425–436 (2005)
52. Wang, H., Cao, J., Ross, D.: Role-based delegation with negative authorization. In: Frontiers of WWW Research and Development—APWeb 2006, pp. 307–318. Springer, Berlin (2006)
53. Wang, H., Zhang, Y., Cao, J.: Ubiquitous computing environments and its usage access control. In: Proceedings of the First International Conference on Scalable Information Systems, InfoScale '06. ACM, New York (2006)
54. Wang, H., Cao, J., Zhang, Y.: Delegating revocations and authorizations in collaborative business environments. Inf. Syst. Front. **11**(3), 293 (2008)
55. Wang, H., Sun, L., Varadharajan, V.: Purpose-based access control policies and conflicting analysis. In: Security and Privacy—Silver Linings in the Cloud, pp. 217–228. Springer, Berlin (2010)
56. Wang, H., Zhang, Z., Taleb, T.: Editorial: special issue on security and privacy of IoT. World Wide Web **21**(1), 1–6 (2018)
57. Wang, Z., Zhan, Z., Lin, Y., Yu, W., Wang, H., Kwong, S., Zhang, J.: Automatic niching differential evolution with contour prediction approach for multimodal optimization problems. IEEE Trans. Evol. Comput. **24**(1), 114–128 (2020)
58. Zhang, F., Wang, Y., Wang, H.: Gradient correlation: are ensemble classifiers more robust against evasion attacks in practical settings? In: Web Information Systems Engineering—WISE 2018, pp. 96–110. Springer, Cham (2018)

59. Zhang, Y., Shen, Y., Wang, H., Zhang, Y., Jiang, X.: On secure wireless communications for service oriented computing. IEEE Trans. Serv. Comput. **11**(2), 318–328 (2018)
60. Zhang, Y. Gong, Y., Gao, Y., Wang, H., Zhang, J.: Parameter-free Voronoi neighborhood for evolutionary multimodal optimization. IEEE Trans. Evol. Comput. **24**(2), 335–349 (2020)

Chapter 5
A Self-Scalable Anonymity Payment Approach in Cloud Environment

An efficient electronic cash scheme has been developed in the last chapter. This chapter proposes a secure, anonymity scalable and practical payment protocol for Internet purchases, and analyses its role-based user-role assignment. The protocol uses electronic cash for payment transactions. In this new protocol, from the viewpoint of banks, consumers can improve anonymity if they worried about disclosure of their identities. An agent provides a higher anonymous certificate and improves the security of the consumers. The agent will certify re-encrypted data after verifying the validity of the content from consumers, but with no private information of the consumers required. With this new method, each consumer can get the required anonymity level, depending on the available time, computation and cost.

This chapter will analyze role-based user-role assignment for the system such as how to grant or revoke memberships of users. Each user may be assigned one or more roles, and each role can be assigned one or more privileges that are permitted to users in that role. User-role assignment is a particularly critical administrative activity. RBAC can reduce conflicts of different roles. The complexities with RBAC can be decreased by mutually exclusive roles and role hierarchies.

5.1 Introduction

Recent advances in the Internet and WWW have enabled rapid development in e-commerce [12, 16, 25, 40]. More and more businesses have begun to develop or adopt e-commerce systems to support their selling/business activities. While this brings convenience for both consumers and vendors, many consumers have concerns about security and their private information when purchasing over the Internet, especially with electronic payment or e-cash payment. Consumers often prefer to have some degree of anonymity when shopping over the Internet [17, 23, 41, 55].

© Springer Nature Switzerland AG 2020
H. Wang et al., *Access Control Management in Cloud Environments*,
https://doi.org/10.1007/978-3-030-31729-4_5

There are a number of proposals for electronic cash systems [6, 10, 26]. All of them lack flexibility in anonymity. For instance, Chaum [6] first proposed an on-line payment system that guarantees receiving valid coins. This system provides some anonymity against a collaboration between shops and banks. However, users have no flexible anonymity and banks have to keep a very big database for users and coins.

Systems mentioned above are on-line payment systems. They need sophisti-cated cryptographic functions for each coin, and require additional computational resources for the bank to validate the purchases [7, 9, 51, 52]. Forcing the bank to be on-line at payment is a very strict requirement. On-line payment systems protect the merchant and the bank against customer fraud, since every payment needs to be approved by the customer's bank. This will increase the computation cost, proportional to the size of the database of spent coins. If a large number of people start using the system, the size of this database could become very large and unmanageable. Keeping a database of the coins ever spent in the system is not a scalable solution. Digicash [7] plans to use multiple banks each minting and managing their own currency with inter-bank clearing to handle the problems of scalability. It seems likely that the host bank machine has an internal scalable structure so that it can even be set up for a 1,000,000 user bank. Under the circumstances, the task of maintaining and querying a database of spent coins is probably beyond today's state-of-the-art database systems.

In an off-line protocol, the merchant verifies the payment using cryptographic techniques, and commits the payment to the payment authority later in an off-line batch process [14, 45, 61]. Off-line payment systems were designed to lower the cost of transactions due to the delay in verifying batch processes. Off-line payment systems, however, suffer from the potential of double spending, whereby the electronic currency might be duplicated and spent repeatedly.

The first off-line anonymous electronic cash was introduced by Chaum et al. [9]. The security of their scheme relied on some restricted assumptions such as requiring a function which is similar to random oracle and maps from the second argument onto a special range. There is also no formal proof attempted. Although hardly practical, their system demonstrated how off-line e-cash can be constructed and laid the foundation for more secure and efficient schemes. In 1995, Chan et al. [5] presented a provable secure off-line e-cash scheme that relied only on the security of RSA [29]. This scheme extended the work of Franklin and Yung [15] who aimed to achieve provable security without the use of general computation protocols. The anonymity of consumers is based on the security of RSA and it cannot be changed dynamically after the system is established. In 2000, Pointcheval [28] presented a payment scheme in which the consumer's identity can be found any time by a certification authority. So the privacy of a consumer cannot be protected.

Recently, role based access control (RBAC) has been widely used in database system management and operating system products [4, 46, 53]. In 1993, the National Institute of Standards and Technology (NIST) developed prototype implementations, sponsored external research [12], and published formal RBAC models [13, 16]. Since then, many RBAC practical applications have been implemented [1, 14, 31], because RBAC has many advantages such as reducing administration cost and complexity. Another use of RBAC is to support integrity. Integrity is a requirement that data and processes be modified only in authorized ways by authorized users. Within a role-based system, the principal concern is protecting the integrity of information: who can perform what acts on what information [38, 47, 54].

As mentioned above, the on-line e-cash payments need more computing resources. Most of the previously designed off-line schemes are only for micro payments and without scalable anonymity for users [49, 56, 58]. They rely on the heuristic proofs of security and therefore do not formally prevent fraud and counterfeit money. Under these conditions, most on-line and off-line payment schemes do not provide efficient anonymity for consumers. Furthermore, there has been little research done on the usage of RBAC in payment scheme management [32]. Hence, a new payment scheme for the purchases over the Internet with the following properties will be useful.

1. Off-line, it spends less computational resources and reduces network communication.
2. Flexible anonymity, it can provide a high level anonymity for some consumers with high secure requirements [22, 24, 37].
3. Untrace ability, no one can trace consumers from cash. However, the identity of a consumer can be found if he/she uses a coin twice.
4. RBAC management, it can decrease the complexities of a system and improve system security such as integrity [21, 35, 36, 48].

In this chapter, we analyse the electronic-payment model first, then propose a new off-line electronic cash scheme, in which the anonymity of consumers is scalable and can be done by consumers themselves. Consumers can get the required anonymity without showing their identities to any third party. Furthermore, to reduce administration cost and complexity and to improve the security of management, we will analyse user-role assignment of the new payment scheme.

The chapter is organized as follows. In the first two section, some basic definitions and simple examples are reviewed. The payment model and the anonymity provider agent are described in Sect. 5.3. The design of a new off-line electronic cash scheme and its security analysis are detailed in Sect. 5.4. User-role assignment and the relation of roles are presented in Sect. 5.5. An example of the new e-cash scheme and how to use it for Internet purchases are given in Sect. 5.6. Conclusions are included in Sect. 5.7.

5.2   Some Basic Definitions

5.2.1   Hash Functions

$H(x)$ is a hash function. For a given value W it is computationally hard to find an x such that $H(x) = W$, i.e. collisions are hard to find, where x might be a vector.

Hash function is a major building block for several cryptographic protocols, including pseudo-random generators [2], digital signatures [3], and message authentication.

5.2.2   DLA and ElGamal Encryption System

Discrete Logarithm Assumption (DLA) is an assumption that the discrete logarithm problem is believed to be difficult.

The discrete logarithm problem is as follows: given an element g in a group G of order q, and another element y of G, find x, where $0 < x < q - 1$, such that y is the result of multiplying g with itself x times, i.e. $y = g^x$. In some groups there exist elements that can generate all the elements of G by exponentiation (i.e. applying the group operation repeatedly) with all the integers from 0 to $q - 1$. When this occurs, the element is called a generator and the group is called cyclic. Rivest [30] has analyzed the expected time to solve the discrete logarithm problem both in terms of computing power and cost and shown that it is computational hard to get y from x.

For this reason, it has been used for the basis of several public-key cryptosystems, including the famous ElGamal encryption system. The ElGamal encryption system [11] is a public key encryption scheme which provides semantic security. Let us briefly recall it.

Table 5.1 indicates that the message m can be obtained only by the person who has the secret key X.

Table 5.1 ElGamal encryption scheme

Step 1. The system needs a group G of order q, and a generator g. The secret key is an element $X \in Z_p = \{0, 1, \ldots, q - 1\}$ and the public key is $Y = g^X$
Step 2. For any message $m \in G$, the cipher text of m is $c = (g^r, Y^r m)$, for a random $r \in Z_p - \{0\}$
Step 3. For any cipher text $c = (a, b)$, the message m can be retrieved by $m = b/a^X$

5.2.3 Undeniable Signature Scheme and Schnorr Signature Scheme

The undeniable signature scheme, devised by Chaum and van Antwerpen [8], is a non-self-authenticating signature schemes, where signatures can only be verified with the signer's consent. However, if a signature is only verifiable with the aid of a signer, a dishonest signer may refuse to authenticate a genuine document. Undeniable signatures solve this problem by adding a new component called the disavowal protocol in addition to the normal components of signature and verification.

An undeniable proof scheme consists of the following algorithms:

1. The key generation algorithm K which outputs random pairs of secret and public keys (sk, pk).
2. The proof algorithm $P(sk, m)$ which inputs a message m, returns an "undeniable signature" S on m.

   However this proof "S" does not convince anybody by itself. To be convinced of the validity of the pair (m, S), relative to the public key pk, one has to interact with the owner of the secret key sk.
3. The confirmation process confirms (sk, pk, m, S), which is an interactive protocol between the signer and the verifier, where the signer tries to convince of the validity of the pair (m, S).
4. The disavowal process is an interactive protocol between the signer and the verifier, where the signer tries to prove that the pair (m, S) is not valid (i.e. has not been produced by him).

Schnorr, for example, proposed an undeniable signature scheme in 1991 [34]. We simply recall it (Table 5.2).

The signer is not able to deny the signature $S = (e, y)$ because the signature can be produced by the owner of the secret key sk only.

Table 5.2 Schnorr signature scheme

The system needs primes p and q such that q is divided by $(p - 1)$, i.e. $q|(p - 1)$, $g \in Z_p$ with order q, i.e. $g^q = 1(mod p)$, $g \neq 1$. A consumer generates by himself a private key sk which is a random number in Z_q. The corresponding public key pk is the number $pk = g^{-sk}(mod p)$

To sign message m with the private key sk the consumer performs the following steps:

1. Computes $x = g^r(mod p)$, where $r \in Z_q$ is a random number
2. Computes $e = H(x, m)$, where H is a hash function
3. Computes $y = r + sk * e(mod q)$ and output the signature $S = (e, y)$

To verify the signature $S = (e, y)$ for message m with the public key pk a verifier computes $\bar{x} = g^y pk^e(mod p)$ and checks $e = h(\bar{x}, m)$

5.2.4   Role Based Access Control

RBAC is described in terms of individual users being associated with roles as well as roles being associated with permissions (Each permission is a pair of objects and operations) [17, 39, 41]. As such, a role is used to associate with users and permissions. A user in this model is a human being. A role is a job function or job title within the organization associated with the authority and responsibility.

Permission is an approval of a particular operation to be performed on one or more objects. The relationship between roles and permissions is shown in Fig. 5.1, arrows indicate a many to many relationship (i.e. a permission can be associated with one or more roles, and a role can be associated with one or more permissions). The RBAC security model has two components: MC_0 and MC_1. Model component MC_0, called the RBAC authorization database model, defines the RBAC security properties for authorization of static roles. Static properties of a RBAC authorization database include role hierarchy, inheritance, cardinality, and static separation of duty. MC_1 called the RBAC activation model, defines the RBAC security properties for dynamic activation of roles. Dynamic properties include role activation, permission execution, dynamic separation of duties, and object access [23, 25, 40]. In particular, the RBAC model supports the specification of:

(a) User/role associations; the constraints specifying user authorizations to perform roles [42, 43, 55],
(b) Role hierarchies; the constraints specifying which role may inherit all of the permissions of another role,
(c) Duty separation constraints; these are role/role associations indicating conflict of interest:

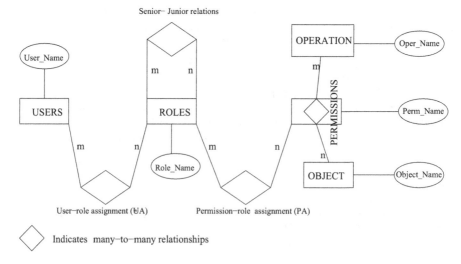

Fig. 5.1 RBAC relationship

(c1) Static separated duty (SSD); a constraint specifying that a user cannot be authorized for two different roles,

(c2) Dynamic separated duty (DSD); a constraint specifying that a user can be authorized for two different roles but cannot act simultaneously in both,

(d) Cardinality; the maximum number of users allowed, i.e. how many users can be authorized for any particular role (role cardinality), e.g., only one manager.

A comprehensive administrative model for RBAC must account for all four issues mentioned above, among others. However, user-role assignment is a particularly critical administrative activity [19, 50, 57]. It is the first adminstrative function for decentralized and delegated systems. Assigning people to tasks is a normal managerial function. Assigning users to roles should be a natural part of assigning users to tasks. Therefore, this chapter will focus on user-role assignment.

5.3 Basic Model and New Payment Model

We will show the basic payment model and then discuss the new payment model in this section.

5.3.1 Basic Payment Model

Electronic cash has sparked wide interest among cryptographers ([27, 30, 59], etc.). In its simplest form, an e-cash system consists of three parts (a bank B, a consumer U and a shop S) and three main procedures as shown in Fig. 5.2 (withdrawal, payment and deposit). In a coin's life-cycle, the consumer U first performs an account establishment protocol to open an account with the bank B.

The consumers and the shops maintain an account with the bank, while

1. U withdraws electronic coins from his account, by performing a withdrawal protocol with the bank B over an authenticated channel.

Fig. 5.2 Basic processes of an electronic cash system

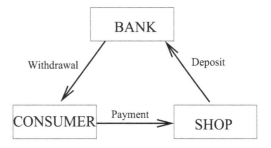

2. U spends a coin by participating in a payment protocol with a shop S over an anonymous channel, and
3. S performs a deposit protocol with the bank B, to deposit the consumer's coin into his account.

The system is *off-line* if the shop S does not communicate with the bank B during payment. It is *untraceable* if there is no p.p.t. TM (probabilistic polynomial-time Turing Machine) that can identify a coin's origin even if one has all the information of withdrawal, payment and deposit transactions. It is *anonymous* if the bank B, in collaboration with the shop S, cannot trace the coin to the consumer. However, in the absence of tamper-proof hardware, electronic coins can be copied and spent multiple times by the consumer U. This has been traditionally referred to as double-spending. In on-line e-cash, double-spending is prevented by having the bank check if the coin has been deposited before. In off-line e-cash, however, this solution is not possible; instead, as proposed by Chaum et al. [9], the system guarantees that if a coin is double-spent the consumer's identity is revealed with overwhelming probability.

There are also three additional processes such as the bank setup, the shop setup, and the consumer setup (account opening). They describe the system initialization, namely creation and posting of public keys and opening of bank accounts. Although they are certainly parts of a complete system, these are often omitted as their functionalities can be easily inferred from the description of the three main procedures. For clarity we will only describe the bank setup and the consumer setup for the new scheme in the next section because the shop setup is similar to the consumer setup.

Besides the basic participants, a third party named Anonymity Provider (AP) agent will be involved in the scheme. The AP agent will help the consumer to get the required anonymity but will not be involved in the purchase process. The new model can be shown in Fig. 5.3. The AP agent gives a certificate to the consumer when s/he needs a higher level of anonymity [18, 20, 44].

Fig. 5.3 New electronic cash model

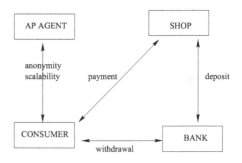

5.3.2 Anonymity Provider Agent

Here we explain what an AP agent is. Assume a consumer owns a valid coin $c = \varphi(pk_B, pk_u, y)$ with its certificate $Cert_c$, which guarantees correct withdrawal from the bank, where $\varphi(pk_B, pk_u, y)$ is a function of the public keys of the bank, the user and a variable y, i.e. (pk_B, pk_u, y). Whether a coin is valid or not depends on its certificate. Therefore the bank can revoke the anonymity of the consumer if it finds that a consumer spends a coin twice. After the following processes with the AP agent, the consumer owns a new valid coin $c' = \varphi(pk_B, pk_u, y + t)$ with its certificate $Cert_{c'}$, where t is a variable.

1. The consumer re-encrypts the coin c into $c' = \varphi(pk_B, pk_u, y + t)$.
2. The consumer provides an undeniable signature S, using c as a public key associated with the secret key sk_u of the user, of the equivalence between c and c'. This equivalence is guaranteed by the variable t.
3. The consumer confirms the validity of this signature S to the AP agent.
4. The AP agent certifies the new coin c' and sends $Cert_{c'}$ to the consumer.

Indeed, after steps 2 and 3, the AP is convinced that the conversion has been performed by the owner of the coin c; c' is equivalent to c. The owner of c will not be able to deny S (the relation between c and c'). The AP agent should be an electronic notarized participant in the system. It does not need to know any private information about consumers, it only verifies the information of consumers.

5.3.3 Proof of Ownership of a Coin

This subsection will show how users prove the ownership of a coin. Let us assume that Y is the public key of the bank, x_u is a secret key of a consumer, and $I = g^{x_u}$ the identity of a consumer. $H(x, y)$ is a hash function. A coin is the encryption of I: $c = (a = g^r, b = Y^r I^s)$ which is afterwards certified by the bank, where r, s are random numbers. With the certificate of the bank, one knows that the encryption is valid. Therefore, in order to prove his ownership, the consumer has just to convince of his knowledge of (x_u, r, s) such that $b = Y^r I^s$. This can be expressed as follows (Table 5.3).

Table 5.3 Proof of validity of a coin $c = Y^r I^s$

1. Consumers choose a random $k \in Z_p$, then compute $t = Y^k g^s \pmod{p}$ and $e = H(m, t)$ where m is a mixed message of c, current time etc.
2. Then compute $u = k - re$, $v = s - x_u e$, and $t_1 = g^{(s-1)x_u e} \pmod{p}$
3. The signature finally consists of (e, u, v, t_1)
4. In order to verify it, one has just to compute $t' = Y^u g^v b^e \pmod{p}$ and check whether $t' = tt_1 \pmod{p}$ and $e = H(m, t'/t_1)$

Then, a scrambled coin is got by multiplying both parts of the old one by respective bases, g and Y, both to the same random exponent ρ:

$$c' = (a' = g^\rho a, b' = Y^\rho b) = (g^{r+\rho}, Y^{r+\rho} I^s).$$

Then, if the owner of the old coin has certified the message $m' = h^\rho$, equivalence of both coins can be proven with the proof of equivalence of three discrete logarithms:

$$log_h m' = log_g(a'/a) = log_Y(b'/b).$$

Where h is a public variable.

5.4 Self-Scalable Anonymity Payment Scheme

In this section, we propose an anonymity self-scalable payment scheme. The new payment scheme has two main features, the first is that a consumer can have a higher level of anonymity himself, the second is that the identity of a consumer cannot be traced unless the consumer spends the same coin twice.

Our scheme includes two basic processes in system initialization (bank setup and consumer setup) and three main protocols: a new withdrawal protocol with which U withdraws electronic coins from B while his account is debited; a new payment protocol with which U pays the coin to S; and a new deposit protocol with which S deposits the coin to B and has his account credited. If a consumer wants to get a higher level of anonymity after getting a coin from the bank (withdrawal), s/he can contact the AP agent.

5.4.1 System Initialization

The bank setup and the consumer setup are described as follows, and the details of the shop setup are omitted (because the shop setup is similar to the consumer setup).

Bank Setup (Performed once by B)
Primes p and q are chosen such that $|p - 1| = \delta + k$ for a specified constant δ, and $p = \gamma q + 1$, for a specified small integer γ. Then a unique subgroup G_q of prime order q of the multiplicative group Z_p and generator g of G_q are defined. Secret key $x_B \in_R Z_q$ for a denomination is created, where $a \in_R A$ means that the element a is selected randomly from the set A with uniform distribution. Hash function H from a family of collision intractable hash function is also defined. B publishes p, q, g, H and its public key $Y = g^{x_B} \pmod p$.

The secret key x_B is safe under the DLA. The hash function will be used in payment transactions.

Consumer Setup (Performed for each consumer U)

The bank B associates the consumer U with $I = g^{x_u} (\text{mod } p)$ where $x_u \in G_q$ is the secret key of the consumer and is generated by the consumer.

After the consumer's account and the shop's account are opened, the new payment scheme can be described.

5.4.2 New Off-line Payment Scheme

We now describe the new anonymity scalable electronic cash scheme, which includes withdrawal, payment and deposit.

Withdrawal (Consumers withdraw coins from the bank)

Usually, an anonymous coin is a certified message, which embeds the public key of a consumer. In our scheme, the message is an encryption of this consumer's public key, using the public key Y of the bank.

Instead of using intricate zero-knowledge proofs to convince the bank of the validity of the encryption, the consumer shows some information to the bank including a signature. So the bank certifies the encryption with full confidence.

The consumer $I = g^{x_u}$ constructs a coin $c = (a = g^r, b = Y^r I^s)$ using the public key Y of the bank, where s is a secret key of the coin, which is kept by the consumer and r is a random number in Z_q. Using the private key x_u, the consumer signs a Schnorr signature S on the message of c together with the date etc. She/He sends (c, S) to the bank together with r, I. Then the bank can verify whether the encryption is correct or not. With the signature of the coin and the date, only the legitimate consumer could have done it. After having modified the consumer's account, the bank sends back a certificate $Cert_c$. The consumer just has to remember $(r, s, Cert_c)$.

Anonymity Scalability (Performed between consumers and the AP agent)

The consumer can use the coin now without a higher anonymity since the bank can easily trace any transaction performed through the coin. This is because some information of the consumer such as $I, Cert_c$ has been known by the bank. To solve this problem, an AP agent is established to help the consumer to achieve a higher level of anonymity: the consumer can derive a new encryption of his identity in an indistinguishable way. However, the consumer will need a new certificate for a new issued cipher text. The AP agent can provide this new certificate. Before certifying, the consumer requires both the previous coin $(c, Cert_c)$ and the proof of equivalence between the two cipher texts. Details are described below.

The consumer contacts the AP agent if s/he needs to get a higher level of anonymity. The consumer chooses a random ρ and re-encrypts the coin:

$$c' = (a' = g^\rho a, b' = Y^\rho b).$$

1. The consumer generates a Schnorr signature S on $m = h^\rho$ using the secret key x_u as shown in Sect. 5.2.3. Because of S, the consumer will not be able to deny his knowledge of ρ later. Furthermore, nobody can impersonate the consumer at this step, since the discrete logarithm x_u of I is required to produce a valid signature. So there is no existential forgery.
2. The consumer also provides a designated -verifier proof of equality of discrete logarithms

$$log_h m = log_g(a'/a) = log_Y(b'/b). \tag{5.1}$$

3. The consumer finally sends c, c', S, m to the AP agent.
4. The AP agent checks the certificate $Cert_c$ on c, the validity of the signature S on the message m, then certifies c' and sends back a certificate $Cert_{c'}$ to the consumer.

After these processes the consumer gets a new certified coin $c' = (a' = g^\rho a, b' = Y^\rho b)$ and a new certification $Cert_{c'}$ which is now strongly anonymous from the point of view of the bank. The AP agent has to keep (c, c', m, S) to be able to prove the link between c and c', with the help of the consumer.

Following the process, the AP agent can also give many smaller new coins for an old one since the amount of new one can be embedded in the certificate $Cert_{c'}$.

Payment (Performed between the consumer and the shop over an anonymous channel)
When a consumer possesses a coin, s/he can simply spend it at shops by proving knowledge of the secret key (x_u, s) associated with the coin c or c'. This proof is a signature $S = (e, u, v, t_1)$ of the new certificate $Cert_{c'}$, purchase, date, etc. with the secret key (x_u, s) associating the coin to the receiver (which is later forwarded to the bank).

Deposit (The receiver deposits a coin to a bank)
Since the system is off-line, the shop will send the payment transcript to the bank B later. The transcript consists of the coin c or c' (if the consumer applied a higher level of anonymity), the signature and the date/time of the transaction. The bank will verify the correctness of payment and credit the coin into the shop's account.

The receiver (shop) deposits the coin into its bank account with a transcript of the payment. If the consumer uses the same coin c twice, then the consumer will be traced: two different receivers will send the same coin c to the bank. The bank can easily search its records to ensure that c has not been used before. If the consumer uses c twice, then the bank has two different signatures. Thus, the bank can isolate the consumer and trace the payment to the consumer's account I.

5.4.3   Security Analysis

An off-line e-cash scheme is secure [15] if the following requirements are satisfied:

1. *Unreusable*: If any consumer uses the same coin twice, the identity of the consumer can be computed.
2. *Untraceable*: With n withdrawal processes, no p.p.t. (Probabilistic polynomial time) Turing Machine can compute $(n + 1)$th distinct and valid coin.
3. *Unforgeable*: With any number of the customer's withdrawal, payment and deposit protocols, no p.p.t. Turing Machine can compute a single valid coin.
4. *Unexpandable*: With any number of the customer's valid withdrawal, payment and deposit protocols, no p.p.t. Turing Machine can compute a legal consumer's identity.

The security in the e-cash scheme is based on the hardness of Discrete Logarithms [60] and hash functions. The system preserves the above four requirements.

Unreusable   When a consumer spends a coin, s/he hands over the coin together with a signature $S = (e, u, v, t_1)$ to a shop. If the consumer uses a coin twice, then we have two signatures $S_1 = (e_1, u_1, v_1, t_{11})$ and $S_2 = (e_2, u_2, v_2, t_{12})$, where

$$u_1 = k_1 - re_1 (mod q), \quad v_1 = s - x_u e_1 (mod q).$$

$$u_2 = k_2 - re_2 (mod q), \quad v_2 = s - x_u e_2 (mod q).$$

Then $(v_2 - v_1)/(e_1 - e_2) = x_u$, this is the secret key of the consumer I. So, a coin in the new scheme cannot be reused.

Untraceable   When a consumer constructs a coin, s/he uses the secret keys x_u and s, both of which are not shown to any other parts in the purchase process. So no one can trace the consumer and the coin.

Unforgeable   We first discuss whether the bank and the AP agent can forge a valid coin or not. To produce a valid coin, the first requirement is making a encryption $c = (a = g^r, b = Y^r I^s)$ of I. The second requirement is using the secret key x_u of the consumer to sign a Schnorr signature of c together with the current time. The bank can do the first step but cannot do the second step since it does not know the secret key x_u. This means the bank cannot forge a valid coin. Similarly, the AP agent cannot forge a valid coin either. It should be noted that even though both the bank and the AP agent know a valid coin, they still couldn't use it. This is because there is a signature in payment process, which can only be done by the user.

As already seen, the secret key x_u of a consumer is never revealed, only used in some signatures. A consumer is therefore protected against any impersonation, even from a collusion of the bank, the AP agent, and the shop. Only the consumer can construct a valid coin since there is a undeniable signature embedded in the coin. To prevent the bank from framing the consumer as a multiple spender in the scheme, we use digital signature I^s for s which is known only by the consumer. Then the system is unforgeable.

Unexpandable For a legal consumer and a valid coin, the secret key x_u and the random number s are never shown to others at anytime. Furthermore, usually, the random number s will be changed for different coins. With n withdrawal proceedings, the random number s will be changed n times. Then, no one can compute the $(n + 1)$th distinct and valid coin even if they see n proceeding withdrawals.

5.5   User-Role Assignment

RBAC administration encompasses the issues of assigning users to roles, assigning permissions to roles, and assigning roles to roles to define a role hierarchy. These activities are all required to bring users and permissions together. However, in many cases, they are best done by different administrators. Assigning permissions to roles is typically the job of application administrators. Assigning roles to roles has aspects of user-role assignment and role-permission assignment. Role-role relationships establish broad policy. A comprehensive administrative model for RBAC must account for all three issues mentioned above. However, user-role assignment is a particularly critical administrative activity. It is likely to be the first administrative function that is decentralized and delegated to users rather than system adminstrators. Assigning people to tasks is a normal managerial function. Assigning users to roles should be a natural part of assigning users to tasks. Sandhu and Bhamidipati developed a model called URA97 in which RBAC is used to manage user-role assignment [33]. However, there is little work on how to use User-role assignment in an electronic commerce [32]. We will analyse user-role assignment for the new scheme in this section. Before analysing user-role assignment of the new scheme, we need to see the relationships of roles.

5.5.1   Duty Separation Constraints

With RBAC, users cannot associate with permissions directly. Permissions must be authorized for roles, and roles must be authorized for users. In RBAC administration, two different types of associations must be managed, i.e. associations between users and roles, and associations between roles and permissions. When a user's job position changes, only the user/role associations change. If the job position is represented by a single role, then when a user's job position changes, only two user/role associations need to be changed: the removal of the association between the user and the user's current role, and the addition of an association between the user and the user's new role.

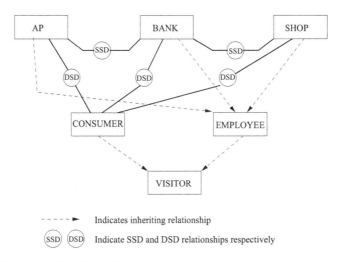

Fig. 5.4 The relationships of the roles in the new scheme

As we mentioned in Sect. 5.2.4, relationships of roles such as Role hierarchies, SSD and DSD have to be decided when a system is designed. Some relationships like cardinality, the maximum number of users etc., can be decided when the system is in operation.

There are four major roles in the system, the AP agent, the consumer, the bank and the shop. The AP agent, the bank and the shop, would be companies comprising many participants. We will not discuss the relationships of all the participants in these companies since they are beyond the scope of this chapter. We will only consider duty separation constraints. In Fig. 5.4, for example, since all staff in the AP agent, the bank and the shop are employees, their corresponding roles inherit the employee role. Similarly, the consumer inherits the visitor role. The roles AP agent, the shop and the bank have a DSD relationship with the role consumer. This indicates that an individual consumer cannot act the roles of the AP agent, the shop or the bank simultaneously. The staff in these three companies have to first log out if they want to register as consumers. For example, a consumer, who is a staff member of the AP agent, can ask the AP agent to help him to get a higher anonymity. But as a consumer, since the shop and the bank need to check the new coin's certificate $Cert_{c'}$ and signature, s/he cannot give herself/himself a new certificate $Cert_{c'}$ of a coin when s/he works for the AP agent. Another staff member of the AP agent should do the job for this person.

The AP agent has an SSD relationship with the bank. This is because the duty of the AP agent is to help a consumer to get a higher anonymity. The bank knows the old coin $c = (g^r, Y^r I^s)$ and its certificate $Cert_c$. The AP agent sends the new certificate $Cert_{c'}$ of the new coin $c' = (g^{r+\rho}, Y^{r+\rho} I^s)$ to the consumer. The bank will know the new certificate $Cert_{c'}$ when the same staff from the AP agent and processing the coin of the consumer.

The AP agent and the bank are authorized by a staff member common in both. If so, the consumer cannot have the required anonymity of coin. The shop also has an SSD relationship with the bank since the bank verifies the payment as well as depositing the coin to the shop's account. The SSD relationship is also a conflict of interest relationship like the DSD relationship but much stronger. If two roles have a SSD relationship, then they may not even be authorized to the same individual. Thus, these three roles may never be authorized to the same individual.

5.5.2   Grant Model

A hierarchy of roles and a hierarchy of administrative roles are shown in Figs. 5.5 and 5.6 respectively.

The sets of roles and administrative roles are required to be disjoint. Senior roles are shown towards the top of the hierarchies and junior are to the bottom. Senior roles inherit permissions from junior roles. Let $x > y$ denote x is senior to y with obvious extension to $x \geq y$. The notion of a prerequisite condition is a key part in the processes of user_role assignment [33].

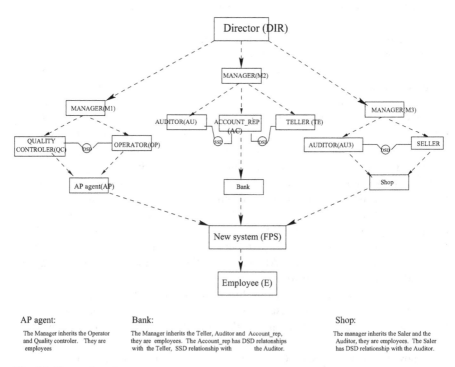

AP agent:

The Manager inherits the Operator and Quality controler. They are employees

Bank:

The Manager inherits the Teller, Auditor and Account_rep, they are employees. The Account_rep has DSD relatonships with the Teller, SSD relationship with   the Auditor.

Shop:

The manager inherits the Saler and the Auditor, they are employees. The Saler has DSD relationship with the Auditor.

Fig. 5.5 User_role assignment

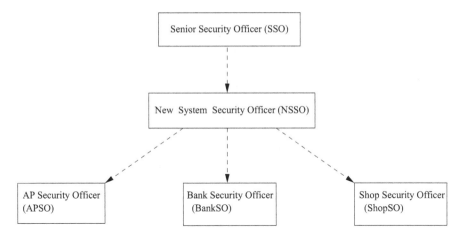

Fig. 5.6 Administrative role assignment

Definition 5.1 A **prerequisite condition** is a boolean expression using the usual $\wedge$ and $\vee$ operators on terms of the form x and $\bar{x}$ where x is a role. A prerequisite condition is evauated for a user u by interpreting x to be ture if $(\exists x' \geq x)$, $(u, x') \in UA$ and $\bar{x}$ to be ture if $(\forall x' \geq x)$, $(u, x') \notin UA$, where UA is a set of user-role assignment. For a given set of roles R let CR denotes all possible prerequisite conditions that can be formed using the roles in R.   ◇

Definition 5.2 User-role assignments are controlled by the relations of *can-assign* $\subseteq AR \times CR \times 2^R$, where AR is a set of administrative roles.   ◇

The meaning of *can-assign* $(x, y, \{a, b, c\})$ is that a member of the administrative role x can assign a user whose currect membership, or non-memebership, in roles satisfies the prerequisite condition y to be a member of roles a, b or c. Table 5.4 is shown the can-assign relations with the prerequisite conditions in the new scheme. To identify a role range within the role hierarchy of Fig. 6.4, we use the familiar closed and open interval notation.

$$[x, y] = \{r \in R | x \geq r \wedge r \geq y\}$$

$$(x, y] = \{r \in R | x > r \wedge r \geq y\}$$

$$[x, y) = \{r \in R | x \geq r \wedge r > y\}$$

$$(x, y) = \{r \in R | x > r \wedge r > y\}$$

Let us consider the APSO tuples (the analysis for BankSO and ShopSO are similar). The first tuple authorizes APSO to assign users with the prerequisite role FPS into AP agent. The second one authorizes APSO to assign users with the prerequisite condition $FPS \wedge \overline{OP}$ to QC. Similarly, the third tuple authorizes APSO

Table 5.4 Can-assign

Admin.role	Prereq. condition	Role range
APSO	FPS	[AP, AP]
APSO	FPS $\wedge \overline{OP}$	[QC, QC]
APSO	FPS $\wedge \overline{QC}$	[OP, OP]
APSO	QC $\wedge$ OP	[M1, M1]
BankSO	FPS	[Bank, Bank]
BankSO	FPS $\wedge \overline{TE} \wedge \overline{AU}$	[AC, AC]
BankSO	FPS $\wedge \overline{TE} \wedge \overline{AC}$	[AU, AU]
BankSO	FPS $\wedge \overline{AU} \wedge \overline{AC}$	[TE, TE]
BankSO	TE $\wedge AU \wedge$ AC	[M2, M2]
ShopSO	FPS	[Shop, Shop]
ShopSO	FPS $\wedge \overline{SALER}$	[lAUDITOR, lAUDITOR]
ShopSO	FPS $\wedge \overline{lAUDITOR}$	[SALER, SALER]
ShopSO	SALER $\wedge$ lAUDITOR	[M3, M3]
NSSO	FPS	(FPS, DIR)
SSO	E	[FPS, FPS]
SSO	FPS	(FPS, DIR)

to assign users with the prerequisite condition $FPS \wedge \overline{QC}$ to OP. Taken together the second and third tuple authorize APSO to put a user who is a member of AP agent into one but not both of QC and OP. This illustrates how mutually exclusive roles can be forced. However, for the NSSO and SSO these are not mutually exclusive. The fourth tuple authorizes APSO to put a user who is a member of both QC and OP into M1 (manager). Of course, a user could have become a member of both QC and OP only by actions of a more powerful administrator than APSO.

5.5.3 Revoke Model

There are related subtleties that arise in RBAC concerning the interaction between granting and revocation of user-role membership and the role hierarchy.

Definition 5.3 A user-role revocation is a relation *can-revoke* $\subseteq AR \times 2^R$, where AR is a set of administrative roles. The meaning of *can-revoke*(x, Y) is that a member of the administrative role x (or a member of an administrative role that is senior to x) can revoke membership of a user from any role $y \in Y$, where Y defines the *range of revocation*. Table 5.5 gives an example of the can-revoke relation.

There are two kinds of revocations. The first one is weak revocation, the second one is strong revocation.

Table 5.5 Can-revoke

Admin.role	Role range
APSO	[AP, M1)
BankSO	[Bank, M2)
ShopSO	[Shop, M3)
NSSO	(FPS, DIR)
SSO	[FPS, DIR]

Definition 5.4 A user U is an explicit member of a role x if $(U, x) \in UA$, and that U is an implicit member of role x if for some $x' > x$, $(U, x') \in UA$.

Weak revocation has an impact only on explicit membership. For weak revocation, the membership of a user in a role is revoked only if the user is an explicit member of the role. Suppose a user Bob is an explicit member of M1, QC, AU, IAUDITOR, AP, FPS and E. If Alice with the activated administrative role APSO weakly revokes Bob's membership from AP, he continues to be a member of the senior roles to AP and therefore can use the permission of AP. Alice should have enough power in the session to weakly revoke Bob's membership from his explicitly assigned roles. For instance, if Alice has activated APSO and then tries to weakly revoke Bob's membership from M1, she is not allowed to proceed because APSO does not have the authority of weak revocation from M1 according to the can-revoke relation in Table 5.2.

Therefore, if Alice wants to revoke Bob's explicit membership as well as implicit membership from AP by weakly revocation, she needs to activate SSO and weakly revoke Bob's membership from AP, QC and M1. This brings out the same result as the one after strong revocation from AP by SSO. However, Alice does not need to revoke Bob's membership from FPS, AU, IAUDITOR and E, because they are not senior roles to AP based on the role hierarchy of Fig. 6.4.

Strong revocation requires revocation of both explicit and implicit membership. Strong revocation of $U's$ membership in x requires that U be removed not only from explicit membership in x, but also from explicit (implicit) membership in all roles senior to x. Strong revocation therefore has a cascading effect up-wards in the role hierarchy. For example, Bob is an explicit member of M1, QC, IAUDITOR, FPS and AP. If Alice with the activated administrative role SSO strongly revokes Bob's membership from AP, then he is removed not only from explicit membership in AP, but also from explicit (or implicit) membership in all roles senior to AP. Actually, after the strong revocation from AP, Bob has been removed from M1, QC as well as AP. However, he still has a membership of FPS and IAUDITOR, since they are not senior roles to AP based on the role hierarchy of Fig. 6.4. This brings out the same result as the one after weak revocation from AP, QC, M1 by SSO. Note that all implied revocations upward in the role hierarchy should within the revocation range of the administrative roles that are active in a session. For instance, if Alice activates APSO and tries to strongly revoke Bob's membership from M1, she is not allowed to proceed because M1 is out of the APSO's can-revoke range in Table 5.2.

5.6   Implementations

In this section, we will analyse two different purchase procedures. We will show how to use the new e-cash for Internet purchases and how to get some smaller coins from the AP agent. This will demonstrate the efficiency of the payment protocol.

Purchase Procedure 1

In purchase procedure 1 a consumer decides how much money should be paid to the shop, withdraws the money from the bank, and pays it to the shop.

1. *Consumer to shop*: The consumer wants to buy some goods in a shop, so contacts the shop for the price.
2. *Consumer to bank*: The consumer gets the money from the bank, the amount being embedded in the signature.
3. *Anonymity scalability*: If the consumer wants to maintain higher level of anonymity, s/he can ask the AP agent to certify a new coin which can be then used in the shop.
4. *Consumer to shop*: The consumer proves to the shop that s/he is the owner of the money, and pays it to the shop. Then the shop sends the goods to the consumer.
5. *Shop to bank*: The shop deposits the e-cash in the bank. The bank checks the validation and that there is no double spending of the coin. The bank transfers the money to the shop's account.

Purchase Procedure 2

In purchase procedure 2 the consumer does not have to ask the bank to send money since the consumer already has enough e-cash in his "wallet". All the consumer needs to do is to get some smaller e-cash from the AP agent to pay the shop.

There are 4 steps in the purchase procedure 2. They are: (1) *consumer to shop*; (2) *consumer to AP agent*; (3) *consumer to shop* again and (4) *shop to bank*. Step 2, *consumer to AP agent* is different from step 3 in procedure 1 but the other three steps are similar to those in procedure 1. Therefore we will focus only on step 2 *consumer to AP agent*. It should be noted that electronic-cash is a digital message and a certification. We say that the AP agent can provide certificates of coins then provide a service in changing to small coin.

Consumer to AP Agent   The consumer advises the AP agent of the amount of money to pay the shop from his wallet. She/He then asks the AP agent to make some smaller coins. By doing this, the consumer can also get a higher level of anonymity. After checking the old money sent by the consumer, the AP agent creates some new coins of an equivalent value to the original coin. One of these new coins can be used in the shop.

We have already seen that the consumer can keep money in his wallet or get money from the bank. In both purchase procedures 1 and 2 most computations are done by the consumers, so the system is very convenient for Internet purchases.

5.7 Conclusions

In this chapter, a new electronic cash scheme is designed to provide different degrees of anonymity for consumers. Consumers can decide the levels of anonymity. They can have a low level of anonymity if they want to spend coins directly after withdrawing them from the bank. Consumers can achieve a higher level of anonymity through the AP agent without revealing their private information and are more secure in relation to the bank because the new certificate of a coin comes from the AP agent who is not involved in the payment process. This system does not need a trusted party to manage consumers' identities. It is an off-line scheme with low communication and computation. With its scalable anonymity, the new payment protocol can effectively prevent eavesdropping, tampering and impersonation. Finally, we have analysed the user-role assignment of the new payment scheme.

Appendix: An Example of the New Scheme

This example will show the main steps in the e-cash scheme. We omit the details of two undeniable signatures in withdrawal and the scalable anonymity process, because they are only used for verifying the user. In the following example, the module 47 is used.

Bank Setup
Suppose $(p, q, \gamma, k) = (47, 23, 2, 4)$, then $G_q = \{0, 1, 2, \ldots, 22\}$ is a subgroup of order 23. $g = 3$ is a generator of G_q. The bank's secret key $x_B = 4$ and hash function $H(x, y) = 3^x * 5^y$. The bank publishes $H(x, y)$ and $\{p, q, g\} = \{47, 23, 3\}$. The public key of the bank is $Y = g^{x_B} = 34$.

User Setup
We assume the secret of a user is $x_u = 7$ and the user sends $I = g^{x_u} = 32$ to the bank. After checking some identifications like social security card or driver's licence, the bank authorizes the user (consumer) with I.

After the bank setup and the user setup, the user can purchase.

Withdrawal
The user chooses $(r, s) = (2, 3)$ and computes $c = (g^r, Y^r I^s) = (9, 2)$, then signs a Schnorr signature S for the message $m = (c, t)$, where t is the current time. The user sends $c = (9, 2)$ and S to the bank, the latter sends back a certificate $Cert_c$.

The user contacts the AP agent if s/he needs a high level of anonymity, or uses the coin in a shop directly (See Payment). The user and the AP agent follow the processes below. We suppose $h = 37$ is a public number.

Anonymity Scalability

The user re-encrypts the coin c, chooses $\rho = 4$ and computes $c' = (a' = g^\rho a, b' = Y^\rho b) = (24, 14)$ and signs a Schnorr signature S on $m = h^\rho = 36$. Finally, the user sends (c, c', S, m) to the AP agent. The latter verifies the Schnorr signature S and the equation (1), and sends a certificate $Cert_{c'}$ to the user if they are correct.

Since the new coin $c' = (24, 14)$ and its certificate $Cert_{c'}$ have no relationship with the bank, the user has a high anonymity.

Payment

The user signs a signature $S = (e, u, v, t_1)$ of a message m which includes c', $Cert_{c'}$ and purchase time etc. to prove the ownership of the new coin. For convenience, we assume $m = 11$. The user chooses $k = 5$ then computes $t = Y^k g^s = 19$, $e = H(m, t) = 40$, $u = 18$, $v = 5$, $t_1 = 28$.

The shop who is convinced that the user is the owner of the coin computes $t' = 15$ if the equation of $t' = tt_1$ and the signature S are successful. She/He does not know who the user is.

Deposit

The bank will put the money into the shop's account when the checking of the coin $C' = (24, 14)$ and the signature $S = (e, u, v, t_1) = (40, 18, 5, 28)$ are correct. The shop can also see that the money in his account is added.

5.8 Problems and Exercises

5.8.1 Problems

1. What is a Hash function? How does a Hash function work for e-payment?
2. What is a public key encryption scheme? Why a public key encryption scheme is required for e-payment?
3. What is the difference between Weak revocation and strong revocation?
4. Why Duty separation constraints are important?
5. What is anonymity for a coin? Why anonymity is necessary?

5.8.2 Exercises

1. An example of a public key encryption scheme, prime numbers p and q are needed.
2. Design a revocation model, it has examples of weak revocation and strong revocation.
3. Design an e-payment scheme, analysing duty separation constraints in the scheme.
4. Design an anonymous payment protocal, verifying its anonymity feature.

References

1. Barkley, J.F., Beznosov, K., Uppal, J.: Supporting relationships in access control using role based access control. In: Third ACM Workshop on Role Based Access Control, pp. 55–65 (1999)
2. Bellare, M., Goldreich, O., Krawczyk, H.: Stateless evaluation of pseudorandom functions: security beyond the birthday barrier. In: Advances in Cryptology—Crypto 99. Lectures Notes in Computer Science, vol. 1666. Springer, Berlin (1999)
3. Canetti, R., Goldreich, O., Halevi, S.: The random Oracle methodology. In: Proceedings of the 30th ACM STOC '98, pp. 209–218. IEEE, New York (1998)
4. Cao, J. et al.: Towards secure XML document with usage control. In: Web Technologies Research and Development—APWeb 2005, pp. 296–307. Springer, Berlin (2005)
5. Chan, A., Frankel, Y., Tsiounis, Y.: An Efficient Off-line Electronic Cash Scheme as Secure as RSA, Research report NU-CCS-96-03. Northeastern University, Boston (1995)
6. Chaum, D.: Blind signature for untraceable payments. In: Advances in Cryptology—Crypto 82, pp. 199–203. Plenum, New York (1983)
7. Chaum, D. (ed.): An Introduction to E-Cash. DigiCash (1995). http://www.digicash.com
8. Chaum, D., Van Antwerpen, H.: Undeniable signatures. In: Advances in Cryptology–Crypto89. Lectures Notes in Computer Science, vol. 435, pp. 212–216. Springer, Berlin (1990)
9. Chaum, D., Fiat, A., Naor, M.: Untraceable electronic cash. In: Advances in Cryptology—Crypto 88. Lectures Notes in Computer Science, vol. 403, pp. 319–327. Springer, Berlin (1990)
10. Cox, B., Tygar, J.D., Sirbu, M.: Netbill security and transaction protocol. In: The first USENIX Workshop on Electronic Commerce, New York (1995)
11. ElGamal, T.: A public key cryptosystem and a signature scheme based on discrete logarithms. IEEE Trans. Inf. Theory **IT-31**(4), 469–472 (1985)
12. Feinstein, H.L.: Final report: NIST small business innovative research (SBIR) grant: role based access control: phase 1, Technical report. In: *Proceedings of the SETA Corporation* (1995)
13. Ferraiolo, D.F., Kuhn, D.R.: Role based access control. In: Proceedings of the 15th National Computer Security Conference, pp. 554–563 (1992). ferraiolo92rolebased.html
14. Ferraiolo, D.F., Barkley, J.F., Kuhn, D.R.: Role-based access control model and reference implementation within a corporate intranet. In: Proceedings of the TISSEC, vol. 2, pp. 34–64 (1999)
15. Franklin, M., Yung, M.: Secure and efficient off-line digital money. In: Proceedings of the Twentieth International Colloquium on Automata, Languages and Programming. Lectures Notes in Computer Science, vol. 700, pp. 265–276. Springer, New York (1993)
16. Goldschlag, D., Reed, M., Syverson, P.: Onion routing for anonymous and private Internet connections. Commun. ACM **24**(2), 39–41 (1999)
17. Kabir, E., Wang, H.: Conditional purpose based access control model for privacy protection. In: Proceedings of the Twentieth Australasian Conference on Australasian Database (ADC '09), vol. 92, pp. 135–142. Australian Computer Society, Australian (2009)
18. Kabir, M., Wang, H., Bertino E.: A conditional purpose-based access control model with dynamic roles. Expert Syst. Appl. **38**(3), 1482–1489 (2011)
19. Kabir, M., Wang, H., Bertino, E.: A conditional role-involved purpose-based access control model. J. Org. Comput. E. Commerce **21**, 71–91 (2011)
20. Kabir, M., Wang, H., Bertino, E.: Efficient systematic clustering method for k-anonymization. Acta Inf. **48**(1), 51–66 (2011)
21. Khalil, F., Li, J., Wang, H.: Integrating recommendation models for improved web page prediction accuracy. In: Proceedings of the Thirty-first Australasian Conference on Computer Science (ACSC '08), vol. 74, pp. 91–100. Australian Computer Society, Darlinghurst (2008)
22. Li, M., et al.: Advanced permission-role relationship in role-based access control. In: Information Security and Privacy, pp. 391–403. Springer, Berlin (2008)

23. Li, M., et al.: Optimal privacy-aware path in hippocratic databases. In: Database Systems for Advanced Applications, pp. 441–455. Springer, Berlin (2009)

24. Li, M., Wang, H.: ABDM: an extended flexible delegation model in RBAC. In: Proceedings of the 2008 8th IEEE International Conference on Computer and Information Technology, pp. 390–395 (2008)

25. Li, M., Wang, H., Plank, A.: Privacy-aware access control with generalization boundaries. In: Proceedings of the Thirty-Second Australasian Conference on Computer Science (ACSC '09), vol. 91, pp. 105–112. Australian Computer Society, Darlinghurst (2009)

26. MastercardVisa (ed.): SET 1.0—Secure Electronic Transaction Specification (1997). http://www.mastercard.com/set.html

27. Okamoto, T.: An efficient divisible electronic cash scheme. In: Advances in Cryptology—Crypto'95. Lectures Notes in Computer Science, vol. 963, pp. 438–451. Springer, Berlin (1995)

28. Pointcheval, D.: Self-scrambling anonymizers. In:Proceedings of Financial Cryptography. Springer, Anguilla (2000)

29. Rivest, R.L., Shamir, A., Adleman, L.M.: A method for obtaining digital signatures and public-key cryptosystems. Commun. ACM $21(2)$, 120–126 (1978)

30. Rivest, R.T.: The MD5 message digest algorithm. Internet RFC 1321 (1992)

31. Sandhu, R.: Role activation hierarchies. In: Third ACM Workshop on Role Based Access Control, pp. 33–40. ACM, New York (1998)

32. Sandhu, R.: Future directions in role-based access control models. In: MMS, 2001 (2001). http://www.list.gmu.edu/confrnc/misconf/

33. Sandhu, R., Bhamidipati, V.: The URA97 model for role-based administration of user-role assignment. In: Lin, T.Y., Qian, X. (eds.) Database Security XI: Status and Prospects, pp. 262–275. North-Holland, Amsterdam (1997)

34. Schnorr, C.P.: Efficient signature generation by smart cards. J. Cryptol. $4(3)$, 161–174 (1991)

35. Sun, X,. et al.: An efficient hash-based algorithm for minimal k-anonymity. In: Proceedings of the Thirty-first Australasian Conference on Computer Science (ACSC '08), vol. 74, pp. 101–107. Australian Computer Society, Darlinghurst (2008)

36. Sun, X., et al.: Enhanced p-sensitive k-anonymity models for privacy preserving data publishing. Trans. Data Privacy $1(2)$, 53–66 (2008)

37. Sun, X., et al.: (p^+, α)-sensitive k-anonymity: a new enhanced privacy protection model. In:Proceeding of the 2008 8th IEEE International Conference on Computer and Information Technology, pp. 59–64 (2008)

38. Sun, L., Li, Y., Wang H.: M-service and its framework. In: Proceedings of the 2005 Asia-Pacific Conference on Communications, pp. 837–841 (2005)

39. Sun, X., Wang, H., Li, J.: Priority driven k-anonymisation for privacy protection. In: Proceedings of the 7th Australasian Data Mining Conference, vol. 87, pp. 73–78 (2008)

40. Sun, X., Wang, H., Li, J.: Microdata protection through approximate microaggregation. In: Proceedings of the Thirty-Second Australasian Conference on Computer Science (ACSC '09), vol. 91, pp. 161–168. Australian Computer Society, Darlinghurst (2009)

41. Sun, L., Wang, H., Yong, J.: Authorization algorithms for permission-role assignments. J. UCS 15, 1782–1798 (2009)

42. Sun, X., Wang, H., Sun, L.: Extended k-anonymity models against attribute disclosure. In: Proceedings of the 2009 Third International Conference on Network and System Security, pp. 130–136 (2009)

43. Sun, X., Wang, H., Li, J.: Satisfying privacy requirements: one step before anonymization. In: Advances in Knowledge Discovery and Data Mining, pp. 181–188. Springer, Berlin (2010)

44. Sun, X., Li, M., Wang, H.: A family of enhanced (L, α)-diversity models for privacy preserving data publishing. Future Gener. Comput. Syst. $27(3)$, 348–356 (2011)

45. Sun, X., Sun, L., Wang, H.: Extended k-anonymity models against sensitive attribute disclosure. Comput. Commun. $34(4)$, 526–535 (2011). Special issue: Building Secure Parallel and Distributed Networks and Systems

46. Wang, H., et al.: Authorization algorithms for the mobility of user-role relationship. In: Proceedings of the Twenty-eighth Australasian Conference on Computer Science (ACSC '05), vol. 38, pp. 69–77. Australian Computer Society, Darlinghurst (2005)

47. Wang, H., et al.: A framework for role-based group deligation in distributed environments. In: Proceedings of the 29th Australasian Computer Science Conference, vol. 48, pp. 321–328 (2006)

48. Wang, H., et al.: Authorization approaches for advanced permission-role assignments. In: Proceedings of the 2008 12th International Conference on Computer Supported Cooperative Work in Design, pp. 277–282 (2008)

49. Wang, H., Li, Q.: Secure and efficient information sharing in multi-university e-learning environments. In: Advances in Web Based Learning—ICWL 2007, pp. 542–553. Springer Berlin (2008)

50. Wang, H., Sun, L.: Trust-involved access control in collaborative open social networks. In: Proceedings of the 2010 Fourth International Conference on Network and System Security, pp. 239–246 (2010)

51. Wang, H., Cao, J., Zhang, Y.: A consumer anonymity scalable payment scheme with role based access control. In: Proceeding of the Second International Conference on Web Information Systems Engineering (WISE01), pp. 53–62 (2001)

52. Wang, H., Cao, J., Kambayashi, Y.: Building a consumer anonymity scalable payment protocol for the internet purchases. In: Proceedings of the 12th International Workshop on Research Issues on Data Engineering: Engineering E-Commerce/E-Business Systems, San Jose, USA (2002)

53. Wang, H., Cao, J., Zhang, Y.: A flexible payment scheme and its role-based access control. IEEE Trans. Knowl. Data Eng. **17**(3), 425–436 (2005)

54. Wang, H., Cao, J., Ross, D.: Role-based delegation with negative authorization. In: Frontiers of WWW Research and Development—APWeb 2006, pp. 307–318. Springer, Berlin (2006)

55. Wang, H., Cao, J., Zhang, Y.: Delegating revocations and authorizations in collaborative business environments. Inf. Syst. Front. **11**(3), 293 (2008)

56. Wang, H., Cao, J., Zhang, Y.: Delegating revocations and authorizations in collaborative business environments. Inf. Syst. Frontiers **11**(3), 293 (2008)

57. Wang, H., Sun, L., Varadharajan, V.: Purpose-based access control policies and conflicting analysis. In: Security and Privacy—Silver Linings in the Cloud, pp. 217–228. Springer, Berlin (2010)

58. Wang, H., Zhang, Y., Cao, J.: Ubiquitous computing environments and its usage access control. In: Proceedings of the First International Conference on Scalable Information Systems (InfoScale '06). ACM, New York (2006)

59. Yiannis, T.: Fair off-line cash made easy. In: Advances in Cryptology–Asiacrypt'98. Lectures Notes in Computer Science, vol. 1346, pp. 240–252. Springer, Berlin (1998)

60. Yiannis, T., Yung, M.: On the security of ElGamal-based encryption. In: International Workshop on Practice and Theory in Public Key Cryptography (PKC '98). Lectures Notes in Computer Science, vol. 1346. Springer, Yokohama (1998)

61. Zhang, J., et al.: Detecting anomalies from high-dimensional wireless network data streams: a case study. Soft Comput. **15**(6), 1195–1215 (2011)

Chapter 6
Using RBAC to Secure Payment Process in Cloud

This chapter presents basic definitions of role based access control RBAC such as user-role assignment, permission-role assignment and role-role assignment and so on. The advantages and significance of RBAC are discussed. Based on the payment model designed in the previous chapter, the use of RBAC to manage the electronic payment system is analyzed.

6.1 Introduction

With people's increased consciousness of the need for electronic commerce to protect their private information and to provide security of applications, system administrators are continuing to implement access control mechanisms and retain a critical and complex aspect of security administration [9, 14, 61]. Traditional administrations of access control are mandatory, discretionary and role-based access control [6, 58, 65]. Mandatory access controls (MAC) restrict access to data based on varying degrees of security requirements for information contained in the objects. Information is associated with multi-level security requirements with labels such as TOP SECRET, SECRET, and CONFIDENTIAL [2]. An assigned right cannot be changed and modifications are permitted only to administrators. Users may need to register on a number of different servers of different operating system types, various databases and multiple business applications [11, 32, 71]. Furthermore, an object classification reflects the sensitivity of the information contained in the object, that is, the potential damage that may come from unauthorized disclosure of information. Registration of each user with each facility is needed to control and prevent unauthorized use. Managing a system with MAC is a challenging task, especially when dealing with the changes on user positions and other access rights. Discretionary access controls (DAC) allow users to grant or revoke access to any authority under their control without the intercession of a system administrator [12].

© Springer Nature Switzerland AG 2020

H. Wang et al., *Access Control Management in Cloud Environments*,

https://doi.org/10.1007/978-3-030-31729-4_6

Access rights to resources are based on the identity of persons and/or groups to which they belong. When the number of users increases, the management is costly. DAC grants authorization or privileges to users directly, authorized statically when they set up an account. Though it is convenient for users to pass on the authorization directly to other users, it brings a serious security problems. For example, when a user passes on some access controls to another user, it may change the level of access privilege of the second user who may then able to access or derive high level information based on the level of access control gained.

The concept of role based access control RBAC started with multi-user and multi-on-line application systems pioneered in the early 1970s [4, 5, 26, 28]. The major notion of RBAC is that permissions are assigned to roles and users are associated with appropriate roles [49, 59, 67]. Users cannot associate with permissions directly. In other words, RBAC is described in terms of individual users being associated with roles as well as roles being associated with permissions (Each permission is a pair of objects and operations). As such, a role is used to associate with users and permissions. A user in this model is a human being. Roles are created for the various job functions in an organization and users are assigned roles based on their authority and qualifications. Users can be easily reassigned from one role to another. Roles can be granted new permissions as new applications and systems are incorporated and permissions can be revoked from roles as needed [21, 62, 66, 68].

Permission is an approval of a particular operation to be performed on one or more objects. The relationship between roles and permissions is shown in Fig. 6.1, arrows indicate a many to many relationship (that is, a permission can be associated with one or more roles, and a role can be associated with one or more permissions). As shown in the figure, RBAC has the capability to establish relations between

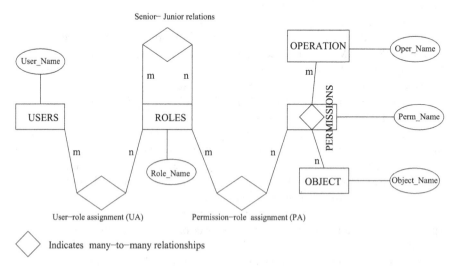

Fig. 6.1 RBAC relationship

roles as well as between permissions and roles and between users and roles [38–40, 60]. For example when two roles are established as mutually exclusive then the same user is not allowed to take on both roles. This problem may happen in user-role assignment. Another example is for permission-role relations, conflicting permissions cannot be assigned to the same role. Therefore in a bank, the permission for approving loan and that of funding loan are conflicting, these two permissions cannot be assigned to a role. In role-role assignment, roles have inheritance relations whereby one role inherits permissions assigned to another role. These relations between users and roles, permissions and roles and between roles and roles are used to establish security policies that include separation of duties and delegation of authority. The security policy of the organization determines role membership and the allocation of each role's capabilities [16, 22, 24, 50].

With RBAC it is possible to predefine role permission relationships, which makes it simple to assign users to the predefined roles. It can also be difficult, without RBAC, to determine what permissions have been authorized to what users.

There are three advantages of RBAC management. Firstly, it is much easier to manage a system using RBAC. In RBAC, a security administrator adds transactions to roles or deletes transactions from roles, where transactions can be a program object associated with data [12]. Security problems are addressed by associating programming code and data into a transaction. Access control does not require any checks on the user's or the program's right to access a data item, since the accesses are built into the transaction. Secondly, RBAC can reduce administration cost and complexity [34]. Usually, there is a relationship between the cost of administration and the number of associations which must be managed in order to administer an access control policy. The larger the number of associations, the more cost and more error prone the access control administration is likely to be, but the use of RBAC reduces the number of associations to be managed. Thirdly, RBAC is better than a typical access control list (ACL) model [27]. RBAC can authorize and audit capabilities so that people are simply assigned new roles while they change responsibilities. This allows for the authorities of a person to be easily documented. By contrast, in ACL, the entire set of authorities must be searched to develop a clear picture of a person's rights because ACLs only support the specification of user/permission and group/permission relationships.

The important feature of RBAC is policy neutral [23, 25, 51, 53]. However, it directly supports three well known security principles: least privilege, separation of duties and data abstraction [33]. RBAC gives support to the least privilege because RBAC can be configured so only those permissions required for the tasks are assigned to roles. Separation of duties is performed by ensuring that mutually exclusive roles must be invoked to complete a sensitive task, for instance, both an accounting manager and account clerk are required to participate in issuing a check. Data abstraction is achieved by means of abstract permissions such as credit and debit for an account object, rather than the read, write, execute permissions typically provided by the database system.

6.2 Administrative Issues in RBAC

It has shown that there are many components to RBAC. RBAC administration is therefore multi-faceted. The components include the issues of assigning users to roles, assigning permissions to role, and assigning roles to roles [52, 54, 69, 70]. This section analyzes these issues.

6.2.1 User-Role Assignments

The user-role assignment (URA) model was originally defined by Sandhu and Bhamidipati [37]. Figure 6.2 shows the regular roles in a shop and an administrative role. There is a junior-most role SHOP to which all employees belong and a senior-most role MANAGER. Roles AUDITOR and SELLER inherit the permissions of role SHOP while MANAGER inherit the permissions of roles AUDITOR and SELLER. The member of administrative role ShopSO are authorized to modify membership in the roles of the figure.

There are two kinds of work in user role assignment [19, 20, 55, 63]. The first is to specify what membership between user and role can be modified by an administrative role. The second is how many users can be assigned to a role. For example, user-role assignment requires that the administrative role ShopSO can assign users to the roles AUDITOR, SELLER and MANAGER, but these users must already be members of the shop, that is, the role SHOP. This is an example of a prerequisite role. More generally user-role assignment allows for a prerequisite condition [10, 15]. The prerequisite conditions is used later in RBAC applications [73, 74].

Fig. 6.2 Administrative role and role relationships in a shop

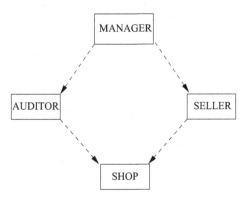

A *session* is a mapping of a user to possibly many roles. In other words, users establish sessions during that users activate some roles. Both users and sessions are important conceptions in RBAC management. The distinction between a user and a session is a fundamental aspect of RBAC and consequently arises in RBAC. To achieve the principle of least privilege a user should be allowed to login to a system with only those roles appropriate for a given session. With constraints it may not be possible for a user to activate all their roles simultaneously [18, 41, 56, 72]. For example, a constraint limits that two roles can be assigned to the same user but cannot be simultaneously activated in a session. Therefore, a person may be qualified to be a car driver and pilot but he/she can activate at most one of these roles at any time. The person cannot perform a single session with all the persons' roles activated. On the other hand, for the security reason, RBAC has dynamic separation duty constraint related to roles. In Fig. 6.2, role AUDITOR and role SELLER has dynamic separation duty relationship. These two roles can be assigned to a person but cannot activate in a session.

The opposite operation of assignment is revocation. There are two kinds of revocations. One is weak revocation and the other one is strong revocation. The revocation operation is said to be weak because it only an assignment from user to role that is directly revoked. On the other hand, strong revocation applies to all roles that include senior roles. Strong revocation cascades upwards in the role hierarchy. For example, suppose Bob is a member of AUDITOR and SHOP. If Alice has administrative role ShopSO revokes Bob's membership from SHOP, he continues to be a member of the senior role AUDITOR and therefore can still use permissions of role SHOP. If Alice strongly revokes Bob's membership from SHOP, his membership in AUDITOR is also revoked. Both revocations are analyzed in the applications of RBAC.

6.2.2 Permission-Role Assignments

Permission-role assignment applies to assign permissions to roles and revoke permissions from roles. From the perspective of a role, permissions character is similar to user's character. Both of users and permissions are basic entities that are brought together by roles [17, 42, 43, 47]. There are two aspects in permission-role assignment. One is that not all permissions can be assigned to roles by an administrator. For example in Fig. 6.2, only permissions which belong to roles SHOP and AUDITOR can assign to role SELLER. It means there are prerequisite conditions for the operations of permission-role assignment.

Prerequisite conditionp is an expression using Boolean operators $\land$ and $\lor$ on terms of the form x and $\bar{x}$ where x is a role and $\land$ means "and", $\lor$ means "or". A prerequisite condition is evaluated for a permission p by interpreting x to be true if $(\exists x' \geq x), (p, x') \in PA$ and $\bar{x}$ to be true if $(\forall x' \geq x), (p, x') \notin PA$, where PA is a set of permission-role assignments. ◇

For a given set of roles R let CR denote all possible prerequisite conditions that can be formed using the roles in R. Not every administrator can assign a permission to a role. The relation of **Can-assignp** $\subseteq AR \times CR \times 2^R$ provides what permissions can be assigned by administrators with prerequisite conditions, where AR is a set of administrative roles.

For example, the meaning of *Can-assignp* (x, y, Z) is that a member of the administrative role x can assign a permission whose current membership satisfies the prerequisite condition y to be a member of roles in range Z. Permission-role assignment (PA) is authorized by *Can-assignp* relation.

6.2.3 Role-Role Assignment

There are three kinds of roles. They are Ability-roles, Group-roles and UP-roles [33].

Ability-roles (ABR) are roles that can only have permissions and other ability-roles as members.

Group-roles (GR) are roles that can only have users and other group-roles as members.

UP-roles (UPR) are roles that have no restriction on membership, in other words, their membership can include users, permissions, group-roles, ability-roles and other UP-roles.

No role can be in two different kinds of roles. It means that the three kinds of roles are mutually disjoint. An Ability-role is a set of permissions that should be assigned as a single unit to a role. Administrators can treat these permissions as a single unit ABR. Assigning ABR to role likes assigning permissions to roles. It is convenient for developers to package basic permissions into an ABR with a task. For example, opening an account in bank includes different permissions such as show identity, check identity, save necessary information in bank system and so on. These permissions are same for everyone. Therefore, they can be setup as an ABR.

Similar to an Ability-role, a Group-role is a set of users who are assigned as a single unit to a role. A GR can be viewed as a team in system application. It can simplify system management. For example, a developing team as a GR which can be assigned to the direct role of the team.

Can-Modify $AR \rightarrow 2^{UPR}$ defines which administrative roles can create and delete roles, assign and revoke memberships between roles.

Table 6.1 shows an example of *Can-modify*. The meaning of *Can-modify (ShopSO, [SHOP, MANAGER))* is that a member of the administrative role SHOP or a member of an administrative role that is senior to SHOP can create and delete roles in the range [SHOP, MANAGER) except for the endpoints of MANGER and can modify relationships between roles in the range [SHOP, MANAGER).

Administrative.role	UP-role range
ShopSO	[SHOP, MANAGER)

Table 6.1 Example of can-modify

6.2.4 Duty Separation Constraints

Separation of duty (SOD) relations are used to enforce conflict of interest policies that prevent users from processing conflicting authorities for their positions. As a security principle, SOD has been widely recognized for its wide application [57], [8]. It ensures that failures of commission within an organization can be caused only as a result of collusion among individuals. To minimize collusion, different skills are assigned to separate tasks required in the performance of a system. SOD can protect that fraud and major errors if no deliberate collusion of multiple users. There are two types of SOD in RBAC. One is static separation of duty, and the other one is dynamic separation of duty.

Static Separation of Duty

In a role-based system, a user may authorize permissions associated with conflicting roles. Static separation of duty (SSD) limits constraints on the assignment of users to roles to prevent this form of conflict. RBAC models have defined SSD relations with respect to constraints on RBAC management. That is no user can be simultaneously assigned to both roles in SSD. SSD relations may exist within hierarchical RBAC. When applying SSD relations in the presence of a role hierarchy, it should be ensured that user inheritance does not undermine SSD policies. For example, the role bank supervisor inherits the role of accounts clerk, and the clerk has an SSD relationship with the role of billing clerk, then supervisor also has an SSD relationship with the billing clerk.

Dynamic Separation of Duty

Dynamic separation of duty (DSD) relations, like SSD relations, are intended to limit the permissions that are available to a user. However DSD relations differ from SSD relations by the context. SSD relations define constraints on a user's total permission space. DSD properties specify the availability of the permissions over a user's permission space that can be activated in a user's sessions. DSD provides support in security management policy for the principle of least privilege in that each user requires different permissions at different times. SSD relations provide the capability to address potential conflict issues that a user is assigned to a role. DSD allows two or more roles that do not create a conflict of interest when acted on independently to be assigned to a user. DSD concerns activated simultaneously. In a bank, for instance, a user may be authorized for both the roles of Teller and

Manager, where the Manager is allowed to acknowledge corrections to a Teller's open cash drawer. If a person acting in the role Teller attempted to switch to the role Manager, DSD relation would require the user to drop the Teller role. A conflict of interest situation does not arise as long as the same user is not allowed to be both of these roles at the same time.

However, RBAC cannot compel systems to use these principles. The security officer can configure RBAC so it implements these principles. In the next two sections, applications of user-role assignment and permission-role assignment including SSD, DSD are discussed. The user-role assignments for the flexible payment scheme are described, and then followed by its permission-role assignments.

6.3   User-Role Assignments for a Flexible Payment Scheme

Using role-based access controls (RBAC) to manage user-role assignments for electronic payments is one of the most challenging problems [44, 46, 48]. There are two types of problems which may arise in user-role assignment with RBAC. One is related to authorization granting process. Mutually exclusive roles may be granted to a user and the user may have or derive a high level of authority. Another is related to authorization revocation. When a role is revoked from a user, the user may still have the role since role hierarchies. This section presents user-role assignments for a flexible electronic payment scheme. To solve these problems, we first analyze the duty separation constraints of the roles and role hierarchies in the scheme, then discuss granting a role to a user, weak revocation and strong revocation for the scheme. The aim of this section is to provide a way to manage electronic payments with RBAC.

Recently, role-based access control (RBAC) has been widely used in database system management and operating system products. RBAC involves individual users being associated with roles as well as roles being associated with permissions (each permission is a pair of objects and operations). As such, a role is used to associate users and permissions. A user in this model is a human being (for example, a staff member in a bank). A role is a job function or job title within an organization associated with authority and responsibility (for example, role BANK manages money for consumers). Permission is an approval of a particular operation to be performed on one or more objects. There are many relationships between users and roles, and between roles and permissions as shown in Fig. 6.1. Assigning people to tasks is a normal managerial function. The assignments of users to roles is a natural part of assigning users to tasks. Hence, user-role assignment is a basic issue of RBAC.

Many RBAC practical applications have been implemented [3, 13, 45] and [34] since 1993. However, there has been little research done on the usage of RBAC in payment scheme management [35]. This section analyzes duty separation constraints such as role-role relationship in a payment scheme and then discuss user-role assignment for the payment scheme.

A scalable anonymity electronic cash scheme has been published [64]. It differs from other electronic payment schemes [7, 31] and it is significant because consumers in the scalable scheme can get a required anonymity without showing their identities to any third party. This scheme is a benefit for consumers who are worried about their identities being traced by banks. However, how to manage the scheme with RBAC is a remained challenging problem.

Duty Separation Constraints of the Scheme
Sandhu and Bhamidipati developed a model called URA97 in which RBAC is used to manage user-role assignment [37]. It did not discuss user-role assignments with electronic commerce. We consider the relationships of the four roles. Duty separation constraints are role-role associations indicating conflicts of interest. Static separated duty (SSD) specifies that a user cannot be authorized for two different roles while dynamic separated duty (DSD) specifies that a user can be authorized for two different roles but cannot act simultaneously in both.

Role hierarchies specify which role may inherit all of the permissions of another role. In Fig. 6.3, for example, since all staff in the AP agent, the bank and the shop are employees, their corresponding roles inherit the employee role. The role AP, SHOP and BANK have DSD relationships with the role CONSUMER. This indicates that an individual consumer cannot play the roles of AP, SHOP or BANK simultaneously. The staff in these three participants have to first log out if they want to register as consumers. For example, a consumer, who is a staff member of the AP agent and is able to act the role AP, can ask the AP agent to help him to get a coin with a high level anonymity. But as a consumer, she/he cannot give herself/himself a new certificate $Cert_{c'}$ of a coin when she/he works for the AP agent. Another staff member of the AP agent should do the job for this person.

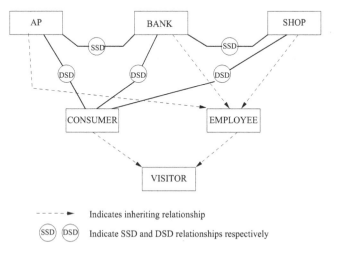

Fig. 6.3 The relationships of the roles in the scheme

The role AP has an SSD relationship with BANK. This is because the duty of the AP is to help a consumer to get a coin with a high level of anonymity. The BANK knows the old coin $c = (g^r, Y^r I^s)$ and its certificate $Cert_c$. The AP sends the new certificate $Cert_{c'}$ of the new coin $c' = (g^{r+\rho}, Y^{r+\rho} I^s)$ to the consumer. The role BANK knows the new certificate $Cert_{c'}$ and new coin c' if the same staff member from the AP agent and the bank processed the coin for the consumer. If this occurs, the consumer cannot have a coin with the required anonymity because the BANK has known the new coin. The SHOP also has an SSD relationship with the BANK since the BANK verifies the payment as well as depositing the coin to the shop's account. The SSD relationship is also a conflict of interest relationship like the DSD relationship but much stronger. If two roles have a SSD relationship, then they may not even be authorized to the same individual. Thus, the role AP, BANK, and SHOP may never be authorized to the same individual.

User-Role Assignments

To discuss user-role assignments, we add a manager role (M1) etc. in an AP agent, a manager role (M2) etc. in a bank, a manager role (M3) etc. in a shop and some administrative roles Senior Officer(SSO) etc. in the system as shown in Figs. 6.4 and 6.5. A hierarchy of roles and a hierarchy of administrative roles are also

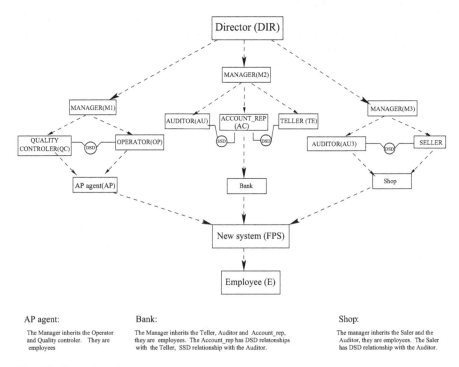

AP agent:	Bank:	Shop:
The Manager inherits the Operator and Quality controler. They are employees	The Manager inherits the Teller, Auditor and Account_rep, they are employees. The Account_rep has DSD relatonships with the Teller, SSD relationship with the Auditor.	The manager inherits the Saler and the Auditor, they are employees. The Saler has DSD relationship with the Auditor.

Fig. 6.4 User_role assignment

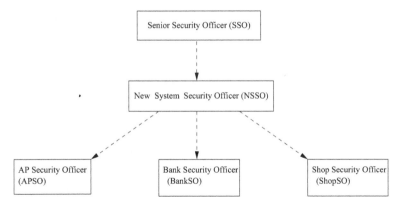

Fig. 6.5 Administrative role assignment

shown in these two figures. The roles in Fig. 6.4 can be granted and revoked by the administrative roles in Fig. 6.5.

Let $x > y$ denote role x is senior to role y with obvious extension to $x \geq y$. The notion of a prerequisite condition is a key part in the processes of user-role assignment [37].

Prerequisite Condition is an expression using Boolean operators $\wedge$ and $\vee$ on terms of the form x and $\bar{x}$ where x is a role and $\wedge$ means "and", $\vee$ means "or". A prerequisite condition is evaluated for a user u by interpreting x to be true if $(\exists x' \geq x), (u, x') \in UA$ and $\bar{x}$ to be true if $(\forall x' \geq x), (u, x') \notin UA$, where UA is a set of user-role assignments. ◇

For a given set of roles R let CR denote all possible prerequisite conditions that can be formed using the roles in R. Not every administrator can assign a role to a user. The relation of **Can-assign** $\subseteq AR \times CR \times 2^R$ provides what roles an administrator can assign with prerequisite conditions, where AR is a set of administrative roles.

Table 6.2 shows the *Can-assign* relation with the prerequisite conditions in the scheme. To identify a role range within the role hierarchy of Fig. 6.4, we use the familiar closed and open interval notation.

$$[x, y] = \{r \in R | x \geq r \wedge r \geq y\}$$

$$(x, y] = \{r \in R | x > r \wedge r \geq y\}$$

$$[x, y) = \{r \in R | x \geq r \wedge r > y\}$$

$$(x, y) = \{r \in R | x > r \wedge r > y\}$$

Let us consider the APSO tuples (the analysis for BankSO and ShopSO are similar). The first tuple authorizes APSO to assign users with the prerequisite role

Table 6.2 Can-assign

Admin.role	Prereq. condition	Role range
APSO	FPS	[AP, AP]
APSO	FPS $\wedge \overline{OP}$	[QC, QC]
APSO	FPS $\wedge \overline{QC}$	[OP, OP]
APSO	QC $\wedge$ OP	[M1, M1]
BankSO	FPS	[Bank, Bank]
BankSO	FPS $\wedge \overline{TE} \wedge \overline{AU}$	[AC, AC]
BankSO	FPS $\wedge \overline{TE} \wedge \overline{AC}$	[AU, AU]
BankSO	FPS $\wedge \overline{AU} \wedge \overline{AC}$	[TE, TE]
BankSO	TE $\wedge AU \wedge$ AC	[M2, M2]
ShopSO	FPS	[Shop, Shop]
ShopSO	FPS $\wedge \overline{SELLER}$	[AUDITOR, AUDITOR]
ShopSO	FPS $\wedge \overline{AUDITOR}$	[SELLER, SELLER]
ShopSO	SELLER $\wedge$ AUDITOR	[M3, M3]
NSSO	FPS	(FPS, DIR)
SSO	E	[FPS, FPS]
SSO	FPS	(FPS, DIR]

FPS into members in the AP agent (AP). The second one authorizes APSO to assign users with the prerequisite condition $FPS \wedge \overline{OP}$ to be quality controllers (QC). Similarly, the third tuple authorizes APSO to assign users with the prerequisite condition $FPS \wedge \overline{QC}$ to be operators (OP). The second and third tuple show that the APSO can grant a user who is a member of the AP agent into one but not both of QC and OP. This illustrates how mutually exclusive roles can be forced. However, for the NSSO and SSO these are not mutually exclusive. The fourth tuple authorizes APSO to put a user who is a member of both QC and OP into a manager (M1). Of course, a user could have become a member of both QC and OP only by actions of a more powerful administrator than APSO.

There are related subtleties that arise in RBAC concerning the interaction between granting and revocation of user-role membership. A relation **Can-revoke** $\subseteq AR \times 2^R$ shows which role range administrative roles can revoke, where AR is a set of administrative roles. The meaning of *Can-revoke* (x, Y) is that a member of the administrative role x (or a member of an administrative role that is senior to x) can revoke membership of a user from any role $y \in Y$, where Y defines the *range of revocation*. Table 6.3 gives an example of the it Can-revoke relation. There are two kinds of revocations [37]. The first one is weak revocation, the second one is strong revocation.

A user U is an *explicit member* of a role x if $(U, x) \in UA$, and U is an *implicit member* of role x if for some role $x' > x$, $(U, x') \in UA$. Weak revocation has an impact only on explicit membership. For weak revocation, the membership of a user is revoked only if the user is an explicit member of the role. Therefore, weak

Table 6.3 Can-revoke

Admin.role	Role range
APSO	[AP, M1)
BankSO	[Bank, M2)
ShopSO	[Shop, M3)
NSSO	(FPS, DIR)
SSO	[FPS, DIR]

revocation from a role x has no effect when a user is not an explicit member of the role x. The following is an example of weak revocation for the flexible scheme where Alice and Bob are users.

Suppose Bob is an explicit member of role M1, QC, AU, AUDITOR, AP, FPS and E in the scheme. If Alice, with the activated administrative role APSO, weakly revokes Bob's membership from AP, he continues to be a member of the senior roles to AP since both M1 and QC are senior roles to AP, therefore he still has the permission of AP. It is necessary to note that Alice should have enough power in the session to weakly revoke Bob's membership from his explicitly assigned roles. For instance, if Alice has activated APSO and then tries to weakly revoke Bob's membership from M1, she is not allowed to proceed because APSO does not have the authority of weak revocation from M1 according to the *Can-revoke* relation in Table 6.3. Therefore, if Alice wants to revoke Bob's explicit membership as well as implicit membership from AP by weak revocation, she needs to activate SSO or NSSO and weakly revoke Bob's membership from AP, QC and M1.

Strong revocation requires revocation of both explicit and implicit membership. Strong revocation of a user's membership in role x requires that the user be removed not only from explicit membership in x, but also from explicit (implicit) membership in all roles senior to x. Strong revocation therefore has a cascading effect up-wards in the role hierarchy.

In the scheme, for example, Bob is an explicit member of role M1, QC, AU, AP, AUDITOR, FPS and E. If Alice, with the activated administrative role SSO, strongly revokes Bob's membership from AP, then he is removed not only from explicit membership in AP, but also from explicit (and implicit) membership in all roles senior to AP. Actually, after the strong revocation from AP, Bob has been removed from M1, QC as well as AP. However, he still has a membership of FPS, AU, AUDITOR and E, since they are not senior roles to AP based on the role hierarchy of Fig. 6.4. This brings about the same result as weak revocation from AP, QC, M1 by SSO. Note that all implied revocations upward in the role hierarchy should be within the revocation range of the administrative roles that are active in a session. For instance, if Alice activates APSO and tries to strongly revoke Bob's membership from M1, she is not allowed to proceed because M1 is out of the APSO's *Can-revoke* range in Table 6.3.

Weak revocation revokes explicit memberships only and strong revocation revokes both explicit and implicit memberships. Therefore a user may not have the permissions of a role if the user's membership is strongly revoked from the role.

6.4   Permission-Role Assignments with the Payment Scheme

The user-role assignment relation UA and permission-role assignment relation PA are many-to-many relations between users and roles, and between roles and permissions as shown in Fig. 6.1. Assigning permissions to roles is typically the province of application administrators. Thus a banking application can be implemented so credit and debit operations are assigned to a teller role. However, approval and funding operations cannot be assigned to a teller role since they are conflicting permissions. Users are authorized to use the permissions of roles to which they are assigned. This is the essence of RBAC [1].

Similar to user-role assignment, there are two types of conflicting problems that may arise in permission-role assignments. One is related to authorization granting process. Conflicting permissions may be granted to a role, and as a result, users with the role may have or derive a high level of authority. Another is related to authorization revocation. When a permission is revoked from a role, the role may still have the permission from other roles. This section discusses how to solve these problems with the payment scheme in [64]. The duty separation constraints of the roles and role hierarchies in the scheme has been analyzed in the last section, this section considers granting a permission to a role, weak revocation permissions and strong revocation permissions for the scheme.

There are a few applications with permission-role assignment [29, 30, 36]. For example, Sandhu and Bhamidipati developed an oracle implementation for permission-role assignment [36]. It does not discuss permission-role assignments for electronic commerce. We analyze permission-role assignment for the payment scheme in this section.

Granting and Revocation Models

RBAC administration encompasses the issues of assigning users to roles, assigning permissions to roles, and assigning roles to roles to define a role hierarchy. These activities are all required to bring users and permissions together. In many cases, they are best done by different administrators. To analyze granting and revocation models, we add a manager role (M1) etc. in an AP agent, a manager role (M2) etc. in a bank, a manager role (M3) etc. in a shop and some administrative roles Senior Officer(SSO) etc. in the system as shown in Figs. 6.4 and 6.5. A hierarchy of roles and a hierarchy of administrative roles are also shown in these two figures. Senior roles are shown towards the top of the hierarchies and junior are to the bottom. Senior roles inherit permissions from junior roles. Permissions can be granted to or revoked from the roles in Fig. 6.4 by the administrative roles in Fig. 6.5.

Let $x > y$ denote x is senior to y with obvious extension to $x \geq y$. The notion of a *prerequisite condition* p is used to restrict on what permissions can be assigned to a role. A *prerequisite condition* p is evaluated for a permission p by interpreting x to be true if $(\exists x' \geq x), (p, x') \in PA$ and $\bar{x}$ to be true if $(\forall x' \geq x), (p, x') \notin PA$, where PA is a set of permission-role assignments. It means that only permissions satisfy the conditions may be assigned to roles. On the other hand, whether an administrator can establish the relationship between permissions and roles depends on the relation

Table 6.4 Can-assignp

Admin.role	Prereq. conditionP	Role range
NSSO	DIR	[M1, M1]
NSSO	DIR	[M2, M2]
NSSO	DIR	[M3, M3]
APSO	FPS $\wedge \overline{OP}$	[QC, QC]
APSO	FPS $\wedge \overline{QC}$	[OP, OP]
BankSO	FPS $\wedge \overline{TE} \wedge \overline{AU}$	[AC, AC]
BankSO	FPS $\wedge \overline{TE} \wedge \overline{AC}$	[AU, AU]
BankSO	FPS $\wedge \overline{AU} \wedge \overline{AC}$	[TE, TE]
ShopSO	FPS $\wedge \overline{SELLER}$	[AUDITOR, AUDITOR]
ShopSO	FPS $\wedge \overline{AUDITOR}$	[SELLER, SELLER]

Table 6.5 Can-revokep

Admin.role	Role range
NSSO	[FPS, DIR)
APSO	[AP, M1)
BankSO	[Bank, M2)
ShopSO	[Shop, M3)

of **Can-assignp** $\subseteq AR \times CR \times 2^R$. That means that permission-role assignment (PA) is authorized by *Can-assignp* relation.

For example, the meaning of *Can-assignp* $(NSSO, DIR, [M1, M1])$ in Table 6.4 is that a member of the administrative role NSSO can assign a permission whose current membership satisfies the prerequisite condition DIR to be a member of roles in range [M1, M1].

The motivation behinds the *Can-revokep* relation is in Figs. 6.4 and 6.5. Figure 6.4 shows that role E is junior-most to which all employees in the new system and role Director (DIR) is senior-most to all employees. Figure 6.5 shows the administrative role hierarchy which co-exist with the roles in Fig. 6.4. The senior-most role is the Senior Security Officer (SSO). Our interest is in the administrative roles junior to SSO. These consist of three security officer roles (APSO, BankSO and ShopSO) with the relationships illustrated in Fig. 6.5.

Based on the role hierarchy in Fig. 6.4 and administrative role hierarchy in Fig. 6.5, we define the *Can-revokep* relation shown in Table 6.4.

There are related subtleties that arise in RBAC concerning the interaction between granting and revocation of permission-role membership. A relation **Can-revokep** $\subseteq AR \times 2^R$ shows which permissions in what role range can be revoked by administrative, where AR is a set of administrative roles. The meaning of *Can-revokep* (x, Y) is that a member of the administrative role x (or a member of an administrative role that is senior to x) can revoke membership of a permission from any role $y \in Y$, where Y defines the *range of revocation*. Table 6.5 gives an example of the *Can-revokep* relation.

A permission P is an *explicit member* of a role x if $(P, x) \in PA$, and P is an *implicit member* of role x if for some role $x' < x$, $(P, x') \in PA$. Weak revocation has an impact only on explicit membership. For weak revocation, the membership of a permission is revoked only if the permission is an explicit member of the role. Therefore, weak revocation from a role x has no effect when a permission is not an explicit member of the role x. We show an example of weak revocation for the flexible scheme.

Suppose P is an explicit member of role M1, QC, AU, AP and FPS in the scheme. If Alice, with the activated administrative role APSO, can weakly revoke P's membership from QC, P continues to be an implicit member of QC since AP is junior to QC and P is an explicit member of AP. It is necessary to note that Alice should have enough power in the session to weakly revoke P's membership from explicitly assigned roles. For instance, if Alice has activated APSO and then tries to weakly revoke P from FPS, she is not allowed to proceed because APSO does not have the authority of weak revocation from FPS according to the *Can-revokep* relation in Table 6.5. Therefore, if Alice wants to revoke P's explicit membership as well as implicit membership from QC by weak revocation, she needs to activate NSSO and weakly revoke P's membership from QC, AP and FPS.

Strong revocation requires revocation of both explicit and implicit membership. Strong revocation of a permission's membership in role x requires that the permission be removed not only from explicit membership in x, but also from explicit (implicit) membership in all roles junior to x. Strong revocation therefore has a cascading effect downwards in the role hierarchy.

In the scheme, for example, P is an explicit member of role M1, QC, AU, AP and FPS. If Alice, with the activated administrative role NSSO, strongly revokes P's membership from QC, then P is removed not only from explicit membership in QC, but also from explicit (and implicit) membership in all roles junior to QC. Actually, after the strong revocation from QC, P has been removed from FPS, AP as well as QC. However, P still has a membership of AU and M1 since they are not junior roles to QC based on the role hierarchy of Fig. 6.4. This brings about the same result as weak revocation from QC, AP and FPS by NSSO. Note that all implied revocations downward in the role hierarchy should be within the revocation range of the administrative roles that are active in a session. For instance, if Alice activates APSO and tries to strongly revoke P's membership from QC, she is not allowed to proceed because FPS is junior to QC but it is out of the APSO's *Can-revokep* range in Table 6.5.

6.5   Related Work

Comparing with previous designed off-line payment schemes, the new payment scheme provides a flexible level of anonymity for consumers. This section continues to discuss the related work on user-role assignments and permission-role assignments. There are several other related works on these two assignments such as role-based access control models [1], role activation hierarchies [34].

A role-based separation of duty language (RSL 99) has been recently proposed [1]. It has given a formal syntax and semantics for RSL99 and has demonstrated its soundness and completeness by using functions on conflicting permission sets. The proposal is different from ours in two aspects. First, It does not consider the case of the management for conflicting roles and permissions. Therefore, there is no support to deal administrative roles with permissions in the proposal. By contrast, our work provide a rich variety of options that can deal the document of administrative roles with roles and permissions. Second, the algorithm RSL99 does not provide access control models. It only gives separation of duty (SOD) policies. By contrast, we present a number of specialized authorization methods for access control which allow administrators to authorize a permission and user to role or revoke a permission and user from roles.

A separate role activation hierarchy which extends the permission-usage hierarchy has been proposed in [34]. The authors indicated two things. The first is to describe RBAC with respect to read-write access, and its relationship to traditional lattice-based access control (LBAC). The second is that roles are required to have dynamic separation of duty. RBAC with dynamic separation of duties is respected to write roles. However, our work substantially differs from that proposal. The main difference is that the paper [34] focuses on separated role activation hierarchy and we focus on an application of RBAC with a payment scheme. Furthermore, there is no e-commerce application test for role activation hierarchies in [34]. By contrast, we analyze the dynamic separation of duty (DSD) of roles in the payment scheme and use DSD to reduce conflicts between various roles and between various permissions in RBAC management.

6.6 Conclusions

The basic structure of RBAC has reviewed in this chapter. The user-role assignments and permission-role assignments and how to use RBAC with an electronic payment system are introduced.

Firstly, user-role assignments for the scalable anonymity payment scheme with RBAC are presented. It provides a way for using RBAC to manage electronic payment schemes. The duty separation constraints of the four roles in the scheme are analyzed. These constraints can be used to prevent unauthorized use of messages in the scheme. Based on the duty separation constraints, we have discussed how to grant a role to a user associated with a *Can-assign* relation. Because of role hierarchies, a user may still have a role which has been revoked by an administrative role. We have demonstrated this case in detail with weak revocation and strong revocation for the scheme.

Furthermore, permission-role assignments for electronic payment are analyzed. To address the problems that arise in permission-role assignment, how to grant a permission to a role associated with a *Can-revokep* relation are discussed. A role may still have a permission which has been revoked by an administrative role. The weak permission revocation and strong permission revocation for the scheme are also detailed disclosed.

6.7   Problems and Exercises

6.7.1   Problems

1. What are advantages of RBAC management?
2. What are the features of static separated duty (SSD) and dynamic separated duty (DSD), what differences have between SSD and DSD?
3. What are Granting and revocation models in RBAC management?
4. What are the differences between explicit membership and implicit membership? why they are important in real situations?

6.7.2   Exercises

1. Given an example of Role-role assignment including three kinds of rolesAbility-roles, Group-roles and UP-roles;
2. Given an example of hierarchy of roles and hierarchy of administrative roles;
3. Design an RBAC management model, analysing static separated duty (SSD) and dynamic separated duty (DSD)?

References

1. Ahn, G.J., Sandhu, R.: The rsl99 language for role-based separation of duty constraints. In: Proceedings of the Fourth ACM Workshop on Role-Based Access Control, pp. 43–54. Fairfax, Toronto (1999)
2. Barkley, J.F.: Application engineering in health care. In: Second Annual CHIN (1995). http://hissa.ncsl.nist.gov/rbac/proj/paper/paper.html
3. Barkley, J.F., Beznosov, K., Uppal, J.: Supporting relationships in access control using role based access control. In: Third ACM Workshop on Role Based Access Control, pp. 55–65 (1999)
4. Boris, K., Jajodia, S.: Concurrency control in multilevel-secure databases based on replicated architecture. In: Proceedings of the 1990 ACM SIGMOD International Conference on Management of Data, pp. 153–162. ACM, New York (1990)
5. Lampson, B.W.: A note on the confinement problem. Commun. ACM **16**(10), 613–615 (1973)
6. Cao, J., et al.: Towards secure XML document with usage control. In: Web Technologies Research and Development (APWeb 2005), pp. 296–307. Springer, Berlin (2005)

7. Chan, A., Frankel, Y., Tsiounis, Y.: An efficient off-line electronic cash scheme as secure as RSA, Research report NU-CCS-96-03. Northeastern University, Boston (1995)

8. Limoges, C.G., Nelson, R.R., Heimann, J.H., Becker, D.S.: Versatile integrity and security environment (vise) for computer systems. In: Proceedings of the 1994 Workshop on New Security Paradigms, pp. 109–118. IEEE Computer Society Press, New York (1994)

9. Chenthara, S., et al.: Security and privacy-preserving challenges of e-health solutions in cloud computing. IEEE Access **7**, 74361–74382 (2019)

10. David, F.F., Riva, S., Serban, G., Kuhn, D., Ramaswamy, C.: Proposed NIST standard for role-based access control. ACM Trans. Inf. Syst. Secur. **4**(3), 224–274 (2001)

11. Du, J., et al.: Feature selection for helpfulness prediction of online product reviews: an empirical study. PLOS ONE **14**, e0226902 (2019)

12. Ferraiolo, D.F., Kuhn, D.R.: Role based access control. In: Proceedings of the 15th National Computer Security Conference, pp. 554–563 (1992). ferraiolo92rolebased.html

13. Ferraiolo, D.F., Barkley, J.F., Kuhn, D.R.: Role-based access control model and reference implementation within a corporate intranet. In: *TISSEC*, vol. 2, pp. 34–64 (1999)

14. Ge, Y., et al.: A benefit-driven genetic algorithm for balancing privacy and utility in database fragmentation. In: Proceedings of the Genetic and Evolutionary Computation Conference, pp. 771–776. Association for Computing Machinery, New York (2019)

15. James, J., Elisa, B., Arif, G.: Temporal hierarchies and inheritance semantics for GTRBAC. In: Proceedings of the Seventh ACM Symposium on Access Control Models and Technologies, pp. 74–83. ACM, New York (2002)

16. Kabir, E., Wang, H.: Conditional purpose based access control model for privacy protection. In: Proceedings of the Twentieth Australasian Conference on Australasian Database (ADC '09), vol. 92, pp. 135–142. Australian Computer Society, Darlinghurst (2009)

17. Kabir, M., Wang, H.: Microdata protection method through microaggregation: a median-based approach. Inf. Secur. J. Global Perspect. **20**, 1–8 (2011)

18. Kabir, M., Wang, H., Bertino, E.: A conditional purpose-based access control model with dynamic roles. Expert Syst. Appl. **38**(3), 1482–1489 (2011)

19. Kabir, M., Wang, H., Bertino, E.: A conditional role-involved purpose-based access control model. J. Org. Comput. E. Commer. **21**, 71–91 (2011)

20. Kabir, M., Wang, H., Bertino, E.: Efficient systematic clustering method for k-anonymization. Acta Inf. **48**(1), 51–66 (2011)

21. Khalil, F., Li, J., Wang, H.: Integrating recommendation models for improved web page prediction accuracy. In: Proceedings of the Thirty-First Australasian Conference on Computer Science (ACSC '08), vol. 74, pp. 91–100. Australian Computer Society, Darlinghurst (2008)

22. Li, M., et al.: Advanced permission-role relationship in role-based access control. In: Information Security and Privacy, pp. 391–403. Springer, Berlin (2008)

23. Li, M., et al.: Optimal privacy-aware path in hippocratic databases. In: Database Systems for Advanced Applications, pp. 441–455. Springer, Berlin (2009)

24. Li, M., Wang, H.: ABDM: an extended flexible delegation model in RBAC. In: Proceedings of the 2008 Eighth IEEE International Conference on Computer and Information Technology, pp. 390–395 (2008)

25. Li, M., Wang, H., Plank, A.: Privacy-aware access control with generalization boundaries. In: Proceedings of the Thirty-Second Australasian Conference on Computer Science (ACSC '09), vol. 91, pp. 105–112. Australian Computer Society, Darlinghurst (2009)

26. Lipner, S.: A comment on the confinement problem. In: Proceedings of the Fifth Symposium on Operating Systems Principles, pp. 192–196 (1975)

27. Lupu, E., Marriott, D., Sloman, M., Yialelis, N.: A policy based role framework for access control. In: ACM/NIST Workshop on Role-Based Access Control (1995). http://www-dse.doc.ic.ac.uk/~ecl1/papers/rbac95/rbac95.pdf

28. Schroeder, M.D., Saltzer, J.H.: A hardware architecture for implementing protection rings. Commun. ACM **15**(3), 157–170 (1972)

29. Najam, P.: Structured management of role-permission relationships. In: Proceedings of the Sixth ACM Symposium on Access Control Models and Technologies, pp. 163–169. ACM, New York (2001)
30. Oh, S., Sandhu, R.: A model for role administration using organization structure. In: Proceedings of the Seventh ACM Symposium on Access Control Models and Technologies, pp. 155–162. ACM, New York (2002)
31. Pointcheval, D.: Self-scrambling anonymizers. In: Proceedings of Financial Cryptography, Anguilla, British West Indies. Springer, Berlin (2000)
32. Rasool, R., et al.: Cyberpulse: a machine learning based link flooding attack mitigation system for software defined networks. IEEE Access **7**, 34885–34899 (2019)
33. Sandhu, R.: Rational for the *RBAC96* family of access control models. In: Proceedings of First ACM Workshop on Role-Based Access Control, pp. 64–72. ACM, New York (1997)
34. Sandhu, R.: Role activation hierarchies. In: Third ACM Workshop on Role Based Access Control, pp. 33–40. ACM, New York (1998)
35. Sandhu, R.: Future directions in role-based access control models. In: MMS, 2001 (2001). http://www.list.gmu.edu/confrnc/misconf/
36. Sandhu, R., Bhamidipati, V.: An oracle implementation of the PRA97 model for permission-role assignment. In: ACM Workshop on Role-Based Access Control, pp. 13–21 (1998). http://citeseer.nj.nec.com/27106.html
37. Sandhu, R., Bhamidipati, V.: The URA97 model for role-based administration of user-role assignment. In: Lin, T.Y., Qian, X. (eds.) Database Security XI: Status and Prospects, pp. 262–275. North-Holland, Amsterdam (1997)
38. Sun, X., et al.: An efficient hash-based algorithm for minimal k-anonymity. In: Proceedings of the Thirty-First Australasian Conference on Computer Science (ACSC '08), vol. 74, pp. 101–107. Australian Computer Society, Darlinghurst (2008)
39. Sun, X., et al.: Enhanced p-sensitive k-anonymity models for privacy preserving data publishing. Trans. Data Privacy **1**(2), 53–66 (2008)
40. Sun, X., et al.: (p^+, α)-sensitive k-anonymity: a new enhanced privacy protection model. In: Proceedings of the 2008 8th IEEE International Conference on Computer and Information Technology, pp. 59–64 (2008)
41. Sun, X., et al.: Injecting purpose and trust into data anonymisation. Comput. Secur. **30**, 332–345 (2011)
42. Sun, X., et al.: Privacy-aware access control with trust management in web service. World Wide Web **14**(4), 407–430 (2011)
43. Sun, X., et al.: Publishing anonymous survey rating data. Data Min. Knowl. Discovery **23**(3), 379–406 (2011)
44. Sun, X., et al.: An approximate microaggregation approach for microdata protection. Expert Syst. Appl. **39**(2), 2211–2219 (2012)
45. Sun, X., et al.: Satisfying privacy requirements before data anonymization. Comput. J. **55**(4), 422–437 (2012)
46. Sun, L., et al.: Purpose based access control for privacy protection in e-healthcare services. JSW **7**, 2443–2449 (2012)
47. Sun, L., Wang, H.: Access control and authorization for protecting disseminative information in e-learning workflow. Concurrency Comput. Pract. Experience **23**, 2034–2042 (2011)
48. Sun, L., Wang, H.: A purpose-based access control in native XML databases. Concurrency Comput. Pract. Experience **24**(10), 1154–1166 (2012)
49. Sun, L., Li, Y., Wang, H.: M-service and its framework. In: Proceedings of the 2005 Asia-Pacific Conference on Communications, pp. 837–841 (2005)
50. Sun, X., Wang, H., Li, J.: Priority driven k-anonymisation for privacy protection. In: Proceedings of the Seventh Australasian Data Mining Conference, vol. 87, pp. 73–78 (2008)
51. Sun, X., Wang, H., Li, J.: Microdata protection through approximate microaggregation. In: Proceedings of the Thirty-Second Australasian Conference on Computer Science (ACSC '09), vol. 91, pp. 161–168. Australian Computer Society, Darlinghurst (2009)

52. Sun, X., Wang, H., Sun, L.: Extended k-anonymity models against attribute disclosure. In: Proceedings of the 2009 Third International Conference on Network and System Security, pp. 130–136 (2009)
53. Sun, L., Wang, H., Yong, J.: Authorization algorithms for permission-role assignments. J. UCS **15**, 1782–1798 (2009)
54. Sun, X., Wang, H., Li, J.: Satisfying privacy requirements: One step before anonymization. In: Advances in Knowledge Discovery and Data Mining, pp. 181–188. Springer, Berlin (2010)
55. Sun, X., Li, M., Wang, H.: A family of enhanced (L, α)-diversity models for privacy preserving data publishing. Future Gener. Comput. Syst. **27**(3), 348–356 (2011)
56. Sun, X., Sun, L., Wang, H.: Extended k-anonymity models against sensitive attribute disclosure. Comput. Commun. **34**(4), 526–535 (2011). Special issue: Building Secure Parallel and Distributed Networks and Systems
57. Terry, R.: Application level security using an object-oriented graphical user interface. In: Proceedings of the 1992–1993 Workshop on New Security Paradigms, pp. 105–108. ACM, New York (1993)
58. Wang, H., et al.: Authorization algorithms for the mobility of user-role relationship. In: Proceedings of the Twenty-Eighth Australasian Conference on Computer Science (ACSC '05), vol. 38, pp. 69–77. Australian Computer Society, Darlinghurst (2005)
59. Wang, H., et al.: A framework for role-based group deligation in distributed environments. In: Proceedings of the 29th Australasian Computer Science Conference, vol. 48, pp. 321–328 (2006)
60. Wang, H., et al.: Authorization approaches for advanced permission-role assignments. In: Proceedings of the 2008 Twelfth International Conference on Computer Supported Cooperative Work in Design, pp. 277–282 (2008)
61. Wang, H., et al.: Editorial: Special issue on security and privacy in network computing. World Wide Web **23**, 951–957 (2020)
62. Wang, H., Li, Q.: Secure and efficient information sharing in multi-university e-learning environments. In: Advances in Web Based Learning—ICWL 2007, pp. 542–553. Springer, Berlin (2008)
63. Wang, H., Sun, L.: Trust-involved access control in collaborative open social networks. In: Proceedings of the 2010 Fourth International Conference on Network and System Security, pp. 239–246 (2010)
64. Wang, H., Cao, J., Kambayashi, Y.: Building a consumer anonymity scalable payment protocol for the internet purchases. In: Proceedings of the Twelfth International Workshop on Research Issues on Data Engineering: Engineering E-Commerce/E-Business Systems, San Jose, USA (2002)
65. Wang, H., Cao, J., Zhang, Y.: A flexible payment scheme and its role-based access control. IEEE Trans. Knowl. Data Eng. **17**(3), 425–436 (2005)
66. Wang, H., Zhang, Y., Cao, J.: Ubiquitous computing environments and its usage access control. In: Proceedings of the First International Conference on Scalable Information Systems (InfoScale '06). ACM, New York (2006)
67. Wang, H., Cao, J., Ross, D.: Role-based delegation with negative authorization. In: Frontiers of WWW Research and Development—APWeb 2006, pp. 307–318. Springer, Berlin (2006)
68. Wang, H., Cao, J., Zhang, Y.: Delegating revocations and authorizations in collaborative business environments. Inf. Syst. Front. **11**(3), 293 (2008)
69. Wang, H., Cao, J., Zhang, Y.: Delegating revocations and authorizations in collaborative business environments. Inf. Syst. Front. **11**(3), 293 (2008)
70. Wang, H., Sun, L., Varadharajan, V.: Purpose-based access control policies and conflicting analysis. In: Security and Privacy—Silver Linings in the Cloud, pp. 217–228. Springer, Berlin (2010)
71. Wang, Z., Zhan, Z., Lin, Y., Yu, W., Wang, H., Kwong, S., Zhang, J.: Automatic niching differential evolution with contour prediction approach for multimodal optimization problems. IEEE Trans. Evol. Comput., pp. 1–1 (2019)

72. Zhang, J., et al.: Detecting anomalies from high-dimensional wireless network data streams: a case study. Soft Comput. **15**(6), 1195–1215 (2011)
73. Zhang, Y., Gong, Y., Gao, Y., Wang, H., Zhang, J.: Parameter-free Voronoi neighborhood for evolutionary multimodal optimization. IEEE Trans. Evol. Comput., pp. 1–1 (2019)
74. Zheng, H., He, J., Huang, G., Zhang, Y., Wang, H.: Dynamic optimisation based fuzzy association rule mining method. Int. J. Mach. Learn. Cybern. **10**(8), 2187–2198 (2019)

Part III
RBAC with OCL and Negative Authorization

The Part III consists of two Chaps. 7 and 8. Chapter 7 presents A de facto constraints specification language in software engineering that is applied to the major relationships in RBAC such as user-role assignments and permission-role assignments. Object Constraints Language (OCL), a part of the Unified Modelling Language (UML) used in object-oriented analysis and design is applied to express various constraints in RBAC. Chapter 8 aims to analyse role-based group delegation features that has not studied before, and to provide an approach for the conflicting problem by adopting negative authorization. It presents granting and revocation delegating models first, and then discuss user delegation authorization and the impact of negative authorization on role hierarchies.

Chapter 7
Role-Based Access Control Constraints and Object Constraint Language

Constraints are an important aspect of role-based access control management (RBAC). Constraints have to be satisfied in user—role assignment and permission—role assignment. The importance of constraints associated with user-role assignments and permission-role assignments in RBAC has been recognized but the modelling of these constraints has not received much attention. In this chapter we use a de facto constraints specification language in software engineering to analyze the constraints in user-role assignments and permission-role assignments. Object Constraints Language (OCL), a part of the Unified Modelling Language (UML) widely used in object-oriented analysis and design is applied to express various constraints in RBAC. We analyse elements, relationships, constraints and structure of RBAC adopting class diagram method in UML. Then the representations of role-based access constraints such as separation, prerequisite, cardinality and mobility constraints with OCL are identified. Finally, comparisons with other related work and our future work are presented.

7.1 Introduction

The National Institute of Standards and Technology (NIST) developed role-based access control (RBAC) prototype in 1995 [10] and published a formal model [11]. Many organizations prefer to centrally control and maintain access rights, not so much at the system administrator's personal discretion but more in accordance with the organization's protection guidelines [9, 34, 44, 45]. RBAC is being considered as part of the emerging SQL3 standard for database management systems, based on their implementation in Oracle 7 [24]. Many RBAC practical applications in Web database process management have been implemented [4, 12, 25, 36, 38].

RBAC involves individual users being associated with roles as well as roles being associated with permissions (Each permission is a pair of objects and operations)

© Springer Nature Switzerland AG 2020
H. Wang et al., *Access Control Management in Cloud Environments*,
https://doi.org/10.1007/978-3-030-31729-4_7

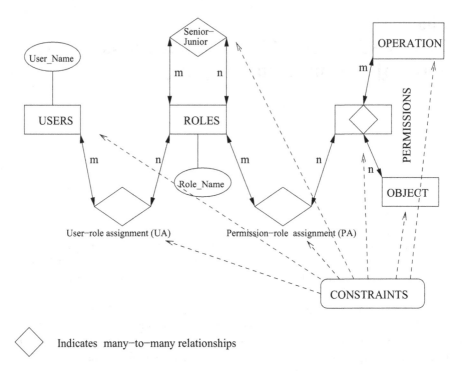

◇ Indicates many–to–many relationships

Fig. 7.1 RBAC relationship

[5, 28, 36]. As such, a role is used to associate users and permissions. A user in this model is a human being. A role is a job function or job title within the organization associated with authority and responsibility. As shown in Fig. 7.1, the relationships between users and roles, and between roles and permissions are many-to-many. Roles are in two categories within RBAC, one is administrative roles (admin.role), the other is regular roles (role) that need to be assigned to or revoked from users by administrative roles. The relationship of Senior-Junior shows hierarchies between roles. Senior roles inherit permissions from junior roles. Let $x > y$ denote x is senior to y with obvious extension to $x \geq y$. Constraints exist within user-role assignment (UA), permission-role assignment (PA) and Senior-Junior relationships etc.

There are three advantages of RBAC management. Firstly, it is much easier to manage a system using RBAC. In RBAC, a security administrator adds transactions to roles or deletes transactions from roles, where transactions can be a program object associated with data [11]. Security issues are addressed by associating programming code and data into a transaction. Access control does not require any checks on the user's or the program's right to access a data item, since the accesses are built into the transaction. Secondly, RBAC can reduce administration cost and complexity [25]. Usually, there is a relationship between the cost of administration and the number of associations, which must be managed in order to administer an access control policy. The larger the number of associations, the costlier and more error prone the access control administration is likely to be, but the use of RBAC reduces the number of associations to be managed. Thirdly, RBAC is better than a typical access control list (ACL) model [18]. RBAC can authorize and audit capabilities so that people are simply assigned new roles when they change responsibilities. This allows for the authorities of a person to be easily documented. By contrast, in ACL, the entire set of authorities must be searched to develop a clear picture of a person's rights because ACLs only support the specification of user/permission and group/permission relationships.

There are various constraints in RBAC as shown in Fig. 7.1. Constraints can be described in natural languages, such as English, German or in other formal languages. Practice has shown that constraints in natural languages will always result in ambiguities [2] and constraints in formal language are usable to persons with a strong mathematical background, but difficult for the average business or system modeler to use. For instance, Ahn and Sandhu [3] proposed a formal language called RCL99 (Role-based constraints specification language 1999) and identified authorization constraints such as prohibition and obligation constraints. The authors of RCL99 are security experts and system developers may not understand the constraints language before they accept training of roles, users and permissions etc in RBAC. This chapter focuses on constraints specification, that is how constraints can be represented.

The paper is organized as follows. In the next section, the motivation of this chapter is identified and the related technologies such as RBAC, Unified Modelling Language (UML) and OCL are reviewed. We discuss various constraints in user-role assignment and permission-role assignment in Sect. 7.3. The constraints are Dynamic Separation of Duty (DSD), Static Separation of Duty (SSD) and Operation authorization and so on. In Sect. 7.4, the constraints with OCL are detailed analyzed. Comparisons with other related work are presented in Sect. 7.5. Conclusions and future work are in Sect. 7.6.

7.2 Motivation and Related Technologies

RBAC constraints are one of the most important components that have involved in the principal motivations of RBAC analysis and design [17, 31, 40]. While RBAC is used by people with different background and brings us sufficient economic impact [13], the constraints in RBAC have to be fulfilled in user-role assignment and permission-role assignment. However, the constraints described by mathematic expressions are difficult to understand and use for business people and system developers. OCL, as an industrial standard constraints specification language, has been used to describe constraints in system analysis and design. Approaches represented by OCL are easy for system developers and modelers to specify and to understand the constraints in different kinds of RBAC management. This chapter targets these approaches.

7.2.1 Role-Based Access Control

With RBAC, users cannot associate with permissions directly. Permissions must be authorized for roles, and roles must be authorized for users [33, 38, 39, 43]. In RBAC administration, two different types of associations must be managed, i.e. associations between users and roles, and associations between roles and permissions. When a user's job position changes, only the user/role associations change. If the job position is represented by a single role, then when a user's job position changes, only two user/role associations need to be changed: remove the association between the user and the user's current role, and add an association between the user and the user's new role.

The RBAC security model has two components: MC_0 and MC_1. Model component MC_0, called the RBAC authorization database model, defines the RBAC security properties for authorization of static roles. Static properties of a RBAC authorization database include role hierarchy, inheritance, cardinality, and static separation of duty. MC_1 called the RBAC activation model, defines the RBAC security properties for dynamic activation of roles. Dynamic properties include role activation, permission execution, dynamic separation of duties, and object access. In particular, the RBAC model supports the specification of:

(a) User/role associations; the constraints specifying user authorizations to perform roles,
(b) Permission/role associations; the constraints identifying role authorizations to run permissions,
(c) Role hierarchies; the constraints specifying which role may inherit all of the permissions of another role,
(d) Duty separation constraints; these are role/role associations indicating conflict of interest:

   (d1) Static separated duty (SSD); a constraint specifying that a user cannot be authorized for two different roles,
   (d2) Dynamic separated duty (DSD); a constraint specifying that a user can be authorized for two different roles but cannot act simultaneously in both,

(f) Cardinality; the maximum number of users allowed, i.e. how many users can be authorized for any particular role (role cardinality), e.g., only one manager.

7.2.2 Unified Modelling Language and Object Constraints Language

The UML is the industry-standard language for specifying, visualizing, constructing, and documenting the artifacts of software systems [8, 16, 23]. It simplifies the complex process of system analysis and design and further software implementation. The UML has become a standard modelling language in the field of software engineering.

UML can be used for database analysis and design. Using the UML for database systems allows the business and application teams who are already using the UML for their designs to share a common language and to communicate with the database team.

The Object Constraint Language (OCL), developed by IBM, is part of the Unified Modelling Language (UML) from version 1.1 [22]. This extension has been designed to augment a class diagram with additional information which cannot be otherwise expressed by UML diagrams; previous versions of UML have only allowed the definition of constraints as annotations in an informal textual way. OCL allows the definition of integrity constraints at the user level, and it has also been used for the formalization of the metamodel of UML. The introduction of a constraint language is an important step towards the formalization of system specification. Constraints represent necessary conditions for a domain to constitute a model of the static aspects of the specified system. OCL is based on standard set theory and it was used to specify invariants on classes and types in the class model, to specify type invariant for stereotypes, to describe pre- and post-conditions on operations and methods, to describe guards, and it is also suited to specify queries in the database sense. That is, OCL can be used to write expressions that evaluate to "true" or "false" and also to write expressions that once evaluated return the values respectively satisfying the constraint specified by those query expressions.

Expressions with OCL are described with the context of an instance of a specific type [14, 27, 41, 46]. In an OCL expression, the word **self** is used to indicate the contextual instance. The keyword **context** is used to present the type of the context instance of an OCL expression. The label **invar** means that the constraint is an invariant constraint. For example, suppose that students study in a University and they register in a course. These relationships can be modelled with the class model of the UML. If the context is University, then *self* refers to an instance of University. The following shows an example of OCL constraint expression describing a University that has more 20,000 students:

context University **invar**:
self.student $\rightarrow$ size > 20,000

The self.student is a set of students that is selected by navigating from University class to Student class though an association. The "." stands for a navigation. A property of a set is accessed by using an arrow "$\rightarrow$" followed by the name of the property. A property of the set of students is expressed using a keyword "size" in the example.

The following shows another example describing that a student can join a course *A* only if the student is already involved in a course *B*.

context Student **invar**:
self.course $\rightarrow$ involves('A') *implies* self.course $\rightarrow$ involves('B')

The self.course → involves('A') means that the course *A* is an element of courses in which a student is involved. An OCL expression delivers a subset of a collection. That is, the OCL has special constructs to specify a selection from a specific collection. For instance, the following OCL expression specifies that the collection of students whose age is less than 15 is empty:

context University **invar:**
slef.student → select($age < 15$) → *is Empty*

The **select** takes a student from self.student and evaluates an expression ($age <$ 15) for the student. If this evaluation is true, then the student is in the result set.

7.3 Constraints in RBAC

Constraints are an important issue when assigning a role to a user and a permission to a role [15, 32, 37]. This issue has received little attention in the research literature. Most prior work has focused on separation of duty constraints. For example, Chen and Sandhu [6] suggested how constraints can be specified. It may work for a Database Administrator (DBA) or Security Officer to specify constraints. The basic idea to apply constraints is to lay out higher level organizational policy. It does not provide details for the applications of other components in RBAC such as user-role assignment and permission-role assignment. Wang et al. [35] introduced a formal authorization allocation approaches and identified the major classes of constraints in RBAC such as *Separation Constraints*, *Prerequisite Constraint* and *Cardinality Constraints*.

7.3.1 Separation Constraints

There are two kinds of separation constraint. One is Static Separation of Duty while the other one is Dynamic Separation of Duty.

The policy of Static Separation of Duty (SSD) can be centrally specified and can then be uniformly imposed on specific roles. The principle reason with SSD is that a user being authorized as a member of one role, the user is not authorized as a member of a second role. For example, a user is a member of the role Teller in a bank cannot be a member of the role Auditor of the same bank. The mutually exclusive roles for a given role and the Static Separation of Duty property can be specified as follows:

mutually-exclusive-authorization(r: roles) = {the list of roles that are mutually exclusive with role "r" }.

Static Separation of Duty: A user is authorized as a member of a role only if that role is not mutually exclusive with any of the other roles for which the user already possesses membership. Suppose u is a user and $r_i, r_j (i \neq j)$ are roles, we have:

$\forall u, r_i, r_j :$
(u is a member of r_i) $\wedge$ (u is a member of r_j) $\Longrightarrow r_i \notin \{$ mutually-exclusive-authorization(r_j) $\}$

RBAC also provides administrators with the capability to enforce an organization-specific policy of Dynamic Separation of Duty. Static Separation of Duty provides an enterpriser with the capability to address potential conflicts of interest issues at the time a user's membership is authorized for a role. However, in some organizations it is permissible for a user to be a member of two roles which do not constitute a conflict of interest when acted independently, but introduce policy concerns when allowed to be acted simultaneously.

For example, a static policy could require that no individual who is a member of role *Payment Initiator* can also be a member of role *Payment Authorizer*. Although such an approach may be adequate for some organizations, for others it may prove too rigid, making the cost of separation greater than the loss that might be expected. The objective behind Dynamic Separation of Duty is to allow more flexibility in operations. Dynamic Separation of Duty places constraints on the simultaneous activation of roles, so for example, an individual user can be authorized for both the roles *Payment Initiator* and *Authorizer*, but can dynamically assume only one of these roles at the same time.

The mutually exclusive roles for the proposed active role is specified by the following function:

mutually-exclusive-activation(r: roles) = {the list of active roles that are mutually exclusive with the proposed role "r"}.

The role-based Dynamic Separation of Duty rule is defined as:

Dynamic Separation of Duty A user can become a member of a new role only if the proposed role is not mutually exclusive with any of the roles in which the user is already a member. Suppose u is a user and $r_i, r_j (i \neq j)$ are roles, we have:

$\forall u, r_i, r_j :$
(r_i is a member of u) $\wedge$ (r_j is a member of u) $\Longrightarrow r_i \notin \{$mutually-exclusive-activation(r_j) $\}$.

The above role-based Dynamic Separation provides a flexibility of that one user can have two mutually exclusive roles but not dynamic active at the same time. Furthermore, we have the object-based separation of duty that means one user may have two mutually exclusive roles and may assume both roles at the same time, but the user cannot act upon an object that the user has previously acted upon. For instance, a user can be authorized for both the roles *Payment Initiator* and *Authorizer*, and also can assume these roles at the same time, but the user cannot handle the same payment process. In another words, we can have the following definition:

Object-Based Separation of Duty An object can become active in a new role only if the proposed role is not mutually exclusive with any of the roles in which the object is currently active.

$\forall ob, r_i, r_j$:

(r_i is an active role of *ob*) $\wedge$ (r_j is an active role of *ob*) $\Longrightarrow r_i \notin \{$mutually-exclusive-activation(r_j) $\}$.

Where *ob* is an object and r_i, r_j are roles.

7.3.2   Prerequisite Constraints

Prerequisite constraints are important aspects in RBAC that are used as conditions when a role is assigned to a user in user-role assignment and a permission is assigned to a role in permission-role assignment [29, 30, 35]. For example, a user can be assigned to the academic role only if the user has already been assigned to the employee role in a university. It ensures that only users who are already assigned to the employee role can be assigned to the academic role. This constraint is called Prerequisite constraint. The Prerequisite constraints in user-role assignment can be expressed as below:

Prerequisite condition is an expression using Boolean operators $\wedge$ and $\vee$ on terms of the form x and $\bar{x}$ where x is a role and $\wedge$ means "and", $\vee$ means "or". A prerequisite condition is evaluated for a user u by interpreting x to be true if $(\exists x' \geq x), (u, x') \in UA$ and $\bar{x}$ to be true if $(\forall x' \geq x), (u, x') \notin UA$, where UA is a set of user-role assignments.   ◇

Where $(\exists x' \geq x), (u, x') \in UA$ means that there exists a role x', x' is senior to role x, or $x' = x$, u is a member of role $x', (\forall x' \geq x), (u, x') \notin UA$ means that there is no role x', x' is senior to role x, or $x' = x$, u is a member of role x'.

We use OCL to express prerequisite constraints in the next section.

7.3.3   Cardinality Constraints

The Cardinality Constraints are a numerical limitation that exist when granting roles to user in user-role assignment. Some roles can only be occupied by a certain number of employees at any given period of time [7, 42, 47]. For example, consider the role of Manager. Although other employees may act in that role, only one employee may assume the responsibilities of a manager at any given time. A user can become a new member of a role as long as the number of members allowed for the role is not exceeded. The number of users allowed for a role and the existing number of users associated with a role is specified by the following two functions:

membership-limit (r: roles) = the membership limit for role "r".
number-of-members(r: roles) = N (> 0) the number of existing members in role "r".

Role capacity can now be described as:

Cardinality: The capacity of a role cannot be exceeded by an additional role member:

$\forall r : roles :$

membership-limit (r) $\geq$ number-of-members (r).

7.3.4 Mobility Constraints

The mobility of user-role relationship is a new feature in user-role assignments. When an administrative role assigns a role to a user with a mobile membership, this allows the user to use the permissions of the role and to be further assigned other roles by administrators. Immobile membership grants the user the authority to use the permissions, but does not make the user eligible for further role assignment [20, 21, 48].

This distinction between mobile and immobile memberships can be very important in practice [19, 26]. For example, in a University, a guest can be granted immobile membership in a role as an observer by an administrative role but he/she cannot be granted a staff role before the immobile membership is removed. Therefore, the guest is able to visit the University but cannot access students' data as a staff member.

7.4 Constraints Expression with OCL

A class diagram for RBAC depicted in Fig. 7.2 shows user, role, permission class. A permission presents which operations work on what objects, hence we have object and operation classes. Each class has attributes and methods. For example, the *Role* class has *Name* attribute and *Grant( ), Revoke( )* methods. Roles are in two categories, user and administrative roles, and the user role is combined by mobile and immobile roles. The permission is specialized by mobile and immobile permissions. The *UA* and *PA* relations mean that user-role assignment and permissions-role assignment, respectively. As we analyzed before, constraints are involved in *UA* and *PA* relationships. The constraints such as separation of duty constraints, prerequisite constraints, mobility constraints etc are identified in this section.

7.4.1 Separation of Duty Constraints

Separation of duty is a security principle used to formulate multi-person control policies, requiring that two or more different people be responsible for the comple-

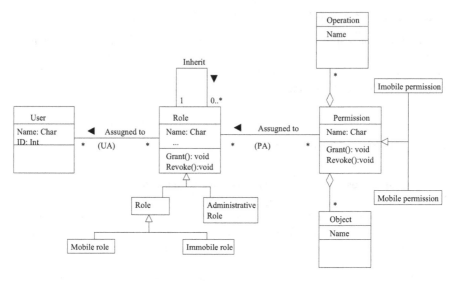

Fig. 7.2 Class diagram for RBAC

tion of a task. The objective of separation of duty is to discourage fraud by spreading the responsibility and authority for an action or task over multiple people. There are two kinds of separation duty. The first one is dynamic separation of duty while the other one is static separation of duty. The objective behind Dynamic Separation of Duty is to allow more flexibility in operations. Dynamic Separation of Duty places constraints on the simultaneous activation of roles. We now specify these constraints with OCL.

context User **invar:**
let M: Set = { { mutually-exclusive-activation(r: roles)}, ... } **in**
M → select($m \mid self.role$ → intersection (m) → $size > 1$) → *is Empty*

This constraint expression selects all mutually exclusive sets, checks all roles assigned to each user, and enforces above requirements.

Static Separation of Duty means that by virtue of a user being authorized as a member of one role, the user is not authorized as a member of a second role. The SSD constraints are expressed by OCL as below.

context User **invar:**
let M: Set = { { mutually-exclusive-authorization(r: roles)}, ... } **in**
M→ select($m \mid self.role$ → intersection (m) → $size > 1$) → *is Empty*

This constraint expresses that no two roles in the set of a mutually exclusive authorization can be assigned to a user. The OCL representation for object-based separation of duty is:

Fig. 7.3 Hierarchies of
administrative roles

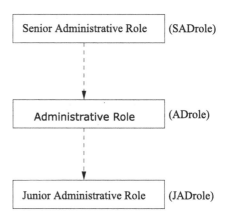

context User **invar:**
let M: Set = { { mutually-exclusive-authorization(r: roles)}, . . . } **in**
M→ select(m | m →intersection (self.session.object) → $size > 1$) → *is Empty*

This constraint indicates that no object associated mutually exclusive roles can be acted by a user at the same time.

7.4.2   Mobility Constraints

It may have hierarchies between roles. We use administrative roles in Fig. 7.3 to explain the mobility of user-role membership. The Figure shows hierarchies of administrative roles. The administrative role SAR is senior to role AR ($SAR > AR$) (or AR is junior to SAR), and role AR is senior to role JAR ($AR > JAR$) (or JAR is junior to AR). The administrative role SAR inherits administrative role AR with all permissions of AR. Similarly, AR inherits junior administrative role JAR. When the membership between user and role is mobile (immobile), we say the user is a mobile (immobile) member of the role or the role is a mobile (immobile) member of the user. Supposing the administrative role AR assigns a role to a user as a mobile member, it means the user can use permissions of the role and other administrative roles including junior administrative role JAR may further assign other roles to the user. If the user is assigned a role as an immobile member by AR, it grants the user the authority to use permissions of the role but cannot be assigned other roles to the user by JAR because JAR is junior to AR.

Each role r is separated into two sub-roles Mr and IMr. Membership in Mr is mobile while membership in IMr is immobile. Assignment of Mr to a user specifies that the user has a mobile membership of r. Similarly, assignment of IMr to a user specifies that the role x is an immobile member of u.

The explicit members of a role r is the set of users $\{u|(u, r) \in UA\}$ and the implicit members of role r is the set of users $\{u|\exists r' > r, (u, r') \in UA\}$ where

UA is user-role assignment. Based on the mobile and immobile membership with the notion of explicit and implicit membership, there are four kinds of user-role membership for a given role r [26].

1. *Explicit Mobile Member EMr:*
   $EMr = \{u, |(u, Mr) \in UA\}$
   EMr is a set of users that have mobile membership with role r.
2. *Explicit Immobile Member EIMr:*
   $EIMr = \{u, |(u, IMr) \in UA\}$
   $EIMr$ is a set of users that have immobile membership with role r.
3. *Implicit Mobile Member ImMr:*
   $ImMr = \{u, |\exists r' > r, (u, Mr') \in UA\}$
   $ImMr$ is a set of users that have implicit mobile membership with role r. It means that role r has a senior role r', the user in $ImMr$ is a mobile member of r'.
4. *Implicit Immobile Member ImIMr:*
   $ImIMr = \{u, |\exists r' > r, (u, IMr') \in UA\}$
   $ImIMr$ is a set of users that have implicit immobile membership with role r. It means that role r has a senior role r', the user in $ImMr$ is a immobile member of r'.

A user may have all four kinds of membership in a role at the same time. However, we limit strict precedence amongst these four kinds of membership as follows:

$$EMr > EIMr > ImMr > ImIMr$$

Therefore only one of the membership is actually in effect at any time even though a user has multiple kinds of membership in a role. By the definition of mobile membership, the r has mobile membership with a user when the user is in EMr or in $ImMr$. However, the role is not a mobile role of a user if the user belongs to both $ImMr$ and $EIMr$ because the strict precedence listed above. Therefore, the Mobility constraints of a user that has mobile membership of roles can be specified as below:

context Mobile Role **invar:**
self.user $\rightarrow$ select $\{\{u|u \in EMr\} \vee \{\{u|u \in ImMr\} \wedge \{u|u \notin EIMr\}\} \rightarrow$ size ≥ 1

Where $\{u|u \in EMr\}$ is a set of users with mobile membership of r, and $\{\{u|u \in ImMr\} \wedge \{u|u \notin EIMr\}\}$ is a set of users with implicit mobile membership of r but not an explicit immobile member of r.

Similarly, since the strict precedence, we have the following expression for immobile membership.

context Immobile Role **invar:**
self.user $\rightarrow$ select $\{\{u|u \in EIMr\} \vee \{\{u|u \in ImIMr\} \wedge \{u|u \notin ImMr\}\} \rightarrow$ size ≥ 1.

7.4.3 Prerequisite Constraints

The following example shows that OCL can also specify prerequisite constraints. Suppose a senior role set of a role r is indicated by *Seniorset (r)*.

Seniorset$(r) = \{r' \mid r'$ *is senior to r* $\}$

The *Seniorset (r)* is used for the judgement of whether or not prerequisite conditions are satisfied. For instance, the prerequisite condition of assigning a role r_1 to user u is that the user is already a member of role r_2. Including inheritance, the constraint can be specified as follows:

context User **invar:**
self.role $\rightarrow$ includes(r_1) *implies* (self.role $\rightarrow$ includes (r_2)) $\vee$(self.role $\rightarrow$ includes $(r \mid r \in Seniorset(r_2)))$

The (self.role $\rightarrow$ includes (r_2)) means that the user is a member of role r_2 while the (self.role $\rightarrow$ includes $(r \mid r \in Seniorset(r_2))$) means that the user is a member of a role in the role set $Seniorset(r_2)$.

This constraint is used for user-role assignment (UA). For permission-role assignment (PA), a prerequisite constraint means that a permission p can be assigned to a role only if the role already possesses permission q. For instance, permission to read a student's exam result requires permission to access the course in which the student has involved. Without the latter permission, assigning the former permission is incomplete. This constraint on PA can be specified with OCL expression as follows:

context Permission **invar:**
self.role $\rightarrow$ includes('read exam result') *implies* self.role $\rightarrow$ includes ('access course')

7.4.4 Cardinality Constraints

Another important constraint in RBAC is a numerical limitation for classes. For example, there is only one person in the role of the head of a department. The head role should be assigned to only one user. The OCL expression for this constraint on UA is as below:

context User **invar:**
self.role $\rightarrow$ select $\{r \mid$ self.name = 'head role' $\} \rightarrow$ size =1

We have represented separation of duty constraints, mobility constraints etc in RBAC by using object constraint language. The significance of the work in this chapter is demonstrated by comparing related works in the next section.

7.5   Comparisons

There is no much work related to role-based access control models with OCL. The paper of Gail and Michael [2] is the only one that we have found which introduced role-based authorization constraints specification using object constraint language.

The authors in [2] have demonstrated that how to specify role-based authorization constraints using an industrial standard constraints specification language OCL. They specified separation of duty constraints, prerequisite constraints and cardinality constraints and then as a result, utilized constraints identified by a formal language such as role-based constraints specification language (RCL2000) [1] when they designed and analyzed role-based systems. The RCL2000 introduced an intuitive formal language for specifying role-based authorization constraints which provides elements, syntax, and semantics. The language was built on RBAC96 [24] components and had two selection functions. The work in [2] helps system developer understand constraints and requirements on secure systems development. However, our work substantially differs from that proposal in three aspects. First, our paper has significantly extended the work in [2]. the paper [2] introduced role-based constraints with OCL based on RBAC96 model. RBAC96 model is the first general model for role-based access control that does not even include new conceptions such as mobility etc. By contrast, we deeply discuss various constraint cases in the advanced RBAC model, ARBAC99 [26]. We have provided OCL with not only separation duty constraints, prerequisite conditions but also mobility of user-role assignment and permission-role assignment. Further more, the results in [2] depend on a special model and examples. Second, the discussion area in this chapter is much wide than that in paper [2]. The authors in paper [2] focus on role-based authorization constraints but we have discussed details for how to express constraints in RBAC using OCL. The authorization constraints are a part of constraints only in RBAC. For example, the object-based separation of duty is a constraint in RBAC but not an authorization constraint. Third, the OCL expression in our paper is more general. The special examples in [2] are used to represent OCL for role-based authorization constraints and hence there is no formal expression. By contrast, we present a number of constraints for role-based access control which allows administrators to authorize a role to users as mobile and immobile member or revoke them from users. The OCL expressions in this chapter provide a rich variety of options that can deal the document of administrative roles with regular roles as mobile and immobile members and the expressions have no limits on special examples.

7.6   Conclusions

This chapter has discussed the constraints in RBAC and provided various kinds of constraints representation with object constraint language. We have analysed the constraints in RBAC such as object-based dynamic separation of duty constraints and mobility constraints etc. The constraints including static separation of duty constraints, role-based dynamic and object-based dynamic separation of duty constraints, prerequisite constraints and mobility constraints in user-role assignment and permission-role assignment have been specified by using OCL. The work in this chapter has significantly extended previous work in several aspects, for example, the object-based dynamic separation of duty and mobility constraints with OCL. As a result, we can use object constraints language to represent the constraints in RBAC when we design and analyze role-based access management. This work can help people to understand constraints and requirements on group work with UML for RBAC.

RBAC is a powerful Web data management system with various constraints. We have analyzed main constraints in RBAC such as separation of duty constraints and mobility constraints etc. The future work is to prove whether all constraints in RBAC can expressed by OCL or not.

7.7   Problems and Exercises

7.7.1   Problems

1. Constraints are important concepts in role-based access control management. What are the differences of constraints between user-role assignments and permission-role assignments? What arc the fundamental ideas of the constraints between senior-junior relationships and operation-object relationships?
2. What are the importance of mobility constraints and separation constraints?
3. This chapter has discussed lots of constraints such as prerequisite constraints and cardinality constraints, however, advanced analysis is preferred.
4. RBAC is a powerful Web data management system with various constraints. We have analyzed main constraints in RBAC such as separation of duty constraints and mobility constraints etc. The future work is to prove whether all constraints in RBAC can expressed by OCL or not.

7.7.2   Exercises

I. Developing OCL algorithms for user-role assignments and permission-role assignments;
2. Given a real example including constraints of both senior-junior relationships and operation-object relationships;
3. Analysing prerequisite constraints and cardinality constraints, developing OCL algorithms for the constraints.

References

1. Ahn, G., Sandhu, R.: Role-based authorization constraints specification. Inf. Syst. Secur. **3**(4), 207–226 (2000)
2. Ahn, G., Shin, M.: Role-based authorization constraints specification using object constraint language. In: Tenth IEEE International Workshops on Enabling Technologies: Infrastructure for Collaborative Enterprises, Massachusetts, pp. 157–165 (2001)
3. Ahn, G.J., Sandhu, R.: The rsl99 language for role-based separation of duty constraints. In: 4th ACM Workshop on Role-Based Access Control, Fairfax (1999), pp. 43–54
4. Barkley, J.F., Beznosov, K., Uppal, J.: Supporting relationships in access control using role based access control. In: Third ACM Workshop on Role Based Access Control, pp. 55–65 (1999)
5. Cao, J., et al.: Towards secure xml document with usage control. In: Web Technologies Research and Development - APWeb 2005, Berlin. Springer, Berlin (2005)
6. Chen, F., Sandhu, R.: Constraints for role-based access control. In: Proceedings of the First ACM Workshop on Role-Based Access Control, pp. 39–46 (1995)
7. Chenthara, S., et al.: Security and privacy-preserving challenges of e-health solutions in cloud computing. IEEE Access **7**, 74361–74382 (2019)
8. Corno, F., Tosato, S., Velardocchla, M.: Specifications for integrated UML-based system-level. Technical Report (2002)
9. David, F.F., Dennis, M.G., Nickilyn, L.: An examination of federal and commercial access control policy needs. In: NIST NCSC National Computer Security Conference, Baltimore, pp. 107–116 (1993)
10. Feinstein, H.L.: Final report: NIST small business innovative research (SBIR) grant: role based access control: phase 1. Technical Report. SETA Corp. (1995)
11. Ferraiolo, D.F., Kuhn, D.R.: Role based access control. In: 15th National Computer Security Conference, pp. 554–563 (1992). ferraiolo92rolebased.html
12. Ferraiolo, D.F., Barkley, J.F., Kuhn, D.R.: Role-based access control model and reference implementation within a corporate intranet. In: Transactions on Information and System Security (TISSEC), vol. 2, pp. 34–64 (1999)
13. Gallaher, M.P., O'Connor, A.C., Kropp, B.: The economic impact of role-based access control. Final Report, National Institute of Standards and Technology, Gaithersburg, 20899-0001 (2002)
14. Kabir, E., et al.: Microaggregation sorting framework for k-anonymity statistical disclosure control in cloud computing. IEEE Trans. Cloud Comput. **8**, 408–417 (2020)
15. Khalil, F., Li, J., Wang, H.: Integrating recommendation models for improved web page prediction accuracy. In: Proceedings of the Thirty-First Australasian Conference on Computer Science - Volume74, ACSC'08, Darlinghurst, pp. 91–100. Australian Computer Society, Darlinghurst (2008)
16. Lau, K., Ornaghi, M.: A formal approach to software component specification. Technical Report (1995)
17. Li, M., et al.: Advanced permission-role relationship in role-based access control. In: Information Security and Privacy, Berlin, pp. 391–403. Springer, Berlin (2008)
18. Lupu, E., Marriott, D., Sloman, M., Yialelis, N.: A policy based role framework for access control. In: ACM/NIST Workshop on Role-Based Access Contro (1995). http://www-dse.doc.ic.ac.uk/~ecl1/papers/rbac95/rbac95.pdf
19. Oh, S., Sandhu, R.: A model for role administration using organization structure. In: Seventh ACM Symposium on Access Control Models and Technologies, pp. 155–162. ACM Press, New York (2002)
20. Peng, M., et al.: Pattern filtering attention for distant supervised relation extraction via online clustering. In Web Information Systems Engineering – WISE 2019, pp. 310–325. Springer, Cham (2019)

21. Rasool, R., et al.: Cyberpulse: a machine learning based link flooding attack mitigation system for software defined networks. IEEE Access **7**, 34885–34899 (2019)
22. Richters, M., Gogolla, M.: On formalizing the UML object constraint language OCL. In: Ling, T.-W., Ram, S., Lee, M.L. (eds.) Proceedings of the 17th International Conference on Conceptual Modeling (ER), vol. 1507, pp. 449–464. Springer, Berlin (1998)
23. Rumbaugh, J., Jacobson, I., Booch, G.: The Unified Modeling Language Reference Manual. Addison-Wesley, Reading (1999)
24. Sandhu, R.: Rational for the *RBAC*96 family of access control models. In: Proceedings of 1st ACM Workshop on Role-Based Access Control, pp. 64–72. ACM Press, New York (1997)
25. Sandhu, R.: Role activation hierarchies. In: Third ACM Workshop on Role Based Access Control, pp. 33–40. ACM Press, New York (1998)
26. Sandhu, R., Munawer, Q.: The arbac99 model for administration of roles. In: The Annual Computer Security Applications Conference, pp. 229–238. ACM Press, New York (1999)
27. Shu, J., et al.: Privacy-preserving task recommendation Services for Crowdsourcing. IEEE Trans. Serv. Comput. (2018) https://doi.org/10.1109/TSC.2018.2791601
28. Sun, L., Li, Y., Wang, H.: M-service and its framework. In: 2005 Asia-Pacific Conference on Communications, pp. 837–841 (2005)
29. Sun, X., et al.: An efficient hash-based algorithm for minimal k-anonymity. In: Proceedings of the Thirty-First Australasian Conference on Computer Science, ACSC'08, Darlinghurst, vol. 74, pp. 101–107. Australian Computer Society, Darlinghurst (2008)
30. Sun X., et al.: Enhanced p-sensitive k-anonymity models for privacy preserving data publishing. Trans. Data Privacy **1**(2), 53–66 (2008)
31. Sun, X., et al.: (p+, α)-sensitive k-anonymity: a new enhanced privacy protection model. In: 2008 8th IEEE International Conference on Computer and Information Technology, pp. 59–64 (2008)
32. Wang, H., Li, Q.: Secure and efficient information sharing in multi-university e-learning environments. In: Advances in Web Based Learning – ICWL 2007, Berlin, pp. 542–553. Springer, Berlin (2008)
33. Wang, H., Cao, J., Ross, D.: Role-based delegation with negative authorization. In: Frontiers of WWW Research and Development - APWeb, Berlin, pp. 307–3182006. Springer, Berlin (2006)
34. Wang, H., Cao, J., Zhang, Y.: A consumer anonymity scalable payment scheme with role based access control. In: 2nd International Conference on Web Information Systems Engineering (WISE01), Kyoto, pp. 53–62 (2001)
35. Wang, H., Cao, J., Zhang, Y.: Formal authorization allocation approaches for role-based access control based on relational algebra operations. In: 3nd International Conference on Web Information Systems Engineering (WISE02), Singapore, pp. 301–312 (2002)
36. Wang, H., Cao, J., Zhang, Y.: A flexible payment scheme and its role-based access control. IEEE Trans. Knowl. Data Eng. **17**(3), 425–436 (2005)
37. Wang, H., Cao, J., Zhang, Y.: Delegating revocations and authorizations in collaborative business environments. Inf. Syst. Front. **11**(3), 293 (2008)
38. Wang, H., et al.: Authorization algorithms for the mobility of user-role relationship. In: Proceedings of the Twenty-eighth Australasian Conference on Computer Science, ACSC'05, vol. 38, pp. 69–77. Australian Computer Society, Darlinghurst (2005)
39. Wang, H., et al.: A framework for role-based group deligation in distributed environments. In: Proceedings of the 29th Australasian Computer Science Conference, vol. 48, pp. 321–328 (2006)
40. Wang, H., et al. Authorization approaches for advanced permission-role assignments. In: 2008 12th International Conference on Computer Supported Cooperative Work in Design, pp. 277–282 (2008)
41. Wang, H., et al.: Protecting outsourced data in cloud computing through access management. Concurrency Comput. Pract. Exp. **28**(3), 600–615 (2016)
42. Wang, H., et al.: Editorial: special issue on security and privacy in network computing. World Wide Web (2019)

43. Wang, H., Zhang, Y., Cao, J.: Ubiquitous computing environments and its usage access control. In: Proceedings of the 1st International Conference on Scalable Information Systems, InfoScale'06, New York. ACM, New York (2006)
44. Wang, H., Zhang, Y., Cao, J., Kambayahsi, Y.: A global ticket-based access scheme for mobile users. Special Issue on Object-Oriented Client/Server Internet Environments, Information Systems Frontiers 6(1), 35–46 (2004)
45. Wang, H., Zhang, Y., Cao, J., Varadharajan, V.: Achieving secure and flexible m-services through tickets. IEEE Trans. Syst. Man Cybern. A Syst. Hum. 33, 697–708 (2003)
46. Wang, H., Zhang, Z., Taleb, T.: Editorial: special issue on security and privacy of IoT. World Wide Web 21(1), 1–6 (2018)
47. Wang, Z., Zhan, Z., Lin, Y., Yu, W., Wang, H., Kwong, S., Zhang, J.: Automatic niching differential evolution with contour prediction approach for multimodal optimization problems. IEEE Trans. Evol. Comput. 24, 114–128 (2019)
48. Zhang, F., Wang, Y., Wang, H.: Gradient correlation: are ensemble classifiers more robust against evasion attacks in practical settings? In: Web Information Systems Engineering – WISE 2018, pp. 96–110. Springer, Cham (2018)

Chapter 8
Role-Based Delegation with Negative Authorization

Role-based delegation model (*RBDM*) based on role-based access control (*RBAC*) has proven to be a flexible and useful access control model for information sharing on distributed collaborative environment. Authorization is an important functionality for *RBDM* in distributed environment where a conflicting problem may arise when one user grants permission of a role to a delegated user and another user grants the negative permission to the delegated user.

This chapter aims to analyse role-based group delegation features that has not studied before, and to provide an approach for the conflicting problem by adopting negative authorization. We present granting and revocation delegating models first, and then discuss user delegation authorization and the impact of negative authorization on role hierarchies. Finally, comparisons with other related work are indicated.

8.1 Introduction

Delegation is the process whereby an active entity grants access resource permissions to another entity in a distributed environment. In today's highly dynamic distributed systems, a user often needs to act on another user's behalf with part of the user's rights. To solve such delegation requirements, ad-hoc mechanisms are used in most systems by compromising existing disorganized policies or additional components to their applications [37, 44, 49, 89]. The basic idea of delegation is to enable someone to do a job, for example, a secretary. Effective delegation not only makes management systems ultimately more satisfactory, but also frees the delegating users to focus on other important issues. In access control management systems, the delegation arises when users need to act on another user's behalf in accessing resources. The delegation might be for a short time, for example, sharing resources temporarily with others during 1 week holiday. Otherwise, users

© Springer Nature Switzerland AG 2020
H. Wang et al., *Access Control Management in Cloud Environments*,
https://doi.org/10.1007/978-3-030-31729-4_8

may perceive security as an obstacle of the resources sharing. With delegation, the delegated user has the privileges to access information without referring back to the delegating user [16, 65, 68, 84].

Delegation is recognised as vital in a secure distributed computing environment [1, 4, 87, 93]. However, a conflicting secure problem may arise when one user grants permission of a role to a delegated user and another user does reject the permission to the delegated user. The most common delegation types include user-to-machine, user-to-user, and machine-to-machine delegation. They all have the same consequence, namely the propagation of access permission. Propagation of access rights in decentralized collaborative systems presents challenges for traditional access mechanisms because authorization decisions are made based on the identity of the resource requester. Unfortunately, access control based on identity may be ineffective when the requester is unknown to the resource owner [14, 19, 30, 83]. Recently some distributed access control mechanisms have been proposed: Lampson et al. present an example on how a person can delegate its authority to others [43]; Blaze et al. introduced trust management for decentralized authorization [12]; Abadi et al. showed an application of express delegation with access control calculus [1]; and Aura described a delegation mechanism to support access management in a distributed computing environment [3]. All these papers have not analysed the conflicting secure problem.

The National Institute of Standards and Technology developed role-based access control (*RBAC*) prototype [26] and published a formal model [27]. *RBAC* enables managing and enforcing security in large-scale and enterprise-wide systems. Many enhancements of *RBAC* models have been developed in the past decade. In *RBAC* models, permissions are associated with roles, users are assigned to appropriate roles, and users acquire permissions through roles. Users can be easily reassigned from one role to another. Roles can be granted new permissions and permissions can be easily revoked from roles as needed. Therefore, *RBAC* provides a means for empowering individual users through role-based delegation in distributed collaboration environments. However, there is little work on delegation with *RBAC* [21, 71, 87].

This chapter analyses role-based delegation model based on *RBAC* and provides a solution for the conflicting problem adopting negative authorization [75, 77, 80, 81]. The remainder of this chapter is organized as follows: Sect. 8.2 presents the related work associated to delegation model and *RBAC*. As the results of this section, we find that both of group-based delegation with *RBAC* and negative authorization for delegation model has never analysed in the literature. Section 8.3 proposes a delegation framework which includes group-based delegation. Granting authorization with pre-requisite conditions and revocation authorization are discussed. Section 8.4 provides an approach for the conflicting problem by adopting negative authorization and briefly discusses how to use negative authorization in delegation framework. Section 8.5 compares our work with the previous work on delegation with *RBAC*. The differences between this work from others are presented. Section 8.6 concludes the paper and outlines our future work.

8.2 Related Work

Delegation is an important feature in many collaboration applications [58, 67, 82, 86]. For example, the Immigration Department is developing partnerships between immigration agencies and people in local areas to address possible problems. Immigration officers are able to prevent illegal stay and crime if they efficiently collaborate with the people. The problem-oriented immigrating system (*POIS*) is proposed to improve the service as a part of the Immigration Department's on going community efforts including identifying potential problems and resolving them before they become significant. With efficient delegation, officers respond quickly to urgent messages and increase the time spent confronting problems.

In *POIS*, officers might be involved in many concurrent activities such as conducting initial investigations, analysing and confronting crimes, preparing immigration reports, and assessing projects [9, 17, 63, 83]. In order to achieve this, users may have one or more roles such as lead officer, participant officer, or reporter. In this example, Tony, a director, needs to coordinate analysing and confronting crimes and assessing projects. Collaboration is necessary for information sharing with members from these two projects. To collaborate closely and make two projects more successful, Tony would like to delegate certain responsibilities to Christine and her staff. The prerequisite conditions are to secure these processes and to monitor the progress of the delegation. Furthermore, Christine may need to delegate the delegated role to her staff as necessary or to delegate a role to all members of a group at the same time. Without delegation skill, security officers have to do excessive work since the involvement of every single collaborative activity. The major requirements of role-based delegation in this example are:

1. Group-based delegation means that a delegating user may need to delegate a role to all members of a group at the same time.
2. Multistep delegation occurs when a delegation can be further delegated. Single-step delegation means that the delegated role cannot be further delegated.
3. Revocation schemes are important character in collaboration. They take away the delegated permissions. There are different revoking schemes, among them are strong and weak revocations, cascading and noncascading revocations, as well as grant-dependent and grant-independent revocations [62, 64, 82].
4. Constraints are an important factor in *RBAC* for laying out higher-level organizational policies [75, 78, 79]. It defines whether or not the delegation or revocation process is valid.
5. Partial delegation means only subsets of the permissions are delegated while total delegation means all permissions are delegated. Partial delegation is an important feature because it allows users only to delegate required permissions. The well-known least privilege security principle can be implemented through partial delegation [72–74].

Although the concept of delegation is not new in authorizations [3, 4, 68], role-based delegation received attention only recently [4, 5, 91, 92]. Aura [3] introduced key-oriented discretionary access control systems that are based on delegation of access rights with public-key certificates. A certificate denotes a signed message that includes both the signature and the original message. With the certificate, the issuer delegates the rights R to someone. The systems emphasized decentralization of authority and operations but their approach is a form of discretionary access control. Hence, they can neither express mandatory policies like Bell-LaPadula model, nor possible to verify that someone does not have a certificate. Furthermore, some important policies such as separation of duty policies cannot be expressed with only certificates. They need some additional mechanism to maintain the previously granted rights and the histories must be updated in real time when new certificates are issued. Delegation is also applied in decentralized trust management [12, 44]. Blaze et al. [12] identified the trust management problem as a distinct and important component of security in network services and Li and Grosof [44] made a logic-based knowledge representation for authorization with tractable trust-management in large-scale, open, distributed systems. Delegation was used to address the trust management problem including formulating security policies and security credentials, determining whether particular sets of credentials satisfy the relevant policies, and deferring trust to third parties. Other researchers have investigated machine to machine and human to machine delegations [1, 76]. For example, [75] proposed a secure, scalable anonymity payment protocol for Internet purchases through an agent which provided a higher anonymous certificate and improved the security of consumers. The agent certified re-encrypted data after verifying the validity of the content from consumers. The agent is a human to machine delegation which can provide new certificates. However, many important role-based concepts, for example, role hierarchies, constraints, revocation were not mentioned.

A rule-based framework for role-based delegation including *RDM2000* model was proposed [20, 47, 66, 91]. *RDM2000* model is based on *RBDM0* model which is a simple delegation model supporting only flat roles and single step delegation. Furthermore, as a delegation model, it does not support group-based delegation.

This chapter focuses exclusively on a role-based delegation model which supports group-based delegation and provides a solution of the conflicting problem with negative authorization in the role-based delegation model. We will extend our previous work and propose a delegation framework including delegation granting and revocation models, group-based delegation. To provide sufficient functions with the framework, this chapter will analyse how does original role assignment changes impact delegation results. This kind of group-based delegation and negative authorization within delegation framework have not been studied before [14, 15, 25, 29].

8.3   Delegation Framework

In this section we propose a role -based delegation model called RBDM which supports role hierarchy and group delegation by introducing the delegation relation [8, 13, 26].

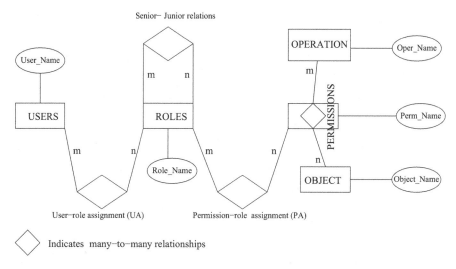

Fig. 8.1 RBAC relationship

8.3.1 Basic Elements and Components

RBAC involves individual users being associated with roles as well as roles being associated with permissions (Each permission is a pair of objects and operations). As such, a role is used to associate users and permissions. A user in this model is a human being. A role is a job function or job title within the organization associated with authority and responsibility [7, 10, 42]. As shown in Fig. 8.1, the relationships between users and roles, and between roles and permissions are many-to-many.

Many organizations prefer to centrally control and maintain access rights, not so much at the system administrator's personal discretion but more in accordance with the organization's protection guidelines [22]. RBAC is being considered as part of the emerging SQL3 standard for database management systems, based on their implementation in Oracle 7 [55]. Many RBAC practical applications have been implemented [6, 56].

A session is a mapping between a user and possibly many roles [2, 35, 41]. For example, a user may establish a session by activating some subset of assigned roles. A session is always associated with a single user and each user may establish zero or more sessions. There may be hierarchies within roles. Senior roles are shown at the top of the hierarchies. Senior roles inherit permissions from junior roles. Let $x > y$ denote x is senior to y with obvious extension to $x \geq y$. Role hierarchies provide a powerful and convenient means to enforce the principle of least privilege since only required permissions to perform a task are assigned to the role.

Although the concept of a user can be extended to include intelligent autonomous agents, machines, even networks, we limit a user to a human being in our model for simplicity.

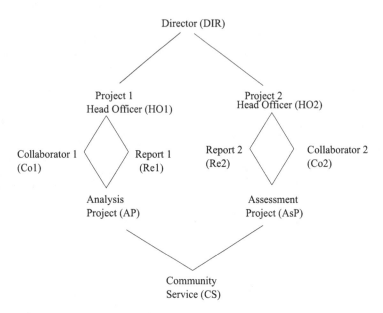

Fig. 8.2 Role hierarchy in *POIS*

Table 8.1 User-Role
relationship

Role name	User name
DIR	Tony
HO1	Christine
HO2	Mike
Co1	Richard
Re1	John
CS	Ahn

Figure 8.2 shows the role hierarchy structure of *RBAC* in *POIS*.

The following Table 8.1 expresses an example of user-role assignment in *POIS*.
There are two sets of users associated with role r:

Original users are those users who are assigned to the role r;
Delegated users are those users who are delegated to the role r.

The same user can be an original user of one role and a delegated user of
another role [28, 32, 54]. Also it is possible for a user to be both an original user
and a delegated user of the same role. For example, if Christine delegates her role
HO1 to Richard, then Richard is both an original user (explicitly) and a delegated
user (implicitly) of role Co1 because the role HO1 is senior to the role Co1. The
original user assignment (UAO) is a many-to-many user assignment relation
between original users and roles. The delegated user assignment (UAD) is a many-
to-many user assignment relation between delegated users and roles.

We have the following components for RBDM model:

U, R, P and S are sets of users, roles, permissions, and sessions, respectively.

1. $UAO \subseteq U \times R$ is a many-to-many original user to role assignment relation.
2. $UAD \subseteq U \times R$ is a many-to-many delegated user to role assignment relation.
3. $UA = UAO \cup UAD$.
4. Users: $R \Rightarrow 2^U$ is a function mapping each role to a set of users. $Users(r) = \{u | (u, r) \in UA\}$ where UA is user-role assignment.
5. $Users(r) = Users\_O(r) \cup Users\_D(r)$ where

$$Users\_O(r) = \{u | \exists r' > r, (u, r) \in UAO\}$$
$$Users\_D(r) = \{u | \exists r' > r, (u, r) \in UAD\}$$

8.3.2 Role-Based Delegation

The scope of our model is to address user-to-user delegation supporting role hierarchies and group delegations [23, 34, 60, 90]. We consider only the regular role delegation in this chapter, even though it is possible and desirable to delegate an administrative role.

A delegation relation (DELR) is existed in the role-based delegation model which includes three elements: original user assignments UAO, delegated user assignment UAD, and constraints. The motivation behind this relation is to address the relationships among different components involved in a delegation. In a user-to-user delegation, there are five components: a delegating user, a delegating role, a delegated user, a delegated role, and associated constraints. For example, ((Tony, DIR), (Christine, DIR), Friday) means Tony acting in role DIR delegates role DIR to Christine on Friday. We assume each delegation is associated with zero or more constraints. The delegation relation supports partial delegation in a role hierarchies: a user who is authorized to delegate a role r can also delegate a role r' that is junior to r. For example, ((Tony, DIR), (Ahn, Re1), Friday) means Tony acting in role DIR delegates a junior role Re1 to Ahn on Friday. A delegation relation is one-to-many relationship on user assignments. It consists of original user delegation (ORID) and delegated user delegation (DELD). Figure 8.3 illustrates components and their relations in a role-based delegation model.

From the above discussions, the following components are formalized:

1. $DELR \subseteq UA \times UA \times Cons$ is one-to-many delegation relation. A delegation relation can be represented by $((u, r), (u', r'), Cons) \in DELR$, which means the delegating user u with role r delegated role r' to user u' who satisfies the constraint $Cons$.
2. $ORID \subseteq UAO \times UAD \times Cons$ is an original user delegation relation.
3. $DELD \subseteq UAD \times UAD \times Cons$ is a delegated user delegation relation.
4. $DELR = ORID \cup DELD$

In some cases, we may need to define whether or not a user can delegate a role to a group and for how many times, or up to the maximum delegation depth

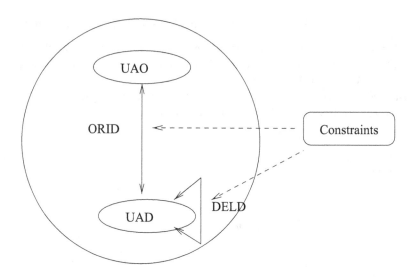

Fig. 8.3 Role-based delegation model

[40, 70, 94]. We only analyze one-step group delegation in this chapter which means the maximum delegation path is 1. The new relation of group delegation is defined as delegation group relation (DELGR) which includes: original user assignments UAO, delegated user assignments UAD, delegated group assignments GAD, and constraints. In a user-group delegation, there are five components: a delegating user (or a delegated user), a delegating role, a delegated group, a delegated role, and associated constrains. For example, ((Tony, DIR), (Project 1, DIR), 1:00pm–3:00pm Monday) means Tony acting in role DIR delegates role DIR to All people involved in Project 1 during 1:00pm–3:00pm on Monday. A group delegation relation is one-to-many relationship on user assignments. It consists of original user group delegation (ORIGD) and delegated user group delegation (DELGD). Figure 8.4 illustrates components and their relations in role-based delegation model.

We provide elements and functions in group delegation:

1. G is a set of users.
2. $DELGR \subseteq UA \times GA \times Cons$ is one-to-many delegation relation. A delegation relation can be represented by $((u, r), (G, r?), Cons) \in DELR$, which means the delegating user u with role r delegated role r to group G who satisfies the constraint $Cons$.
3. $ORIGD \subseteq UAO \times GAD \times Cons$ is a relation of an original user and a group.
4. $DELGD \subseteq UAD \times GAD \times Cons$ is a relation of a delegated user and a group.
5. $DELGR = ORIGD \cup DELGD$

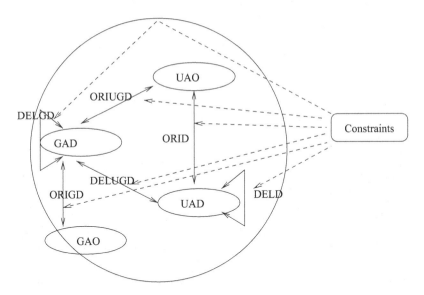

Fig. 8.4 Role-based group delegation model

8.4 Delegation Authorization

This section analyses delegation authorization and provides an approach for the conflicting secure problem with negative authorization.

8.4.1 Authorization Models

The delegation authorization goal imposes restrictions on which role can be delegated to whom [39, 46, 61, 69]. We partially adopt the notion of prerequisite condition from Wang et al. [82] to introduce delegation authorization in the delegation framework.

A prerequisite condition CR is an expression using Boolean operators '$\wedge$' and '$\vee$' on terms r and $\bar{r}$ where r is a role and '$\wedge$' means "and", '$\vee$' means "or", for example, $CR = r_1 \wedge r_2 \vee r_3$.

The following relation authorizes user-to-user delegation in this framework:

$$Can\_delegate \subseteq R \times CR \times N$$

where R, CR, N are sets of roles, prerequisite conditions, and maximum delegation depth, respectively. For group-based delegation mentioned last section, $N = 1$. The meaning of $(r, cr, n) \in Can\_delegate$ is that a user who is a member of role r (or a role senior to r) can delegate role r (or a role junior to r) to any user whose current

Table 8.2 Can-revoke

RoleName	Role Range
HO1	[Co1, CS]

entitlements in roles satisfy the prerequisite condition CR without exceeding the maximum delegation depth n.

There are related subtleties that arise in RBDM concerning the interaction between delegating and revocation of user-user delegation membership and the role hierarchy [30, 33, 48, 50].

Definition 8.1 A user-user delegation revocation is a relation $Can - revoke \subseteq R \times 2^R$, where R is a set of roles.   ◇

The meaning of Can-revoke (x, Y) is that a member of role x (or a member of an role that is senior to x) can revoke delegation relationship of a user from any role $y \in Y$, where Y defines the *range of revocation*. Table 8.2 gives the Can-revoke relation in Fig. 8.2.

There are two kinds of revocations [82]. The first one is weak revocation; the second one is strong revocation.

Definition 8.2 A user U is an explicit member of a role x if $(U, x) \in UA$, and that U is an implicit member of role x if for some $x' > x, (U, x') \in UA$.   ◇

Weak revocation only revokes explicit membership from a user and do not revoke implicit membership [24, 52, 53, 57]. On the other hand, strong revocation requires revocation of both explicit and implicit membership. Strong revocation of $U's$ membership in x requires that U be removed not only from explicit membership in x, but also from explicit (implicit) membership in all roles senior to x. Strong revocation therefore has a cascading effect up-wards in the role hierarchy. For example, suppose there are two delegations $((Tony, DIR), (Ahn, AP), Friday)$ and $((John, Re1), (Ahn, AP), Friday)$ and Tony wants to remove the membership of AP from Ahn on Friday. With weak revocation, the first delegation relationship is removed, but the second delegation has not yet removed. It means that Ahn is still a member of AP. With strong revocation two delegation relationships are removed and hence Ahn is not a member of AP.

8.4.2 An Approach for the Conflicting Problem

In the real world of access control, there are two well-known decision policies [11]:

(a) Closed policy: This policy allows access if there exists a corresponding positive authorization and denies it otherwise.
(b) Open policy: This policy denies access if there exists a corresponding negative authorization and allows it otherwise.

It is quite popular to apply closed policy in centralize management system. However, in uncentralised environment, the closed policy approach has a major problem in that the lack of a given authorization for a given user does not prevent this user from receiving this authorization later on. Bertino et al. [11] proposed an explicit negative authorization as blocking authorizations. Whenever a user receives a negative authorization, his positive authorizations become blocked. Negative authorization is typically discussed in the context of access control systems that adopt open policy. The introduction of negative authorization brings with it the possibility of conflict in authorization, an issue that needs to be resolved in order for the access control model to give a conclusive result. The types of conflicts brought about by the negative authorization are beyond this chapter. Negative authorization is rarely mentioned in *RBAC* literature, mainly because *RBAC* Models such as RBAC96 and the proposed NIST standard model are based on positive permissions that confer the ability to do something on holders of the permissions [38, 51, 59, 88].

As we previously discussed a delegation relation $((u1, r1), (u', r'), Cons1) \in DELR$, which means the delegating user $u1$ with role $r1$ delegated role r' to user u' who satisfies the constraint $Cons1$. What will happen if there is another delegation $((u2, r2), (u', \neg r'), Cons2) \in DELR$ which means the delegating user $u2$ with role $r2$ rejected to delegate role r' to user u' who satisfies the constraint $Cons2$. We analyse the solution of this conflicting problem with role hierarchy. We may use one of the following policies:

1. Denial takes precedence (DTP): Negative authorizations are always adopted when conflict exists.
2. Permission takes precedence (PTP): Positive authorizations are always adopted when conflicts exists.

These two policies are too simple for enterprise collaborations since it is not an efficient solution. In enterprise environment, role hierarchy is a very important feature since a senior role has all permissions of its junior roles. It means a senior role is more powerful than a junior role. Therefore, some differences with negative authorization between a senior role and its junior role are necessary [18, 31, 36, 45]. A practical solution for the above conflicting problem is:

1. Role r' can delegate to user u' if $r1$ is senior to $r2$,
2. Role r' cannot delegate to user u' if $r1$ is junior to $r2$.

For the security reason, we suggest using DTP policy for two roles without hierarchy relationship when a conflicting problem happens. We summarize the above discussion for the conflicting problem.

1. Role r' can delegate to user u' if $r1$ is senior to $r2$,
2. Role r' cannot delegate to user u' if either $r1$ is junior to $r2$ or there is no hierarchy relationship between $r1$ and $r2$.

8.5   Comparisons

To the best of our knowledge, there is no research work on role-based delegation with negative authorization. The closed work to this chapter are on mobility of user-role assignment [85] and role-based delegation [4].

Our previous work [85] discussed the mobility of user-role relationship in *RBAC* management and provided new authorization allocation algorithms for *RBAC* along with the mobility that are based on relational algebra operations. They are the authorization granting algorithm, weak revocation algorithm and strong revocation algorithm. The paper does not use role delegation but instead defines the role mobility, whereby a user with an mobile role may further grant other roles but she/he cannot accept other roles if she/he has an immobile role. The mobility could be viewed as a special case of role-based delegation in their work. But some important delegation features such as delegation conflicts and delegation revocation have not been considered. By contrast, the work in this chapter provides a rich variety of options that can deal with delegation authorization and revocation.

Barka and Sandhu [4] proposed a simple model for role-based delegation called *RBDM0* within *RBAC0*, the simplest form of *RBAC96* [Sandhu et al. 1996]. They developed a framework for identifying interesting cases that can be used for building role-based delegation models. This is accomplished by identifying the characteristics related to delegation, using these characteristics to generate possible delegation cases. Their work is different from ours in three aspects. First, it focuses on a simple delegation model supporting only flat roles and single step delegation. Some important features such as role hierarchies, constraints and revocations were not supported. By contrast, our work has analysed delegation authorization and revocation models with constraints involving role hierarchies. Second, they neither gave the definition of role-based delegation relation, which is a critical notion to the delegation model nor discussed the relationships among original user and delegated user. By contrast, the delegation framework in this chapter is based on original user and delegated user since the delegating relationship in this chapter has five components $((u, r), (u', r'), Cons)$ in which (u, r) is original user-role relationship and (u', r') be delegated user-role relationship. Third, they have not discussed group-based delegation, but we have analysed elements and functions in group delegation.

8.6   Conclusions

This chapter has discussed role-based delegation model and negative authorization for a solution of conflicting secure problems which may easy arise in distributed environment. We have analysed not only delegating framework including delegating authorization and revocation with constraints, but also group-based delegation. To provide a practical solution for the conflicting problem, we have analysed role hierarchies, the relationship of senior and junior role, and positive and negative authorizations. The work in this chapter has significantly extended previous work in several aspects, for example, the group-based delegation and negative authorizations. It also begins a new direction of negative authorizations.

8.7 Problems and Exercises

8.7.1 Problems

1. What is a Delegation between individuals, between individual and groups, and between groups to groups?
2. What are the possible constrains of delegations?
3. Negative authorizations are very important in system management, is that possible to have a negative authorization structure?

8.7.2 Exercises

1. Developing algorithms based on the framework and solution proposed in this chapter;
2. Developing a delegating revocation model including constraints, analysing revocation process.
3. Based on the developed model in the second exercise, analysing negative authorization.

References

1. Abadi, M., Burrows, M., Lampson, B., Plotkin, G.: A calculus for access control in distributed systems. ACM Trans. Program. Lang. Syst. **15**(4), 706–734 (1993)
2. Andreoli, J., Pacull, F., Pagani, D., Pareschi, R.: Multiparty negotiation of dynamic distributed object services. J. Sci. Comput. Program. **31**(2-3), 179–203 (1998)
3. Aura, T.: Distributed access-rights management with delegation certificates. In: Security Internet Programming, pp. 211–235 (1999)
4. Barka, E., Sandhu, R.: Framework for role-based delegation models and some extensions. In: Proceedings of the 16 Annual Computer Security Applications Conference, New Orleans, pp. 168–177 (2000a)
5. Barka, E., Sandhu, R.: Framework for role-based delegation models. In: Proceedings of the 23rd National Information Systems Security Conference, Baltimore, pp. 101–114 (2000b)
6. Barkley, J.F., Beznosov, K., Uppal, J.: Supporting relationships in access control using role based access control. In: Proceedings of the third ACM Workshop on Role Based Access Control, pp. 55–65 (1999)

7. Beam, C., Segev, A.: Electronic Catalogs and Negotiations. CITM Working Paper 96-WP-1016 (1996)
8. Bellare, M., Roga way, P.: Random oracles are practical: a paradigm for designing efficient protocols. In: Proceedings of the first ACM Conference on Computer and Communications Security, pp. 62–73. IEEE, New York (1993)
9. Bellare, M., Goldreich, O., Krawczyk, H.: Stateless evaluation of pseudorandom functions: Security beyond the birthday barrier. In: Advances in Cryptology—Crypto 99. Lectures Notes in Computer Science, vol. 1666. Springer, Berlin (1999)
10. Ben-Shaul, I., Gidron, Y., Holder, O. (eds.): A Negotiation Model for Dynamic Composition of Distributed Applications. Institute of Electrical and Electronics Engineers, Piscataway (1998)
11. Bertino, E., Bettini, C., Ferrari, E., Samarati, P.: An access control model supporting periodicity constraints and temporal reasoning. ACM Trans. Database Syst. 23(3), 231–285 (1998)
12. Blaze, M., Feigenbaum, J., Ioannidis, J., Keromytis, A.: The role of trust management in distributed system security. Secur. Int. Program., pp. 185–210 (1999)
13. Boyko, V., Peinado, M., Venkatesan, R.: Speeding up discrete log and factoring based schemes via precomputations. In: Advances in Cryptology—Eurocrypt'98. Lectures Notes in Computer Science, vol. 1807. Springer, Berlin (1998)
14. Canetti, R., Goldreich, O., Halevi, S.: The random oracle methodology. In: Proceedings of the 30th ACM STOC '98, pp. ,209–218. IEEE, New York (1998)
15. Canetti, R., Micciancio, D., Reingold, O.: Perfectly One-Way Probabilistic Hash Functions. In: Proceedings of the 30th ACM STOC '98. IEEE, New York (1998)
16. Cao, J., et al.: Towards secure xml document with usage control. In: Web Technologies Research and Development—APWeb 2005, pp. 296–307. Springer, Berlin (2005)
17. Chan, A., Frankel, Y., Tsiounis, Y.: An efficient off-line electronic cash scheme as secure as RSA, Research report nu-ccs-96-03. Northeastern University, Boston (1995)
18. Chaum, D.: An Introduction to e-cash, DigiCash (1995). http://www.digicash.com
19. Chaum, D., Van Antwerpen, H.: Undeniable signatures. In: Advances in Cryptology–Crypto89. Lectures Notes in Computer Science, vol. 435, pp. 212–216. Springer, Berlin (1990)
20. Chen, Z., Lee, M., Cheung, C.: A framework for mobile commerce. In: Proceedings of the Americas Conference on Information Systems 2001, E-Commerce: Wireless/Mobile. AISeL (2001)
21. Chenthara, S., et al.: Security and privacy-preserving challenges of e-health solutions in cloud computing. IEEE Access 7, 74361–74382 (2019)
22. David, F.F., Dennis, M.G., Nickilyn, L.: An examination of federal and commercial access control policy needs. In: NIST NCSC National Computer Security Conference, Baltimore, MD, pp. 107–116 (1993)
23. Dogac, A.: Survey of the Current State-of-the-Art in Electronic Commerce and Research Issues in Enabling Technologies. In: Proceeding of uro-Med Net 98 Conference, Electronic Commerce Track (1998)
24. ElGamal, T.: A public key cryptosystem and a signature scheme based on discrete logarithms. IEEE Trans. Inf. Theory IT-31(4), 469–472 (1985)
25. Eng, T., Okamoto, T.: Single-trem divisible electronic coins. In: Advances in cryptology–Eurocrypt'94. Lectures Notes in Computer Science, vol. 950, pp. 306–319. Springer, Berlin (1995)
26. Feinstein, H.L.: Final report: nist small business innovative research (SBIR) grant: role based access control: phase 1, technical report. In: SETA Corporation (1995)
27. Ferraiolo, D.F., Kuhn, D.R.: Role based access control. In: Proceedings of the 15th National Computer Security Conference, pp. 554–563 (1992). ferraiolo92rolebased.html
28. Ford, W., Baum, M.: Secure Electronic Commerce: Building the Infrastructure for Digital Signatures and Encryption. Prentice Hall PTR, Englewood Cliffs (1997)
29. Frankel, Y., Yiannis, T., Yung, M.: Indirect discourse proofs: achieving fair off-line electronic cash. In: Advances in cryptology—Asiacrypt'96. Lectures Notes in Computer Science, vol. 1163, pp. 286–300. Springer, Berlin (1996)

30. Franklin, M., Yung, M.: Secure and efficient off-line digital money. In: Proceedings of the Twentieth International Colloquium on Automata, Languages and Programming. Lectures Notes in Computer Science, vol. 700, pp. 265–276. Springer, Berlin (1993)

31. Gabber, E., Silberschatz, A.: Agora: a minimal distributed protocol for electronic commerce. In: The 2rd USENIX workshop on electronic commerce, Oakland, CA (1996)

32. Garfinkel, S., Spafford, G.: Web Security and Commerce Risks, Technologies, and Strategies. O'Reilly and Associates, New York (1997)

33. Goldreich, O., Krawczyk, H.: On the composition of zero-knowledge proof systems. SIAM J. Comput. 25(1):159–192 (1996)

34. Green, S., et al.: Software Agents: A review. Tcd-cs-1997-06, Trinity College Dublin and Broadcom Eireann Research, Ireland (1997)

35. Guttman, R.H., Maes, P.: Cooperative vs. competitive multi-agent negotiations in retail electronic commerce. In: Proceedings of the Second International Workshop on Cooperative information Agents (CIA'98)., Paris, France (1998)

36. Herzberg, A., Yochai, H.: Mini-Pay: Charging per Click on the Web (1996). http://www.ibm.net.il

37. Jansen, W., et al.: Security policy management for handheld devices. In: Proceedings of the 2003 International Conference on Security and Management (SAM'03) (2003)

38. Juels, A., Luby, M., Ostrovsky, R.: Security of blind digital signatures. In: Advances in Cryptology—Crypto 97. Lectures Notes in Computer Science, vol. 1294, pp. 150–164. Springer, Berlin (1997)

39. Kabir, E., et al.: Microaggregation sorting framework for k-anonymity statistical disclosure control in cloud computing. IEEE Trans. Cloud Comput. 8(2), 1–1 (2018)

40. Kabir, M., et al.: A novel statistical technique for intrusion detection systems. Future Gener. Comput. Syst. 79, 303–318 (2018)

41. Ketchpel, S.P., Garcia-Molina, H.: Making trust explicit in distributed commerce transactions. In: IEEE Proceedings of the 16th ICDCS, pp. 270–281 (1996)

42. Klusch, M.: Intelligent Information Agents: Agent-Based Information Discovery and Management on the Internet. Springer, Berlin (1998)

43. Lampson, B.W., Abadi, M., Burrows, M.L., Wobber, E.: Authentication in distributed systems: theory and practice. ACM Trans. Comput. Syst. 10(4), 265–310 (1992)

44. Li, N., Grosof, B.N.: A practically implementation and tractable delegation logic. In: IEEE Symposium on Security and Privacy, pp. 27–42 (2000)

45. Loudon, D., Della, B.: Consumer Behavior: Concepts and Applications Fourth Edition. McGraw-Hill, New York (1993)

46. Lynn, B., Xun, Y.: Off-line digital cash schemes providing untraceability, anonymity and change. Electron. Commerce Res. 19(10), 81–110 (2018)

47. Neubert, R., et al.: Virtual enterprises—challenges from a database persperctive. In: Proceedings of ADC'01, GoldCoast, Australia. IEEE, New York (2001)

48. Okamoto, T., Ohta, K.: Disposable zero-knowledge authentication and their applications to untraceable electronic cash. In: Advances in Cryptology–Crypto89 Lectures Notes in Computer Science, vol. 435, pp. 481–496. Springer, Berlin (1990)

49. Papazoglou, M., ATsalgatidou, A.: Special issue on information systems support for electronic commerce. Inf. Syst. 24(6), 425–427 (1999)

50. Pfitzmann, B., Waidner, M.: How to break and repair a 'provably secure' untraceable payment system. In: Advances in Cryptology—Crypto'91. Lectures Notes in Computer Science, vol. 576, pp. 338–350. Springer, Berlin (1992)

51. Pointcheval, D., Stern, J.: Security arguments for digital signatures and blind signatures . J. Cryptology 13(3), 361–396 (2000)

52. Poutanen, T., Hinton, H., Stumm, M.: Netcents: a lightweight protocol for secure micropayments. In: Proceedings of the 3rd USENIX Workshop on Electronic Commerce, Boston, Massachusetts (1998)

53. Rivest ,R.T.: The MD5 message digest algorithm. In: Internet RFC 1321 (1992)

54. Rohm, A.W., Pernul, G.: COPS: a model and infrastructure for secure and fair electronic markets. In: Proceedings of the 32nd Hawaii International Conference on System Sciences (HICSS-32). IEEE Computer Society, Hawaii (1999)

55. Sandhu, R.: Rational for the RBAC96 family of access control models. In: Proceedings of 1st ACM Workshop on Role-based Access Control, pp. 64–72. ACM, New York (1997)

56. Sandhu, R.: Role activation hierarchies. In: Proceedings of the Third ACM Workshop on Role Based Access Control, pp. 33–40. ACM, New York (1998)

57. Schnorr, C.P.: Efficient signature generation by smart cards. J. Cryptology 4(3), 161–174 (1991)

58. Shu, J., et al.: Privacy-preserving task recommendation Services for Crowdsourcing. IEEE Trans. Serv. Comput. (2018) https://doi.org/10.1109/TSC.2018.2791601

59. Simon, D.: Anonymous communication and anonymous cash. In: Advances in Cryptology—Crypto'96. Lectures Notes in Computer Science, vol. 1109, pp. 61–73. Springer, Berlin (1997)

60. Spegel, N., Rogers, B., Buckley, R.: Negotiation Theory and Techniques. In: Skills Series. Chatswood, N.S.W., Butterworths (1998)

61. Sun, L., et al.: Purpose based access control for privacy protection in e-healthcare services. JSW 7, 2443–2449 (2012)

62. Sun, X., et al.: An approximate microaggregation approach for microdata protection. Expert Syst. Appl. 39(2), 2211–2219 (2012)

63. Sun, X., et al.: Satisfying privacy requirements before data anonymization. Comput. J. 55(4), 422–437 (2012)

64. Sun, L., Wang, H.: A purpose-based access control in native xml databases. Concurrency Comput. Pract. Experience 24(10), 1154–1166 (2012)

65. Sun, L., Li, Y., Wang, H.: M-service and its framework. In: Proceedings of the 2005 Asia-Pacific Conference on Communications, pp. 837–841 (2005)

66. Timmers, P.: Global and Local in Electronic Commerce. In: Proceedings of EC-Web. Lectures Notes in Computer Science, London, vol. 1875. Springer, Berlin (2000)

67. Vimalachandran, P., et al.: Preserving patient-centred controls in electronic health record systems: a reliance-based model implication. In: Proceedings of the 2017 International Conference on Orange Technologies (ICOT), pp. 37–44 (2017)

68. Wang, H., et al.: Authorization algorithms for the mobility of user-role relationship. In: Proceedings of the Twenty-eighth Australasian Conference on Computer Science (ACSC '05), vol. 38, pp. 69–77. Australian Computer Society, Australia (2005)

69. Wang, H., et al.: Protecting outsourced data in cloud computing through access management. Concurrency Comput. Pract. Experience 28(3), 600–615 (2016)

70. Wang, Y., et al.: MTMR: Ensuring mapreduce computation integrity with merkle tree-based verifications. IEEE Trans. Big Data 4(3), 418–431 (2018)

71. Wang, H., et al.: Editorial: special issue on security and privacy in network computing. In: World Wide Web (2019)

72. Wang, H., Duan, T.: A signature scheme for security of e-commerce. Comput. Eng. 25, 79–80 (1999)

73. Wang, H., Zhang, Y.: A protocol for untraceable electronic cash. In Lu, H., Zhou, A. (eds.) Proceedings of the First International Conference on Web-Age Information Management. Lectures Notes in Computer Science, Shanghai, China, vol. 1846, pp. 189–197. Springer, Berlin (2000)

74. Wang, H., Zhang, Y.: Untraceable off-line electronic cash flow in e-commerce. In: Proceedings of the 24th Australian Computer Science Conference ACSC2001, GoldCoast, Australia, pp. 191–198. IEEE Computer Society, New York (2001)

75. Wang, H., Cao, J., Zhang, Y.: A consumer anonymity scalable payment scheme with role based access control. In: Proceedings of the 2nd International Conference on Web Information Systems Engineering (WISE01), Kyoto, Japan, pp. 53–62 (2001)

76. Wang, H., Cao, J., Zhang, Y.: A consumer scalable anonymity payment scheme with role based access control. In: Proceedings of the Second International Conference on Web Information Systems Engineering, vol. 1, pp. 53–62 (2001)

77. Wang, H., Cao, J., Kambayashi, Y.: Building a consumer anonymity scalable payment protocol for the internet purchases. In: Proceedings of the 12th International Workshop on Research Issues on Data Engineering: Engineering E-Commerce/E-Business Systems, San Jose, USA (2002)

78. Wang, H., Cao, J., Zhang, Y.: A flexible payment scheme and its role-based user-role assignment. In: Proceedings of the second International Workshop on Cooperative Internet Computing (CIC2002), Hong Kong, China, pp. 58–68 (2002)

79. Wang, H., Cao, J., Zhang, Y.: A flexible payment scheme and its user-role assignment. In: Chan, A., et al. (eds.) Cooperative Internet Computing, pp. 107–128. Kluwer Academic, Dordrecht (2002)

80. Wang, H., Cao, J., Zhang, Y.: Formal authorization allocation approaches for role-based access control based on relational algebra operations. In: Proceedings of the 3rd International Conference on Web Information Systems Engineering (WISE02), Singapore, pp. 301–312 (2002)

81. Wang, H., Cao, J., Zhang, Y.: Ticket-based service access scheme for mobile users. In: Proceedings of the Twenty-Fifth Australasian Computer Science Conference (ACSC2002). Monash University, Melbourne (2002)

82. Wang, H., Cao, J., Zhang, Y.: Formal authorization allocation approaches for permission-role assignments using relational algebra operations. In: Proceedings of the 14th Australian Database Conference ADC2003, Adelaide, Australia (2003)

83. Wang, H., Zhang, Y., Cao, J., Varadharajan, V.: Achieving secure and flexible m-services through tickets. In: IEEE Transactions System Man Cybernetics A Specification Issue M-Service, pp. 697–708 (2003)

84. Wang, H., Cao, J., Zhang, Y.: A flexible payment scheme and its role-based access control. IEEE Trans. Knowl. Data Eng. **17**(3), 425–436 (2005)

85. Wang, H., Sun, L., Zhang, Y., Cao, J.: Authorization Algorithms for the Mobility of User-Role Relationship. In: Proceedings of the 28th Australasian Computer Science Conference (ACSC2005), Newcastle, Australia, pp. 167–176 (2005)

86. Wang, H., Zhang, Z., Taleb, T.: Editorial: special issue on security and privacy of IoT. World Wide Web **21**(1), 1–6 (2018)

87. Wang, Z., Zhan, Z., Lin, Y., Yu, W., Wang, H., Kwong, S., Zhang, J.: Automatic niching differential evolution with contour prediction approach for multimodal optimization problems. IEEE Trans. Evol. Comput. **24**(1), 1–1 (2019)

88. Yacobi, Y.: Efficient electronic money. In: Advances in Cryptology–Asiacrypt'94. Lectures Notes in Computer Science, vol. 917, pp. 153–163. Springer, Berlin (1995)

89. Yao, W., Moody, K., Bacon, J.: A model of oasis role-based access control and its support for active security. In: Proceedings of ACM Symposium on Access Control Models and Technologies (SACMAT), Chantilly, VA, pp. 171–181 (2001)

90. Zhang, Y., Jia, X.: Transaction processing. Wiley Encycl. Electr. Electron. Eng. **22**, 298–311 (1999)

91. Zhang, L., Ahn, G., Chu, B.: A rule-based framework for role-based delegation. In: Proceedings of ACM Symposium on Access Control Models and Technologies (SACMAT 2001), Chantilly, VA, pp. 153–162 (2001)

92. Zhang, L., Ahn, G., Chu, B.: A role-based delegation framework for healthcare information systems. In: Proceedings of ACM Symposium on Access Control Models and Technologies (SACMAT 2002), Monterey, CA, pp. 125–134 (2002)

93. Zhang, F., Wang, Y., Wang, H.: Gradient correlation: Are ensemble classifiers more robust against evasion attacks in practical settings? In: Web Information Systems Engineering (WISE 2018), pp. 96–110. Springer, Cham (2018)

94. Zhang, Y., Shen, Y., Wang, H., Zhang, Y., Jiang, X.: On secure wireless communications for service oriented computing. IEEE Trans. Serv. Comput. **11**(2), 318–328 (2018)

Part IV
Ubiquitous Computing and Social Networks

This part includes two Chaps. 9 and 10. Chapter 9 focuses on ubiquitous computing and security challenges. The purpose of ubiquitous computing is anywhere and anytime access to information within computing infrastructures that is blended into a background and no longer be reminded. This ubiquitous computing poses new security challenges while the information can be accessed at anywhere and anytime because it may be applied by criminal users. Chapter 9 presents a usage control model to protect services and devices in ubiquitous computing environments, which allows the access restrictions directly on services and object documents.

As social network is a hot area and lots of privacy and security issues raised recently, Chap. 10 works in social network. A trust involved access management framework for supporting privacy preserving access control policies and mechanisms is proposed in Chap. 10. The mechanism enforces access policy to data containing personally identifiable information. The key component of the framework is an access control model that provides full support for expressing highly complex privacy-related policies, taking into account features like purposes and obligations.

Chapter 9
Access Control Management for Ubiquitous Computing

The purpose of ubiquitous computing is anywhere and anytime access to information within computing infrastructures that is blended into a background and no longer be reminded. This ubiquitous computing poses new security challenges while the information can be accessed at anywhere and anytime because it may be applied by criminal users. Additionally, the information may contain private information that cannot be shared by all user communities. Several approaches are developed to protect information for pervasive environments against malicious users. However, ad-hoc mechanisms or protocols are typically added in the approaches by compromising disorganized policies or additional components to protect from unauthorized access.

In this chapter, we present a usage control model to protect services and devices in ubiquitous computing environments, which allows the access restrictions directly on services and object documents. The model not only supports complex constraints for pervasive computing, such as services, devices and data types but also provides a mechanism to build rich reuse relationships between models and objects. Finally, comparisons with related works are analysed.

9.1 Introduction

Ubiquitous computing has been started to be investigated since 1993 by Weiser [104]. The widely used definition of ubiquitous computing is the method of enhancing computer use by making many computers available throughout the physical environment, but making them effectively invisible to the user. The major character of ubiquitous computing is to create a user centric and application oriented computing environment. Such environments are different from the traditional computing models since a physical space within the environments supported by associated hardware and software facilitates interactive information exchange between users

© Springer Nature Switzerland AG 2020
H. Wang et al., *Access Control Management in Cloud Environments*,
https://doi.org/10.1007/978-3-030-31729-4_9

and the space [16, 47, 95, 96]. The availability of cheap computing devices and wireless networks are making such spaces possible. A user does not require to log into a single personal computer as in traditional computing environments, but communicates with a variety of computing devices in the space. Scalable configuration is an important aspect in such space since the same space is often used for different tasks at different times. Contextual information, such as the current users in the space, or the current activity, is important for the configuration.

Resources and information in ubiquitous computing environments are shared by users, heterogeneous sensors and so on. Security makes it vital in the environments since contextual information such as sensor locations and applications become an integral part of the system authorization [24, 93, 96, 102]. On the other hand, a variety of applications and users interaction with the pervasive environment poses new security challenges to the traditional user-password approach for computer security [58, 88, 92, 101]. The heterogeneous devices and mobile users in such dynamic pervasive computing environments make security management difficult, especially the access to authorized users since it is a basic security requirement for guaranteeing user's privacy, information confidentiality, integrity and availability [44, 52, 69, 98].

The security research of ubiquitous computing and its applications are still in infant stage, but an active research area [31, 82, 110]. Several papers have analysed the security requirements for ubiquitous computing [53, 79, 82, 89, 100]. An active space is proposed in [79] which can be configured for different types of applications at different times. Role-based access control [80] techniques for easy administration of users and permissions are applied to create and enforce access control policies for different configurations of the active space. Through an example scenario, dynamic protection domains are built for the assignments of permissions to roles and roles to users based on context information. A security architecture is designed for a research project GAIA operation system [89]. The architecture provides dynamism and flexibility to manage the security concerns in such a computing system with physical spaces of hundreds of computational devices extending the user's view of the computational environment beyond the physical limitations of a traditional distributed system. A protocol is presented in [53] which preserves the privacy of users and keeps their communication anonymous. In this protocol, a "MIST" is created that can protect user's ID from the system and other users and users are able to enjoy seamless interaction with services and other entities within the ubiquitous computing environment.

An application of payment prototype in ubiquitous computing is analysed in [82]. Computational models of trust are proposed for use in pervasive environments for deciding whether or not customers are allowed to pay with an e-purse. Authors have built a scheme (and its prototype) that mitigates this kind of loss of privacy without forbidding the use of trust for smoothing payment by giving the opportunity to the user to divide trust (i.e. transactions) according to context.

There are several security issues that need to be addressed in the application of ubiquitous computing [14, 86, 90, 97]. In particular, the following requirements are critical to developing a secure and flexible access control architecture.

1. Access based on contextual information.
   Existing access approaches are developed in the context of traditional distributed and multi-user systems which specify the allowed accesses for users or subjects to resources or objects [3, 8, 35, 80, 81]. The users and objects in traditional systems are static, but in ubiquitous environments both subjects and objects may enter and leave the space dynamically. For instance, people have to use their membership number and password to login IEEE digital library; but it may not have user ID and password in ubiquitous environments. There is no mechanism for expressing other factors that may influence authorization.
2. Access control in a collaborative environment. Ubiquitous computing is often used for collaborative services, where many users work together to complete a task [40, 49, 73, 99]. An access control model in ubiquitous environments has to provide a secure collaboration structure for the users sharing of permissions in the collaborative task between dynamic users. For example, Tony as the director of project A wants to share full or part of permissions with Christine who is a member of the project B. How to organise this sharing process?
3. Decentralized administration. A physical space in ubiquitous computing is usually part of a larger system, and the access control policy may be organized by the administrators of the larger systems and the space.
4. Access for different users and devices. Ubiquitous computing may also be used for non-technical applications [79]. For example, customers have been checked by security systems in airport for safety issues where the customers do not know what are the systems and how they work. the Users in the pervasive environment may not have any special training and prefer the easy use of the devices in the environments.

The last requirement is about human computer interface which is beyond this chapter. We focus on the remaining three requirements. This chapter presents authorization models which adopt usage control to manage access to the space and secure architectures to perform the authorization models. Traditional access control has analyzed authorization decisions on a subject's access to target resources. "Obligations" are requirements that have to be followed by the subject for allowing accessing resources. "Conditions" are subject and object independent requirements that have to be passed. In ubiquitous environments, both users and objects are highly dynamic, obligations and conditions of new hosts are decision factors for the access management.

Traditional authorization decisions are generally made at the time of requests but do not consider ongoing controls for long access or for revocation [7, 27, 78]. The objects including devices in pervasive computing space are used by various users. There are complex relationships among users, objects, and arbitrary authorizations between users and objects. An object can be a device, a file, dynamically generated documents, and so on. Because of the complex ubiquitous environment, users are required to obey obligations and satisfy conditions and ongoing control with different security policies. Usage control [69] has been recognized as the next generation access control to be efficient in security administration. Authorizations, obligations and conditions are used to build a secure architecture. The ongoing control provides dynamic access verification for contextual information.

The remainder of this chapter is organized as follows: Sect. 9.2 presents usage control and ubiquitous computing model including the relationships between space objects and users, and space objects and applications. Three decision factors *Authorization, Obligation, Conditions* and Continuity properties *pre* and *ongoing* are introduced in this section. Section 9.3 develops authorization models with usage control for ubiquitous computing. It includes the procedures of *pre-Authorizations, ongoing-Authorizations, pre-Obligations, ongoing-Obligations, pre-Conditions* and *ongoing-Conditions*. Section 9.4 discusses how to build secure architectures for collaborations in distributed administration by using reference monitors in details. Section 9.5 compares our work with the previous work on pervasive computing security. The difference between this work from others is presented. Section 9.6 concludes the paper and outlines our future work.

9.2 Related Technologies

9.2.1 Usage Control

There are eight components: subjects, subject attributes, objects, object attributes, rights, authorizations, obligations, and conditions in usage control model [46, 61, 62, 69] (see Fig. 9.1). Subjects and objects are familiar concepts from the traditional access control, and are used in their familiar sense in this chapter [23, 28, 68]. A right represents access of a subject to an object, such as read or write. The existence of the right is determined when the access is attempted by the subject. The usage decision functions indicated in Fig. 9.1 make this determination based on subject attributes, object attributes, authorizations, obligations and conditions at the time of usage requests.

Subject and object attributes can be used during the access decision process [57, 64, 84, 91]. Examples of subject attributes are identities, group names, roles, memberships, credits, etc. Examples of object attributes are security labels, ownerships, classes, access control lists, etc. In an on-line shop a price could be an object attribute, for instance, the book Harry Potter is priced at $20 for a 'read' right and priced at $1000 price for a 'resell' right.

Authorizations, obligations and conditions are decision factors used by decision functions to determine whether a subject should be allowed to access an object [55, 102, 105, 112]. Authorizations are based on subject and object attributes and the specific right. Authorization is usually required prior to the access, but in addition it is possible to require ongoing authorization during the access, e.g., a certificate revocation list (CRL) may be periodically checked while the access is in progress. An access is immediately revoked if the relevant certificate appears on the CRL.

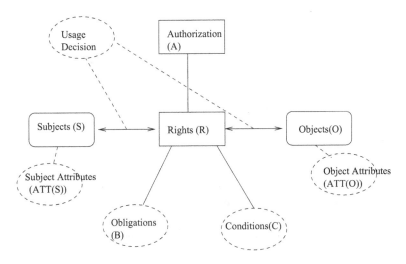

Fig. 9.1 Components of model

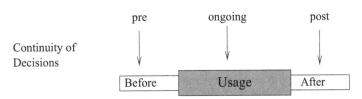

Fig. 9.2 Continuity properties

Authorizations may require updates on subject and object attributes. These updates can be either 'pre', 'ongoing', or 'post' that are called continuity properties shown in Fig. 9.2.

Conditions are decision factors that depend on environmental and system-oriented requirements. For example, IEEE member can access full papers in the IEEE digital library. They can also include the security status of the system, such as low level, normal, high alert, etc.

As discussed above, continuity is another decision factor as shown in Fig. 9.2. In traditional access control, authorization is assumed to be done before access is allowed (pre). However, the dynamic changes of contextual information in ubiquitous computing environments, it is quite reasonable to extend this for continuous enforcement by evaluating usage requirements throughout usages (ongoing) [5, 13, 17, 21].

9.2.2   Ubiquitous Computing Model

The basic concept in usage control is the access right to an object, which is called usage. Users are assigned usage when they enter a special space of ubiquitous computing environments, and access policies for services in the space are generated by assigning access rights to users. The objects in pervasive environments are services, devices, dynamic generated objects. The access rights, for example, to a device are the set of operations that can be performed by users and to a service are the set of operations that can be applied by users [43, 67, 71, 75].

We introduce the concept of a space object, with associated space rights, which are permissions to resources within the space [2, 36, 41, 77]. Access control policies for the space are described by space objects and rights, and this simplifies the task of the space administrator. The main features of ubiquitous computing are to create a user centric and application oriented computing environment. Therefore, we consider users and applications in this pervasive environments. Users who want to access the space have their accounts created by system administrators and are assigned a usage of access space objects based on their rights and responsibilities within the space. When a user with a usage enters to a space, the user is automatically assigned a space object, which is restricted to a set of rights that make sense within the space. Figure 9.3 shows how users are assigned to space usages.

For instance, a space administrator could create a usage of interview-room that is allowed to setup the space as an interview room, and decide that only users of human resource offices could be assigned this usage. An officer in human resource may have many other permissions in the entire system, but when the office is assigned into the usage of interview-room, it is only allowed rights related to that task [1, 70, 83].

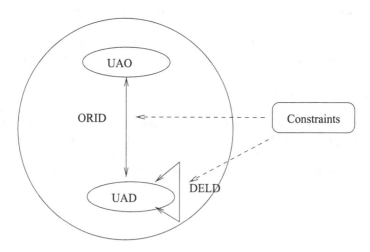

Fig. 9.3 User—space usage assignments

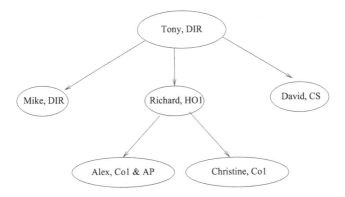

Fig. 9.4 Application—space usage assignments

A user's rights in a space are a subset of his rights within the entire system, it means that rights assigned to a space object are always a part of rights to the corresponding system.

Application usages are used to specify access control policies for applications [30, 76, 111, 113]. These application usages are mapped into space usages by the space administrator. For example, as shown in Fig. 9.4, an application for an interview may have two application usages: committee members and candidates. These two usages are decided with the functions of different participants in the application. Candidates should access to a presentation device and committee members must have read access to the slides presented. The specific rights that a candidate requires depends on the devices in the space that are running the application. Application usages and users are assigned by the space administrator to appropriate space objects and their access rights, and access control within a space is only enforced in terms of these space usages.

The protection domains in our model are defined by authorization approaches in the space. When the space switches modes, new objects may be dynamically created, based on the context of the space, and rights automatically assigned to them.

9.3 Authorization Models

We now discuss authorization models for space objects adopting usage control in this section [29, 45, 85, 109]. Based on three decision factors: authorizations, obligations, and conditions, we develop a family of core models for usage control. By core models, we mean that they focus on the enforcement process and do not include administrative issues. We assume there exists a usage request on space object. Decision-making can be done either before (pre) or during (ongoing) exercise of the requested right. Decision-making after the usage has no influence on the decision of current usage. Based on these criteria, we have 6 possible cases as a core model for usage control in the space: pre-Authorizations, ongoing-Authorizations, pre-Obligations, ongoing-Obligations, pre-Conditions and ongoing-Conditions. Depending on the access requirements on pervasive computing environments in real world, it is possible to utilize more than one case.

For simplicity we consider only the pure cases consisting of *Authorizations, Obligations* or *Conditions* alone with *pre* or *ongoing* decisions only. We focus on developing comprehensive usage control models for the space objects. Next we present usage control models (UCM) with different pure cases.

A. UCM_{preA}: **Pre-authorizations Model**

In an UCM_{preA} model, the decision process is performed before access is allowed. The UCM_{preA} model has the following components:

1. $S, Obj, App, ObjR, AppR, ATT(S), ATT(Obj), ATT(App)$ and usage decision Boolean functions $preA, preA_1$ on Obj for S and App, respectively.

   Where $S, Obj, App, ObjR, AppR$ represent Subject, Space object, Application in a pervasive computing environment and Rights required on the object and on the application (e.g. read, write) respectively. $ATT(S)$, $ATT(Obj), ATT(App)$ represent attributes of subjects, objects and applications in the environments respectively. $preA$ and $preA_1$ are predicates about authorization functions. Fox example, when users enter the space, $preA$, or $preA_1$ is a function on users' account and password (subject attributes) or service tickets, objects and rights (read, write or resell) that are used to check whether users can access the objects with the rights or not,

2. $allowed(S, Obj, ObjR) \Rightarrow preA(ATT(S), ATT(Obj), ObjR)$,

   Where $A \Rightarrow B$ means B is a necessary condition for A. This predicate indicates that if subject S is allowed to access object Obj with right $ObjR$ then the indicated condition $preA$ must be true.

3. $allowed(App, Obj, ObjR, AppR) \Rightarrow$
   $preA_1(ATT(App), ATT(Obj), ObjR, AppR)$.

   The $allowed(App, Obj, ObjR, AppR)$ predicate indicates that if application App is allowed to map a space object Obj with right $ObjR$ then the decision function $preA_1$ is true.

The UCM_{preA} model provides an authorization method on whether a subject can access an object or not, and whether an application can map to an object or not. The $allowed(S, Obj, ObjR)$ predicate shows that subject S can access some part of information in the space. At this stage, private information in the ubiquitous computing environments is restricted.

B. UCM_{onA}: **Ongoing-Authorizations Model**

An UCM_{onA} model is used to check ongoing authorizations during access processes. The UCM_{onA} model has the following components:

1. $S, Obj, App, ObjR, AppR, ATT(S), ATT(Obj), ATT(App)$ as before, and ongoing usage decision functions onA on Obj (Space object) and onA_1 on both

Obj and App, onA is used to check whether S can continue to access the object or not, and onA_1 is to check whether App can continue to map the object or not.

2. $allowed(S, Obj, ObjR) \Rightarrow true$,

   This is a prerequisite for ongoing authorization on Obj.

3. $allowed(App, Obj, ObjR, AppR) \Rightarrow true$,

   This is a prerequisite for ongoing authorization on Obj.

4. $stopped(S, Obj, ObjR) \Leftarrow \neg onA(ATT(S), ATT(Obj), ObjR)$,

   The access of subject S to Obj is terminated if the ongoing authorization onA is failed.

5. $stopped(App, Obj, ObjR, AppR) \Leftarrow \neg onA_1(ATT(App), ATT(Obj),$
   $ObjR, AppR)$.

   The map of App to Obj is terminated if the ongoing authorization onA_1 is failed.

UCM_{onA} introduces the onA, onA_1 predicate instead of $preA$, $preA_1$, $allowed(S, Obj, ObjR)$ and $allowed(App, Obj, ObjR, AppR)$ are required to be $true$, otherwise ongoing authorization should not be initiated. Ongoing authorization is active throughout the usage of the requested right, and the onA and onA_1 predicates are repeatedly checked for continuation access. These checks are performed periodically based on time or event. The model does not specify exactly how this should be done. When attributes are changed and requirements are no longer satisfied, $stopped$ procedures are performed. We use $stopped(S, Obj, ObjR)$ and $stopped(App, Obj, ObjR, AppR)$ to indicate that rights $ObjR$ of subject S on object Obj and $AppR$ of application App are revoked and the ongoing access terminated. For example, suppose only one candidate can access the presentation device in an interview room simultaneously. If another person requests access and passed the pre-authorization, the user with the earlier time access is terminated. While this is a case of ongoing authorizations, it is important that the certificate should be evaluated in a pre decision.

C. UCM_{preB}: Pre-obligations Model

UCM_{preB} introduces pre-obligations that have to be fulfilled before access is permitted [12, 33, 37, 38]. Examples of pre-obligations are requiring a student to register by filling forms before accessing an education website, requiring the student to click the ACCEPT box on a license agreement to run some software such as "$Slide-show$" and "$Sample-demo$", etc. The pre-obligation action may perform on a different object (e.g., register, license agreement) than the object that the user is trying to access (e.g., Slide-show). It means that the pre-obligation action may be done by some other subject. Hence obligation subjects, objects, and actions are added in the following UCM_{preB} model.

For simplicity, the following model is described for subject and object only. It can directly be used for any part of restricted information in the space.

The UCM_{preB} model has the following components:

1. $S, Obj, ObjR, ATT(S), ATT(Obj)$ as before,

2. OBS, OBO, and OBA represent obligation subjects, objects, and actions, respectively; decision function $preObfilled : OBS \times OBO \times OBA \rightarrow \{true, false\}$,

   As mentioned above, subject S and access object may be different from OBS and OBO, hence, we separately describe them. The function $preObfilled(s, xd, r)$ is used to check if obligations are obeyed or not.

3. $allowed(S, Obj, ObjR) \Rightarrow preObfilled(S, Obj, ObjR)$.

   The $preObfilled(S, Obj, ObjR)$ function must be true if S is allowed to access Obj with right $ObjR$.

The model indicates that obligations have to be fulfilled before S can access Obj. Note that each obligation has to be true if there are more than two obligations.

D. UCM_{onB}: **Ongoing-Obligations Model**

Obligations are required to fulfil in UCM_{onB} models while rights are exercised [65, 72, 107, 108]. Ongoing-obligations may have to be fulfilled periodically or continuously. For example, a user may have to open a security policy window at least every 30 min. Alternatively, a user may have to leave the window active all the time with inconvenience. The model concerns obligations that have to be fulfilled.

The UCM_{onB} model has the following components:

1. $S, Obj, ObjR, ATT(S), ATT(Obj)$ as before,
2. OBS, OBO, and OBA represent obligation subjects, objects, and actions, respectively; an ongoing decision function $onObfilled : OBS \times OBO \times OBA \rightarrow \{true, false\}$,

   The ongoing function $preObfilled(S, Obj, ObjR)$ is used to check if obligations are continually obeyed or not.

3. $allowed(S, Obj, ObjR) = true$,

   A prerequisite for UCM_{onB}. It means S is accessing Obj.

4. $stopped(S, Obj, ObjR) \Leftarrow \neg onObfilled(S, Obj, ObjR)$.

Where $stopped(S, Obj, ObjR)$ indicates that the access of S on Obj with $ObjR$ is revoked if the ongoing obligations are failed.

E. $UCM_{(preC)}$: **pre-Conditions Model**

As described earlier, conditions are not directly related to subjects and objects since they define environmental and system restrictions. We focus on this model for subject and space object. The model can also be used for restricted device in the space.

The UCM_{preC} model has the following components:

1. $S, Obj, ObjR, ATT(S), ATT(Obj)$ as before,
2. $preCON$(a set of pre-conditions), verify conditions function $preConSatisfied : preCON \rightarrow \{true, false\}$. The function $preCon$ $Satisfied$ is used to check whether the pre-conditions are satisfied or not.
3. $preC(S, Obj, ObjR) = \bigwedge_{preCon_i \in preCON} preConSatisfied(preCon_i)$.

   All pre-conditions have to be checked if there are more than two conditions.
4. $allowed(S, Obj, ObjR) \Rightarrow preC(S, Obj, ObjR)$.

The third component indicates situations with more than two conditions and the $allowed(S, Obj, ObjR)$ expresses that all conditions have to be satisfied before access is approved.

F. UCM_{onC}: Ongoing-Conditions Model

UCM_{onC} model requires conditions to be satisfied while rights are in active use. For example, *realOne player* does not work when Windows XP system works on safe mode.

The UCM_{onC} model has the following components:

1. $S, Obj, ObjR, ATT(S), ATT(Obj)$ as before,
2. $onCON$(a set of ongoing conditions), verify ongoing conditions function
   $onConSatisfied : onCON \rightarrow \{true, false\}$,
   The function $onConSatisfied$ is used to check whether ongoing conditions are satisfied or not.
3. $onC(S, Obj, ObjR) = \bigwedge_{onCon_i \in onCON} onConSatisfied(onCon_i)$,
   All ongoing conditions are required to check.
4. $allowed(S, Obj, ObjR) = true$,
   A prerequisite for UCM_{onC}.
5. $stopped(S, Obj, ObjR) \Leftarrow \neg onC(S, Obj, ObjR)$.

$stopped(S, Obj, ObjR)$ indicates that the access of S on Obj is stopped if ongoing conditions are not satisfied. In practice, the above six models may need to be combined for an access control. The following algorithm is based on these models and introduces how to manage an ubiquitous computing access control when a user (subject) applies to access an object (Obj) with right $ObjR$ (Table 9.1).

We obtain an authorization method for users access objects in the space by checking users' (subjects') authorizations, obligations and conditions with continuity properties. The algorithm provides a solution of the first two requirements described in Sect. 9.1. For other two requirements, we analyse security architectures in the next section in which both client and server sides is required to be monitored. The results of the security architectures are applied for decentralized administration and for various users as well [6, 54, 66, 87].

9.4 Security Architecture

In this section, we discuss architecture solutions for ubiquitous computing access control based on reference monitors. Reference monitors have been discussed extensively in access control community [4, 59, 60]. Subjects can access objects only through the reference monitor since it provides control mechanisms on access space objects such as services and devices in the space.

Table 9.1 Authorization algorithm

Authorization Algorithm:

Input: Access request: (S, ObjR, Obj)

Output: result.xml

Method:

// Verify UCM_preA:

1) **if** $preA(ATT(S), ATT(Obj), ObjR) = false$

// The process in pre-Authorization is not successful

2) ACCESS denied;

3) **endif**

// Verify UCM_onA:

4) **if** $preA(ATT(S), ATT(Obj), ObjR) = false$

// The process in pre-Authorization is failed, do not need further verification.

5) Application denied;

6) **endif**

7) $onA(ATT(S), ATT(Obj), ObjR) = false$

// The process in ongoing-Authorization is not successful

8) ACCESS stopped;

// Verify UCM_preB:

9) **if** $preObfill(S, Obj, ObjR) = false$

// Obligations are not fulfilled and pre-Obligation is not passed.

10) ACCESS denied;

11) **endif**

//Verify UCM_onB:

12) **if** $allowed(S, Obj, ObjR) = false$

13) Stop verification.

14) **endif**

15) **if** $onObfill(S, Obj, ObjR) = false$

// Obligations are not continually fulfilled and on-Obligation is not passed.

16) ACCESS is stopped;

17) **endif**

// Verify UCM_preC:

18) **if** $preC(S, Obj, ObjR) = false$

// Conditions are not satisfied and pre-Condition verification is not passed.

19) ACCESS denied;

20) **endif**

//Verify UCM_onC:

21) **if** $allowed(S, Obj, ObjR) = false$

22) Stop verification.

23) **endif**

24) **if** $onC(S, Obj, ObjR) = false$

// Conditions are not continually satisfied and on-Condition is not passed.

25) ACCESS is stopped;

26) **endif**

27) ACCESS Obj is permitted;

28) Output result.xml;

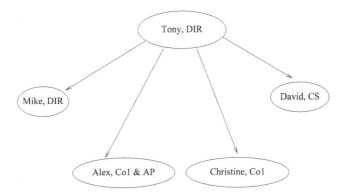

Fig. 9.5 Space access reference monitor

9.4.1 Structure of Reference Monitor

ISO has published a standard for access control framework by using reference monitors [51]. Based on the standard, a reference monitor consists of Usage Decision Facility (UDF) and Usage Enforcement Facility (UEF) as shown in Fig. 9.5. Each facility includes several functional modules.

UEF includes *Customization, Monitor and Update modules* and UDF includes *authorization, conditions and obligations decision modules.* When a subject sends an access request through *Customization module* to *Authorization module, Authorization module* verifies authorization process and checks whether the request is allowed or not. It may return yes or no or metadata information of the authorization result. This metadata information can be used for approved access on objects by *Customization module* in UEF. *Condition module* is used to make a decision for whether the conditional requirements are satisfied or not. *Obligation module* is applied to verify whether obligations have been performed or not before or during the requested usage. When any obligation is changed, it must be monitored by *monitor module* and the result has to be resolved by *Update module* in UEF. Applications of these modules rely on ubiquitous computing requirements.

9.4.2 Architectures

There are two kinds of reference monitors: Server-side (or Space-side) Reference Monitor (SRM), and Client-side Reference Monitor (CRM). Servers provide objects such as services and devices in the space and clients require access to the objects [18, 20, 21, 26]. Like a traditional reference monitor, an SRM works in server space environment and manages access to objects in the space. On the other hand, a CRM works in the client environment and controls access to the objects when it works as a server for other clients. For example, the client acts as a server when a file or a document is delegated or disseminated to other users. SRM and CRM can coexist within a system. For real implementations, both CRM and SRM should be used for better security. We analyse architectures according to reference monitors on space (server) side only (SRM-only), on client side only (CRM-only) and on both server and client sides (SRM and CRM).

SRM-Only Architecture

A system with SRM-only facilitates works on server side only to control subjects access objects. In this case an object may or may not be stored in client-side. If the object (e.g. a file) is allowed to reside in client-side, it means the saved client copy of the object is no longer valid and doesn't have to be controlled. It can be used and changed freely at client-side [19, 56, 63, 106]. For example, a cookie file can be saved at a client's local machine for his records and the server doesn't care how the copy will be used by the client since the system keeps original account information safe. However if the file or some parts of the document has to be protected and controlled centrally, the document must remain at server-side storage and is not allowed to be stored in client-side. This is the main topics of traditional access control and trust management system [10, 15, 48, 94].

CRM-Only Architecture

No reference monitor exists on the server-side in a system with CRM-only environment. Rather, a reference monitor exists at the client system for controlling usage of delegated or disseminated objects. In this environment objects can be stored either centrally or locally. The usage of the objects saved at the client-side on behalf of a server is still under the control of CRM. Distributed ubiquitous computing environments are associated with certain usage rules and users may need to prove they have sufficient credentials to access the document [12, 22, 38, 50].

SRM and CRM Architecture

With both SRM to CRM, this architecture can provide a comprehensive access control. SRM may be used for distribution related control while CRM can be used for object delegation or dissemination. For instance, in SRM, objects can be pre-customized for distribution. The pre-customized objects can be further controlled and customized by CRM. As a result, server can restrict or eliminate unnecessary exposure of objects that do not have to be distributed. If a user requests certain object document that includes some secret information, SRM can pre-customize the requested objects before distribution such that the distributed version of the objects doesn't include any secret information [32, 34, 44, 74]. If the document cannot be delegated or disseminated, the CRM at client side can do this work.

The SRM and CRM architecture provides a solution for restricting access to objects and protecting the objects from malicious delegation and dissemination in collaborative and distributed environments.

9.5 Comparisons

Related work has been done on Context-Aware Dynamic Access Control for Pervasive Applications [110], Role-based access control in ambient and remote space [103], Access Control for Active Spaces [79], and Coordinated access controlnext term with temporal and spatial constraints on mobile execution in coalition environments [39].

Zhang and Parashar [110] proposed a context-based access control model for ubiquitous computing through dynamic role-based access control (DRBAC) model which is an extension of role-based access control (RBAC). DRBAC borrowed the definitions of users, roles, permissions and role hierarchy structure from RBAC, and dynamically adjusts two key requirements based on context information: (1) A user's access privileges must change when the user's context changes, and (2) A resource must adjust its access permission when its system information changes. The operation of the model was illustrated using a sample application scenario of smart building. Compared to traditional access control mechanisms, the DRBAC model provides improved security for pervasive applications. Their work is different from ours in two aspects. First, it focused on the updating of user-role assignments and permission-role assignments based on the context. Therefore, it only discussed the management in server side and without any management about how to control the object accessed by users. By contrast, our work provides a rich variety of options that can deal with objects in both server and user sides. Second, role-based access control was used in DRBAC which must be combined with feasible authentication mechanisms to secure pervasive applications in the real world. In our scheme, a security architecture has been designed to support the authorization processes such as pre-Authorizations, pre-Obligations and pre-Conditions as well as ongoing-Authorizations, ongoing-Obligations, and ongoing-Conditions.

Role-based access control in ambient and remote space was described by H. Wedde and M. Lischka in 2004 [103]. Their work was based on a distributed and layered RBAC approach that allows at the same time for (1) more efficient evaluation, (2) avoiding evaluation circles, due to the layered trust level and access rules, and (3) more flexibility and more efficient administration. This chapter restricts itself to presenting a distributed and location- dependent RBAC approach which is multilayered. The main difference between our scheme and the work in [103] is that we focus on a systematic level for objects in pervasive computing by using usage control model and consider a solution for different kinds of authorizations, whereas the latter is a discussion of providing a secure infrastructure with efficient evaluation and negotiation to objects.

G. Sampemane, P. Naldurg and R. Campbell presented an access control system that automates the creation and enforcement of access control policies for different configurations of an Active Space [79]. The Active Space is a physical space augmented with heterogeneous computing and communication devices along with supporting software infrastructure. The system explicitly recognizes different modes of cooperation between groups of users, and the dependence between physical and virtual aspects of security in Active Spaces. The access model in the system provides support for both discretionary and mandatory access control policies, and uses role-based access control techniques for easy administration of users and permissions. However, our work substantially differs from that access control system. Differences arise in the following three aspects. First, their system is based on role based access control (RBAC) and hence it focuses on permissions-role assignment, objects hierarchies and constrains. By comparison, based on usage control, we have analyzed the characteristics of various access authorizations and presented detailed models for different kinds of authorizations. Second, the approach addresses the problems of Active Spaces in the server side. It does not discuss a secure architecture for objects. By contrast, we have discussed a security architecture for access control by considering both server and client sides. Finally, their approach is based on RBAC, and hence does not mention how to update users' permissions on objects when their conditions or obligations have changed. It is an important state for objects in an Active Space since users always alter their conditions or obligations. By contrast, users in our scheme have to pass pre-Authorizations and ongoing-Authorizations as well as pre-Obligations, pre-Conditions and ongoing-Obligations and ongoing-Conditions. It means our approach is much more powerful in dynamic environment.

Song Fu and Cheng-Zhong Xu have presented a coordinated access control model with temporal and spatial constraints for secure mobile execution in grids [39]. Various access patterns of mobile entities are expressed by the SRAL language. The specification of a security policy with temporal and spatial constraints is included in a text file protected by cryptography. Authors are going to investigate the privilege delegation among mobile entities and trust management in their coordinated access control system. Their work are different from the work in this chapter at the following two aspects. First, their work focused on the problem in mobile environment since the dynamic mobile environment poses new challenges to access control. Resource sharing in the grid coalition environment creates certain temporal and spatial requirements for access by mobile entities. They formalized the mobile execution of grid entities by using the mobile code model. By contrast, we focus on ubiquitous computing that is more wider area than the mobile environment, and challenges and a security architecture solution have been proposed in the paper. Second, their work is a practical work that has been demonstrated by a constraint language *SRAC*. *SRAC* is defined to specify spatial constraints for shared resource. To prove the concept and technical feasibility of the coordinated access control model, the language has implemented it in a mobile agent system. We have theoretically analysed detailed secure characteristics in ubiquitous computing and have built various authorizations, obligations and conditions.

9.6   Conclusions

This chapter has discussed access management and architectures for pervasive computing by using usage control. We have analysed not only decision factors in usage control such as authorizations, obligations and conditions, but also the continuity. Different kinds of models are built for ubiquitous computing. To protect objects from malicious delegation and dissemination in collaborative and distributed management, we have analysed reference monitors on both server and client sides and obtained several secure architecture solutions. The work in this chapter has significantly extended previous work in several aspects, for example, the ongoing continuity for authorizations, obligations and conditions. These methods can be used to control objects in a dynamic environment since they provide a robust access control for ubiquitous computing environments and can protect sensitive messages from dissemination. It also begins a new application with usage control.

9.7   Problems and Exercises

9.7.1   Problems

1. Secure XML documents with usage control: XML Web Service is a platform-independent Web application that accepts requests from different systems on the Internet and can involve a range of web technologies such as XML [11], SOAP [9], WSDL[25] and HTTP [42]. XML is used to store and exchange data in the Internet that may include private message of customers. For example, the following XML document displays customer's information.

   XML document not only shows the contents of data but also the constraints and relationships between data. In Table 9.2, the element *customerInfo* includes *ssn, name* and *creditCardInfo* sub-elements. The sub-element *ssn* is a simple type while sub-elements *name* and *creditCardInfo* are combined with their own sub-elements. An XML document may be generated from various resources with varying security requirements due to its ability to express complex relationship between data. Alternatively, a user may like to limit access to particular parts of an XML document. In the example above, Tony objects that everyone can read all information on his Mastercard. Another example may happen in an University, when an XML document can consist of information from applications among several faculties and multiple databases. When an internal or external user accesses this document, his/her access permission has to be monitored according to security

Table 9.2 XML document example

```
<?xml version="1.0" encoding="UTF-8"? >
<customerInfo xmlns="http://www.hotel.com/CustomerInfo" gender="Male">
<ssn>123-45-6789</ssn >
<name>
<firstName> Tony </firstName >
<lastName> Wang > </lastName >
</name >
<creditCardInfo >
<type >Master card </type >
<cardNo >88888888888888888 </cardNo >
<expireDate >12/05 </expireDate >
<nameOnCard > Tony Wang </nameOnCard >
</creditCardInfo >
</customerInfo >
```

policies in all these faculties and databases. These examples show that secure XML document is an significant topic.

There are several security issues that need to be addressed in the application of XML documents. In particular, the following problems are critical to developing a secure and flexible access control architecture.

1. Restricting access to XML documents to authorized users.
2. Protecting XML documents from malicious dissemination.
3. What are the challenges to apply RBAC to ubiquitous computing environment?

9.7.2 Exercises

1. Developing algorithms with *XML* based on the models and architectures proposed in this chapter;
2. Analysing applications of the developed algorithms in a real example.

References

1. Alqhatani, A., Lipford, H.: "There is nothing that i need to keep secret": sharing practices and concerns of wearable fitness data. In: Proceedings of the Fifteenth Symposium on Usable Privacy and Security (SOUPS 2019). USENIX Association, Santa Clara (2019)
2. Andreoli, J., Pacull, F., Pagani, D., Pareschi R.: Multiparty negotiation of dynamic distributed object services. J. Sci. Comput. Program. **31**, 2–3 (1998)

3. Barkley, J.F., Beznosov, K., Uppal, J.: Supporting relationships in access control using role based access control. In: Proceedings of the Third ACM Workshop on Role Based Access Control, pp. 55–65 (1999)

4. Beam, C., Segev, A.: Electronic Catalogs and Negotiations. CITM Working Paper 96-WP-1016 (1996)

5. Bellare, M., Roga way, P.: Random oracles are practical: a paradigm for designing efficient protocols. In: First ACM Conference on Computer and Communications Security, pp. 62–73. IEEE, New York (1993)

6. Ben-Shaul, I., Gidron, Y., Holder, O. (eds.): A Negotiation Model for Dynamic Composition of Distributed Applications. Institute of Electrical and Electronics Engineers, Piscataway (1998)

7. Bertino, E.,Castano, S., Ferrari, E., Mesiti, M.: Controlled access and dissemination of xml documents. In: Proceedings of the Second International Workshop on Web Information and Data Management, pp. 22–27. ACM, New York (1999)

8. Bertino, E., Castano, S., Ferrari, E., Mesiti, M.: Specifying and enforcing access control policies for XML document sources. World Wide Web **3**, 139–151 (2000)

9. Box, D.: Simple Object Access Protocol (SOAP) 1.1. World Wide Web Consortium (W3C), Cambridge, (2000)

10. Boyko, V., Peinado, M., Venkatesan, R.: Speeding up discrete log and factoring based schemes via precomputations. In: Advances in Cryptology—Eurocrypt'98. Lectures Notes in Computer Science, vol. 1807. Springer, Berlin (1998)

11. Bray, T., Paoli, J., Sperberg, M., Maler, E.: Extensible Markup Language (XML) 1.1, 2nd ed. World Wide Web Consortium (W3C), Cambridge (2000)

12. Canetti, R., Goldreich, O., Halevi, S.: The random oracle methodology. In: Proceedings of the 30th ACM STOC '98, pp. 209–218. IEEE, New York (1998)

13. Canetti, R., Micciancio, D., Reingold, O.: Perfectly One-Way Probabilistic Hash Functions. In: Proceedings of the 30th ACM STOC '98. IEEE, New York (1998)

14. Cao, J., et al.: Towards secure xml document with usage control. In: Web Technologies Research and Development—APWeb 2005, pp. 296–307. Springer, Berlin (2005)

15. Chan, A., Frankel, Y., Tsiounis, Y.: An efficient off-line electronic cash scheme as secure as RSA. In: Research report nu-ccs-96-03. Northeastern University, Boston (1995)

16. Chang, B., et al.: Active security management based on secure zone cooperation. Future Gener. Comput. Syst. **20**(2), 283–293 (2004)

17. Chaum, D.: Blind signature for untraceable payments. In: Advances in Cryptology—Crypto 82, pp. 199–203. Plenum Press, New York (1983)

18. Chaum, D. (ed.): An Introduction to e–cash, DigiCash (1995). http://www.digicash.com

19. Chaum, D.: An Introduction to e-cash, DigiCash (1995). http://www.digicash.com

20. Chaum, D., Van Antwerpen, H.: Undeniable signatures. In: Advances in Cryptology–Crypto89. Lectures Notes in Computer Science, vol. 435, pp. 212–216. Springer, Berlin (1990)

21. Chaum, D., Fiat, A., Naor, M.: Untraceable electronic cash. In: Advances in Cryptology—Crypto 88. Lectures Notes in Computer Science, vol. 403, pp. 319–327. Springer, Berlin (1990)

22. Chen, Z., et al.: Distributed individuals for multiple peaks: a novel differential evolution for multimodal optimization problems. IEEE Trans. Evol. Comput. **99**, 1–1 (2019)

23. Chen, Z., Lee, M., Cheung, C.: A framework for mobile commerce. In: Proceedings of the Americas Conference on Information Systems 2001, E-Commerce: Wireless/Mobile. AISeL (2001)

24. Chenthara, S., et al.: Security and privacy-preserving challenges of e-health solutions in cloud computing. IEEE Access **7**, 74361–74382 (2019)

25. Chinnici, R., Gudgin, M., Moreau, J., Weerawarana S.: Web Services Description Language (WSDL) 1.2. World Wide Web Consortium (W3C), Cambridge (2002)

26. Cox, B., Tygar, J.D., Sirbu, M.: Netbill security and transaction protocol. In: The first USENIX Workshop on Electronic Commerce, New York (1995)

27. Damiani, E., Sabrina, D., Paraboschi, S., Samarati, P.: Fine grained access control for soap e-services. In: Proceedings of the tenth international conference on World Wide Web, pp. 504–513. ACM, New York (2001)

28. Dini, G.: A secure and available electronic voting service for a large-scale distributed system. Future Gener. Comput. Syst. **19**(1), 69–85 (2003). Selected papers of the 29th SPEEDUP workshop on distributed computing and high-speed networks, 22–23 March 2001, Bern, Switzerland

29. Dogac, A.: Survey of the current state-of-the-art in electronic commerce and research issues in enabling technologies. In: Proceeding of uro-Med Net 98 Conference, Electronic Commerce Track (1998)

30. Du, J., et al.: Feature selection for helpfulness prediction of online product reviews: an empirical study. PLOS ONE **14**, e0226902 (2019)

31. Edwards, W., Newman, M., Sedivy, J.: Building the ubiquitous computing user experience. In: CHI '01: CHI '01 extended abstracts on Human factors in computing systems, pp. 501–502. ACM Press, New York (2001)

32. ElGamal, T.: A public key cryptosystem and a signature scheme based on discrete logarithms. IEEE Trans. Inf. Theory **IT-31**(4), 469–472 (1985)

33. Eng, T., Okamoto, T.: Single-trem divisible electronic coins. In: Advances in cryptology–Eurocrypt'94. Lectures Notes in Computer Science, vol. 950, pp. 306–319. Springer, Berlin (1995)

34. Ferraiolo, D.F., Kuhn, D.R.: Role based access control. In: Proceedings of the 15th National Computer Security Conference, pp. 554–563 (1992). ferraiolo92rolebased.html

35. Ferraiolo, D.F., Barkley, J.F., Kuhn, D.R.: Role-based access control model and reference implementation within a corporate intranet. In: TISSEC, vol. 2, pp. 34–64 (1999)

36. Ford, W., Baum, M.: Secure electronic commerce: Building the Infrastructure for Digital Signatures and Encryption. Prentice Hall PTR, Englewood (1997)

37. Frankel, Y., Yiannis, T., Yung, M.: Indirect discourse proofs: achieving fair off-line electronic cash. In: Advances in cryptology—Asiacrypt'96. Lectures Notes in Computer Science, vol. 1163, pp. 286–300. Springer, Berlin (1996)

38. Franklin, M., Yung, M.: Secure and efficient off-line digital money. In: Proceedings of the Twentieth International Colloquium on Automata, Languages and Programming. Lectures Notes in Computer Science, vol. 700, pp. 265–276. Springer, Berlin (1993)

39. Fu, S., Xu, C.: Coordinated access control with temporal and spatial constraints on mobile execution in coalition environments. Future Gener. Comput. Syst. **23**(6), 804–815 (2007)

40. Gabber, E., Silberschatz, A.: Agora: a minimal distributed protocol for electronic commerce. In: The 2rd USENIX workshop on electronic commerce, Oakland, CA (1996)

41. Garfinkel, S., Spafford, G.: Web Security and Commerce Risks, Technologies, and Strategies. O'Reilly and Associates, New York (1997)

42. Gettys, J., Mogul, J., Frystyk, H., Masinter, L., Leach, P., Berners-Lee, T.: Hypertext Transfer Protocol - http/1.1 (1999). http://www.ietf.org/rfc/rfc2616.txt

43. Goldreich, O., Krawczyk, H.: On the composition of zero-knowledge proof systems. SIAM J. Comput. **25**(1), 159–192 (1996)

44. Goldschlag, D., Reed, M., Syverson, P.: Onion routing for anonymous and private Internet connections. Commun. ACM **24**(2), 39–41 (1999)

45. Green, S., et al.: Software Agents: A review. Tcd-cs-1997-06, Trinity College Dublin and Broadcom Eireann Research, Ireland (1997)

46. Guan, S., Wang, T., Ong S.: Migration control for mobile agents based on passport and visa. Future Gener. Comput. Syst. **19**, 173–186 (2003)

47. Guttman, R.H., Maes, P.: Cooperative vs. Competitive Multi-Agent Negotiations in Retail Electronic Commerce. In: Proceedings of the Second International Workshop on Cooperative information Agents (CIA'98), Paris, France (1998)

48. Han, W., et al.: DTC: Transfer learning for commonsense machine comprehension. Neurocomputing **396**, 102–112 (2019)

49. Herzberg, A., Yochai, H.: Mini-Pay: Charging per Click on the Web (1996). http://www.ibm. net.il

50. Huang, T., et al.: A niching memetic algorithm for multi-solution traveling salesman problem. IEEE Trans. Evol. Comput. **24**(3), 1–1 (2019)

51. ISO: Security frameworks for open systems: Access control framework. Technical report, ISO/IEC 10181-3 (1996)

52. Jajodia, S., Samarati, P., Subrahmanian, V., Bertino, E.: A unified framework for enforcing multiple access control policies. In: Proceedings of the 1997 ACM SIGMOD international conference on Management of data, pp. 474–485. ACM, New York (1997)

53. JAl-Muhtadi, J., Campbell, R., Kapadia, A., Mickunas, M., Yi, S.: Routing through the mist: Privacy preserving communication in ubiquitous computing environments. In: ICDCS '02: Proceedings of the 22 nd International Conference on Distributed Computing Systems (ICDCS'02), p. 74. IEEE Computer Society, Washington (2002)

54. Jansen, W., et al.: Security policy management for handheld devices. In: Proceedings of the 2003 International Conference on Security and Management (SAM'03) (2003)

55. Jordi, P. et al.: Distributed access control with blockchain. CoRR, abs/(1901)03568 (2019)

56. Juels, A., Luby, M., Ostrovsky, R.: Security of blind digital signatures. In: Advances in Cryptology—Crypto 97. Lectures Notes in Computer Science, vol. 1294, pp. 150–164. Springer, Berlin (1997)

57. Kabir, E., et al.: Microaggregation sorting framework for K-anonymity statistical disclosure control in cloud computing. IEEE Transactions on Cloud Computing. **8**(2), 408–417 (2020)

58. Kabir, M., et al.: A novel statistical technique for intrusion detection systems. Future Gener. Comput. Syst. **79**, 303–318 (2018)

59. Ketchpel, S.P., Garcia-Molina, H.: Making Trust Explicit in Distributed Commerce Transactions. In: IEEE Proceedings of the 16th ICDCS, pp. 270–281 (1996)

60. Klusch, M.: Intelligent Information Agents: Agent-Based Information Discovery and Management on the Internet. Springer, Berlin (1998)

61. Laccetti, G., Schmid, G.: A framework model for grid security. Future Gener. Comput. Syst. **23**(5), 702–713 (2007)

62. Li, Q., Atluri, V.: Concept-level access control for the semantic web. In: Proceedings of the 2003 ACM workshop on XML security, pp. 94–103. ACM, New York (2003)

63. Loudon, D., Della, B.: CONSUMER BEHAVIOR: Concepts and Applications Fourth Edition. McGraw-Hill, New York (1993)

64. Batten, L., Yi, X.: Off-line digital cash schemes providing untraceability, anonymity and change. Electron. Commer. Res. **19**(1), 81–110 (2019)

65. MastercardVisa, (ed.): SET 1.0—Secure electronic transaction specification (1997). http:// www.mastercard.com/set.html

66. Neubert, R., et al.: Virtual enterprises—challenges from a database persperctive. In: Proceedings of ADC'01, GoldCoast, Australia. IEEE, New York (2001)

67. Okamoto, T., Ohta, K.: Disposable zero-knowledge authentication and their applications to untraceable electronic cash. In: Advances in Cryptology–Crypto89. Lectures Notes in Computer Science, vol. 435, pp. 481–496. Springer, New York (1990)

68. Papazoglou, M., ATsalgatidou, A.: Special issue on information systems support for electronic commerce. Inf. Syst. **24**(6), 425–427 (1999)

69. Park, J., Sandhu, R.: Towards usage control models: beyond traditional access control. In: Proceedings of the Seventh ACM Symposium on Access Control Models and Technologies, pp. 57–64. ACM, New York (2002)

70. Peng, M., et al.: Pattern filtering attention for distant supervised relation extraction via online clustering. In: Web Information Systems Engineering—WISE 2019, pp. 310–325. Springer, Cham (2019)

71. Pfitzmann, B., Waidner, M.: How to break and repair a 'provably secure' untraceable payment system. In: Advances in Cryptology—Crypto'91. Lectures Notes in Computer Science, vol. 576, pp. 338–350. Springer, Berlin (1992)

72. Pointcheval, D.: Self-scrambling anonymizers. In: Proceedings of Financial Cryptography, Anguilla, British West Indies. Springer, Berlin (2000)

73. Pointcheval, D., Stern, J.: Security arguments for digital signatures and blind signatures. J. Cryptology **13**(3), 361–396 (2000)
74. Poutanen, T., Hinton, H., Stumm, M.: Netcents: a lightweight protocol for secure micro-payments. In: Proceedings of the 3rd USENIX Workshop on Electronic Commerce, Boston, Massachusetts (1998)
75. Rabin, M.: Digital Signatures, Foundations of secure communication. Academic Press, New York (1978)
76. Rasool, R., et al.: Cyberpulse: a machine learning based link flooding attack mitigation system for software defined networks. IEEE Access **7**, 34885–34899 (2019)
77. Rohm, A.W., Pernul, G.: COPS: A Model and Infrastructure for Secure and Fair Electronic Markets. In: Proceedings of the 32nd Hawaii International Conference on System Sciences (HICSS-32). IEEE Computer Society, Hawaii (1999)
78. Sabrina, D.: An authorization model for temporal xml documents. In: Proceedings of the 2002 ACM symposium on Applied computing, pp. 1088–(1093). ACM, New York (2002)
79. Sampemane, G., Naldurg, P., Campbell, R.: Access control for active spaces. In: ACSAC '02: Proceedings of the 18th Annual Computer Security Applications Conference, Washington, DC, USA, p. 343. IEEE Computer Society, New York (2002)
80. Sandhu, R.: Role activation hierarchies. In: Proceedings of the Third ACM Workshop on Role Based Access Control, pp. 33–40. ACM, New York (1998)
81. Schnorr, C.P.: Efficient signature generation by smart cards. J. cryptology **4**(3), 161–174 (1991)
82. Seigneur, J., Jensen, C.: Trust enhanced ubiquitous payment without too much privacy loss. In: SAC '04: Proceedings of the 2004 ACM symposium on Applied computing, pp. 1593–1599. ACM, New York (2004)
83. Shenoy, J., et al. Jive: Spatially-constrained encryption key sharing using visible light communication. In: Proceedings of the 16th EAI International Conference on Mobile and Ubiquitous Systems: Computing, Networking and Services (2019)
84. Shu, J., et al.: Privacy-preserving task recommendation Services for Crowdsourcing. IEEE Trans. Serv. Comput. (2018). https://doi.org/10.1109/TSC.2018.2791601
85. Spegel, N., Rogers, B., Buckley, R.: Negotiation Theory and Techniques. Skills Series. Butterworths, London (1998)
86. Sun, L., Li, Y., Wang, H.: M-service and its framework. In: Proceedings of the 2005 Asia-Pacific Conference on Communications, pp. 837–841 (2005)
87. Timmers, P.: Global and local in electronic commerce. In: Proceedings of EC-Web. Lectures Notes in Computer Science, London, vol. 1875. Springer, New York (2000)
88. Vimalachandran, P., et al.: Preserving patient-centred controls in electronic health record systems: a reliance-based model implication. In: Proceedings of the 2017 International Conference on Orange Technologies (ICOT), pp. 37–44 (2017)
89. Viswanathan, P., Gill, B., Campbell, R.: Security architecture in gaia. Technical report, Champaign, IL, USA (2001)
90. Wang, H., et al.: Authorization algorithms for the mobility of user-role relationship. In: Proceedings of the Twenty-eighth Australasian Conference on Computer Science (ACSC '05), vol. 38, pp. 69–77. Australian Computer Society, New York (2005)
91. Wang, H., et al.: Protecting outsourced data in cloud computing through access management. Concurrency Comput. Pract. Experience **28**(3), 600–615 (2016)
92. Wang, Y., et al.: MTMR: Ensuring mapreduce computation integrity with merkle tree-based verifications. IEEE Trans. Big Data **4**(3), 418–431 (2018)
93. Wang, H., et al.: Editorial: special issue on security and privacy in network computing. World Wide Web **23**(2), 951–957 (2019)
94. Wang, G., et al.: Incorporating word embeddings into topic modeling of short text. Knowl. Inf. Syst. **61**(2), 1123–1145 (2019)
95. Wang, H., Cao, J., Zhang, Y.: Formal authorization allocation approaches for permission-role assignments using relational algebra operations. In: Proceedings of the 14th Australian Database Conference ADC2003, Adelaide, Australia (2003)

96. Wang, H., Zhang, Y., Cao, J., Varadharajan, V.: Achieving secure and flexible m-services through tickets. In: IEEE Transaction System Man, Cybernetics, A Special Issue M-Service, pp. 697–708 (2003)

97. Wang, H., Cao, J., Zhang, Y.: A flexible payment scheme and its role-based access control. IEEE Trans. Knowl. Data Eng. **17**(3), 425–436 (2005)

98. Wang, H., Cao, J., Zhang, Y.: A flexible payment scheme and its role based access control. IEEE Trans. Knowl. Data Eng. **17**(3), 425–436 (2005)

99. Wang, H., Li, J., Addie, R., Dekeyser, S., Watson R.: A framework for role-based group delegation in distributed environment. In: Proceedings of the 29th Australasian Computer Science Conference. Australian Computer Society, New York (2006)

100. Wang, H., Zhang, Y., Cao, J.: Ubiquitous computing environments and its usage access control. In: Proceedings of the 1st International Conference on Scalable Information Systems (InfoScale '06). ACM, New York (2006)

101. Wang, H., Zhang, Z., Taleb, T.: Editorial: special issue on security and privacy of IoT. World Wide Web **21**(1), 1–6 (2018)

102. Wang, Z., Zhan, Z., Lin, Y., Yu, W., Wang, H., Kwong, S., Zhang, J.: Automatic niching differential evolution with contour prediction approach for multimodal optimization problems. IEEE Trans. Evol. Comput. **24**(1), 114–128 (2019)

103. Wedde, H., Lischka, M.: Role-based access control in ambient and remote space. In: SACMAT '04: Proceedings of the Ninth ACM Symposium on Access Control Models and Technologies, pp. 21–30. ACM, New York (2004)

104. Weiser, M.: Hot topics-ubiquitous computing. Computer **26**(10), 71–72 (1993)

105. Xiao, Y., Jia, Y., Liu, C., Cheng, X., Yu, J., Lv, W.: Edge computing security: State of the art and challenges. Proc. IEEE **107**(8), 1608–1631 (2019)

106. Yacobi, Y.: Efficient electronic money. In: Advances in Cryptology–Asiacrypt'94. Lectures Notes in Computer Science, vol. 917, pp. 153–163. Springer, Brlin (1995)

107. Yiannis, T.: Fair off-line cash made easy. In: Advances in Cryptology–Asiacrypt'98. Lectures Notes in Computer Science, vol. 1346, pp. 240–252. Springer, Berlin (1998)

108. Yiannis, T., Yung, M.: On the security of ElGamal-based encryption. In: International Workshop on Practice and Theory in Public Key Cryptography (PKC '98). Lectures Notes in Computer Science, vol. 1346. Springer, Yokohama (1998)

109. Zhang, Y., Jia, X.: Transaction processing. Wiley Encyclopedia of Electrical and Electronics Eng. **22**, 298–311 (1999)

110. Zhang, G., Parashar, M.: Context-aware dynamic access control for pervasive applications. In: CND'04: Proceedings of the Communication Networks and Distributed Systems Modeling and Simulation Conference, pp. 21–30. Society for Modeling and Simulation International, New York (2004)

111. Zhang, F., Wang, Y., Wang, H.: Gradient correlation: are ensemble classifiers more robust against evasion attacks in practical settings? In: Web Information Systems Engineering (WISE 2018), pp. 96–110. Springer, Cham (2018)

112. Zhang, Y., Shen, Y., Wang, H., Zhang, Y., Jiang, X.: On secure wireless communications for service oriented computing. IEEE Trans. Serv. Comput. **11**(2), 318–328 (2018)

113. Zhang, Y., Gong, Y., Gao, Y., Wang, H., Zhang, J.: Parameter-free voronoi neighborhood for evolutionary multimodal optimization. IEEE Trans. Evol. Comput. **24**(2), 335-349 (2019)

Chapter 10
Trust-Based Access Control Management in Collaborative Open Social Networks

This chapter proposes a trust involved access management framework for supporting privacy preserving access control policies and mechanisms. The mechanism enforces access policy to data containing personally identifiable information. The key component of the framework is an access control model that provides full support for expressing highly complex privacy-related policies, taking into account features like purposes and obligations. A policy refers to an access right that a subject can have on an object, based on relationship, trust, purpose and obligations. The structure of purpose involved access control policy is studied and the authorization approaches are discussed including positive authorization and negative authorizations. Finally a discussion of our work in comparison with other access control and frameworks such as *EPAL* is discussed.

10.1 Introduction

Social networks have received dramatic interests in research and development due to the global applications. One principle of participating web-based social network (*WBSN*) is to share and exchange information with other users including strangers [17]. For example, Facebook (www.facebook.com) has more than 350 million active users who are able to publish resources and to record and/or establish relationships with other users including how much they trust people.

As the number of users and the number of sites themselves explode, securing individuals privacy to avoid threats such as misuse becomes an increasingly important issue [40]. An example of misuse is that users happen to share various types of sensitive data which trigger undesired consequences of job firing (Popkin, H.: Twitter Gets you Fired in 140 Characters or Less (March 23, 2009), http://www.msnbc.msn.com/id/29796962). Indeed, Facebook receives the complaints of informing users with the latest personal information related to their online friends.

© Springer Nature Switzerland AG 2020
H. Wang et al., *Access Control Management in Cloud Environments*,
https://doi.org/10.1007/978-3-030-31729-4_10

These complaints result in an online petition, signed by over 700,000 users, demanding the company to stop this service. The fact that the sensitive message is collected and shared without any consent or awareness violates privacy for many people [16, 64, 74].

The importance for protecting privacy has been recognized since it becomes a major concern for both customers and enterprises in today's corporate marketing strategies [11, 53, 61, 67]. This raises challenging questions and problems regarding the use and protection of private message. One principle of protecting private information is based on who is allowed to access private information and for what purpose [36]. For example, personal information provided by patients to hospitals may only be used with record purpose, not with advertising purpose. Purposes are reasons for data collection and data access. The motivations of adopting purpose are (1) the fundamental policies for private information concern with which data object is used for what purposes (for example, customers' age and email address are used for the purpose of marketing analysis), and (2) customers agreed data usage varies from individual to individual. Information technology provides the capability to store various types of users' information required during their business activities. Indeed, it was shown that 97% of web sites were collecting at least one type of identifying information such as name, e-mail address, or postal address of consumers [39].

Data privacy is defined by policies describing to whom the data may be disclosed and what are the purposes of using the data [1, 62, 68, 69]. For example, a policy may specify that price of an air ticket from an agent may be disclosed, but only with "opted-in" customers, or that the price will be disclosed unless the agent has specifically "opted-out" of this default. While there is recent work on defining languages for specifying privacy policies [https:www.w3.org/Submission/2003/SUBM-EPAL-20031110, https:www.w3.org/P3P/], access control mechanisms for enforcing such policies have not been investigated [34, 41] analysed a conditional privacy management with role based access control, which supports expressive condition languages and flexible relations among permission assignments for complex privacy policies. But many interested problems remain, for example, developing a formal method to describe and manage access control policy with purposes. As stated by Adams and Sasse [2]: "Most invasions of privacy are not intentional but due to designers' inability to anticipate how this data could be used, by whom, and how this might affect users"?

This chapter develops a trust-based framework for information sharing in social networks [36, 38, 55, 72]. Trust is a key role when performing access control in social network since it is one of the fundamental parameters to decide whom can share information, from whom can accept information [23]. A trust model for *WBSN* should keep into account that, in this scenario, the semantics of trust should be also related the compliance with the specified access control policies and privacy preferences. Another important point is how to compute trust [35, 37, 54]. Indeed, it is quite evident that assigning a wrong trust value to a potential malicious user could imply unauthorized releasing of information or unauthorized disclosure of personal relationships. Liu and Terzi [40] analysed trust involved privacy scores of users in

Table 10.1 WBSNs comparative information

WBSN	Purpose	Relatinoship	Trust	Protection
FaceBook	General	Friend	None	Basic
RepCheck	Reputation	Generic	Personal, business	None
Myspace	General	Friend	None	Basic
LinkedIn	Business	Various (colleague, classmate, friend)	Business	Limited length connection

Online Social Networks. Another important point is how to compute trust. Indeed, it is quite evident that assigning a wrong trust value to a potential malicious user could imply unauthorized releasing of information or unauthorized disclosure of personal relationships. Therefore, some mechanisms and strategies should be devised to help in trust computation. The area of trust modeling, computation and protection in collaborative communities is new and therefore a lot of research issues still remain open. We adopt the trust definition and do not discuss trust models since it is out of the scope of the paper.

Privacy preserving approaches, such as password, have nearly always been available for standard web pages, blogs, webmail, and bulletin boards [7, 20, 51, 52]. However, as aspects of Web 2.0 continue to be adopted, the ability to protect information within the same page will be required. For example, a blogger might maintain a single blog, but wish to control access to particular entries based on the reader's relationship to the blogger. The ability to perform this type of fine-grained access control will not only become essential in the world of Web 2.0, it will largely determine the success or failure of many social, political, and economic realms in the Web 2.0 world. Access control and the related privacy issues is a new research area and only few work have been done in this field. Indeed, most of today WBNSs enforce access control according to a very simple model (referred as basic in Table 10.1), according to which the owner of a resource has only 3 options wrt its protection: (1) defining it as public, (2) defining it as private, or (3) defining it as accessible only by his/her direct neighbors. Examples of *WBSN*s adopting this model are FaceBook, MySpace, and LinkedIn. Some *WBSN*s enforce variants of the basic model, in order to give more flexibility, but the principle is the same. All these approaches have the advantage of being easy to be implemented, but they lack in flexibility in terms of the access control requirements that can be specified [19, 45, 50, 76]. This chapter will design a fine-grained access control scheme for social network.

The remainder of this chapter is organized as follows: Sect. 10.2 presents the motivations behind our work in this chapter. We find that both purpose-based access control for privacy preserving in social network and the analysis of access control policies have not been widely studied in the literature. Section 10.3 proposes a trust involved purpose based access framework which includes detailed information of trust, relation type, purposes and so on. Section 10.4 provides access control policy structure and authorization models as well as illustrates the impact of generating a new access policy through examples. The access control authorizations are analysed in Sect. 10.5 while Sect. 10.6 compares the work in this chapter and related previous work, the comparisons demonstrate the significance of the work in this chapter. Finally, the conclusions and further work are given in Sect. 10.7.

10.2   Motivations

The direct victims of privacy violations are consumers, but many enterprises and organizations are deeply concerned about privacy issues as well [18, 24, 29, 60]. By demonstrating good privacy practices, many companies, such as FaceBook and MySpace, try to build solid trust with customers, thereby attracting more customers. This chapter provides theory and a practical demonstration of how to protect reliably and strongly private information in *WBSN*.

Access control in WBSNs is a new research area. Research on security in *WBSN* has mainly focused on privacy-preserving techniques to allow statistical analysis on social network data without compromising the privacy of members [12, 30, 66].

Suppose, for instance, that Alice is the owner of a set of resources RA, and that she wishes to share them with some of her friends. In this simple scenario, traditional access control like *RBAC* fit very well [25, 46, 70, 71]. Indeed, since an access control policy basically states who can access what and under which modes, and since Alice knows a priori her friends, she is able to set up a set of authorizations to properly grant the access only to (a subset of) her friends. However, if we consider a more general scenario, the traditional way of specifying policies is not enough. For instance, let us suppose that Alice decides to make available her resources not only to her friends, but also to their friends, the friends of their friends, and so on. The problem is that Alice may not know a priori all her possible indirect friends, and thus she may not be able to specify a set of access control policies applying to them. Moreover, if we consider that relationships among users of a *WBSN* could change dynamically over time, this solution implies a complex policy management. An access control model for *WBSNs* should therefore take into account that usually a node in the network wishes to share its data with other nodes on the basis of both direct and indirect relationships existing among them. Thus the data owner can control the release of their personal information in the same manner he would control it in the analog world–based on their relationship with the data receiver rather than the receiver's role. One result is that people can hold multiple relationships with someone (e.g., both sister and close friend), and can even be present in what might be considered to be conflicting relationships (e.g., a mother might generally be considered to be a friend, yet a daughter might not want to reveal everything she reveals to her friends to her mother as well). Some social networking sites, such as FaceBook (http://www.facebook.com), have started to develop these forms of control, however the relationships that they can represent are still limited [5, 8, 31, 59].

Let us consider again the *WBSN* depicted in Fig. 10.1, and assume once again that Alice wishes to share her data with some of her direct and indirect friends. In

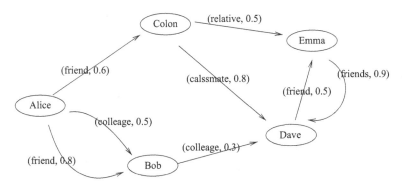

Fig. 10.1 Type and trust level of relationships

particular, she wants to grant access to Bob (B) and Colon who are direct friends of hers. She wants to allow also Dave to access her data, even if Alice does not know them directly, because they are direct friends of Bob and Colon. In contrast, Alice may not want to give Emma (E) access to her resources, since she does not know how Dave chooses his friends. In conclusion, when considering a *WBSN*, the length of the path connecting two nodes (i.e., the depth of a relationship) is a relevant information for access control purposes. Thus, an access control model for *WBSNs* should make a user able to state in a policy not only the type but also the maximum depth of a relationship.

Although the notions of depth and trust may be related, they are not equivalent [47, 48, 63]. For instance, let us suppose that Alice does not trust Bob very much, and that, in contrast, she considers Colon highly trustworthy. In this case, the depth of the relationship is the same for both Bob and Colon, but the trust level is different. Therefore, access control policies should support also constraints on the minimum trust level of a relationship.

Social network security is becoming a more and more relevant research topic [12, 28, 49], two position articles recognize the relevance of addressing access control issues in *WBSNs*. In particular, Gates [22] describes relationship-based access control as one of the new security paradigms that addresses the requirements of the so-called Web 2.0. Whereas Hart et al. [26] identify content-based and relationship-based access control as the key requirements for protecting *WBSN* resources which makes use of relationship information available in *WBSNs* for denoting authorized subjects. However, those articles do not address access control and privacy requirements enforcement, an issue that is fundamental to make any security solution usable in real-world scenarios. For example, only direct relationships are considered in Hart et al. [26], and the notion of trust level is not taken into account as one of the possible parameters to be used in access authorizations. As far as privacy is concerned, research on this issue is currently focusing mainly on privacy preserving data mining techniques that allow social network analysis without disclosing possible sensitive information.

Bader et al. [3] adopt a multi-level security approach, where trust is the only parameter used to determine the security level of both users and resources. More precisely, to each user u a reputation value $r(u)$ is assigned, computed as the average of the trust ratings specified for him/her by other users in the system. Furthermore, Bader et al. [3] consider only direct trust relationships, whereas we consider (a) both direct and indirect relationships, and (b) both purpose and obligations. This has the advantage of giving resource owners the ability to specify more flexible policies, making them able to better denote the constraints to be satisfied by users in order to access a resource. Kruk et al. [33], is primarily a FOAF-based distributed identity management system for social networks, where access rights and trust delegation management are provided as additional services. Kruk et al. [33] discuss only generic relationships, corresponding to the ones modeled by the foaf. Finally, Kruk et al. [33] do not discuss the case of multiple policies associated with the same resource, whereas our model supports the possibility of combining policies by using the AND and OR Boolean operators.

The important techniques for private information happen within distributed systems specifically tailored to support privacy policies [27, 42, 56, 58], such as the well known P3P standard [www.w3.org/P3P/]. In particular, Agrawal et al. [43] introduced the concept of Hippocratic databases, incorporating privacy protection in relational database systems. An important feature of their work is that it uses some privacy metadata, consisting of privacy policies and privacy authorizations stored in privacy-policies tables and privacy-authorizations tables respectively. However, they neither discussed the concepts of purpose with hierarchy structure, nor the prohibition of purpose and association of purposes and data elements. LeFevre et al. [34] presented an approach to enforce privacy policy in database systems. They introduced two models of cell level limited disclosure enforcement, namely table semantics and query semantics, but did not consider access control management. Ni et al. [41] analysed a role-based access model for purpose-based privacy protection, but their work did not consider usage access management and the conflicts between purposes in policies. The development of access technology entails addressing many challenging issues, ranging from modeling to architectures, and may lead to the next-generation of access management. This chapter develops purpose based access technology for privacy violation challenges including complex policy structured models with access control.

This chapter focuses exclusively on how to specify and enforce policies for authorizing purpose-based access management using a rule-based language [21, 65, 72, 75]. We propose a comprehensive framework for purpose and data management where purposes are organized in a hierarchy. In our approach each data element is associated with a set of purposes, as opposed to a single security level in traditional secure applications. Also, the purposes form a hierarchy and can vary dynamically. These requirements are more complex than those concerning traditional secure applications. To provide sufficient functions with the framework, this chapter analyses the explicit prohibition of purpose and the association of a set of purposes with access control policies. This kind of analysis for purpose-based usage control for privacy preserving has not been studied [9, 10, 57, 73].

10.3   A Trust Based Access Framework

This section analyses the terminology included in a trust-based access framework *TBAF*. *TBAF* includes privacy-aware access control and supports trust-based information sharing and granularity of data labeling by introducing personal relationship, sticky policy in social network, fine-grained format and trust modeling [13–15, 32].

Trust in a person is a commitment to an action based on a belief that the future actions of that person will lead to a good outcome [23, 44]. For instance, Alice trusts Bob regarding email if she chooses to read a message (commits to an action) that Bob sends her (based on her belief that Bob will not waste her time). There are three main properties of trust that are relevant to the development of algorithms for computing it, namely, transitivity, asymmetry, and personalization.

The primary property of trust that is used in our work is transitivity. Trust is not perfectly transitive in the mathematical sense, that is, if Alice highly trusts Bob, and Bob highly trusts Chuck, it does not always and exactly follow that Alice will highly trust Chuck. It is also important to note the asymmetry of trust. For two people involved in a relationship, trust is not necessarily identical in both directions. For example, employees typically say they trust their supervisors more than the supervisors trust the employees [36, 51]. One property of trust that is important in social networks and has been frequently overlooked in the past is the personalization of trust. Trust is inherently a personal opinion. Two people often have very different opinions about the trustworthiness of the same person [35, 37, 38, 57].

A trust relationship is usually modeled as a directed edge, connecting two entities A and B, labeled with information stating whether, and, possibly, how much, A considers B trustworthy. The directed edge models a specific property of trust, i.e., its asymmetric nature. In fact, if A trusts B, it does not necessary follow that B trusts A.

The data structure of *WBSN* is a tuple *(VSN, ESN, RTSN, ϕ_{SN})*, where RTSN is the set of supported relationship types, *VSN* and $ESN \subseteq VSN \times VSN \times RTSN$ are, respectively, the nodes and edges of a directed labeled graph $(VSN, ESN, RTSN)$, whereas $\phi_{SN} : ESN \rightarrow [0, 1]$ is a function assigning to each edge $e \in ESN$ a trust level T, which is a rational number in the range [0, 1].

An edge $e = vv' \in ESN$ expresses that node v has established a relationship of a given type rt, $e \in RTSN$ with node v'. We say that such relationship, denoted $rt(v, v')$, is direct, since v and v' are directly connected by edge e. As an example, consider the *WBSN* depicted in Fig. 10.1, where *Alice (A)* has a direct relationship of type *friend* and trust level 0.6 with *Colon (C)*.

Note that, in a given *WBSN*, multiple paths may exist between two nodes, denoting the same type of relationship. For instance, in the *WBSN* depicted in Fig. 10.1, three paths exist from Alice to Dave (D) denoting a relationship of type friendOf—namely, ABD, ACD, and ACED. Trust computation is more accurate when only the shortest paths are taken into account. As such, we adopt this approach throughout the project. Therefore, we extend the notion of relationship by saying that a relationship $rt(v, v')$ is the set of all the shortest paths from v to v' consisting of edges labeled with relationship type rt.

A possible solution is to adopt the same rational applied in the real world: the trust value assigned to a person is estimated on the basis of his/her reputation, which can be assessed taking into account the person behavior. Indeed, it is a matter of fact that people assign to a person with unfair behavior a bad reputation and, as a consequence, a low level of trust. Thus, a possible solution is to estimate the trust level to be assigned to a user in a collaborative community on the basis of his/her reputation, given by his/her behavior with regards to all the other users in the community. In our scenario, this can be done by making a user able to monitor the behavior of the other users wrt the release of private information or resources. However, this solution raises serious privacy concerns, because a participant might not agree in releasing information about the decisions he/she has made, even if these are signals of good behavior.

Purpose

A purpose describes the reason(s) for data collection and data access [41]. A set of purposes P, is organized in a tree structure, referred to as a Purpose Tree PT, where each node represents a purpose in P and each edge represents a hierarchical relation (i.e., specialization and generalization) between two purposes. Figure 10.2 gives an example of a purpose tree.

Let P_i and P_j be two purposes in a purpose tree. P_i is senior to P_j (or P_j is junior to P_i) if there exists a downward path from P_i to P_j in the tree. Based on the tree structure of purposes, the partial relationships between purposes are existed. Suppose PT is a purpose tree and P is a set of purposes in PT. $Pu \in P$ is a purpose, the senior purposes of Pu, denoted by $Senior(Pu)$, is the set of all nodes that are senior to Pu. For example, $Senior(Record) = \{Admin, General\ Purpose\ \}$ in

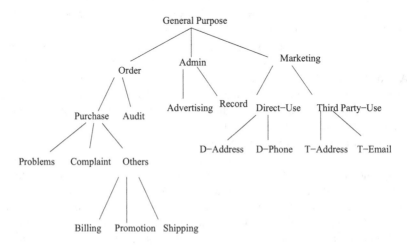

Fig. 10.2 Example of purpose structure

Fig. 10.2. The junior purposes of Pu, denoted by $Junior(Pu)$, is the set of all nodes that are junior to Pu. For instance, $Junior(Admin)= \{Advertise, Record\}$.

Intended purposes are purposes associated with data and thus regulate data accesses. *Access purposes* are purposes for accessing data. An intended purpose consists of two components: Allowed Intended Purposes (*AIP*) and Prohibited Intended Purposes (*PIP*), i.e. $IP = \langle AIP, PIP \rangle$, where $AIP \subset P$, and $PIP \subset P$. Intended purposes can be viewed as brief summaries of privacy policies for data. When an access is requested, the access purpose is checked against the intended purposes for the data item. That is, access is granted if the access purpose is entailed by the *AIP* and not entailed by the *PIP*; in this case we say the access purpose is compliant to the intended purpose. On the other hand, the access is denied if either of these two conditions fails. The access purpose is then not compliant to the intended purpose. The structure of *AIP* and *PIP* allows more compact and flexible policies in the designed model. Moreover, conflicts between *AIP* and *PIP* for the same data element are resolved by applying the denial-takes-precedence policy where *PIP* overrides *AIP*.

Let $IP = \langle AIP, PIP \rangle$, the set of purposes implied by IP is defined as

$$IP^* = (Junior(AIP) \cup AIP) - (Senior(PIP) \cup PIP).$$

The advantages of this definition are: it is reality that an access purpose is compliant to $\langle AIP, PIP \rangle$ if it is compliant to $\langle Junior(AIP), PIP \rangle$. Furthermore, an access purpose is not compliant to $\langle AIP, Senior(PIP) \rangle$ if it is not compliant to $\langle AIP, PIP \rangle$.

Most privacy policies are in two categories. One is a permissive policy that selectively allows data access for a set of purposes. The other one is a prohibitive policy that explicitly prohibits access to data for certain purposes. For example, a company decides not to use any information about children of age under 13 for the marketing purpose. This policy is prohibitive in nature as it explicitly disallows access to the data items belonging to minors for the particular purpose.

10.4 Access Control Policies

We introduce the structure of access control policy. Let us assume a social network system that possesses data or resources that need to be protected from unauthorized accesses. Policies are defined to apply to this system.

Definition 10.1 An access control policy (rule) is a tuple of the form

$$(Data, Sub, RelT, Purp, Dmax, Tmin, Obli)$$

The subjects (*Sub*) terms identifies a user or a group who requests an action onto the resources. The resources (*Data*) term identifies a subset of objects which are normally private information that access to the objects is restricted. The purpose (*Purp*) is selected a pre-defined set of purposes that is reasons subjects intend to execute an action. The *RelT* is a relationship type between the data owner and the user may have the right to access. *Dmax* and *Tmin* are maximal depth and minimal required trust respectively. Obligations (*Obli*) are requirements that have to be followed by the subject for having access to resources. For instance, users are asked to agree to a privacy policy when installing Skype software; otherwise, the software cannot be used.

Subjects, relationship type, and trust are the same concepts in traditional access control policies that specify who can access what with action. Purposes are applied to achieve fine-grained polices. The purpose checks for properties of the context with no intended side effects. If a side effect exists we need to consider other arguments like obligations and conditions in authorization process. We briefly discuss obligations in this chapter but the detailed analysis for obligations is omitted. As we mentioned in the first section, the purpose is the reason to collect the resources and is indispensable to private access policies.

Access control requirements applying to a resource are expressed by specifying one or more access conditions, by which the resource owner Sub determines the type of relationships that a requesting node R must have with a given node along with access purpose, their maximum depth, minimum trust level and obligations. A privacy policy, $\langle Data, Sub, RelT, Purp, Dmax, Tmin, Obli \rangle$, describes the data disclosed to whom must have a relationship, $RelT \in RTSN \cup *$ is a relationship type, whereas $Dmax \in N \cup *$ and $TMmin \in [0, 1] \cup *$ are, respectively, the maximum depth and minimum trust level that the relationship must have and satisfy obligations. If $Sub = *$ and/or $RelT = *$, Sub corresponds to any node in V_{SN}/or $RelT$ corresponds to any relationship in RT_{SN}, whereas, if $Dmax = *$ and/or $Tmin = *$, there is no constraint concerning the depth and/or trust level, respectively.

Consider the *WBSN* depicted in Fig. 10.1, suppose that Alice owns her email address that should be accessed by users that are either friends of Alice with purpose of purchase, constraints on depth 3, trust level 0.8 or direct colleagues of Carl with marketing purpose, independently from their trust level. This can be achieved by specifying two distinct access rules, namely, $(EmailAddress, Alice, Friends, Purchase, 3, 0.8, \phi)$ and $(EmailAddress, Carl, colleague, Marketing, 1, 0, \phi)$.

The following two examples are positive and negative authorizations, respectively. The security policy example includes two rules.

Example 1:   "Hua allows his direct friends with minimal 0.8 trust to access his address for marketing purpose by notify through email";

Example 2:   "Chris does not allow colleague to access his home phone for record purpose".

In the first rule *Data = Address, Sub = Hua, RelT = friends, Purp = Marketing, Dmax = 1, Tmin = 0.8, Obli = Notify (email)*. The second example with negative authorization, *Data = Home phone, S = Chris, RelT = Colleague, Purp = record,*

Dmax = 0, Tmin = 1. Due to the negative policy, we set up the Dmax to 0. There is no obligations in the second example. Therefore,

P1: (Address, Hua, Friends, Marketing, 1, 0.8, Notify (Email))
P2: (Homephone, Chris, Colleague, Record, 0, 1, ϕ)

10.4.1   Policy Operations

This section analyses the impact of generating new policies to an existing Trust-based access control (*TAC*) model. It may have unforeseen problems while a new policy for privacy protection is raised. For example, when Hua moves to the complaint department, a new policy is defined:

3. "Hua allows his direct friends with minimal 0.8 trust to access his address for problem solving purpose by notify through email";

The corresponding expression in *TAC* is:

P3: (Address, Hua, Friends, problem solving, 1, 0.8, Notify (Email)).

Comparing to P1, these are two policies for people access Hua's address for different purposes. What is the results of these two policies if combine them together? Normally, we should apply P1 for access address for Marketing purpose and, apply P3 to access address for Problem solving purpose.

The differences in these two policies are the purposes where one is Marketing purpose while the other one is Problem Solving purpose. How the system will verify?

Should the system verify Marketing purpose for the access to addresses with consent conditions? *TAC* achieves that by considering different access policies as linked by a conjunction.

That is, if a user *Sub* allows to others with relationship type *RelT* and minimal trust *Tmin* to access on *data* for purpose *Purp*, all access polices of *Sub* related to the data, Depth, Trust, Purposes and Obligations must be checked. *Sub* can read the *data* if there exists at least one policy and *Sub* can satisfy all purposes in all policies. If a new access policy is related to the same data, same obligations of some existed private policies, it is not used to relax the access situations but to make the access stricter. If privacy officers want to relax the access environments, they can do so by revising the existed access policies instead of creating a new one.

"Obligations" are requirements that have to be followed by the subject for allowing access resources. For instance, users are asked to agree a privacy policy when install Skype software; otherwise, the software cannot be used.

Consider the following access policies which include conflicting obligations:

P4: (Homephone, Chris, Colleague, Record, 2, 1, Notify())
P5: (Homephone, Chris, Colleague, Record, 2, 1, Notify(Opt-out))

Once a data request is authorized, the system does not know which obligation should be executed (either Notify or Notify with Opt-out); therefore P4 conflicts with P5.

10.4.2   Access Control Architecture

Besides the definition of a suitable policy language, one of the key issues is related to the architecture according to which access control should take place. The traditional way according to which access control is performed in data management systems does not fit very well with the collaborative community scenario. In a traditional data management system, there is a trusted module, called reference monitor, which mediates each access request submitted to the system, and decides whether it can be granted or not, on the basis of the specified access control policies. The access control policies specified by all the users are stored into a centralized policy base, managed by the database server. This architecture is not appropriate for a collaborative community environment for two main reasons. The first is that in a dynamic and highly decentralized environment like collaborative communities, a centralized service in charge of performing access control may become a bottleneck for the whole system. The second reason is that adopting centralized access control enforcement implies to totally delegate to the community manager the administration of user data and the related access control policies and this may lead to some privacy and confidentiality concerns. For instance, a community user might not want that the community manager knows the policies regulating access to his/her resources. Additionally, the increasing privacy concerns about the management of personal information by the community manager lead us to believe that a centralized access control solution is not the most appropriate one, since we believe that, in the next future, collaborative community users would like to have more and more control over their data and the way access control is enforced over them.

10.5   Access Control Authorizations

We have described the access framework through access control policies by adding relationship, trust level and maximal depth and purpose. This section discusses the details of the access authorization and verification based on the framework. Access authorizations are granted to users based on the relationship type, access purpose on the data, minimal trust and obligations. We have already analyzed different authorizations models such as *pre-Authorizations model* and *ongoing-Authorizations model* [70], and create trust-based access authorizations for social network in this section.

The framework supports the access control policies and their authorizations as well. It should be noticed that the authorization is related to the ontology supported by social networks, in that it defines authorizations on the basis of resources and purposes. In general, an access authorization is a triple (Sub, Act, Obj) stating that subject *Sub* has the right to execute permission *Act* on object *Obj*.

In the real world of access control, there are two well-known decision policies [6]:

(a) Closed policy: This policy allows access if there exists a corresponding positive authorization and denies it otherwise.
(b) Open policy: This policy denies access if there exists a corresponding negative authorization and allows it otherwise.

It is quite popular to apply closed policy in centralize management system. However, in social network, the closed policy approach has a major problem in that the lack of a given authorization for a given user does not prevent this user from receiving this authorization later on. Bertino et al. [6] proposed an explicit negative authorization as blocking authorizations. Whenever a user receives a negative authorization, his positive authorizations become blocked. Negative authorization is typically discussed in the context of access control systems that adopt open policy. The introduction of negative authorization brings with it the possibility of conflict in authorization, an issue that needs to be resolved in order for the access control model to give a conclusive result. The perceived advantage of closed policy systems is twofold. First, it is easier to maintain the principle of least privilege in a closed; second, policy administrators cannot write inconsistent rules, i.e., a set of rules in which an access permission is allowed by a positive authorization and simultaneously denied by a negative authorization.

Negative authorization can be implemented by prohibited intended purposes. Similar to positive access control authorization, a negative authorization specifies a relationship between a user and the content that is not authorized or the person prefers not to access. A negative authorization can be represented as a tuple (Sub, Act, Obj, PIP) which implies that a subject *Sub* is prohibited to take the permission *Act* on object *Obj*.

10.6 Comparisons

We present a brief comparison of the trust involved access model *TAC* against other related work. The closely related works to this chapter are Enforcing access control in Web-based social networks [12], Social Network Privacy via Evolving Access Control [17] and the enterprise privacy authorization language (*EPAL*).

Carminati et al. [12] proposed an access control model and related enforcement mechanism for WBSNs that adopt a rule-based approach for specifying access control policies on the resources owned by network participants, and where authorized users were denoted in terms of the type, depth, and trust level of relationships. Different from traditional access control systems, their mechanism made use of a semidecentralized architecture, where the information concerning users relationships is encoded into certificates, stored by a certificate server, whereas access control enforcement was carried out client-side. Their work is different from the work in this chapter in several aspects. Firstly, their work discussed access control models with positive authorization for social network, but the work in this chapter analysed access models with positive authorizations, but also negative authorizations that was described as their future work. Secondly, their work presented a client-side access control mechanism with trust computation. By contrast, our work an access control rules with trust, relationship type, but also purposes and obligations which are not included and analysed in their work.

Crescenzo and Lipton [17] introduced the problem of limiting privacy loss due to data shared in a social network, where the basic underlying assumptions are that users are interested in sharing data. The authors shown that users-regulated access control is unsuccessful for practical social network, and proposed that social networks deploy an additional layer of server-assisted access control which, even under no action from a user, automatically evolves over time, by restricting access to the user's data. The evolving access control mechanism provides non-trivial quantifiable guarantees for formally specified requirements of utility. Their work is different from ours in two aspects. First, their paper is focused on limiting privacy loss while participating to online activity at social networking websites. By contrast, our work has analysed trust-based access framework with different relationship types in social network. Second, their work designed a new model for balancing privacy and utility in social networks, and proposed a solution that achieves non-trivial tradeoffs between these two goals. They neither analyse the trust and depth of relationship nor purpose structure and obligations. By contrast, our work has analysed purpose hierarchical structure and the impact of adding new access control policies.

EPAL is a formal language for writing enterprise privacy policies to govern data handling practices in IT systems according to fine-grained positive and negative authorization rights. It concentrates on the core privacy authorization while abstracting data models and user-authentication from all deployment details such as data model or user-authentication. An EPAL policy defines lists of hierarchies of data-categories, user-categories, and purposes, and sets of (privacy) actions, obligations, and conditions. Purposes model the intended service for which data is used (e.g., processing a travel expense reimbursement or auditing purposes). Compared to EPAL, TAC has the following major differences. First, one of the important design criteria of TAC is to unify privacy policy enforcement and access control policy enforcement into one access control model. By contrast, EPAL is designed independently from any access control model. Second, the conflicting policies problem was not introduced and analysed in EPAL; hence shortcoming exists during answering data access request [4], but TAC supports conflict detection to guarantee that no conflicts arise in the procedures of generating new policies, thus preventing the disclosure of private information. Third, we analyse the policy structure with trust, relationship type, purpose and obligation in social network which are not discussed in EPAL.

10.7 Conclusions

This chapter has discussed trust-based access control policies with purposes and obligations. We have studied the access control framework but also the structure of access policies including subjects, resources, purposes, trust, relationship types and obligations. We have also analysed the impact of adding new policies and the conflicts that they can lead to. The work in this chapter has significantly extended previous work in several aspects, for example, purpose involved access control, and access control policies in collaboration social network.

The research for trust involved access control policies is still in its infancy and much further work remains to be done. There could exist conflicting access policies within *TAC* in social network, and how to develop algorithms to find and fix the conflicts and their applications are possible avenues for our future work. The development of a system approach to test the conflicts between policies is also being considered.

10.8 Problems and Exercises

10.8.1 Problems

1. Trust-based access control is a new research area in system management. Trust relationship can be different in various groups and it is therefore a challenge to manage the relationship and effectively use trust.
2. Role-based access management is a basic access method, how to invlove trust to an RBAC model?
3. In the real world of access control, there are two well-known decision policies (Bertino et al. [6]):

   (a) Closed policy: This policy allows access if there exists a corresponding positive authorization and denies it otherwise.
   (b) Open policy: This policy denies access if there exists a corresponding negative authorization and allows it otherwise.

The problem is how to organise the two decision policies with trust-based access management.

10.8.2 Exercises

1. Developing algorithms developed in this chapter and test the conflicts;
2. Given an example, analysing the developed algorithms;
3. Analysing the two decision policies through examples, trust relationship can be involved.

References

1. Abiteboul, S., et al.: The lowell database research self-assessment. Commun. ACM **48**(5), 111–118 (2005)
2. Adams, A., Angela, S.M.: Privacy in multimedia communications: protecting users, not just data. In: Blandford, A., Vanderdonckt, J., Gray, P. (eds.) People and Computers XVŰInteraction without Frontiers, eds edn. Springer, London. https://doi.org/10.1007/978-1-4471-0353-0_4
3. Bader, A., et al.: A trust based approach for protecting user data in social networks. In: Proceedings of the 2007 Conference of the Center for Advanced Studies on Collaborative Research, CASCON'07, pp. 288–293. IBM Corp., Armonk (2007)
4. Barth, A., Mitchell, J., Rosenstein, J.: Conflict and combination in privacy policy languages (summary). In: Proceedings of the 2004 ACM workshop on Privacy in the Electronic Society (2004)
5. Bellare, M., Roga way, P.: Random oracles are practical: a paradigm for designing efficient protocols. In: First ACM Conference on Computer and Communications Security, pp. 62–73. IEEE, Piscataway (1993)
6. Bertino, E.P., Samarati, P., Jajodia, S.: An extended authorization model for relational databases. IEEE Trans. Knowl. Data Eng. **9**(1), 145–167 (1997)
7. Bertino, E., Castano, S., Ferrari, E., Mesiti, M.: Specifying and enforcing access control policies for XML document sources. World Wide Web **3**, 139–151 (2000)
8. Boyko, V., Peinado, M., Venkatesan, R.: Speeding up discrete log and factoring based schemes via precomputations. In: Advances in Cryptology - Eurocrypt'98. Lectures Notes in Computer Science, vol. 1807. Springer, Berlin (1998)
9. Canetti, R., Goldreich, O., Halevi, S.: The random oracle methodology. In: Proceedings of the 30th ACM STOC'98, pp. 209–218. IEEE, Piscataway (1998)
10. Canetti, R., Micciancio, D., Reingold, O.: Perfectly one-way probabilistic hash functions. In: Proceedings of the 30th ACM STOC'98. IEEE, Piscataway (1998)
11. Cao, J., et al.: Towards secure xml document with usage control. In: Web Technologies Research and Development - APWeb 2005, pp. 296–307. Springer, Berlin (2005)
12. Carminati, B., Ferrari, E., Perego, A.: Enforcing access control in web-based social networks. ACM Trans. Inf. Syst. Secur. **13**(1), 6 (2009)
13. Chan, A., Frankel, Y., Tsiounis, Y.: An efficient off-line electronic cash scheme as secure as RSA. Research report NU-CCS-96-03, Northeastern University, Boston (1995)
14. Chaum, D.: Blind signature for untraceable payments. In: Advances in Cryptology - Crypto 82, pp. 199–203. Plenum Press, New York (1983)
15. Chaum, D., Fiat, A., Naor, M.: Untraceable electronic cash. In: Advances in Cryptology - Crypto'88. Lectures Notes in Computer Science, vol. 403, pp. 319–327. Springer, Berlin (1990)
16. Chenthara, S., et al.: Security and privacy-preserving challenges of e-health solutions in cloud computing. IEEE Access **7**, 74361–74382 (2019)
17. Di Crescenzo, G., Lipton, R.: Social network privacy via evolving access control. In: Wireless Algorithms, Systems, and Applications, pp. 551–560. Springer, Berlin (2009)
18. Feinstein, H.L.: Final report: NIST small business innovative research (SBIR) grant: role based access control: phase 1. Technical Report. SETA Corp. (1995)
19. Ferraiolo, D.F., Kuhn, D.R.: Role based access control. In: 15th National Computer Security Conference. pp. 554–555. 63ferraiolo92rolebased.html
20. Ferraiolo, D.F., Barkley, J.F., Kuhn, D.R.: Role-based access control model and reference implementation within a corporate intranet. In: Transactions on Information and System Security (TISSEC), vol. 2, pp. 34–64 (1999)
21. Gabber, E., Silberschatz, A.: Agora: a minimal distributed protocol for electronic commerce. In: The 2rd USENIX workshop on electronic commerce, Oakland (1996)
22. Gates, C.: Access control requirements for web 2.0 security and privacy. IEEE Web. **2**(0), 12–15 (2007)

23. Golbeck, J.: Trust and nuanced profile similarity in online social networks. ACM Trans. Web **3**(4), 12 (2009)
24. Goldschlag, D., Reed, M., Syverson, P.: Onion routing for anonymous and private Internet connections. Commun. ACM **24**(2), 39–41 (1999)
25. Green, S., et al. Software agents: a review. TCD-CS-1997-06, Trinity College Dublin and Broadcom Eireann Research, Dulbin (1997)
26. Hart, M., Johnson, R., Stent, A.: More content-less control: access control in the web 2.0. IEEE Web 28–42 (2007)
27. Juels, A., Luby, M., Ostrovsky, R.: Security of blind digital signatures. In: Advances in Cryptology - Crypto 97. Lectures Notes in Computer Science, vol. 1294, pp. 150–164. Springer, Berlin (1997)
28. Kabir, E., Wang, H.: Conditional purpose based access control model for privacy protection. In: Proceedings of the Twentieth Australasian Conference on Australasian Database - Volume 92, ADC'09, pp. 135–142. Australian Computer Society, Darlinghurst (2009)
29. Kabir, M., Wang, H., Bertino, E.: A conditional purpose-based access control model with dynamic roles. Expert Syst. Appl. **38**(3), 1482–1489 (2011)
30. Kabir, M., Wang, H., Bertino, E.: A conditional role-involved purpose-based access control model. J. Org. Comput. E. Commerce **21**, 71–91 (2011)
31. Kabir, M., Wang, H., Bertino, E.: Efficient systematic clustering method for k-anonymization. Acta Inform. **48**(1), 51–66 (2011)
32. Khalil, F., Li, J., Wang, H.: Integrating recommendation models for improved web page prediction accuracy. In: Proceedings of the Thirty-First Australasian Conference on Computer Science - Volume 74, ACSC'08, Darlinghurst, pp. 91–100. Australian Computer Society, Darlinghurst (2008)
33. Kruk, S., et al.: D-FOAF: Distributed identity management with access rights delegation. In: The Semantic Web – ASWC'06, Berlin, pp. 140–154. Springer, Berlin (2006)
34. LeFevre, K. et al.: Limiting disclosure in hippocratic databases. In: Proceedings of the Thirtieth International Conference on Very Large Data Bases - Volume 30, VLDB'04, pp. 108–119. VLDB Endowment (2004)
35. Li, M., et al.: Advanced permission-role relationship in role-based access control. In: Information Security and Privacy, Berlin, pp. 391–403. Springer, Berlin (2008)
36. Li, M., et al.: Optimal privacy-aware path in hippocratic databases. In: Database Systems for Advanced Applications, Berlin, pp. 441–455. Springer, Berlin (2009)
37. Li, M., Wang, H.: ABDM: An extended flexible delegation model in RBAC. In: 2008 8th IEEE International Conference on Computer and Information Technology, pp. 390–395 (2008)
38. Li, M., Wang, H., Plank, A.: Privacy-aware access control with generalization boundaries. In: Proceedings of the Thirty-Second Australasian Conference on Computer Science - Volume 91, ACSC'09, Darlinghurst, pp. 105–112. Australian Computer Society, Darlinghurst (2009)
39. Li, M., Wang, H., Ross, D.: Trust-based access control for privacy protection in collaborative environment. In: 2009 IEEE International Conference on e-Business Engineering, pp. 425–430 (2009)
40. Liu, K., Terzi, E.: A framework for computing the privacy scores of users in online social networks. ACM Trans. Knowl. Discov. Data **5**(1), 6 (2010)
41. Ni, Q., et al.: Privacy-aware role-based access control. IEEE Secur. Priv. **7**(4), 35–43 (2009)
42. Pointcheval, D., Stern, J.: Security arguments for digital signatures and blind signatures. J. Cryptol. **13**(3), 361–396 (2000)
43. Rakesh, A.: Hippocratic databases. In: Proceedings of the 28th International Conference on Very Large Data Bases, VLDB'02, pp. 143–154. VLDB Endowment (2002)
44. Rasool, R., et al.: Cyberpulse: a machine learning based link flooding attack mitigation system for software defined networks. IEEE Access **7**, 34885–34899 (2019)
45. Sandhu, R.: Role activation hierarchies. In: Third ACM Workshop on Role Based Access Control, pp. 33–40. ACM Press, New York (1998)
46. Spegel, N., Rogers, B., Buckley, R.: Negotiation Theory and Techniques. Skills Series. Butterworths, London (1998)

47. Sun, X., et al.: An efficient hash-based algorithm for minimal k-anonymity. In: Proceedings of the Thirty-first Australasian Conference on Computer Science - Volume 74, ACSC'08, Darlinghurst, pp. 101–107. Australian Computer Society, Darlinghurst (2008)

48. Sun, X. et al.: Enhanced p-sensitive k-anonymity models for privacy preserving data publishing. Trans. Data Priv. 1(2), 53–66 (2008)

49. Sun, X., et al.: (p+, α)-sensitive k-anonymity: a new enhanced privacy protection model. In: 2008 8th IEEE International Conference on Computer and Information Technology, pp. 59–64 (2008)

50. Sun, X., et al.: Injecting purpose and trust into data anonymisation. Comput. Secur. 30, 332–345 (2011)

51. Sun, X., et al.: Privacy-aware access control with trust management in web service. World Wide Web 14(4), 407–430 (2011)

52. Sun, L., Wang, H.: Access control and authorization for protecting disseminative information in e-learning workflow. Concurrency Comput. Pract. Exp. 23, 2034–2042 (2011)

53. Sun, L., Li, Y., Wang, H.: M-service and its framework. In: 2005 Asia-Pacific Conference on Communications, pp. 837–841 (2005)

54. Sun, X., Wang, H., Li, J.: Priority driven k-anonymisation for privacy protection. In: Proceedings of the 7th Australasian Data Mining Conference, vol. 87, pp. 73–78 (2008)

55. Sun, X., Wang, H., Li, J.: Microdata protection through approximate microaggregation. In: Proceedings of the Thirty-Second Australasian Conference on Computer Science - Volume 91, ACSC'09, pp. 161–168. Australian Computer Society, Darlinghurst (2009)

56. Sun, X., Wang, H., Sun, L.: Extended k-anonymity models against attribute disclosure. In: 2009 Third International Conference on Network and System Security, pp. 130–136 (2009)

57. Sun, L., Wang, H., Yong, J.: Authorization algorithms for permission-role assignments. J. Univ. Comput. Sci. 15, 1782–1798 (2009)

58. Sun, X., Wang, H., Li, J.: Satisfying privacy requirements: one step before anonymization. In: Advances in Knowledge Discovery and Data Mining, Berlin, pp. 181–188. Springer, Berlin (2010)

59. Sun, X., Li, M., Wang, H.: A family of enhanced (l, α)-diversity models for privacy preserving data publishing. Futur. Gener. Comput. Syst. 27(3), 348–356 (2011)

60. Sun, X., Sun, L., Wang, H.: Extended k-anonymity models against sensitive attribute disclosure. Comput. Commun. 34(4), 526–535 (2011). Special issue: Building Secure Parallel and Distributed Networks and Systems

61. Wang, H., et al.: Authorization algorithms for the mobility of user-role relationship. In: Proceedings of the Twenty-eighth Australasian Conference on Computer Science - Volume 38, ACSC'05, pp. 69–77. Australian Computer Society, Darlinghurst (2005)

62. Wang, H. et al.: A framework for role-based group deligation in distributed environments. In: Proceedings of the 29th Australasian Computer Science Conference, vol. 48, pp. 321–328 (2006)

63. Wang, H., et al.: Authorization approaches for advanced permission-role assignments. In: 2008 12th International Conference on Computer Supported Cooperative Work in Design, pp. 277–282 (2008)

64. Wang, H., et al.: Editorial: special issue on security and privacy in network computing. World Wide Web 23, 951–957 (2020)

65. Wang, H., Li, Q.: Secure and efficient information sharing in multi-university e-learning environments. In: Advances in Web Based Learning – ICWL 2007, Berlin, pp. 542–553. Springer, Berlin (2008)

66. Wang, H., Sun, L.: Trust-involved access control in collaborative open social networks. In: 2010 Fourth International Conference on Network and System Security, pp. 239–246 (2010)

67. Wang, H., Cao, J., Zhang, Y.: A flexible payment scheme and its role-based access control. IEEE Trans. Knowl. Data Eng. 17(3), 425–436 (2005)

68. Wang, H., Cao, J., Ross, D.: Role-based delegation with negative authorization. In: Frontiers of WWW Research and Development - APWeb 2006, Berlin, pp. 307–318. Springer, Berlin (2006)

69. Wang, H., Zhang, Y., Cao, J.: Ubiquitous computing environments and its usage access control. In: *Proceedings of the 1st International Conference on Scalable Information Systems*, InfoScale'06, New York. ACM, New York (2006)
70. Wang, H., Zhang, Y., Cao, J.: Access control management for ubiquitous computing. Futur. Gener. Comput. Syst. **24**(8), 870–878 (2008)
71. Wang, H., Zhang, Y., Cao, J.: Effective collaboration with information sharing in virtual universities. IEEE Trans. Knowl. Data Eng. **21**, 840–853 (2008)
72. Wang, H., Cao, J., Zhang, Y.: Delegating revocations and authorizations in collaborative business environments. Inf. Syst. Front. **11**(3), 293–305 (2009)
73. Wang, H., Sun, L., Varadharajan, V.: Purpose-based access control policies and conflicting analysis. In: Security and Privacy – Silver Linings in the Cloud, Berlin, pp. 217–228. Springer, Berlin (2010)
74. Wang, Z., et al.: Automatic niching differential evolution with contour prediction approach for multimodal optimization problems. IEEE Trans. Evol. Comput. **24**(1), 114–128 (2020)
75. Yacobi, Y.: Efficient electronic money. In: Advances in Cryptology–Asiacrypt'94. Lectures Notes in Computer Science, vol. 917, pp. 153–163. Springer, Berlin (1995)
76. Zhang, J. et al.: Detecting anomalies from high-dimensional wireless network data streams: a case study. Soft Comput. **15**(6), 1195–1215 (2011)

Part V
Access Control Policy and Blockchain Technology

Part V consists of three Chaps. 11–13. Privacy preserving is increasing in its importance since privacy becomes a major concern for both customers and enterprises in today's corporate marketing strategies. Chapter 11 proposes a purpose-based access control model in distributed computing environment for privacy preserving policies and mechanisms, and describes algorithms for policy conflicting problems. The mechanism enforces access policy to data containing personally identifiable information. The key component is purpose involved access control models (PAC) that provide full support for expressing highly complex privacy-related policies, taking into account features like purposes, conditions and obligations. As the current COVID 19 situation, universities are all locked down. Both staff and students have to move to online teaching and study. Virtual university is a common situation. Chapter 12 aims to build a new rule-based framework to identify and address issues of sharing in virtual university environments through role-based access control management (RBAC). The framework includes a role-based group delegation granting model, group delegation revocation model, authorization granting and authorization revocation. Various revocations and the impact of revocations on role hierarchies are analysed. The implementation with XML-based tools demonstrates the feasibility of the framework and authorization methods. Chapter 13 concludes the contributions and future work of this book. It also discusses Blockchain Based Access Control and describes Blockchain-based access control framework for the Internet of Things.

Chapter 11
Building Access Control Policy Model for Privacy Preserving and Testing Policy Conflicting Problems

This chapter proposes a purpose-based access control model in distributed computing environment for privacy preserving policies and mechanisms, and describes algorithms for policy conflicting problems. The mechanism enforces access policy to data containing personally identifiable information. The key component is purpose involved access control models (*PAC*) that provide full support for expressing highly complex privacy-related policies, taking into account features like purposes, conditions and obligations. A policy refers to an access right that a subject can have on an object, based on attribute predicates, obligation actions, and system conditions. Policy conflicting problems may arise when new access policies are generated that are possible to be conflicted to existing policies. As a result of the policy conflicts, private information cannot be well protected. The structure of purpose involved access control policy is studied, and efficient conflict-checking algorithms are developed and implemented. Finally a discussion of our work in comparison with other access control and frameworks such as *EPAL* is presented.

11.1 Introduction

Privacy preserving is increasing in its importance since privacy becomes a major concern for both customers and enterprises in today's corporate marketing strategies [59, 80, 94, 95]. This raises challenging questions and problems regarding the use and protection of private messages, especially for context-aware web service. One principle of protecting private information is based on who is allowed to access private information and for what purpose [34, 53, 82, 90]. For example, personal information provided by patients to hospitals may only be used with record purpose, not for advertising purpose. There must be purposes for data collection and data access. The motivations for adopting purpose based approach are (1) the fundamental policies for private information concern with which data object is used

© Springer Nature Switzerland AG 2020   225
H. Wang et al., *Access Control Management in Cloud Environments*,
https://doi.org/10.1007/978-3-030-31729-4_11

for what purposes [49] (for example, customers' age and email address are used for the purpose of marketing analysis), and (2) customers agreed data usage varies from individual to individual. Information technology provides the capability to store various types of users' information required during their business activities. Indeed, Pitofsky [50] showed that 97% of web sites were collecting at least one type of identifying information such as name, home address, e-mail address, or postal address of consumers. The fact that the personal information is collected and can be used without any consent or awareness violates privacy for many people. This chapter analyses purpose based methods to secure private information.

Data privacy is defined by policies describing to whom the data may be disclosed and what are the purposes of using the data [1, 84, 87]. For example, a policy may specify that price of an air ticket from an agent may be disclosed, but only with "opted-in" customers, or that the price will be disclosed unless the agent has specifically "opted-out" of this default. While there is recent work on defining languages for specifying privacy policies [57], access control mechanisms for enforcing such policies have not been investigated [64]. Ni et al. [46] analyzed a conditional privacy management with role based access control, which supports expressive condition languages and flexible relations among permission assignments for complex privacy policies. But many interested problems remain, for example, developing a formal method to describe and manage purposes and to automatically detect possible conflicts between access policies. As stated by Al-Harbi and Osborn [2] and Adams and Sasse [3]: "Most invasions of privacy are not intentional but due to designers' inability to anticipate how this data could be used, by whom, and how this might affect users"?

Access control is significant when disclosing private information in web service [34, 40, 73]. The importance of privacy has been recognized for a long time, but the concept has not been supported in traditional access models, especially purpose based access control systems. A security officer has to check privacy policies if an access is required. Furthermore, administrators are prone to making mistakes when they generate new access policies to access sensitive data [7, 66, 67]. Such an approach significantly increases the management efforts in distributed environments because of the various privacy requirements and the continuous involvement from security officers. This chapter bridges the gap between private information protecting technology and access control models. We start from building a purpose-based access framework and analyzing the conflicts between purposes in access control policies [81, 85, 91].

The remainder of this chapter is organized as follows: Sect. 11.2 presents the motivations behind our work in this chapter. Section 11.3 proposes a purpose based access framework which includes detailed information of purposes and access control evaluation. Section 11.4 provides access control policy structure and authorization models as well as illustrates the impact of generating a new access policy through examples. Section 11.5 describes conflict problems in access purposes and policies, and develops algorithms for detecting conflicts between purposes. The implementation of the conflicting algorithms is described in Sect. 11.6. Section 11.7 compares the work in this chapter and related previous work, the comparisons demonstrate the significance of the work in this chapter. Finally, the conclusion of the paper and further work are given in Sect. 11.8.

11.2 Motivations

The important techniques for private information occur in distributed systems specifically tailored to support privacy policies, such as the well known P3P standard [28, 44, 48, 92]. In particular, Agrawal et al. [53] introduced the concept of Hippocratic databases, incorporating privacy protection in relational database systems. An important feature of their work is that it uses some privacy metadata, consisting of privacy policies and privacy authorizations stored in privacy-policies tables and privacy-authorizations tables respectively. However, they neither discussed the concepts of purpose with hierarchy structure, nor the prohibition of purpose and association of purposes and data elements [8, 14]. LeFevre et al. [38] presented an approach to enforce privacy policy in database systems. They introduced two models of cell level limited disclosure enforcement, namely table semantics and query semantics, but did not consider access control management. Li et al. [64] devised generalization boundary techniques to maximize data usability while, minimizing disclosure of privacy. Inspired by the fact that the permissible generalization level results in a much finer level access control, the authors proposed a privacy-aware access control model in web service environments and also analyzed an access process management through a trust-based decision and ongoing access control policies. However, the concept of purpose was missed. Ni et al. [46] analyzed a role-based access model for purpose-based privacy protection, but their work did not consider usage access management and the conflicts between purposes in policies. The development of access technology entails addressing many challenging issues, ranging from modeling to architectures, and may lead to the next-generation of access management. This chapter develops purpose based access technology for privacy violation challenges including complex policy structured models with access control.

Privacy violations may happen when data are released to third parties [32, 53, 70]. Data once released are not any longer under the control of the organizations owning them, and the data owners are not able to control the way data are used. The most common approach to address the privacy of released data is to modify the data by removing all information that can directly link data items with individuals [63, 68, 98]. It is important to note that simply removing identity information, like names or social-security numbers, from the released data may not be enough to anonymize the data. Many examples show that even when such information is removed from the released data, the remaining data combined with other information sources may still link the information to the individuals it refers to Torra [79]. Sweeney [37] proposed approaches based on the notion of k-anonymity as solutions of the problem. Another secure private information techniques such as density-based clustering algorithms happens in the context of data mining [35, 43, 77].

Data mining techniques are today very effective. Thus even though a database is sanitized by removing private information, the use of data mining techniques may allow one to recover the removed information. These techniques are based on modifying or perturbing the data in some way; for example, techniques specialized for privacy preserving mining of association rules modify the data so to reduce the confidence of sensitive association rules [22–24, 26]. A problem common to those techniques is represented by the quality of the resulting data; if data undergo too many modifications, they may not be useful any longer [16].

Secure private information cannot be easily achieved by traditional access management systems because traditional access management systems focus on which user is performing what action on which data object [11, 12, 93], and privacy policies are concerned with which data object is used for what purpose(s). For example, a common privacy agreement between a data collector and customers is "we use customer information for marketing purposes and to enable help us to resolve problems with services" that does not specify who can access the customer information, but only states that the information can be accessed for the purposes of marketing and customer service. Another challenge in access control policies is the conflict problem when generating new policies [64, 65, 69]. For example, assume three access control policies and no conflicts between two access control policies; however it may lead to conflicts when three access policies are executed.

This chapter focuses exclusively on how to specify and enforce policies for authorizing purpose-based access management using a rule-based language. We propose a comprehensive framework for purpose and data management where purposes are organized in a hierarchy. In our approach each data element is associated with a set of purposes, as opposed to a single security level in traditional secure applications [15, 18, 25, 58]. Also, the purposes form a hierarchy and can vary dynamically. These requirements are more complex than those concerning traditional secure applications. To provide sufficient functions with the framework, this chapter analyses the explicit prohibition of purpose and the association of a set of purposes with access control policies. Furthermore, we discuss the conflict problems with multiple access control policies and develop algorithms for detecting and resolving conflicts. This kind of analysis for purpose-based usage control for privacy preserving has not been studied.

11.3 Purpose Involved Access Control Framework

This section develops a purpose based access control framework called *PACF*. *PACF* includes extended access control models and supports purpose hierarchy by introducing the intended and access purposes, and purpose associated data models. It is supposed authorization approaches in access control models to be applied for access purpose determination in database systems [36, 83].

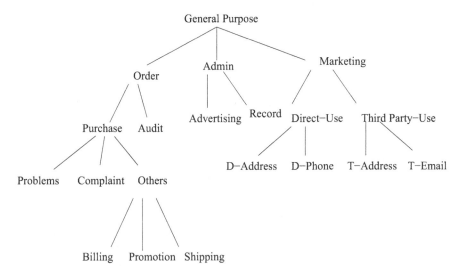

Fig. 11.1 Example of purpose structure

Purpose A purpose describes the reason(s) for data collection and data access [46].
A set of purposes P, is organized in a tree structure, referred to as a Purpose Tree PT,
where each node represents a purpose in P and each edge represents a hierarchical
relation (i.e., specialization and generalization) between two purposes. Figure 11.1
gives an example of a purpose tree.

Let P_i and P_j be two purposes in a purpose tree. P_i is senior to P_j (or P_j is
junior to P_i) if there exists a downward path from P_i to P_j in the tree. Based on the
tree structure of purposes, the partial relationships between purposes are existed.
Suppose PT is a purpose tree and P is a set of purposes in PT. $Pu \in P$ is a purpose,
the senior purposes of Pu, denoted by $Senior(Pu)$, is the set of all nodes that
are senior to Pu. For example, $Senior(Record) = \{Admin, General Purpose\}$ in
Fig. 11.1. The junior purposes of Pu, denoted by $Junior(Pu)$, is the set of all
nodes that are junior to Pu. For instance, $Junior(Admin) = \{Advertise, Record\}$.

We design an access control model by adding purposes and policy language,
and discuss the details of the access purpose authorization and verification based
on the model [39, 62, 89]. Intuitively, an access to a specific data element should
be allowed if the allowed purposes for the data, stated by the privacy policies,
include or imply the purpose of the data access. Access purpose authorizations
are granted to users based on the access purpose on the data, obligations and
conditions. Authorizations approaches in access control such as *pre-Authorizations
model* and *ongoing-Authorizations model* have already been introduced [92], and
access purpose authorizations in access control policies are analyzed in this chapter.

11.4   Access Control Policies

We introduce the structure of access control policy after introducing the basic concepts of purposes [9, 10]. Policies are defined to apply to this system. Let us assume a generic computer system that possesses data or resources that need to be protected from unauthorized accesses. Privacy preserving is achieved by through authorization models and policy operations in the designed access control policies [13, 71, 88].

Definition 11.1   An access control policy (rule) is a tuple of the form
(Subjects, Action, Resources, Purpose, Condition, Obligation)

The subjects terms identifies a user or a group who requests an action onto the resources. The action is any operation (e.g. deleting a file) to a resource in the access application. The resources term identifies a subset of objects which are normally private information that access to the objects is restricted. The purpose is selected pre-defined set of purposes that is reasons subjects intend to execute an action. The condition is a Boolean expression (i.e. a predicate) and "Obligations" are requirements that have to be followed by the subject for having access to resources [41, 60, 61]. For instance, users are asked to accept the agreement of privacy policy when installing Skype software; otherwise, the software cannot be used. We do not discuss conditions in this chapter due to limited space available in this chapter.

Subjects, action, and resources are the same concepts in traditional access control policies that specify who can access what with action [33, 78]. Purposes are applied to achieve fine-grained polices. The purpose checks for properties of the context with no intended side effects. If a side effect exists we need to consider other arguments like obligations and conditions in authorization process. We briefly discuss obligations in this chapter but the detailed analysis for obligations is omitted. As we mentioned in the first section, the purpose is the reason to collect the resources and is indispensable to private access policies.

The following two examples are positive and negative authorizations, respectively. The security policy example includes two rules.

Example 1:   "Hua can access purchase information for marketing purpose during working hours";
Example 2:   "Christine cannot update phone numbers for record purpose anytime".

In the first rule $S = Hua$, $A = read$, $R = purchase\ information$, $P = marketing$, $C = 8:00am-6:00pm$. There is no obligations in the examples. The second example with negative authorization, $S = Christine$, $A = update$, $R = phone\ number$, $P = record$, $C = anytime$.

11.4.1 Authorization Models

Definition 11.2 The *PAC* model is composed of the following components:

1. A set S of Subjects, a set D of Data, a set $Pu = \langle AIP, PIP \rangle$ of purposes (detailed AIP and PIP are in Byun and Li [9]), a set A of actions, a set of O for obligations and a set of C for conditions.
2. A set of data access right $DA = \{(d, a) \mid a \in A, d \in D\}$,
3. A set of private data access right $PDR = \{(da, a, pu, c, o) \mid da \in DA, pu \in Pu, c \in C, o \in O, a \in A\}$,
4. Private data subject assignment $PDS \subseteq S \times PDR$ is a many-to-many relation that decides what subjects with which access purposes can access the private information based on authorizations.

In what follows we provide additional details on the purpose involved language of *PAC* model and elaborate on conflicts among purposes and obligations [4, 21, 42, 86]. To simplify the purpose involved authorization models, we assume that $PIP = \phi$, and then $Pu = AIP$.

We illustrate through an example a privacy preserving expressed with *PAC* model [31, 72]. Suppose that Food and Drug Administration (http://www.fda.gov/) is a web site aiming at audience that deploys its privacy policies with the purpose tree in Fig. 11.1:

1. Subjects = {Hua, Tony, Christine, Den},
2. Action = {Read, Update, Delete},
3. Data = {OrderInfo, HomePhone, PostAdd, EmailAdd},
4. Purpose = {Order, Complaint, Billing, Shipping, ProblemSolving, Others},

The following privacy policies:

1. "Hua can read customers' PostAddress for shipping purpose".
2. "Tony can only read customers' Email address for purchase purpose if they allow to do so".
3. "Christine may read customers' order information for Billing purpose; and customers will be informed by Email".
4. "Den can read customers' Home Phone for Problem solving if it is approved by Hua".

These policies are expressed as follows in *PAC* model:

P1: (Hua, (PostAdd, Read), Shipping, N/A, ϕ))
P2: (Tony, (EmailAdd, Read), Purchase, OwnerConsent='Yes', ϕ)
P3: (Christine, (OrderInfor, Read), Billing, N/A, Notify(ByEmail))
P4: (Den, (HomePhone, Read), Problemsolving, 'Approved by Hua', N/A)

11.4.2   Policy Operations

This section analyses the impact of generating new policies to an existing *PAC* model. It may have unforeseen problems while a new policy for privacy protection is raised [29, 30, 54]. For example, when Tony moves to the complaint department, a new policy is defined:

5. "Tony can only read Email address of customers, for complaint purpose if they allow to do so"

The corresponding expression in *PAC* is:

P5: (Tony, (EmailAdd, Read), Complaint, OwnerConsent='Yes', ϕ).

Comparing to P2, these are two policies for Tony to access Email address for different purposes. What is the results of these two policies if combine them together? Normally, we should apply P2 for Tony to access email address for Purchase purpose and, apply P5 to access email address for Complaint purpose.

The differences in these two policies are the purposes where one is Purchase purpose while the other one is Complaint purpose. How the system will verify? Should the system verify Complaint for the access to email addresses with consent conditions? *PAC* achieves that by considering different access policies as linked by a conjunction.

That is, if a user U wants to access right a on data d for purpose Pu, all access polices of U related to $((d, a), Pu)$ must be checked. U can read the d if there exists at least one policy and U can satisfy all purposes in all policies. If a new access policy is related to the same user, same data, same right and same conditions of some existed private policies, it is not used to relax the access situations but to make the access stricter. If privacy officers want to relax the access environments, they can do so by revising the existed access policies instead of creating a new one.

Suppose two private access policies in *PAC*: $(u_1, (d_1, r_1), pu_1, c_1, \phi)$ and $(u_1, (d_1, r_1), pu_2, c_1, \phi)$, can we simply replace them with a new one as $(u_1, (r_1, d_1), pu_1 \wedge pu_2, c_1, \phi)$? Consider $P2$ and $P5$, we have the following policy:

P6: (Tony, (EmailAdd, Read), Complaint $\wedge$ Purchase, OwnerConsent = 'Yes', ϕ).

From the purpose hierarchy structure in Fig. 11.1, *Complaint* $\wedge$ *Purchase* = *Complaint* since *Complaint* is junior to purpose *Purchase*. Translating $P6$ into plain English, we obtain "Tony can read customers' Email address for Complaint purpose if the customers agree to do so". The translating is not correct since something is lost. Tony cannot access email addresses, for purposes of Problem solving and Other purchase purposes which are not included. The reason for this is the context variable purchase purpose in P5. The variable purchase purpose separates the values of order into three disjoint sets: Complaint, Problem solving and Others not included in the first two purposes. P2 thus applies to all three kinds of customers, while P5 only applies to email addresses for Complaint purpose. Simply combining purposes in P2 with purposes in P5 actually removes all purposes except Complaint purpose for access email addresses.

The notion of splitting context variables is required to analyse this problem [Ni et al. [46]].

Definition 11.3 A splitting context variable (*SCV*) is a context variable that satisfies the following conditions.

1. A *SCV* is related to purpose information.
2. The values of an *SCV* partition purposes into disjoint sets.
3. A *SCV* is not used to represent information about consent.

Based on the *SCV* definition, *Order* is *SCV*, whereas *Admin* and *Direct-Use* are not since the joint sets of *Advertising* and *Record*, *D-Address* and *D-Phone* are not empty. The notion of *SCV* is important and is used in the analysis of the paper. We are now able to give an answer to the aforementioned question: only if both pu_1 and pu_2 do not involve *SCV*, or the *SCV* that they involve have the same values, they could be safely rewritten into $pu_1 \wedge pu_2$.

Consider the following two access policies:

P7: (Tony, (EmailAdd, Read), Complaint, OwnerConsent='Yes', ϕ)
P8: (Tony, (EmailAdd, Read), N/A, OwnerConsent='Yes', ϕ).

*P*7 and *P*8 can be revised as:

P9: (Tony, (EmailAdd, Read), Complaint, OwnerConsent='Yes', ϕ).

Similarly, the following two access policies:

P10: (Tony, (EmailAdd, Read), Shipping, OwnerAge $\leq$ 13, ϕ)
P11: (Tony, (EmailAdd, Read), Record, OwnerAge $\leq$ 13 ϕ)
P12: (Tony, (EmailAdd, Read), Shipping $\wedge$ Record , OwnerAge $\leq$ 13, ϕ)

P12 is equivalent to *P*10 and *P*11. We now rewrite *P*2 and *P*5 as following policies:

P13: (Tony, (EmailAdd, Read), Shipping $\cup$ Billing $\cup$ Problemsolving $\cup$ Promotion, OwnerConsent='Yes', ϕ)
P14: (Tony, (EmailAdd, Read), Complaint, OwnerConsent='Yes', ϕ)

It is easy to understand P13 and P14 rather than P2 and P5. $\cup$ means "or" in the example. We do not have obligations in the discussion above. What may happen if there are obligations? Consider the following example:

P15: (Tony, (EmailAdd, Read), Complaint, OwnerConsent='Yes', NotifybyPhone)
P16: (Tony, (EmailAdd, Read), Purchase, OwnerConsent='Yes', NotifybyEmail)

Intuitively, P15 is fine for Tony reading customers' email address for Complaint purpose. This means that the phone activity should be invoked for Complaint purpose when accessing customers' data for Purchase purpose by notified by Email. Therefore, their equivalent forms are:

P17: (Tony, (EmailAdd, Read), Complaint, OwnerConsent='Yes', NotifybyPhone and NotifybyEmail)

P18: (Tony, (EmailAdd, Read), Shipping ∪ Billing ∪ Problemsolving ∪ Promotion, OwnerConsent='Yes', NotifybyEmail)

In summary, a private data access request related to user u, data d, access right a, purpose Pu is authorized only if all access policies related to $(u, (r, d), Pu)$ are satisfied. If so, obligations in all applicable policies are invoked after the access request.

11.5 Conflicting Algorithms

In the section, we discuss the various cases of conflicting policies in *PAC* model. It is not easy to comply with complex security and privacy policies, especially in large enterprises. The more complex a security policy is, the larger is the probability that such policy contains inconsistent and conflicting parts.

Consider the following policies:

P19: (Christine, (Read, OrderInfor), Shipping, Time=5PM-11PM, ϕ)
P20: (Christine, (Read, OrderInfor), Problem solving, Time=5PM-11PM, ϕ)

These two policies do not conflict with each other because P19 and P20 actually work on different purposes. The *SCV Order* used in these two policies as purposes with different values. It is called incomparable policies because they have incomparable purposes, that is, a *SCV* exists which has two disjoint value sets in the two purposes.

Definition 11.4 Let pu_i and pu_j be two purposes in two access control policies. We say that pu_i and pu_j are incomparable purposes if there exists a common *SCV* that has disjoint value sets in purposes pu_i and pu_i. Otherwise, we say that pu_i and pu_j are comparable purposes, written as $pu_i \approx pu_j$.

Consider the following two permission assignments which include comparable purposes:

P21: (Christine, (Read, OrderInfor), Purchase, Time = 9AM–5PM, ϕ)
P22: (Christine, (Read, OrderInfor), Billing, Time = 9AM–5PM, ϕ)

Because P21 allows data access during 9AM–5PM with Purchase purpose and P22 allows data access during in the same time with Billing purpose, a data request occurs during 9AM–5 PM with Billing purpose could be authorized. These two policies are compatible because they have compatible purposes: the intersection of value sets of context variable *Order* in different access policies is not empty.

Besides compatible purposes, we may have conflicting purposes.

P23: (Christine, (Read, OrderInfor), purchase, Time = 5PM–11PM,ϕ)
P24: (Christine, (Read, OrderInfor), audit, Time = 5PM–11PM, ϕ).

P23 specifies that Christine is authorized to access order information for Purchase during 5PM–11PM, whereas P24 allows partners' access with *Audit* during 5PM–11PM. Hence, when data access request is issued, the access purpose could not be both purchase and audit. Therefore, any data request will be denied according to these two access policies. These two permission assignments conflict with each other because they have conflicting purposes, that is, no value of the context variable *Order* could satisfy both purposes.

Definition 11.5 Let pu_i and pu_j be two comparable purposes in two access policies. We say that pu_i and pu_j are conflicting purposes if there exists at least one common context variable in pu_i and pu_j that has disjoint value sets, written as $pu_i \asymp pu_j$. Otherwise, we say that pu_i and pu_j are compatible purposes.

Consider the following access policies which include conflicting obligations:

P25: (Christine, (Read, OrderInfor), purchase, N/A, Notify())
P26: (Christine, (Read, OrderInfor), purchase, N/A, Notify(Opt-out))

Once a data request is authorized, the system does not know which obligation should be executed (either Notify or Notify with Opt-out); therefore P25 conflicts with P26.

We denote the fact that two obligations o_i and o_j conflict as $o_i \asymp o_j$.

Based on aforementioned definitions and examples, we give the definition of conflicting access policies.

Definition 11.6 Let $Pi = (ui, (ri, di), pui, ci, oi)$ and $Pj = (uj, (rj, dj), puj, cj, oj)$ be two privacy-sensitive data access policies. We say that Pi and Pj are conflicting if one of the following two conditions holds:
$(ui = uj) \wedge (ri = rj) \wedge (di = dj) \wedge (ci = cj) \wedge (pui \asymp puj)$
$(ui = uj) \wedge (ri = rj) \wedge (di = dj) \wedge (ci = cj) \wedge (pui \approx puj) \wedge (oi \asymp oj)$

In *PAC*, conflicting access policies should be detected and one of them should be removed to prevent ambiguities when enforcing access policies.

Detecting Algorithms

Conflicting policies detection is important in order to guarantee the consistency of access control policy. In this section, we present algorithms to detect conflicts between purposes and to check conflicts in access control policies. The key point of the algorithm is that we first sort context variables used in conditions according to their name, then make a disjoint test for the value sets for a variable in the various conditions.

Algorithm 1 Purpose-Conflict(pu1, pu2)
Require: *pu1* and *pu2* are two purposes applied in two access control policies
Outcomes: True //Purposes have conflicts
              False //Otherwise
1: pul_1: Sort context variables used in *pu1* according to their name
2: pul_2: Sort context variables used in *pu2* according to their name
3: for(integer $i = 1$ to $|pul_1|$)

4:     { for(integer $j = 1$ to $|pul_2|$)
5:        { if $pul_1[i].name = pul_2[j].name$ // Common context variable
6:        then
7:           { if $pul_1[i].SCV = True$ // $pul_1[i]$ is a SCV
8:              { if disjointTest($pul_1[i].value$, $pul_2[j].value$) = 'False'
// $pul_1[i].value$ and $pul_2[j].value$ have joint value sets, no conflicts between $pul_1[i]$ and $pul_2[j]$
9:              then j++ //check the next purpose in $pu2$
10:             else
11:             Return True //Conflict purposes }
12:          else j++ //check the next purpose in $pu2$ }
13:       else j++ }
14:    i++ //check the next purpose in $pu1$
15: Return result

Based on the Purpose-Conflict algorithm, the access control policy detection algorithm is given below. The idea of the algorithm is to test the purpose conflicts first, if so the policies are conflict. Otherwise, check the obligations to determine if or not the policies are conflict.

Algorithm 2 Policy-Conflict(po1, po2)
Require: po_1 and po_2 are two access control policies
Outcomes: True //Policies have conflicts
                  False //Otherwise
1: if $po_1.s \neq po_2.s$ or $po_1.d \neq po_2.d$ or $po_1.r \neq po_2.r$ or $po_1.c \neq po_2.c$, then
2: return False
3:     end if
4:     { if Purpose-Conflict($po_1.pu$, $po_2.pu$) = True
5:     //Checking conflicts between two purposes in two policies
7:     return True // policies conflict
8:     else // $po_1.pu \approx po_2.pu$
9:        {if {$(po_1.o \cap po_2.o) = \phi$ //obligations are comparable
10:       then
11:          { if Obligation-Conflict($po_1.o$, $po_2.o$)= True
12:          return True // Obligations conflicts
13:          else return False //no conficts in policies }
14:       else // SCV-Disjoint($po_1.o$, $po_2.o$) = False, Obligation incomparable
15:       return False // No conflicts in policies}
16:       }

Based on Algorithm 1, 2 and the structure of access purpose and policy, we can further develop algorithms with *SQL* to support the purpose and policy management approach presented in this chapter. The detailed methods with *SQL* are omitted.

11.6   Experimental Results

This section presents the implementation of the access control policy algorithms with Microsoft Visual Studio technology. The reason of using Microsoft Visual Studio technology is that we do not need to worry about the data structure including attributes in each access control policy. It is easy to add attributes to the existing *policy* table when another access policy is required to join or create in future [52, 55]. This is a web-based project implemented in *XAMPP* (http:// www.apachefriends.org/en/xampp.html) environment in windows platform using *MySql* database and *Apache* web server. Due to the open source *MySQL* database with high performance, high reliability and ease of use, it is used to store the information of subjects, actions, resources, purposes and obligations in policy in the implementation. We store the structure of policy, purpose hierarchy, resources and so on. *Apache* was the first viable alternative to the Netscape Communications Corporation web server, and since has evolved to dominate other web servers in terms of functionality and performance, making applications easily portable to all of the operating systems on which Google Chrome runs [17, 45, 97]. With Microsoft Visual Studio, it is able to go to the next level with *html5*.

The implementation of the access control policy algorithms includes many components, for example:

1. The structure of database including access control policy, resource and purpose
2. Conflicts of purposes, obligations and policies
3. Conditions and obligations in policies.

Clients are requiring using a modern web browser such as Google Chrome, Mozilla Firebox, Internet Explorer 6 or over and enable cookies. The computer must have an Internet connection in order to be able to access the system.

Database Design

The database to implement the *PAC* model consists of many tables such as *Policy, Resource* and *Purpose*. For example, the policy table named *policy.mdf* is defined in the *PAC* model which is a tuple of form *(Subject, Action, Resources, Purpose, Condition, Obligation)*. The Fig. 11.2 below shows the definition of the *Policy* Table.

User Interface

In order to make the implementation more convenient we developed a graphical user interface which interacts with the procedures of creating and removing policies. The graphical user interface is illustrated in Fig. 11.3. This interface was developed using Microsoft Visual Studio 2010 Ultimate and *MySql* database is used to initiate the generating access control policy instead of typing the above procedure call. This implementation is convenient for administrators since they only need to define the purpose hierarchy and obligation structure.

Figure 11.3 shows the page of all policies defined in database in a data grid. They can be modified by *edit* and *delete*. To access the resource we have to enter policy

Column Name	Data Type	Allow Nulls
▶🔑 PolicyId	bigint	☐
Subject	varchar(50)	☐
Action	varchar(50)	☐
Resourse	varchar(50)	☐
Purpose	varchar(50)	☐
Obligation	varchar(50)	☐

Fig. 11.2 Policy structure

Enter policy Id: [   ]

[Submit]

	PolicyId	Subject	Action	Resourse	Purpose	Obligation
Edit Delete	16	Christine	r	OrderInformation	Billing	NA
Edit Delete	17	Christine	r	OrderInformation	Billing	NAT
Edit Delete	19	Hua01	r	Customers	Audit	yes
Edit Delete	20	Hua01	r	Customers	Research	yes
Edit Delete	22	Hua01	r	Customers	Post	no
Edit Delete	23	Hua01	r	Customers	Purchase	no
Edit Delete	24	Hua01	r	OrderInformation	Purchase	no
Edit Delete	25	Hua	r	Customers	Purchase	yes
Edit Delete	26	Hua	w	Customers	Research	NA

[AddPolicy]

Fig. 11.3 Creating policy

Id in the text box given upper side of data grid and click on *Submit* button. To add new policy we need to click on *Add Policy* button as below.

Comparable Policy

If a new policy is created which consists of the data given below, the new policy is comparable to the existing *policy* 16 which has same Subject, Action, Resource and Obligation except purpose with *Purchase* and here purpose is *Billing* in Fig. 11.4. Due to the comparable property it will show a message of comparable policy and add the new policy to the database [74, 75].

Conflict of Purposes

When a new policy is planed to add which has data like given below, the new policy is now compared to the *policy* 16 which has same Subject, Action, Resource and Obligation and purpose is *Purchase* and here purpose is *Audit*, due to they are incompatible it will give us message of conflict of purpose and the new policy is not able to add to the database as shown in Fig. 11.5.

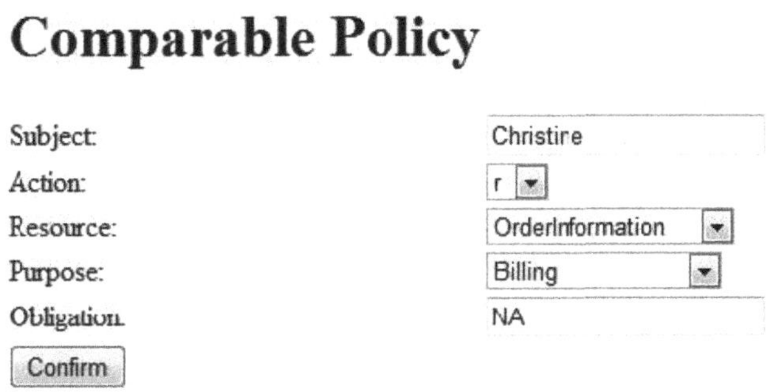

Comparable Policy

Subject: Christire

Action: r ▾

Resource: OrderInformation ▾

Purpose: Billing ▾

Obligation.   NA

[Confirm]

Fig. 11.4   Comparable policy

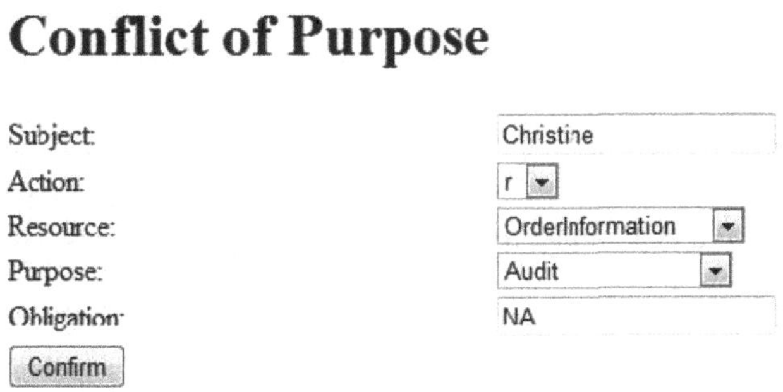

Conflict of Purpose

Subject: Christine

Action: r ▾

Resource: OrderInformation ▾

Purpose: Audit ▾

Obligation: NA

[Confirm]

Fig. 11.5   Conflict of purposes

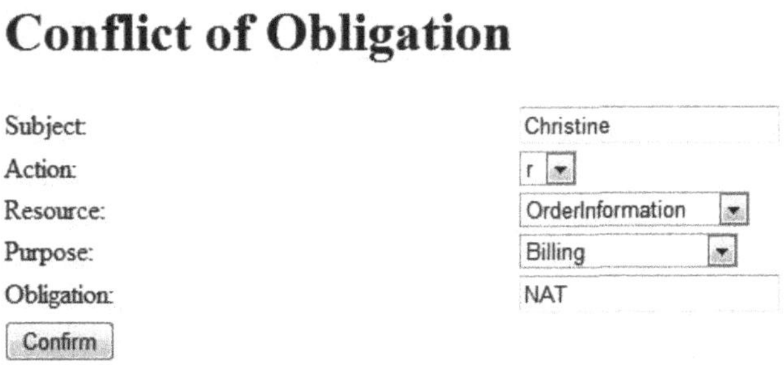

Conflict of Obligation

Subject: Christine

Action: r ▾

Resource: OrderInformation ▾

Purpose: Billing ▾

Obligation: NAT

[Confirm]

Fig. 11.6   Creating policy with conflicting obligation

Conflict of Obligations

It is quite similar to the conflict of purposes when the implementation deals with the obligation conflicts [20, 27, 56, 76]. When a new policy which has data given below, it is compared to the existing *policy* 16 which has same Subject, Action, Resource and Purpose but Obligation is *NA* and here Obligation is *NAT*. Due to they are conflicted it will give us message of conflict of obligation and it is not able to add to the database as shown in Fig. 11.6.

The advantages of the implementation are (1) providing a user interface for administrators to manage access control policies with various purposes and obligations since users can create and delete policy from the database without technical support which is efficient for system organisers; (2) The system provides a solution for conflicting policy problem, it supports not only the conflicts of purpose, but also the conflicts of obligations. (3) Implementation with Microsoft Visual Studio technology which is easy to manage life targeting an increasing number of platforms and technologies in future. However, we do not analyse generalized temporal constraints and the workflow of the policy creating processes, we suppose to complete them in our future work.

11.7 Comparisons

We present a brief comparison of the purpose involved access model *PAC* against other related work. The closely related works to this chapter are privacy-aware role-based access control [6, 19, 47], the enterprise privacy authorization language (*EPAL*) [57] and a conditional role-involved purpose-based access control model [24, 34, 99].

Ni et al. [47] introduced a family of models that extend the well known *RBAC* model in order to provide full support for expressing highly complex privacy-related policies, taking into account features like purposes and obligations. The models include the *Core P-RBAC* model, *Hierarchical P-RBAC* model, *Conditional P-RBAC* and *Universal P-RBAC*. Their work is different from ours in three aspects. First, their paper is focused on the conditions and their relationships in role-based access control. By contrast, our work has analyzed the purpose hierarchy structure in access control policies in usage access control model. Second, the conflicts between two P-RBAC permission assignments discussed in their paper are based on conditions. They neither analyze the access purpose structure nor the impact of adding a new access policy with different purposes. By contrast, our work has analyzed purpose hierarchical structure and the impact of adding new access control policies, specially the conflicting problem between three purposes.

EPAL [57] is a formal language for writing enterprise privacy policies to govern data handling practices in IT systems according to fine-grained positive and negative authorization rights. It concentrates on the core privacy authorization while abstracting data models and user-authentication from all deployment details such as data model or user-authentication. An *EPAL* policy defines lists of hierarchies of data-categories, user-categories, and purposes, and sets of (privacy) actions, obligations, and conditions. Purposes model the intended service for which data is used (e.g., processing a travel expense reimbursement or auditing purposes). Compared to *EPAL*, *PAC* has the following major differences. First, one of the important design criteria of *PAC* is to unify privacy policy enforcement and access control policy enforcement into one access control model. By contrast, EPAL is designed independently from any access control model. Second, the conflicting policies problem was not introduced and analyzed in *EPAL*; hence shortcoming exists during answering data access request [5, 51, 96], but *PAC* supports conflict detection to guarantee that no conflicts arise in the procedures of generating new policies, thus preventing the disclosure of private information. Third, the basic ideas of purpose in *PAC* are borrowed from *EPAL*, the purposes in EPAL represent reasons of data collection without further discussion such as conflicts from a privacy perspective; by contrast purposes in *PAC* have rich analysis and conflict algorithms.

The paper [34] proposed a privacy preserving access control which is based on variety of purposes. Conditional purpose is applied along with allowed purpose and prohibited purpose in the model. The structure of conditional purpose-based access control model is defined and investigated through dynamic roles. An algorithm is developed to achieve the compliance computation between access purposes and intended purposes and is illustrated with Role-based access control (RBAC) in a dynamic manner to support conditional purpose-based access control. However, the paper did not analyze the structure of access control policy, nor the associated access control models, access purposes, obligations and conflicts between access purposes and between access control policies, but instead discussed how to extend traditional access control models to a further coverage of privacy preserving in data mining atmosphere.

11.8 Conclusions

This chapter has discussed purpose-based access control policies with conditions and obligations in distributed computing environments. We have studied the access control framework but also the structure of access policies including subjects, access actions, resources, purposes and obligations. We have also analyzed the impact of adding new policies and the conflicts that they can lead to. Algorithms have been developed and to help a system to detect and solve the problems. Furthermore, the experimental results demonstrate the practicality and performance of the algorithms. The work in this chapter has extended previous work significantly in several aspects, for example, purpose involved access control, access control policies and generating a new access policy without conflicts.

The research for purpose involved access control policies is still in its infancy and much further work remains to be done. There could exist redundant access policies in *PAC*. For instance, P7 is redundant with respect to P8. Formal definitions of the redundancy need to be developed and solutions for addressing them are possible avenues for our future work.

11.9 Problems and Exercises

11.9.1 Problems

1. Purpose is associated to data that describes the reason(s) for data collection and data access. Purposes various in different areas and domains. It is a challenge to define a unified format to describe purposes for all domains.
2. This chapter develops purpose-based access control policies in usage access control, can the policies be able to applied to role-based access control?
3. Purposes will take different functions in customer's level and in administrator's level, the problem is how to manage the differences in real applications.
4. The difficulty of secure private information is that customers' data usage varies from individual to individual. For example, some online consumers may feel that it is acceptable to disclose their purchase history or browsing habits in return for better service, such as site personalization. Other customers, however, believe that such techniques violate their privacy. The problem is to develop a privacy preserving system to satisfy all customers.
5. In database systems, privacy policies are often enforced at the application level: The application generates a query to a database and retrieves a result, then check the result and filters unpermitted information. However, privacy leaks when the approach is applied at the cell Level of a database system. Consider Alice, who has opted to allow an agent releasing her email address but not her phone number to charities. Bob might choose to provide his phone number, but not his address. Row-level enforcement must either filter information that should be permitted, or disclose prohibited information. The challenge is to develop a system to protect the private information in a cell level.
6. The W3C's Platform for Privacy Preference (P3P) [44] is an industry standard that intends to provide an automated method for users to gain control over the use of their personal information collected by the web sites they visit. P3P allows web sites to encode their privacy practice in a machine readable format, such as what data is collected, who can access the data for what purposes, and how long the data will be stored by the sites. Even though P3P provides a standard means for enterprises to make privacy promises to their users, P3P does not provide any mechanism to ensure that these promises are consistent with the internal data processing.

11.9.2 Exercises

1. Given an example with two different domains, purposes are different;
2. Analysing applications of pusposes with role-based access control;

3. Developing a system approach to test conflicts between purposes as well as conflicts between policies. The approach will be surely help system administrators to make less errors when they generate new access control policies.
4. Developing algorithms developed in this chapter and test the conflicts;
5. Given an example, analysing purposes, obligations and conditions;
6. Analysing the privacy features of the P3P system including both positive and negative features.

References

1. Abiteboul, S., et al.: The lowell database research self-assessment. Commun. ACM **48**(5), 111–118 (2005)
2. Aiman, A., Sylvia, O.: Mixing privacy with role-based access control. In: Fourth International Conference on Computer Science & Software Engineering, pp. 1–7 (2011)
3. Adams, A., Angela, S.M.: Privacy in multimedia communications: protecting users, not just data. In: Blandford, A., Vanderdonckt, J., Gray, P. (eds.) People and Computers XVŰInteraction without Frontiers, eds edn. Springer, London. https://doi.org/10.1007/978-1-4471-0353-0_4
4. Barkley, J.F., Beznosov, K., Uppal, J.: Supporting relationships in access control using role based access control. In: Third ACM Workshop on Role Based Access Control, pp. 55–65 (1999)
5. Barth, A., Mitchell, J., Rosenstein, J.: Conflict and combination in privacy policy languages (summary). In: Proceedings of the 2004 ACM Workshop on Privacy in the Electronic Society (2004)
6. Bertino, E., Castano, S., Ferrari, E., Mesiti, M.: Specifying and enforcing access control policies for XML document sources. World Wide Web **3**, 139–151 (2000)
7. Bertino, E., Byun, J., Li, N.: Privacy-Preserving Database Systems, pp. 178–206. Springer, Berlin (2005)
8. Boyko, V., Peinado, M., Venkatesan, R.: Speeding up discrete log and factoring based schemes via precomputations. In: Advances in Cryptology - Eurocrypt'98. Lectures Notes in Computer Science, vol. 1807. Springer, Berlin (1998)
9. Byun, J., Li, N.: Purpose based access control for privacy protection in relational database systems. VLDB J. **17**(4), 603–619 (2008)
10. Byun, J., Bertino, E., Li, N.: Purpose based access control of complex data for privacy protection. In: Proceedings of the Tenth ACM Symposium on Access Control Models and Technologies, SACMAT'05, pp. 102–110. Association for Computing Machinery, New York (2005)
11. Canetti, R., Goldreich, O., Halevi, S.: The random oracle methodology. In: Proceedings of the 30th ACM STOC'98, pp. 209–218. IEEE, Piscataway (1998)
12. Canetti, R., Micciancio, D., Reingold, O.: Perfectly one-way probabilistic hash functions. In: Proceedings of the 30th ACM STOC'98. IEEE, Piscataway (1998)
13. Cao, J., et al.: Towards secure xml document with usage control. In: Web Technologies Research and Development - APWeb 2005, Berlin, pp. 296–307. Springer, Berlin (2005)
14. Chan, A., Frankel, Y., Tsiounis, Y.: An efficient off-line electronic cash scheme as secure as RSA. Research Report nu-ccs-96-03, Northeastern University, Boston (1995)
15. Chaum, D., Fiat, A., Naor, M.: Untraceable electronic cash. In: Advances in Cryptology - Crypto'88. Lectures Notes in Computer Science, vol. 403, pp. 319–327. Springer, Berlin (1990)
16. Clifton, C.: Using sample size to limit exposure to data mining. J. Comput. Secur. **8**(4), 281–307 (2000)

17. Du, J., et al.: Feature selection for helpfulness prediction of online product reviews: an empirical study. Plos One **14**, e0226902 12 (2019)
18. Eng, T., Okamoto, T.: Single-trem divisible electronic coins. In: Advances in Cryptology–Eurocrypt'94. Lectures Notes in Computer Science, vol. 950, pp. 306–319. Springer, Berlin (1995)
19. Feinstein, H.L.: Final report: NIST small business innovative research (SBIR) grant: role based access control: phase 1. Technical Report. SETA Corp. (1995)
20. Ferraiolo, D.F., Kuhn, D.R.: Role based access control. In: 15th National Computer Security Conference, pp. 554–563 (1992). ferraiolo92rolebased.html
21. Ferraiolo, D.F., Barkley, J.F., Kuhn, D.R.: Role-based access control model and reference implementation within a corporate intranet. In: Transactions on Information and System Security (TISSEC), vol. 2, pp. 34–64 (1999)
22. Folino, F., Pizzuti, C.: Combining markov models and association analysis for disease prediction. In: International Conference on Information Technology in Bio-and Medical Informatics, pp. 39–52. Springer, Berlin (2011)
23. Frankel, Y., Yiannis, T., Yung, M.: Indirect discourse proofs: achieving fair off-line electronic cash. In: Advances in Cryptology–Asiacrypt'96. Lectures Notes in Computer Science, vol. 1163, pp. 286–300. Springer, Berlin (1996)
24. Franklin, M., Yung, M.: Secure and efficient off-line digital money. In: Proceedings of the Twentieth International Colloquium on Automata, Languages and Programming. Lectures Notes in Computer Science, vol. 700, pp. 265–276. Springer, Berlin (1993)
25. Ge, Y., et al.: A benefit-driven genetic algorithm for balancing privacy and utility in database fragmentation. In: Proceedings of the Genetic and Evolutionary Computation Conference, pp. 771–776. Association for Computing Machinery, New York (2019)
26. Goldreich, O., Krawczyk, H.: On the composition of zero-knowledge proof systems. SIAM J. Comput. **25**(1), 159–192 (1996)
27. Goldschlag, D., Reed, M., Syverson, P.: Onion routing for anonymous and private Internet connections. Commun. ACM **24**(2), 39–41 (1999)
28. Huang, X., et al.: A generic framework for three-factor authentication: preserving security and privacy in distributed systems. IEEE Trans. Parallel Distrib. Syst. **22**(8), 1390–1397 (2011)
29. Kabir, E., et al.: Microaggregation sorting framework for k-anonymity statistical disclosure control in cloud computing. IEEE Trans. Cloud Comput. **8**, 408–417 (2018)
30. Kabir, M., et al.: A novel statistical technique for intrusion detection systems. Futur. Gener. Comput. Syst. **79**, 303–318 (2018)
31. Kabir, E., Wang, H.: Conditional purpose based access control model for privacy protection. In: Proceedings of the Twentieth Australasian Conference on Australasian Database - Volume 92, ADC'09, pp. 135–142. Australian Computer Society, Darlinghurst (2009)
32. Kabir, M., Wang, H.: Microdata protection method through microaggregation: a median-based approach. Inf. Secur. J. A Global Perspect. **20**, 1–8 (2011)
33. Kabir, M., Wang, H., Bertino, E.: A conditional purpose-based access control model with dynamic roles. Exp. Syst. Appl. **38**(3), 1482–1489 (2011)
34. Kabir, M., Wang, H., Bertino, E.: A conditional role-involved purpose-based access control model. J. Org. Comput. E. Commerce **21**, 71–91 (2011)
35. Kabir, M., Wang, H., Bertino, E.: Efficient systematic clustering method for k-anonymization. Acta Inf. **48**(1), 51–66 (2011)
36. Khalil, F., Li, J., Wang, H.: Integrating recommendation models for improved web page prediction accuracy. In: Proceedings of the Thirty-First Australasian Conference on Computer Science - Volume 74, ACSC '08, pp. 91–100. Australian Computer Society, Darlinghurst (2008)
37. Latanya, S.: Achieving k-anonymity privacy protection using generalization and suppression. Int. J. Uncertain. Fuzziness Knowl.-Based Syst. **10**(5), 571–588 (2002)
38. LeFevre, K., et al.: Limiting disclosure in hippocratic databases. In: Proceedings of the Thirtieth International Conference on Very Large Data Bases - Volume 30, VLDB'04, pp. 108–119. VLDB Endowment (2004)

39. Li, M., et al.: Advanced permission-role relationship in role-based access control. In: Information Security and Privacy, Berlin, pp. 391–403. Springer, Berlin (2008)
40. Li, M., et al.: Optimal privacy-aware path in hippocratic databases. In: Database Systems for Advanced Applications, Berlin, pp. 441–455. Springer, Berlin (2009)
41. Li, M., Wang, H.: ABDM: an extended flexible delegation model in RBAC. In: 2008 8th IEEE International Conference on Computer and Information Technology, pp. 390–395 (2008)
42. Li, M., Wang, H., Plank, A.: Privacy-aware access control with generalization boundaries. In: Proceedings of the Thirty-Second Australasian Conference on Computer Science - Volume 91, ACSC'09, Darlinghurst, pp. 105–112 (2009). Australian Computer Society, Darlinghurst
43. Liu, J., et al.: Privacy preserving distributed dbscan clustering. In: *Proceedings of the 2012 Joint EDBT/ICDT Workshops*, EDBT-ICDT'12, New York, pp. 177–185. Association for Computing Machinery, New York (2012)
44. Lorrie, C., et al.: The platform for privacy preferences 1.0 (p3p1. 0) specification (2002). http://www.w3.org/TR/P3P/ (Cited on pages 31 and 66) (2007)
45. MastercardVisa., (ed.): SET 1.0 - Secure electronic transaction specification (1997). http://www.mastercard.com/set.html
46. Ni, Q., et al.: Privacy-aware role based access control. In: Proceedings of the 12th ACM Symposium on Access Control Models and Technologies, SACMAT '07, New York, pp. 41–50. Association for Computing Machinery, New York (2007)
47. Ni, Q., et al.: Privacy-aware role-based access control. IEEE Secur. Privacy **7**(4), 35–43 (2009)
48. Okamoto, T.: An efficient divisible electronic cash scheme. In: Advances in Cryptology–Crypto'95. Lectures Notes in Computer Science, vol. 963, pp. 438–451. Springer, Berlin (1995).
49. Petković, M., et al.: Purpose control: did you process the data for the intended purpose? In: Secure Data Management, Berlin, pp. 145–168. Springer, Berlin (2011)
50. Pitofsky, R., et al.: Privacy online: fair information practices in the electronic marketplace. Statement of the Federal Trade Commission before the Committee on Commerce, Science and Transportation, United States Senate, Washington (2000)
51. Pointcheval, D.: Self-scrambling anonymizers. In: Proceedings of Financial Cryptography, Anguilla. Springer, Anguilla (2000)
52. Poutanen, T., Hinton, H., Stumm, M.: Netcents: a lightweight protocol for secure micropayments. In: The 3rd USENIX Workshop on Electronic Commerce, Boston (1998)
53. Rakesh, A.: Hippocratic databases. In: Proceedings of the 28th International Conference on Very Large Data Bases, VLDB '02, pp. 143–154. VLDB Endowment (2002)
54. Rasool, R., et al.: Cyberpulse: a machine learning based link flooding attack mitigation system for software defined networks. IEEE Access **7**, 34885–34899 (2019)
55. Rivest, R.T.: The MD5 message digest algorithm. Internet RFC 1321 (1992)
56. Sandhu, R.: Role activation hierarchies. In: Third ACM Workshop on Role Based Access Control, pp. 33–40. ACM Press, New York (1998)
57. Schunter, M., Powers, C.: The enterprise privacy authorization language (epal 1.1) (2003)
58. Shen, Y., et al.: Microthings: a generic iot architecture for flexible data aggregation and scalable service cooperation. IEEE Commun. Mag. **55**(9), 86–93 (2017)
59. Shu, J., et al.: Privacy-preserving task recommendation Services for Crowdsourcing. IEEE Trans. Serv. Comput. (2018). https://doi.org/10.1109/TSC.2018.2791601
60. Sun, X., et al.: An efficient hash-based algorithm for minimal k-anonymity. In: Proceedings of the Thirty-First Australasian Conference on Computer Science - Volume 74, ACSC'08, Darlinghurst, pp. 101–107. Australian Computer Society, Darlinghurst (2008)
61. Sun, X., et al.: Enhanced p-sensitive k-anonymity models for privacy preserving data publishing. Trans. Data Privacy **1**(2), 53–66 (2008)
62. Sun, X., et al.: (p+, α)-sensitive k-anonymity: a new enhanced privacy protection model. In: 2008 8th IEEE International Conference on Computer and Information Technology, pp. 59–64 (2008)
63. Sun, X., et al.: Injecting purpose and trust into data anonymisation. Comput. Secur. **30**, 332–345 (2011)

64. Sun, X., et al.: Privacy-aware access control with trust management in web service. World Wide Web **14**(4), 407–430 (2011)
65. Sun, X., et al.: Publishing anonymous survey rating data. Data Min. Knowl. Disc. **23**(3), 379–406 (2011)
66. Sun, L., et al.: Purpose based access control for privacy protection in e-healthcare services. J.Softw. **7**, 2443–2449 (2012)
67. Sun, X., et al.: An approximate microaggregation approach for microdata protection. Exp. Syst. Appl. **39**(2), 2211–2219 (2012)
68. Sun, X. et al.: Satisfying privacy requirements before data anonymization. Comput. J. **55**(4), 422–437 (2012)
69. Sun, L., Wang, H.: Access control and authorization for protecting disseminative information in e-learning workflow. Concurrency Comput. Pract. Exp. **23**, 2034–2042 (2011)
70. Sun, L., Wang, H.: A purpose-based access control in native xml databases. Concurrency Comput. Pract. Exp. **24**(10), 1154–1166 (2012)
71. Sun, L., Li, Y., Wang, H.: M-service and its framework. In: 2005 Asia-Pacific Conference on Communications, pp. 837–841 (2005)
72. Sun, X., Wang, H., Li, J.: Priority driven k-anonymisation for privacy protection. In: Proceedings of the 7th Australasian Data Mining Conference, vol. 87, pp. 73–78 (2008)
73. Sun, X., Wang, H., Li, J.: Microdata protection through approximate microaggregation. In: Proceedings of the Thirty-Second Australasian Conference on Computer Science - Volume 91, ACSC'09, pp. 161–168. Australian Computer Society, Darlinghurst (2009)
74. Sun, X., Wang, H., Li, J.: Satisfying privacy requirements: one step before anonymization. In: Advances in Knowledge Discovery and Data Mining, Berlin, pp. 181–188. Springer, Berlin (2010)
75. Sun, X., Wang, H., Sun, L.: Extended k-anonymity models against attribute disclosure. In: 2009 Third International Conference on Network and System Security, pp. 130–136 (2009)
76. Sun, L., Wang, H., Yong, J.: Authorization algorithms for permission-role assignments. J. Univ. Comput. Sci. **15**, 1782–1798 (2009)
77. Sun, X., Li, M., Wang, H.: A family of enhanced (l, α)-diversity models for privacy preserving data publishing. Futur. Gener. Comput. Syst. **27**(3), 348–356 (2011)
78. Sun, X., Sun, L., Wang, H.: Extended k-anonymity models against sensitive attribute disclosure. Comput. Commun. **34**(4), 526–535 (2011). Special issue: Building Secure Parallel and Distributed Networks and Systems
79. Vicenç, T.: Towards knowledge intensive data privacy. In: Data Privacy Management and Autonomous Spontaneous Security, pp. 1–7. Springer, Berlin (2010)
80. Vimalachandran, P. et al.: Preserving patient-centred controls in electronic health record systems: a reliance-based model implication. In: 2017 International Conference on Orange Technologies (ICOT), pp. 37–44 (2017)
81. Wang, H., Li, Q.: Secure and efficient information sharing in multi-university e-learning environments. In: *Advances in Web Based Learning – ICWL 2007*, Berlin, pp. 542–553. Springer, Berlin (2008)
82. Wang, H., Sun, L.: Trust-involved access control in collaborative open social networks. In: 2010 Fourth International Conference on Network and System Security, pp. 239–246 (2010)
83. Wang, H., Cao, J., Ross, D.: Role-based delegation with negative authorization. In: Frontiers of WWW Research and Development - APWeb 2006, Berlin, pp. 307–318. Springer, Berlin (2006)
84. Wang, H., Cao, J., Zhang, Y.: A flexible payment scheme and its role-based access control. IEEE Trans. Knowl. Data Eng. **17**(3), 425–436 (2005)
85. Wang, H., Cao, J., Zhang, Y.: Delegating revocations and authorizations in collaborative business environments. Inf. Syst. Front. **11**(3), 293 (2008)
86. Wang, H., Cao, J., Zhang, Y.: Delegating revocations and authorizations in collaborative business environments. Inf. Syst. Front. **11**(3), 293 (2008)
87. Wang, H. et al.: Authorization algorithms for the mobility of user-role relationship. In: Proceedings of the Twenty-Eighth Australasian Conference on Computer Science - Volume 38, ACSC'05, pp. 69–77. Australian Computer Society, Darlinghurst (2005)

88. Wang, H., et al.: A framework for role-based group deligation in distributed environments. In: Proceedings of the 29th Australasian Computer Science Conference, vol. 48, pp. 321–328 (2006)

89. Wang, H., et al.: Authorization approaches for advanced permission-role assignments. In: 2008 12th International Conference on Computer Supported Cooperative Work in Design, pp. 277–282 (2008)

90. Wang, H., Sun, L., Varadharajan, V.: Purpose-based access control policies and conflicting analysis. In: Security and Privacy – Silver Linings in the Cloud, Berlin, pp. 217–228. Springer, Berlin (2010)

91. Wang, H., Zhang, Y., Cao, J.: Ubiquitous computing environments and its usage access control. In: Proceedings of the 1st International Conference on Scalable Information Systems, InfoScale'06. ACM, New York (2006)

92. Wang, H., Zhang, Y., Cao, J.: Access control management for ubiquitous computing. Futur. Gener. Comput. Syst. **24**(8), 870–878 (2008)

93. Wang, H., Zhang, Y., Cao, J.: Effective collaboration with information sharing in virtual universities. IEEE Trans. Knowl. Data Eng. **21**, 840–853 (2008)

94. Wang, H., Zhang, Z., Taleb, T.: Editorial: special issue on security and privacy of IoT. World Wide Web **21**(1), 1–6 (2018)

95. Wang, Z., Zhan, Z., Lin, Y., Yu, W., Wang, H., Kwong, S., Zhang, J.: Automatic niching differential evolution with contour prediction approach for multimodal optimization problems. IEEE Trans. Evol. Comput. **24**, 114–128 (2020)

96. Yiannis, T.: Fair off-line cash made easy. In: Advances in Cryptology–Asiacrypt'98. Lectures Notes in Computer Science, vol. 1346, pp. 240–252. Springer, Berlin (1998)

97. Yiannis, T., Yung, M.: On the security of ElGamal-based encryption. In: International Workshop on Practice and Theory in Public Key Cryptography (PKC '98). Lectures Notes in Computer Science, vol. 1346, Yokohama. Springer, Berlin (1998)

98. Zhang, J., et al.: Detecting anomalies from high-dimensional wireless network data streams: a case study. Soft Comput. **15**(6), 1195–1215 (2011)

99. Zhang, Y., Gong, Y., Gao, Y., Wang, H., Zhang, J.: Parameter-free voronoi neighborhood for evolutionary multimodal optimization. IEEE Tran. Evol. Comput. **24**, 335–349 (2020)

Chapter 12
Effective Collaboration with Information Sharing in Virtual Universities

A global education system, as a key area in future IT, has fostered developers providing various learning systems with low cost. While a variety of E-learning advantages has been recognized for a long time and many advances in E-learning systems have been implemented, the needs for effective information sharing in a secure manner have to date been largely ignored, especially for virtual university collaborative environments. Information sharing of virtual universities usually occurs in broad, highly dynamic network-based environments, and formally accessing the resources in a secure manner poses a difficult and vital challenge.

This chapter aims to build a new rule-based framework to identify and address issues of sharing in virtual university environments through role-based access control management (*RBAC*). The framework includes a role-based group delegation granting model, group delegation revocation model, authorization granting and authorization revocation. We analyze various revocations and the impact of revocations on role hierarchies. The implementation with *XML*—based tools demonstrates the feasibility of the framework and authorization methods. Finally, the current proposal is compared with other related work.

12.1 Introduction

E-learning, as a significant modern education and learning approach and tool, is defined as learning activities performed over electronic devices [12, 93, 97]. E-learning has the potential to become a lower cost and efficient education tool, and one of the key e-commerce applications with a rapidly growing commercial market in the near future [30, 38, 65, 109]. Virtual universities as an example of E-learning have been implemented in many countries, for instance, Canadian Virtual University (http://www.cvu-uvc.ca/) is a group of Canada's leading universities in distance and online learning. Human interaction administration, as a shortcoming of E-learning,

© Springer Nature Switzerland AG 2020

H. Wang et al., *Access Control Management in Cloud Environments*,
https://doi.org/10.1007/978-3-030-31729-4_12

is a critical component of the E-learning market, especially in virtual university environments. There are situations in which learning resources cannot be updated and delivered due to insufficient collaborative management arrangements between partners of virtual universities. It is still an open question how efficiently technical skills can be trained in distributed E-learning environments [70, 75].

Virtual universities are becoming strongly networked and fundamental changes in the organization of education are occurring [90, 98]. Geographical isolation is no longer a factor for virtual universities. Students may study courses and complete qualifications from all over the world without leaving their homes or work offices. In a virtual university, each partner (e.g. a university in Canadian Virtual University) usually has its own accredited subjects which are admired by students. The large numbers of students and their various requirements increasingly encourages collaboration of partners to offer their best subjects to students. The collaboration within a virtual university is found to be a beneficial and enjoyable component of offering a course, but a source of frustration at the same time. Students' evaluations show that the perceived best and worst aspect of the course is communications between and within each partner in the virtual university [29, 84, 101]. Students are sincerely motivated by the expertise of lecturers, but obviously dissatisfied with their collaborations regarding access and updating study materials. The major problem is that students find it difficult to coordinate their schedules at their own university when study materials provided by the university is postponed. Furthermore, the collaborative partners in the virtual university are often distributed and their collaboration occurs across highly dynamic Internet-based environments, and formally accessing the subject materials in a secure manner poses a difficult and vital challenge [47, 48, 89].

Therefore, effective and efficient communication with distant collaborators is required for the collaboration between and within a virtual university environment [74, 88, 94, 117]. This chapter aims to develop a policy-based framework for information sharing in a distributed collaborative virtual university environment with role-based delegation. The inclusion of role-based delegation and revocation allows users themselves to delegate role authorities to others to process some authorized functions and later remove those authorities. Role-based delegation and revocation models are developed with comparison to established technical analysis, laboratory experiments, support hierarchical roles and multistep delegation. The models are implemented to demonstrate the feasibility of the framework and secure protocols for managing delegations and revocations.

Delegation is the process whereby an active entity in a distributed environment grants access resource permissions to another entity. In today's highly dynamic distributed systems, a user often needs to act on another user's behalf with part of the user's rights. To solve such delegation requirements, ad-hoc mechanisms are used in most systems by compromising existing disorganized policies, or additional components to their applications [54, 76, 102, 112]. The most common delegation types are user-to-machine, user-to-user, and machine-to-machine delegations [1, 5, 57]. They all have the same consequence, namely the propagation of access permission. Propagation of access rights in decentralized collaborative systems presents challenges for traditional access mechanisms because authorization decisions are made based on the identity of the resource requester. Unfortunately, access control based on identity may be ineffective when the requester is unknown to the resource owner [92, 106, 110]. Recently some distributed access control mechanisms have been proposed in distributed E-learning environments: Lowe et al. [56] presented a formal access model for vicarious learning based on an informal model arising out of a particular project and implementation of the model with a tool support system; Mendling [59] described business models for E-learning with a delegation mechanism to support access management in a distributed education environment. Weippl et al. [107, 108] have shown the security importance in E-learning environments since e-learning systems are production systems used by many people.

The National Institute of Standards and Technology proposed a role-based access control (*RBAC*) prototype and published a formal model [23]. *RBAC* enables managing and enforcing security in large-scale and enterprise-wide systems and its applications depend on specific system requirements. Many enhancements of *RBAC* models have been developed in the past decade. For example, Joshi et al. introduced a generalized temporal role-based access control (*GTRBAC*) Model that is an extension of the *RBAC* model [40, 41]. In *RBAC* models, permissions are associated with roles, users are assigned to appropriate roles, and users acquire permissions through roles. Users can be easily reassigned from one role to another. Roles can be granted additional permissions and permissions can be easily revoked from roles as needed [25, 34, 69]. Therefore, *RBAC* provides a means for empowering individual users through role-based delegation in distributed virtual university collaboration environments.

The importance of delegation in E-learning has been recognized for a long time [19, 55, 70, 107], but the concept has not been supported in *RBAC* models [24, 26]. An IT administrator (security officer) has to assign a role to the delegated lecturer if the role is required to be delegated to the lecturer. Such a model significantly increases the management efforts in a collaborative virtual university environment because of the dynamic of delegations and the continuous involvement from IT administrators. This chapter provides a bridge of the gap between delegation techniques and *RBAC* models in distributed virtual university environments.

The remainder of this chapter is organized as follows: Sect. 12.2 presents the related work associated with delegation models and *RBAC*. As a result of this section, we find that both group-based delegation within *RBAC* and its implementation with *XML* have not been presented and analysed in the literature. Section 12.3 proposes a delegation framework which includes the structures of role-based delegation, role-based group delegation and revocation models. Section 12.4 discusses the dimensions of revocation and various types of delegating revocations. The impacts of revocation an original role delegation are analysed in detail. Section 12.5 provides delegation authorizations. Granting authorization with prerequisite conditions and revocation authorization are discussed in this section. Definitions of *Can_delegate*, *Can_revoke*, *role range* are introduced and authorization rules for delegation and revocation are presented. Section 12.6 describes the implementation of the role-based group delegation using *XML* technology and Sect. 12.7 compares the work in this chapter to related previous work. Finally, the conclusion of the chapter is in Sect. 12.8.

12.2 Motivations

Effective collaboration is a common and significant process in a virtual university, and delegation is an important feature to achieve the collaborative goal. Effective delegation is defined as "the key aspect of good supervision" in [58]. Effective delegation not only develops people in groups work more efficiently and productive, but also frees the delegating users and groups up to more important issues [46, 105, 116]. For example, imagine that the University of Southern Queensland (USQ), the Victoria University of Technology (VUT) and La trobe University (LaU) are three partners in a virtual university. Lecturer *A* from USQ as a course examiner in the virtual university, wants to apply 2 weeks off to attending a conference and to delegate the examiner role to Lecturer *B* at VUT. The normal procedures are: (1) Lecturer *A* fills an application form sent to his/her Department; (2) The form approved by the Department then needs to be delivered to the Faculty; (3) The form signed by the Dean of the Faculty will be sent to the HR and administrative office at USQ; (4) The HR will send the application to VUT for approval; (5) Administrators assign the examiner role to Lecturer *B* after the form signed by the Department and the Faculty at VUT. The procedure takes a few weeks and costs a lot. This kind of leave application is very common in a university, especially in the virtual university [53, 77, 83].

USQ is developing partnerships between VUT and LaU to address possible problems including the complex leave application. The three universities are able to provide available study materials and also prevent illegal resource access if they efficiently collaborate with the people in other universities. A problem-oriented collaboration system (*POCS*) is proposed to improve the service to students as a part of ongoing community efforts including identifying potential problems and resolving them before they become significant. With efficient delegation, staff members respond quickly to urgent accidents and increase the time spent confronting problems.

In *POCS*, lecturers might be involved in many concurrent activities such as conducting initial majors, analysing student involvement, preparing coordinator reports, and assessing students' employee market reports. In order to achieve this, lecturers may have one or more roles such as head supervisor, participant supervisor, or reporter. In this example, Tony, a director at *USQ*, needs to coordinate analysing student involvement in the virtual university courses and assessing employee market reports. Collaboration is necessary for information sharing with members in other universities from these two projects. To collaborate closely and make two projects more successful, Tony would like to delegate certain responsibilities to Christine and her staff at *VUT*. The prerequisite conditions are to secure these processes and to monitor the progress of the delegation. Furthermore, Christine may need to delegate her delegated role to other staff as necessary or to delegate a role to all members of a group at the same time. Without delegation skill, IT administrators have to do excessive work because of their involvement in every single collaborative activity. The major requirements and challenges of role-based delegation within this collaborative virtual university example are [81, 85, 95]:

1. Group-based delegation means that a delegating user (a lecturer) may need to delegate a role to all members of a group at the same time [50, 51].
2. Multistep delegation occurs when a delegation can be further delegated. Single-step delegation means that the delegated role cannot be further delegated [43, 111].
3. Revocation schemes are an important feature of collaborative virtual university systems. They take away the delegated permissions. There are different revoking schemes; among them are strong and weak revocations, cascading and noncascading revocations, as well as grant-dependent and grant-independent revocations [80, 91, 99].
4. Constraints are an important factor in *RBAC* for laying out higher-level organizational policies. They define whether or not the delegation or revocation process is valid [15, 35, 73].
5. Partial delegation means only subsets of the permissions are delegated while total delegation means all permissions are delegated. Partial delegation is an important feature because it allows users only to delegate required permissions. The well-known least privilege security principle can be implemented through partial delegation [49, 78].

Although the concept of delegation is not new in authorizations [4, 21, 103, 108], role-based delegation has received attention only recently [114, 115]. Aura [4] introduced key-oriented discretionary access control systems that are based on delegation of access rights with public-key certificates. The systems emphasized decentralization of authority and operations but their approach is a form of discretionary access control. Hence, they can neither express mandatory policies like the Bell–LaPadula model [7], nor is it possible to verify that someone does not have a certificate. Furthermore, some important policies such as separation of duty policies cannot be expressed only with certificates. They need some additional mechanism to maintain the previously granted rights and the histories must be updated in real time when new certificates are issued. Delegation is also applied in decentralized trust management [6, 28, 32, 33].

Some researchers have worked on the semantics of authorization, delegation, and revocation [1, 44, 52]. Hagstrom et al. [36] studied various problems of revoking in an ownership-based framework, but their attempt was still not sufficient to model all the revocations required in role-based delegation, for example, strong revocation and weak revocation. Zhang et al. [114, 115] proposed a rule-based framework for role-based delegation. The framework was based on a simple delegation model supporting only flat roles (i.e. no role hierarchy) and single step delegation. Furthermore, as a delegation model, it does not support group-based delegation.

The model does not analyse how original role assignment changes impact on delegations or implement with XML-based language. All these previous works were not successful in addressing the requirements of role-based delegation in virtual university environments.

This chapter focuses exclusively on a role-based delegation model which supports group-based delegation in virtual university environments and its implementation with *XML* technology. We propose a delegation framework including delegation granting and revocation models, and group-based delegation. To provide sufficient functions with the framework, this chapter analyses how changes to original role assignment impact upon delegation results. This kind of role-based group delegation and its implementation with *XML* have not been studied before.

12.3 The Role-Based Delegation and Revocation Framework

In this section we propose a role-based group delegation framework called *RBGDF* which supports role hierarchy and group delegation by introducing a delegation relation.

12.3.1 Role-Based Access Control

The basic elements and relations in *RBAC* are depicted in Fig. 12.1. *RBAC* involves individual users being associated with roles, as well as roles being associated with permissions (each permission is a pair of objects and operations) [23, 79, 82]. As such, a role is used to associate users and permissions. A user in this model of the virtual university environment is a human being, such as a lecturer or professor. A role is a job function or job title within the organization associated with authority and responsibility. There are two types of roles: regular role and administrative role. We only address regular roles in this chapter. Roles have hierarchy structure in *RBAC* model. Senior roles inherit all permissions from junior roles [8, 9, 45]. Therefore, a senior-junior relationship exists in the figure. Permission is an approval for a particular operation to be performed on one or more objects. As shown in the figure, User_name, Role_name, Perm_name, Oper_name and Object_name are attributes of User, Role, Permission, Operation and Object respectively. Four relationships between users and roles, between roles and permissions, between roles and roles, and between operations and objects are many-to-many. The security policy of the organization determines role membership and the allocation of each role's capabilities [22, 27, 96].

The number of roles and users in virtual university environments can be hundreds or thousands. For instance, USQ has five faculties, and each faculty has five departments. Each department has fifty courses and every course has at least two roles of one examiner and one moderator. Managing these roles and users and their

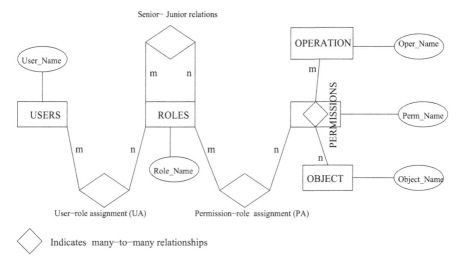

Fig. 12.1 RBAC relationship

interrelationships is a challenge that is often highly decentralized and delegated to a small team of project groups. Role-based delegation is a particularly critical administrative activity because assigning people to tasks is a normal managerial function and assigning users to roles is a natural part of delegating users to tasks. Furthermore, the activities in distributed E-learning environment are decentralized and delegated to users rather than system administrators [10, 11].

Delegation is an important aspect of *RBAC* and often regarded as one of the principal motivations behind *RBAC*. Although the importance of delegation in *RBAC* has been recognized for a long time, it has not received much attention. Zhang et al. [114, 115] recently proposed a rule-based framework for role-based delegation. We use the concept of role-based delegation borrowed from their work. The central contributions of this article are to describe how we can build a framework of role-based group delegation within *RBAC* in a distributed virtual university environment, how the impact of role structures when a role is removed, and to implement the delegation framework with *XML* based tools and languages.

12.3.2   Role-Based Delegation Model

An important concept within *RBAC* is a session, which involves a mapping between a user and possibly many roles [13, 72, 104]. For example, a user may establish a session by activating some subset of assigned roles. A session is always associated with a single user and each user may establish zero or more sessions. There may be hierarchies within roles. Senior roles are shown at the top of the hierarchies. Senior roles inherit permissions from junior roles. Let $x > y$ denote x is senior to y with

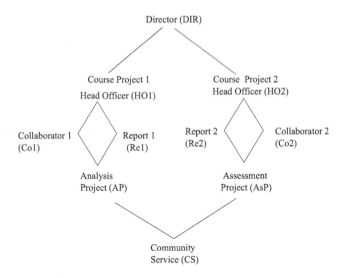

Fig. 12.2 Role hierarchy in *POCS*

Table 12.1 User-role
assignments

Role_name	User_name
DIR	Tony
HO1	Richard
HO2	Mike
Co1	Christine
Re1	John
CS	Ahn

the obvious extension to $x \geq y$. Role hierarchies provide a powerful and convenient means to enforce the principle of least privilege since only required permissions to perform a task are assigned to the role.

Figure 12.2 shows the role hierarchy structure of *RBAC* in *POCS*. The following Table 12.1 expresses an example of user-role assignment in *POCS*. There are two sets of users associated with a role *r*:

Original users are those users who are assigned to *r*;

Delegated users are those users who are delegated to *r*.

The same user can be an original user of one role and a delegated user of another role [42, 86, 119]. Also it is possible for a user to be both an original user and a delegated user of the same role. For example, if Richard delegates his role *HO1* to Christine, then Christine is both an original user (explicitly) and a delegated user (implicitly) of role *Co1* because the role *HO1* is senior to the role *Co1*. The original user assignment (*UAO*) is a many-to-many user assignment relation between original users and roles. The delegated user assignment (*UAD*) is also a many-to-many user assignment relation between delegated users and roles. Figure 12.3 shows the relationships of user and role in *UAO* and *UAD*.

Fig. 12.3 UAO and UAD
realtionships

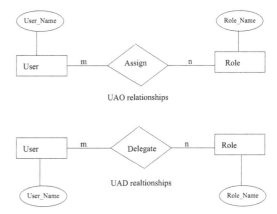

We have the following components for the role-based delegation model in virtual university environments:

U, R, P and S are sets of users (e.g. lecturers, professors), roles (e.g. course examiner, course moderator), permissions (e.g. read gradebook, update gradebook), and sessions, respectively.

1. $UAO \subseteq U \times R$ is a many-to-many original user to role assignment relation.
2. $UAD \subseteq U \times R$ is a many-to-many delegated user to role assignment relation.
3. $UA = UAO \cup UAD$. User-role assignment includes original user-role assignment and delegated user-role assignment.
4. Users: $R \Rightarrow 2^U$ is a function mapping of roles to sets of users.
   $Users(r) = \{u|(u, r) \in UA\}$ where UA is user-role assignment.
5. $Users(r) = Users\_O(r) \cup Users\_D(r)$
   where
   $Users\_O(r) = \{u|\exists r'' \geq r, (u, r'') \in UAO\}$
   $Users\_D(r) = \{u|\exists r'' \geq r, (u, r'') \in UAD\}$
   $Users(r)$ includes all users who are members of role r. The users may be original and delegated users. The original users $Users\_O(r)$ are not only the member of role r but also the member of a senior role r'' of r. This is because the senior role r'' inherits all permissions of its junior role r. With the hierarchy structure of roles, a user who is a member of r'' is also a member of role r. The members in $Users\_D(r)$ are similar to that in $Users\_O(r)$. For instance, according Table 12.1 and the example of Richard delegating role $HO1$ to Christine, we have:
   $Users\_O(HO1) = \{Richard\}$,
   and
   $Users\_D(HO1) = \{Christine\}$.

With these components, we analyse user-to-user delegation supporting role hierarchies and group delegations. As we mentioned before, we consider only the

Fig. 12.4 Role-based
delegation model

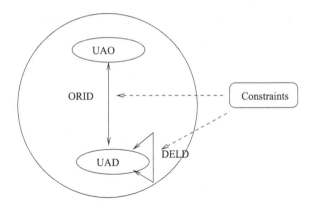

regular role delegation in this chapter, even though it is possible and desirable to delegate an administrative role [16, 62, 64].

A delegation relation (*DELR*) exists in the role-based delegation model which includes three elements: original user assignments *UAO*, delegated user assignment *UAD*, and constraints. The motivation behind this relation is to address the relationships among different components involved in a delegation. In a user-to-user delegation, there are five components: a delegating user, a delegating role, a delegated user, a delegated role, and associated constraints. For example, *((Tony, DIR), (Christine, DIR), Friday)* means Tony acting in role *DIR* delegates role *DIR* to Christine on Friday. We assume each delegation is associated with zero or more constraints. The delegation relation supports partial delegation in role hierarchies: a user who is authorized to delegate a role r can also delegate a role r' that is junior to r. For example, *((Tony, DIR), (Ahn, Re1), Friday)* means Tony acting in role *DIR* delegates a junior role *Re1* to Ahn on Friday. A delegation relation *DELR* is a one-to-many relationship on user assignments. It consists of original user delegation (*ORID*) and delegated user delegation (*DELD*). Figure 12.4 illustrates components and their relations in a role-based delegation model.

From the above discussions, the following components are formalized:

1. $DELR \subseteq UA \times UA \times Cons$ is a one-to-many delegation relation. A delegation relation can be represented by $((u, r), (u', r'), Cons) \in DELR$, which means the delegating user u with role r delegated role r' to user u' when the constraint $Cons$ is satisfied. With the partial delegation requirement in our virtual environments, we emphasize that the user u can only delegate role r or its junior role r' to the user u'.
2. $ORID \subseteq UAO \times UAD \times Cons$ is an original user delegation relation.
3. $DELD \subseteq UAD \times UAD \times Cons$ is a delegated user delegation relation.
4. $DELR = ORID \cup DELD$.

The last equation shows that delegation relations consist of original and delegated user delegation relations. Based on the user-to- user delegation, we now analyse group delegation in the remaining part of this section [18, 31, 100].

12.3.3 Role-Based Group Delegation

The scope of our model is to address role-based group delegation with role hierarchies and constraints that support multistep and partial delegations. There are two kinds of group delegation: user-group delegation and group-group delegation. We first discuss user-group delegations, which consist of original user-group and delegated user-group delegations. The new relation of user-group delegation is defined as delegation group relation ($DELUGR$) which includes: original user assignments UAO; delegated user assignments UAD; delegated group assignments GAD; and *constraints*. In a user-group delegation, there are five components: a delegating user (or a delegated user); a delegating role; a delegated group; a delegated role; and associated constraints. For example, *((Tony, DIR), (Project 1, DIR), 1:00pm–3:00pm Monday)* means Tony acting in role *DIR* delegates role *DIR* to all people involved in Project 1 during 1:00PM–3:00PM on Monday. A user-group delegation relation is a one-to-many relationship on user assignments. It consists of original user group delegation ($ORIUGD$) and delegated user group delegation ($DELUGD$). Figure 12.5 illustrates components and their relations in the role-based delegation model. Hence we have the following elements and functions for user-group delegation:

1. G is a set of users. GA is a group-role assignment which specifies a group of users authorized to perform roles. For example, $(G, r') \in GA$ means the group G has been authorized to perform role r'.
2. $DELUGR \subseteq UA \times GA \times Cons$ is a one-to-many delegation relation. A delegation relation can be represented by $((u, r), (G, r'), Cons) \in DELUGR$, which means the delegating user u with role r delegated role r' to group G if the constraint $Cons$ is satisfied. In virtual university E-learning environments, for instance, role r could be the Computing Coordinator and role r' be the same of role r ($r' = r$) or an examiner in computing (r' is a junior role of role r).
3. $ORIUGD \subseteq UAO \times GAD \times Cons$ is a relation of an original user and a group with constraints.
4. $DELUGD \subseteq UAD \times GAD \times Cons$ is a relation of a delegated user and a group with constraints.
5. $DELUGR = ORIGD \cup DELGD$.

Similar to user-group delegation, group-group delegation consists of original group assignment GAO, delegated group assignment GAD and constraints. As shown in Fig. 12.5, there are the following elements and functions in group-group delegation:

1. G is a set of users. GA is a set of group-role assignments.
2. $DELGGR \subseteq GA \times GA \times Cons$ is a one-to-many delegation relation. A delegation relation can be represented by $((G, r), (G', r'), Cons) \in DELUGR$, which means the delegating group G with role r delegated role r' to group G' if the constraint $Cons$ is satisfied. Where $r' = r$ or r' is a junior role of role r.

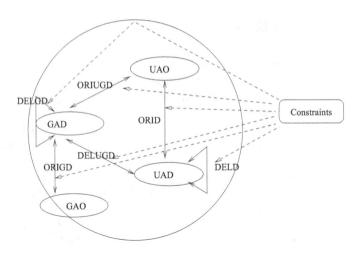

Fig. 12.5 Role-based group delegation model

3. $ORIGGD \subseteq GAO \times GAD \times Cons$ is a relation of a group and a group with constraints.
4. $DELGGD \subseteq GAD \times GAD \times Cons$ is a relation of a delegated group and a group with constraints.
5. $DELGGR = ORIGGD \cup DELGGD$.

The practical group-group delegation is monitored by a powerful person such as a director of the delegated group. The procedure of delegation authorization is analysed in section 12.5.

12.4 Role-Based Delegation Revocations

Revocation is a significant function in role-based group delegations. For example, Tony delegated role *DIR* to group Project 1; if the group moves to another company and does not exist at the university anymore, the delegated role *DIR* has to be revoked instantly. For simplicity, we do not differentiate roles and groups in this section.

12.4.1 Revocation Dimensions

Different revocation models have been proposed for access control systems [36, 91, 115]. For instance, three dimensions were introduced in [36] that are applied for database management system. We gather these dimensions in a unified collections:

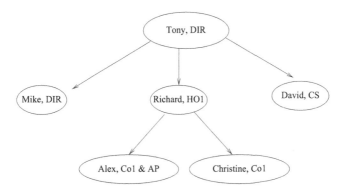

Fig. 12.6 Delegation relationships

dependency, resilience, propagation and dominance. Each dimension is defined in this section adopting examples rather than formal descriptions.

Dependency Dependency refers to the legitimacy of a user who can revoke a delegated role. Dependent revocation means only the delegating user can revoke the delegated user from the delegated role. Independent revocation allows any original user of the delegating role to revoke the user from the delegated role. For example, in Fig. 12.6, suppose Richard acting as role *HO1* delegated role *Co1* to Christine, and the delegation needs to be removed. With dependent revocation Richard can revoke Christine from the delegated role *Co1* but Tony cannot even though Tony acts as role *DIR* that is senior to and an original role of *Co1*, but Tony can take the delegated role *Co1* from Christine with independent revocation.

Resilience This dimension describes revocation through deleting or negative authorization. The effect of a role deleting revocation from a user is acted; another user may grant the user the same role that was just revoked, and as a result the revocation has no affect on the user. The negative authorization has high priority in this dimension that means the authorization overrule any other authorizations until the negative one is in turn revoked. As shown in Fig. 12.6, Richard needs to keep Alex from role *Co1*, he can either delete the current delegating relationship, or give a negative authorization of *Co1* to Alex. In the first case, Alex is denied to act as role *Co1*, but only as long as no other users delegate Alex the role. In the second case, Alex can not act as role *Co1* until the negative authorization is revoked. Therefore, negative authorization is stronger than deleting revocation.

Propagation This dimension distinguishes revocations according to a delegation structure of role locations. There are local revocation and global revocation in the dimension [67, 106]. The local revocation only happens to the direct delegation relationship while the global revocation effects all other users authorized by the revoked user. We use Fig. 12.6 to explain the difference between local and global revocations. Suppose Tony wants to revoke Richard from *HO1* but trusts Alex with roles *AP, Col*, and trusts Christine with role *Col* delegated by Richard, local revocation can be applied; otherwise global revocation is applied to take role *HO1* from Richard as well as both roles *AP, Col* from Alex and *Col* from Christine.

Dominance This dimension deals with role structure in *RBAC*. Roles in *RBAC* have hierarchy relationships and the relationships have transferable features that means when $r_1 > r_2$ and $r_2 > r_3$, then $r_1 > r_3$. Due to role hierarchy, a role r'' has all permissions of role r when $r'' > r$. A revocation problem may arise when a user with two roles $\{r'', r\}$, and the user still has the permissions of r if only to revoke r from the user. An explicit member of a user u is a set of roles $\{r | (u, r) \in UA\}$ where $(u, r) \in UA$ means user u has role r and the implicit member of a user u is a set of roles $\{r | \exists r'' > r, (u, r'') \in UA\}$. We say an explicit membership or implicit membership if a role is an explicit member or implicit member of a user, respectively. The difference between an explicit member and implicit member of a user is the direct relationship between the user and roles. A role may have an explicit and implicit membership of a user. For instance, according Figs. 12.2 and 12.6, role *AP* is an explicit member of Alex, and also an implicit member of Alex since $Col > AP$ and Alex has role *Col*. To solve the authorization revocation problem, we need to revoke the explicit membership first if a user is an explicit member of the role, and then revoke all implicit memberships.

There are two kinds of revocations. The first one is weak revocation which revokes explicit membership only. Weak revocation has an impact only on explicit membership. With weak revocation, the membership of a role with a user is revoked only if the role is an explicit member of the user. Therefore, weak revocation of a role from a user has no effect when the role is not an explicit member of the user. The second one is strong revocation that revokes both explicit and implicit memberships. Strong revocation of a role membership in a user requires that the role be removed not only from explicit membership in the user, but also from explicit and implicit membership in all roles senior to the role. Strong revocation therefore has a cascading effect up-wards in the role hierarchy [2, 63, 71].

In the example mentioned before that the user with two roles $\{r'', r\}$ where $r'' > r$, the user remains all permissions of role r through weak revocation role r from the user since the role r'' remains to the user. With strong revocation role r from the user, not only the role r but the role r'' is removed off from the user since r'' has an explicit membership of the user and is senior to role r. In e-learning environments, Alex has two delegated roles *Col, AP* where role *Col* is senior to role *AP* in Figs. 12.2 and 12.6. If Richard wants to take role *AP* from Alex with strong revocation, both roles *Col* and *AP* are revoked from Alex, but with weak revocation only role *AP* is revoked.

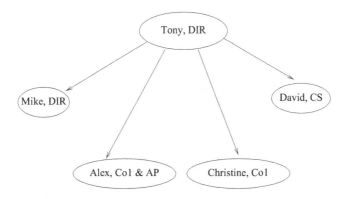

Fig. 12.7 Delegation relationships after *DWLD*

12.4.2   Revoking Delegations

Sixteen different revocations exist based on the dimensions in the previous section. Each scheme, as shown in Table 12.2, has a unique description with respect to the four dimensions. We analyze four delegating revocations in this chapter.

DependentWeakLocalDelete(*DWLD*)
The DependentWeakLocalDelete(*DWLD*), as the first revocation scheme, is the most easy operation. It does neither have resilience, propagation, nor dominance, and only the direct delegating user can remove the delegation relationship. Suppose Tony as the director wants to revoke role *HO1* from Richard since Richard is not an employee any longer in a company. With the scheme of *DWLD*, role *Ho1* only takes away from Richard and the roles of both Alex and Christine are intact; the delegation relationships between Richard and Alex, Richard and Christine come to the relationships between Tony and Alex, Tony and Christine as shown in Fig. 12.7 from Fig. 12.6.

The features of scheme *DWLD* when user U_1 wants to revoke role r from user U_2 are:

1. U_1 does not grant role r to U_2;
2. Role r may still stay with U_2 if users other than U_1 delegate r to him;
3. Roles granted by users other than U_1 are intact;
4. The delegation structure may need to be updated since roles delegated by U_2 have to remain.

DependentStrongLocalDelete(*DSLD*)
The DependentStrongLocalDelete(*DSLD*) is different from *DWLD* in the dominance aspect. It does not have resilience and propagation, but dominance, and only the direct delegating user may take away the delegation relationship. Suppose Mike acting as role *DIR* wants to remove role *Co1* from Richard since Richard is out of

Table 12.2 Revocation types

No.	Dependency	Resilience	Propagation	Dominance	Name
1	No	No	No	No	DependentWeakLocalDelete(*DWLD*)
2	No	No	No	Yes	DependentStrongLocalDelete(*DSLD*)
3	No	No	Yes	No	DependentWeakGlobalDelete(*DWGD*)
4	No	No	Yes	Yes	DependentStrongGlobalDelete(*DSGD*)
5	No	Yes	No	No	DependentWeakLocalNegative(*DWLN*)
6	No	Yes	No	Yes	DependentStrongLocalNegative(*DSLN*)
7	No	Yes	Yes	No	DependentWeakGlobalNegative(*DWLN*)
8	No	Yes	Yes	Yes	DependentStrongGlobalNegative(*DSGN*)
9	Yes	No	No	No	IndependentWeakLocalDelete(*IDWLD*)
10	Yes	No	No	Yes	IndependentStrongLocalDelete(*IDSLD*)
11	Yes	No	Yes	No	IndependentWeakGlobalDelete(*IDWGD*)
12	Yes	No	Yes	Yes	IndependentStrongGlobalDelete(*IDSGD*)
13	Yes	Yes	No	No	IndependentWeakLocalNegative(*IDWLN*)
14	Yes	Yes	No	Yes	IndependentStrongLocalNegative(*IDSLN*)
15	Yes	Yes	Yes	No	IndependentWeakGlobalNegative(*IDWLN*)
16	Yes	Yes	Yes	Yes	IndependentStrongGlobalNegative(*IDSGN*)

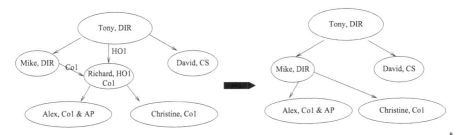

Fig. 12.8 Delegation relationships after *DSLD*

the work as role *Col*. With the scheme of *DSLD*, not only is role *Col* taken away from Richard by Mike, but role *HO1* has to be moved from Richard by Tony since role *HO1* delegated by Tony is senior to role *Col*. New delegation relationships are generated between Mike and Alex, Mike and Christine as shown in Fig. 12.8.

The features of scheme *DSLD* when user U_1 wants to revoke role r from user U_2 are:

1. U_1 does not grant role r to U_2;
2. Implicit role r' that is senior to role r is removed;
3. Roles other than r and its senior role are intact;
4. The delegation structure may need to be updated since roles delegated by U_2 have to remain.

DependentWeakGlobalDelete(*DWGD*)

The DependentWeakGlobalDelete(*DWGD*) is different from *DWLD* in the propagation aspect. It does not have resilience and dominance, but propagation, and only the direct delegating user may remove the delegation relationship. Suppose Mike acting as role *DIR* wants to remove role *Col* from Richard since Richard is out of the work as role *Col*. With the scheme of *DWGD*, role *Col* is taken away from Richard by Mike, but role *HO1* is intact, role *Col* is also revoked from Alex and Christine since the delegation authorization is no longer supported by Richard. The new relationships after the *DWGD* are shown in Fig. 12.9.

The features of scheme *DWGD* when user U_1 wants to revoke role r from user U_2 are:

1. U_1 does not grant role r to U_2;
2. role r delegated by U_2 to users is removed;
3. Roles other than r are intact;
4. The delegation structure may need to be updated since roles other than r delegated by U_2 have to remain.

DependentWeakLocalNegative(*DWLN*)

The DependentWeakLocalNegative(*DWLN*) is the scheme with negative authorization in resilience dimension. When a negative authorization of a role is granted to

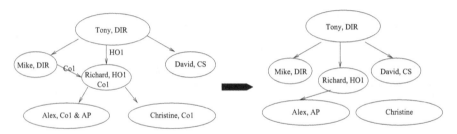

Fig. 12.9 Delegation relationships after *DWGD*

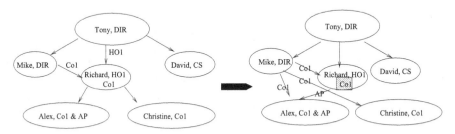

Fig. 12.10 Delegation relationships after *DWLN*

a revokee as weak and local revocation, the negative authorization will remain with the revokee until the authorization is removed, and the revokee cannot act as the role even though the role is delegated to her/him. The negative revocation scheme is different from other revocation schemes in the resilience dimension. We use the black colour for the role with negative authorization in Fig. 12.10. Suppose Mike acting as role *DIR* wants to grant a negative authorization of role *Col* to Richard since Richard is no longer loyal as role *Col*. With the scheme of *DWLN*, role *Col* is taken away from Richard by Mike, but role *HO1* is intact. Role *Col* is not revoked from Alex and Christine since the revocation is weak.

The features of scheme *DWLN* when user U_1 wants to revoke role r from user U_2 as a negative authorization are:

1. role r delegated to U_2 is inactive;
2. roles other than r delegated by U_2 are intact;
3. Roles other than r delegated to U_2 are intact;
4. The delegation structure may need to be updated since roles other than r delegated by U_2 have to remain.

Based on the results of the structure with role-based group delegation, we discuss group delegation and revocation authorizations in the next section.

12.5 Delegation Authorization

We develop delegating and revocation models in this section. The notion of a *prerequisite condition*, *Can_delegate* and *Can_revoke* are key parts in group delegation process.

12.5.1 Authorization Models

The delegation authorization goal imposes restrictions on which roles can be delegated to whom [17, 37, 87, 113]. We partially adopt the notion of prerequisite condition from [91] to introduce delegation authorization in the delegation framework.

A *prerequisite condition* is an expression using Boolean operators '∧' and '∨' on terms of the form r and $\bar{r}$ where r is a role and '∧' means "and", '∨' means "or". A prerequisite condition is evaluated for a user u by interpreting r to be true if $(\exists r'' \geq r)$, $(u, r'') \in UA$ and $\bar{r}$ to be true if $(\forall r'' \geq r)$, $(u, r'') \notin UA$, where UA is a set of user-role assignments. ◇

We say a group satisfies a prerequisite condition if all users in the group satisfy the prerequisite condition.

For a given set of roles R let CR denote all possible prerequisite conditions that can be formed using the roles in R, for example, $CR = r_1 \wedge r_2 \vee \bar{r}_3$. In some cases, we may need to define whether or not a user or a group can delegate a role to a group and for how many times. We define the maximum delegation times as the maximum delegation depth (MDD). MDD is a number to limit the delegation times. A delegation becomes a single-step delegation if its MDD equals to one. Not every user can delegate a role to another user. The following relation provides what roles a user can delegate with prerequisite conditions.

Definition 12.1 *Can_delegate* is a relation of $R \times CR \times MDD$ where R, CR, MDD are sets of roles, prerequisite conditions, and maximum delegation depth, respectively. ◇

The meaning of $(r, cr, mdd) \in Can\_delegate$ is that a user who is a member of role r (or a role senior to r) may delegate role r (or a role junior to r) to a group whose current entitlements in roles satisfy the prerequisite condition cr without exceeding the maximum delegation depth mdd. To identify a role range within the role hierarchy, the closed and open interval notation is used [91].

Role-based group delegation is authorized by *Can_delegate*. Table 12.3 shows the *Can_delegate* relations with the prerequisite conditions in the *POCS* example. The meaning of *Can_delegate* ($DIR, [CS, HO1], 1$) is that a member (a user or group of role DIR may delegate role DIR and all roles in *POCS* (since all roles are junior to DIR) to a group whose current membership satisfies the prerequisite condition *[CS, HO1]* with one-step delegation. The second tuple authorizes that a

Table 12.3 Can delegate relations in POCS

RoleName (R)	Prereq.condition (CR)	Maxi dele depth (MDD)
DIR	[CS, HO1]	1
HO1	[AP, HO1)	2
AP	CS	1
CS	ϕ	2

Table 12.4 Example of can revoke relation

RoleName	Role range
HO1	[Co1, CS]
Re1	[Re1, AP]

user or a group of role *HO1* can assign role *HO1*, and *Co1*, *Re1*, *AP* and *CS* to a group in which users are members of either role *AP*, or *Co1*, or *Re1* (since *AP*, *Co1* and *Re1* are in the range of *[AP, HO1))*.

There are related subtleties that arise in *RBGDF* concerning the interaction between delegating and revocation of user-group delegation membership and the role hierarchy.

Definition 12.2 A role-based group delegation revocation is a relation $Can\_revoke \subseteq R \times 2^R$, where R is a set of roles.   ◇

The meaning of $Can\_revoke(r, Y)$ is that a member of role r (or a member of a role that is senior to r) may revoke the delegation relationship of a group from any role $y \in Y$, where Y defines the *range of revocation*. Table 12.4 gives the Can-revoke relation in Fig. 12.2. The first tuple shows that a member of role *HO1* may revoke a delegation relationship of a group from any role in *[Co1, CS]*.

We extend the definition of explicit and implicit members of a role from a user to a group, and then analyse weak revocation and strong revocation [91].

Definition 12.3 A group G is an explicit member of a role r if $(u, r) \in UA$, for all $u \in G$. G is an implicit member of role r if for some $r'' > r$, $(u, r'') \in UA$, for all $u \in G$.   ◇

Weak revocation only revokes explicit membership from a user and does not revoke implicit membership [118, 120]. On the other hand, strong revocation requires revocation of both explicit and implicit memberships. Strong revocation of $G's$ membership in r requires that G be removed not only from explicit membership in r, but also from explicit (implicit) membership in all roles senior to r. Strong revocation therefore has a cascading effect upwards in the role hierarchy. For example, suppose there are two delegations $((Tony, DIR), (Project1, AP), Friday)$ and $((John, Re1), (Project1, AP), Friday)$ and Tony wants to remove the delegated role AP from the group of Project1 on Friday. With weak revocation, the first delegation relationship is removed, but the second delegation has not yet removed. It means that the group is still a member of AP. With strong revocation two delegation relationships are removed and hence the group is no longer a member of AP.

12.5.2 *Authorization Rules*

The purpose of rule-based authorization is to specify and enforce delegation and revocation authorization policy designed in a virtual university. The benefit of the rules is the entirely declaration and hence it is easier for administrators to define delegation policy [14, 66, 114].

The delegation relations *Can-delegate* and *Can-revoke* have included the basic ideas of authorization on delegation and revocation. There are several steps in practise when a user wants to delegate to or revoke a role from a group. Suppose a user U_1 wants to delegate a group G' role r' with constraints *Cons*, the authorization rules are:

1. Is User U_1 acting as a role r in a session S?
2. Is role r senior or equal to role r'?
3. Does the group G satisfy the *Cons*?
4. Does the *Can-delegate* relation success including the maximum delegation number?

The delegation is passed if all of the above conditions are true, and the group G' is assigned to the delegated role r'; otherwise it is fail and the G' could not act as role r'.

Based on the relation *Can-revoke*, the authorization rules of DependentWeakLocalDelete(*DWLD*) for user U_1 wanting to take off role r' from group G' are:

1. Is U_1 the delegating user of role r' in a session S?
2. Does the *Can-revoke* relation success including the role r' in the revocation range?

This is the simplest revocation since only the delegating user may remove the delegated role r' from the group G'.

The authorization rules of user U_1 wants to take off role r' from group G' with DependentStrongLocalDelete(*DSLD*) are in two rule sets. The first rule set is for weak revocation while the second one is for strong revocation.

Weak Revocation (U_1, G', r')
1. Is U_1 the delegating user of role r' in a session S?
2. Does the *Can-revoke* relation success including the role r' in the revocation range?

Strong Revocation
1. Find all roles r the group G' owns that are senior to role r',
2. Do the Weak revocation of (U_1, G', r).

The *DSLD* authorization rules enforce the movement of role r' but also all its senior roles from the group.

We do not describe all authorization rules of revocation in this section due to the paper length.

12.6 XML Implementation

This section presents the implementation of the group delegation with *XML*-based technology. XML has many advantages: simplicity, extensibility, interoperability and so on [3, 20, 39]. This is a web-based project implemented in XAMPP (http://www.apachefriends.org/en/xampp.html) environment in windows platform using XML and XUL (http://www.xulplanet.com/). XML is used to store the information in the virtual university. We store structure of university, role hierarchy and group hierarchy. XML DOM is used to deal with every node of XML file. All these are server-side scripting pages. Hence all these pages are stored in the root directory of web-server.

The implementation of the role-based delegation framework in the virtual university includes many components, for example:

1. The structure of each university involved in the virtual university
2. Role hierarchy of staff shown in rolehie.xml file and group hierarchy in grouphie.xml file
3. Constraints in delegation and revocation.

XML Schema for multiuniversity structure in Table 12.5 shows that we have a root element with name multiuniversity and which consists of various university elements, programs element and courses element. Using this structure, we can add any number of universities we like in future as the value of attribute MaxOccurs is set to unbounded. Also, it is easy to add various elements with program and courses offered in the multiuniversity.

Many XML schemas are existed in implementation: university, faculty, program, course, user, role, user-role assignment, revocation types schema and so on. For example, user-role assignment schema and revocation types schema in the multiuniversity environment in Tables 12.6 and 12.7. The revocation types schema in Table 12.7 explains structure of revocation types in Table 12.2.

Table 12.5 *XML* Schema for a multiuniversity

```
<xs:element name="multiuniversity">
<xs:complexType >
<xs:sequence >
<xs:element name="university" type="universityType"
MaxOccurs="unbounded" / >
<xs:element name="programs" type="programsType" / >
<xs:element name="courses" type="coursesType" / >
</xs:sequence >
</xs:complexType >
</xs:element >
```

Table 12.6   *XML* Schema for user-role assignment

< xs:element name="UserRoleAssignment" type="URAType" / >

< xs:complexType name="URAType" >

< xs:sequence >

< xs:element name="user"type="xs:IDREF" maxOccurs="2000" / >

< /xs:sequence >

< xs:attribute name="role" type="xs:IDREF" use="required" / >

< /xs:complexType >

Table 12.7   *XML* schema for revocation types

<xs:element name="RevocationTypes" >

<xs:complexType >

<xs:restriction base="xs:string" >

<xs:enumeration value="Dependent Weak Local Delete" / >

<xs:enumeration value="Dependent Strong Local Delete" / >

… … …

<xs:enumeration value="Independent Strong Global Negative" />

</xs:restriction >

<xs:attribute name="revocationID" type="xs:ID" use="required" / >

<xs:attribute name="dependency" type="xs:boolean" use="required" / >

<xs:attribute name="resilience" type="xs:boolean" use="required" / >

<xs:attribute name="propagation" type="xs:boolean" use="required" / >

<xs:attribute name="dominance" type="xs:boolean" use="required" />

Table 12.8   *XML* file for user-role assignment

< UserRoles >

< UserRoleAssignment >

< user userID="usqtwmb0001"> Tony </user >

< role roleID="rl0"> DIR < /role >

< /UserRoleAssignment >

< UserRoleAssignment >

< user userID="usqtwmb0002"> Christine </user>

< role roleID="rl1"> HO1 </role >

< /UserRoleAssignment >

… … …

< /UserRoles >

From the above XML Schemas, we form XML files in Tables 12.8 and 12.9 for the user-role relationships in Table 12.1 and the revocation types in Table 12.2, respectively.

After delegation or revocation took place, all the information regarding delegating user, delegated user, delegated role, revoking user, revoked user, revoked role are stored in an XML file. This information will be shown to a user when he/she

Table 12.9 *XML* file for revocation types

< *RevocationTypes* >

< *Revocation revocationID="01" dependency="no"*

resilience="no" propagation="no" dominance="no">
                                  DWLD</Revocation>

<Revocation revocationID="02" dependency="no"

resilience="no" propagation="no" dominance="yes">
                                  DSLD</Revocation>

... ...

<Revocation revocationID="16" dependency="yes"

resilience="yes" propagation="yes" dominance="yes">
                                  IDSGN</Revocation>

---

logged in and the user will know that he was delegated to some role during some period. By this way delegated or revoked users can interact with each other and to the system.

The format of a role-based group delegation from Sect. 12.3 is $((u, r), (G', r'),$ $Cons)$ and $((G, r), (G', r'), Cons)$. To maintain the relationship between groups, we extend the definition of senior and junior roles to the definition of senior and junior groups.

Definition 12.4 A group $G1$ is senior to a group $G2$ if any member of $G1$ has the power of the member in $G2$ and may have additional power but not vice versa.   ◇

Let $G1 > G2$ signify that $G1$ is senior to $G2$. Hence a member of $G1$ is considered senior to a member of $G2$. If $G1$ is senior to $G2$ we also say that $G2$ is junior to $G1$. For convenience we use the files *grouphie.xml* and *rolehie.xml* to store the group hierarchy and the role hierarchy of the children and parent groups and roles.

Based on Table 12.1, a part of the group hierarchy of Fig. 12.2 is modelled in *grouphie.xml* using *IDREF* attributes [60] as shown in Table 12.10. For simplicity, we say Tony is a group with the only one user. The hierarchy is not a tree but a graph, for clarity and conciseness, Table 12.10 shows the hierarchy as a nested relation. The first column gives the group name, the second column gives the immediate parent groups of that group, and the third column gives the immediate children. ϕ means that the group has no parent or child as the case may be. Using *grouphie.xml*, we can find all seniors and juniors for a group by respectively identifying the parents and children using simple *XPath* query expressions. An example of the role hierarchy of Fig. 12.2 is represented in *rolehie.xml* using *IDREF* attributes as shown in Table 12.11.

Definition 12.3 has described a group to be an *explicit* or *implicit* member of a role. A group may be an *explicit* and *implicit* member of a role simultaneously. To simulate a role hierarchy we use information about explicit and implicit membership in *roleDB*. However, *roleDB* is not sufficient to distinguish the case where a group is both an explicit and implicit member of some role from the case where the group

Table 12.10 Group and its roles hierarchy of Fig. 12.2

Group name	Parent group	Child group
Tony	ϕ	Project1, project2
Project1	Tony	Ahn
Project2	Tony	Ahn
Ahn	Project1, project2	ϕ

Table 12.11 Group hierarchy of Fig. 12.2

Role name	Senior role	Junior role
DIR	ϕ	HO1, HO2
HO1	DIR	Co1, Re1
HO2	DIR	Co2, Re2
Co1	HO1	AP
Re1	HO1	AP
AP	Co1, Re1	CS
CS	AP, AsP	ϕ

is only an implicit member of the role. For this purpose we introduce another file *explicit.xml* that keeps information about explicit membership only.

There is a procedure for delegating a user to a group in our implementation. The procedure call is *Delegate (role, group)*. The parameters role and group specify which role is to be delegated to a group. The delegation function has the following main steps: (1) Select a role to be delegated (or revoked); (2) Select a group to delegate (or revoke); (3) Check whether or not the group satisfies the delegating authorization rules including the prerequisite condition in the relation *Can_delegate* and the *MDD*; (4) Setup constraints; and (5) Update the group delegation relationship *DELGR* database. For delegation revocation, instead of steps (3) and (4), one must check whether or not the revocation authorization rules are successful and the revoked role is in the role range of the relation *Can_revoke*. The *DELGR* database maintains group hierarchy information (*grouphie.xml*), role hierarchy information (*rolehie.xml*), explicit membership (*explicit.xml*), and the *Can_delegate* and *Can_revoke* relation tables.

In order to make our implementation more convenient we developed a graphical user interface which interacts with this procedure to do role-based group delegation. The graphical user interface is illustrated in Fig. 12.11. This interface was developed using *XUL* and is used to initiate group delegation instead of typing the above procedure call. This implementation is convenient for users since they only need to define the group hierarchy and the relations *Can_delegate* and *Can_revocate*.

The advantages of the work in this chapter are (1) providing a framework for efficient information sharing in a virtual university since users can delegate (or revoke) roles to (or from) users and groups without administrators' interaction; (2) The framework supports not only group delegations and various revocations, but also multistep delegations, constraints and partial delegations; (3) analysing the impact of revocations with role hierarchy; and (4) implementation with *XML* based technology which is easy for adding more universities in future. However, we do

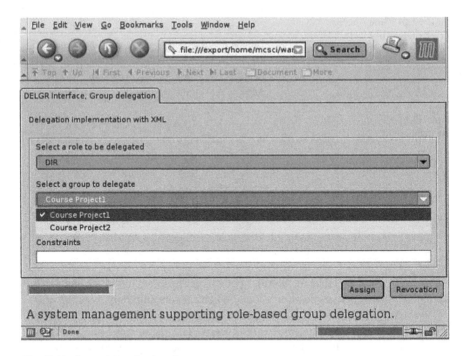

Fig. 12.11 Group delegation interface

not analyse generalized temporal constraints and the workflow of the delegation processes, we suppose to complete them in our future work.

12.7 Comparisons

The closest work to this chapter is on an architecture for supporting vicarious learning in a distributed environment [61], and role-based delegation [5].

Neely et al. [61] discussed that the existing software systems designed to support learning could not adequately provide for vicarious learning in a cross-institutional collaborative environment. The authors developed an architecture based on role-based access control, which provides the necessary security, robustness, flexibility, and explicit formulation of policy. They also planned to improve tool support for writing policies, in particular the development of the user interface and some validation procedures. However, a possible weakness of the system, without better tool support, is that users wishing to use a completely new policy need to be able to write XML files, or at least be able to customize existing ones. The paper did not analyse role-based delegation but instead discussed a case study in a distributed E-learning environment of how to apply *RBAC* on a particular project. The architecture could be viewed as an application of *RBAC* in their work.

However some important features and requirements in distributed E-learning were not addressed such as group delegation, multistep delegation, partial delegation and delegation revocation. As such their work does not fully satisfy the requirements of virtual university learning systems. By contrast, the work in this chapter provides a rich variety of options that can deal with delegation authorization and revocation.

Barka and Sandhu [5] proposed a model for role-based delegation called *RBDM0* within *RBAC0*, the simplest form of *RBAC96* [68]. They developed a framework for identifying interesting cases that can be used for building role-based delegation models. This was accomplished by identifying the characteristics related to delegation, and using those characteristics to generate possible delegation cases. Their work is different from ours in three aspects. Firstly, it focuses on a simple delegation model supporting only flat roles and single step delegation. Some important features such as role hierarchies, constraints and revocations were not supported. By contrast, our work has analysed delegation authorization and revocation models with constraints involving role hierarchies. Secondly, they neither gave the definition of role-based delegation relation a critical notion to the delegation model, nor discussed the relationships among original users and delegated users. By contrast, the delegation framework in this chapter is based on original users and delegated users since the delegating relationship in this chapter has five components $((u, r), (u', r'), Cons)$. Thirdly, they did not discuss group-based delegation, while we have analysed elements and functions in group delegation as well as its implementation with *XML*.

12.8 Conclusions

This chapter has discussed a role-based delegation model for virtual university learning environments and its implementation with *XML*. We have analysed a delegating framework including delegating authorization and revocation with constraints, and extended it to include group-based delegation. The revocation dimensions and delegating revocations are discussed. Furthermore, role assignment changes, as the impact result of original role delegating revocation, are described. To provide a practical solution for role-based group delegations, we have analysed role hierarchies and the relationship of senior and junior roles. The work in this chapter has significantly extended previous work in several aspects, for example group-based delegation, group delegation authorization with prerequisite conditions and revocation authorization. Finally, the proposed role-based delegation framework in this chapter is demonstrated by its implementation with *XML*.

12.9   Problems and Exercises

12.9.1   Problems

1. Analysing constraints in the delegation model at a virtual university. We have mentioned the time temporal duration as a constraint in our delegation model, but it needs more work on constraints including the constraints in *GTRBAC* model [41].
2. One problem is the workflow analysis of delegation processes in the role-based delegation model at a virtual university.

12.9.2   Exercises

1. Analysing time complexity of weak revocation algorithms and strong revocation algorithms;
2. Given an example, analysing a delegating framework including delegating authorization and revocation with constraints, and extending it to group-based delegation.

References

1. Abadi, M., Burrows, M., Lampson, B., Plotkin, G.: A calculus for access control in distributed systems. ACM Trans. Program. Lang. Syst. **15**(4), 706–734 (1993)
2. Alqhatani, A., Lipford, H.: "there is nothing that i need to keep secret": sharing practices and concerns of wearable fitness data. In: Fifteenth Symposium on Usable Privacy and Security (SOUPS 2019), Santa Clara. USENIX Association, Berkeley (2019)
3. Arenas, M., Libkin, L.: A normal form for xml documents. ACM Trans. Database Syst. **29**(1), 195–232 (2004)
4. Aura, T.: Distributed access-rights management with delegation certificates. In: Security Internet Programming, pp. 211–235. Springer, Berlin (1999)
5. Barka, E., Sandhu, R.: Framework for role-based delegation models and some extensions. In: Proceedings of the 16 Annual Computer Security Applications Conference, New Orleans, pp. 168–177 (2000)
6. Baskerville, R.: Hacker wars: E-collaboration by vandals and warriors. Int. J. e-Collaboration **2**(1), 1–16 (2006)
7. Bell, D.E., La Padula, L.J.: Secure computer system: unified exposition and multics interpretation. Technical Report ESD-TR-75-306 (1976)
8. Bellare, M., Roga way, P.: Random oracles are practical: a paradigm for designing efficient protocols. In: First ACM Conference on Computer and Communications Security, pp. 62–73. IEEE, Piscataway (1993)
9. Boyko, V., Peinado, M., Venkatesan, R.: Speeding up discrete log and factoring based schemes via precomputations. In: Advances in Cryptology - Eurocrypt'98. Lectures Notes in Computer Science, vol. 1807. Springer, Berlin (1998)

10. Canetti, R., Goldreich, O., Halevi, S.: The random oracle methodology. In: Proceedings of the 30th ACM STOC '98, pp. 209–218. IEEE, Piscataway (1998)
11. Canetti, R., Micciancio, D., Reingold, O.: Perfectly one-way probabilistic hash functions. In: Proceedings of the 30th ACM STOC'98. IEEE, Piscataway (1998)
12. Cao, J., et al.: Towards secure xml document with usage control. In: Web Technologies Research and Development - APWeb 2005, Berlin, pp. 296–307. Springer, Berlin (2005)
13. Chan, A., Frankel, Y., Tsiounis, Y.: An efficient off-line electronic cash scheme as secure as RSA. Research report NU-CCS-96-03, Northeastern University, Boston (1995)
14. Chaum, D.: Blind signature for untraceable payments. In: Advances in Cryptology - Crypto'82, pp. 199–203. Plenum Press, New York (1983)
15. Chaum, D.: An Introduction to e-cash. DigiCash (1995). http://www.digicash.com
16. Chaum, D., Fiat, A., Naor, M.: Untraceable electronic cash. In: Advances in Cryptology - Crypto'88. Lectures Notes in Computer Science, vol. 403, pp. 319–327. Springer, Berlin (1990)
17. Chen, Z., et al.: Distributed individuals for multiple peaks: a novel differential evolution for multimodal optimization problems. IEEE Trans. Evol. Comput. **24**(4), 708–719 (2020). https://doi.org/10.1109/TEVC.2019.2944180
18. Chenthara, S., et al.: Security and privacy-preserving challenges of e-health solutions in cloud computing. IEEE Access **7**, 74361–74382 (2019)
19. Dogac, A.: Survey of the current state-of-the-art in electronic commerce and research issues in enabling technologies. In: Proceeding of uro-Med Net 98 Conference, Electronic Commerce Track (1998)
20. Du, J., et al.: Feature selection for helpfulness prediction of online product reviews: an empirical study. PLOS ONE **14**, e0226902 (2019)
21. El-Khatib, K., Korba, L., Xu, Y., Yee, G.: Privacy and security in e-learning. Int. J. Distance Edu. Technol. **1**(4), 11–30 (2003)
22. Eng, T., Okamoto, T.: Single-trem divisible electronic coins. In: Advances in Cryptology–Eurocrypt'94. Lectures Notes in Computer Science, vol. 950, pp. 306–319. Springer, Berlin (1995)
23. Feinstein, H.L.: Final report: NIST small business innovative research (SBIR) grant: role based access control: phase 1. Technical Report. SETA Corp. (1995)
24. Ferraiolo, D., Cugini, J., Kuhn, R.: Role-based access control (RBAC): features and motivations. In: The 11th Annual Computer Security Applications Conference, New Orleans, Dec 11–15, pp. 241–48 (1995)
25. Ferraiolo, D.F., Kuhn, D.R.: Role based access control. In: 15th National Computer Security Conference, pp. 554–563 (1992). ferraiolo92rolebased.html
26. Ferraiolo, D.F., Barkley, J.F., Kuhn, D.R.: Role-based access control model and reference implementation within a corporate intranet. In: Transactions on Information and System Security (TISSEC) vol. 2, pp. 34–64 (1999)
27. Frankel, Y., Yiannis, T., Yung, M.: Indirect discourse proofs: achieving fair off-line electronic cash. In: Advances in Cryptology–Asiacrypt'96. Lectures Notes in Computer Science, vol. 1163, pp. 286–300. Springer, Berlin (1996)
28. Franklin, M., Yung, M.: Secure and efficient off-line digital money. In: Proceedings of the Twentieth International Colloquium on Automata, Languages and Programming. Lectures Notes in Computer Science, vol. 700, pp. 265–276. Springer, Berlin (1993)
29. Frolik, J., Weller, T.: Wireless sensor systems: an approach for a multiuniversity design course. IEEE Trans. Edu. **45**(2), 135–141 (2002)
30. Gabber, E., Silberschatz, A.: Agora: a minimal distributed protocol for electronic commerce. In: The 2nd USENIX Workshop on Electronic Commerce, Oakland (1996)
31. Ge, Y., et al.: A benefit-driven genetic algorithm for balancing privacy and utility in database fragmentation. In: Proceedings of the Genetic and Evolutionary Computation Conference, New York, pp. 771–776. Association for Computing Machinery New York (2019)
32. Ghaoui, C., Janvier, W.A.: Interactive e-learning. International Journal of Distance Education Technologies **2**(3), 23–35 (2004)

33. Goldreich, O., Krawczyk, H.: On the composition of zero-knowledge proof systems. SIAM J. Comput. **25**(1), 159–192 (1996)
34. Goldschlag, D., Reed, M., Syverson, P.: Onion routing for anonymous and private Internet connections. Commun. ACM **24**(2), 39–41 (1999)
35. Green, S., et al.: Software agents: a review. TCD-CS-1997-06, Trinity College Dublin and Broadcom Eireann Research, Dublin (1997)
36. Hagstrom, A., Jajodia, S., Presicce, F., Wijesekera, D.: Revocations-a classification. In: Proceedings of 14th IEEE Computer Security Foundations Workshop, Nova Scotia, pp. 44–58 (2001)
37. Han, W., et al.: DTC: Transfer learning for commonsense machine comprehension. Neurocomputing **396**, 102–112 (2019)
38. Herzberg, A., Yochai, H.: Mini-pay: charging per click on the Web (1996). http://www.ibm.net.il
39. Huang, T., et al.: A niching memetic algorithm for multi-solution traveling salesman problem. IEEE Trans. Evol. Comput. **24**, 508–522 (2020)
40. James, B., et al.: An analysis of expressiveness and design issues for the generalized temporal role-based access control model. IEEE Trans. Depend. Secur. Comput. **2**(2), 157–175 (2005)
41. James, B., et al.: A generalized temporal role-based access control model. IEEE Trans. Knowl. Data Eng. **17**(1), 4–23 (2005)
42. Jordi, P., et al.: Distributed access control with blockchain. CoRR, abs/1901.03568 (2019)
43. Juels, A., Luby, M., Ostrovsky, R.: Security of blind digital signatures. In: Advances in Cryptology - Crypto 97. Lectures Notes in Computer Science, vol. 1294, pp. 150–164. Springer, Berlin (1997)
44. Kabir, E., Wang, H.: Conditional purpose based access control model for privacy protection. In: Proceedings of the Twentieth Australasian Conference on Australasian Database - Volume 92, ADC'09, pp. 135–142. Australian Computer Society, Darlinghurst (2009)
45. Kabir, E., et al.: Microaggregation sorting framework for k-anonymity statistical disclosure control in cloud computing. IEEE Trans. Cloud Comput. **8**, 408–417 (2020)
46. Kabir, M., et al.: A novel statistical technique for intrusion detection systems. Futur. Gener. Comput. Syst. **79**, 303–318 (2018)
47. Kabir, M., Wang, H., Bertino, E.: A conditional role-involved purpose-based access control model. J. Org. Comput. E. Commerce **21**, 71–91 (2011)
48. Kabir, M., Wang, H., Bertino, E.: Efficient systematic clustering method for k-anonymization. Acta Inform. **48**(1), 51–66 (2011)
49. Khalil, F., Li, J., Wang, H.: Integrating recommendation models for improved web page prediction accuracy. In: Proceedings of the Thirty-First Australasian Conference on Computer Science - Volume 74, ACSC'08, pp. 91–100. Australian Computer Society, Darlinghurst (2008)
50. Li, M., Wang, H.: ABDM: An extended flexible delegation model in RBAC. In: 2008 8th IEEE International Conference on Computer and Information Technology, pp. 390–395 (2008)
51. Li, M., et al.: Advanced permission-role relationship in role-based access control. In: Inf. Secur. Privacy, Berlin, pp. 391–403. Springer, Berlin (2008)
52. Li, M., et al.: Optimal privacy-aware path in hippocratic databases. In: Database Systems for Advanced Applications, Berlin, pp. 441–455. Springer, Berlin (2009)
53. Li, M., Wang, H., Plank, A.: Privacy-aware access control with generalization boundaries. In: Proceedings of the Thirty-Second Australasian Conference on Computer Science - Volume 91, ACSC'09, Darlinghurst, pp. 105–112 (2009). Australian Computer Society, Darlinghurst
54. Li, N., Grosof, B.N.: A practically implementation and tractable delegation logic. In: IEEE Symposium on Security and Privacy, pp. 27–42 (2000)
55. Loudon, D., Della, B.: Consumer Behavior: Concepts and Applications, 4th edn. Mcgraw-Hill, New York (1993)
56. Lowe, H., Wallis, A.M., Newman, J.: Role-based access control for vicarious learning. In: Proceedings of the European Conference on E-Learning, pp. 43–50. Brunel University, Uxbridge (2002)

57. Lu, H.: Open multi-agent systems for collaborative web-based learning. Int. J. Distance Edu. Technol. **2**(2), 36–45 (2004)
58. McNamara, C.: Basics of delegating (2007). http://www.managementhelp.org/guiding/delegate/basics.htm
59. Mendling, J., Neumann, G., Pinterits, A., Simon, B., Wild, F.: Indirect revenue models for e-learning at universities - the case of learn@wu. In: E-Learning Workshop Hannover - "Einsatzkonzepte und Geschftsmodelle" (ELW 2004), Hannover (2004)
60. Michael, H.: XSLT Programmer's Reference. Wiley, Hoboken (2001)
61. Neely, S., Lowe, H., Eyers, D., Bacon, J., Newman, J., Gong, X.: An architecture for supporting vicarious learning in a distributed environment. In: SAC'04: Proceedings of the 2004 ACM Symposium on Applied Computing, New York, pp. 963–970. ACM Press, New York (2004)
62. Okamoto, T., Ohta, K.: Disposable zero-knowledge authentication and their applications to untraceable electronic cash. In: Advances in Cryptology–Crypto89. Lectures Notes in Computer Science, vol. 435, pp. 481–496. Springer, Berlin (1990)
63. Peng, M., et al.: Pattern filtering attention for distant supervised relation extraction via online clustering. In: Web Information Systems Engineering – WISE 2019, Cham, pp. 310–325. Springer, Cham (2019)
64. Pfitzmann, B., Waidner, M.: How to break and repair a 'provably secure' untraceable payment system. In: Advances in Cryptology - Crypto'91. Lectures Notes in Computer Science, vol. 576, pp. 338–350. Springer, Berlin (1992)
65. Pointcheval, D., Stern, J.: Security arguments for digital signatures and blind signatures. J. Cryptol. **13**(3), 361–396 (2000)
66. Rabin, M.: Digital Signatures, Foundations of Secure Communication. Academic, NewYork (1978)
67. Rasool, R., et al.: Cyberpulse: a machine learning based link flooding attack mitigation system for software defined networks. IEEE Access **7**, 34885–34899 (2019)
68. Sandhu, R.: Rational for the *RBAC96* family of access control models. In: Proceedings of 1st ACM Workshop on Role-based Access Control, pp. 64–72. ACM Press, New York (1997)
69. Sandhu, R.: Role activation hierarchies. In: Third ACM Workshop on Role Based Access Control, pp. 33–40. ACM Press, New York (1998)
70. Seufert, S.: E-learning Business Models: Framework and Best Practice Examples. Idea Group, pp. 11–36 (2001)
71. Shenoy, J., et al.: Jive: spatially-constrained encryption key sharing using visible light communication. In: Proceedings of the 16th EAI International Conference on Mobile and Ubiquitous Systems: Computing, Networking and Services (2019)
72. Shu, J., et al.: Privacy-preserving task recommendation Services for Crowdsourcing. IEEE Trans. Serv. Comput. (2018). https://doi.org/10.1109/TSC.2018.2791601
73. Simon, D.: Anonymous communication and anonymous cash. In: Advances in Cryptology - Crypto'96. Lectures Notes in Computer Science, vol. 1109, pp. 61–73. Springer, Berlin (1997)
74. Spegel, N., Rogers, B., Buckley, R.: Negotiation Theory and Techniques. Skills Series. Butterworths, London (1998)
75. Stafford, T.F.: Understanding motivations for internet use in distance education. IEEE Trans. Edu. **48**(2), 301–306 (2005)
76. Sun, L., Li, Y., Wang, H.: M-service and its framework. In: 2005 Asia-Pacific Conference on Communications, pp. 837–841 (2005)
77. Sun, L., Wang, H., Yong, J.: Authorization algorithms for permission-role assignments. J. Univ. Comput. Sci. **15**, 1782–1798 (2009)
78. Sun, X., et al.: An efficient hash-based algorithm for minimal k-anonymity. In: Proceedings of the Thirty-First Australasian Conference on Computer Science - Volume 74, ACSC'08, Darlinghurst, pp. 101–107. Australian Computer Society, Darlinghurst (2008)
79. Sun, X., et al.: Enhanced p-sensitive k-anonymity models for privacy preserving data publishing. Trans. Data Privacy **1**(2), 53–66 (2008)

80. Sun, X., et al.: (p+, α)-sensitive k-anonymity: a new enhanced privacy protection model. In: 2008 8th IEEE International Conference on Computer and Information Technology, pp. 59–64 (2008)
81. Sun, X., Li, M., Wang, H.: A family of enhanced (l, α)-diversity models for privacy preserving data publishing. Futur. Gener. Comput. Syst. **27**(3), 348–356 (2011)
82. Sun, X., Wang, H., Li, J.: Priority driven k-anonymisation for privacy protection. In: Proceedings of the 7th Australasian Data Mining Conference, vol. 87, pp. 73–78 (2008)
83. Sun, X., Wang, H., Li, J.: Microdata protection through approximate microaggregation. In: Proceedings of the Thirty-Second Australasian Conference on Computer Science - Volume 91, ACSC'09, pp. 161–168. Australian Computer Society, Darlinghurst (2009)
84. Sun, X., Wang, H., Li, J.: Satisfying privacy requirements: one step before anonymization. In: Advances in Knowledge Discovery and Data Mining, Berlin, pp. 181–188. Springer, Berlin (2010)
85. Sun, X., Wang, H., Sun, L.: Extended k-anonymity models against attribute disclosure. In: 2009 Third International Conference on Network and System Security, pp. 130–136 (2009)
86. Vimalachandran, P., et al.: Preserving patient-centred controls in electronic health record systems: a reliance-based model implication. In: 2017 International Conference on Orange Technologies (ICOT), pp. 37–44 (2017)
87. Wang, G., et al.: Incorporating word embeddings into topic modeling of short text. Knowl. Inf. Syst. **61**(2), 1123–1145 (2019)
88. Wang, H., Li, Q.: Secure and efficient information sharing in multi-university e-learning environments. In: Advances in Web Based Learning – ICWL 2007, Berlin, pp. 542–553. Springer, Berlin (2008)
89. Wang, H., Sun, L.: Trust-involved access control in collaborative open social networks. In: 2010 Fourth International Conference on Network and System Security, pp. 239–246 (2010)
90. Wang, H., Cao, J., Ross, D.: Role-based delegation with negative authorization. In: Frontiers of WWW Research and Development - APWeb 2006, Berlin, pp. 307–318. Springer, Berlin (2006)
91. Wang, H., Cao, J., Zhang, Y.: Formal authorization allocation approaches for permission-role assignments using relational algebra operations. In: Proceedings of the 14th Australian Database Conference ADC2003, Adelaide (2003)
92. Wang, H., Cao, J., Zhang, Y.: An electronic payment scheme and its RBAC management. Concurrent Eng. Res. Appl. **12**(3), 247–275 (2004)
93. Wang, H., Cao, J., Zhang, Y.: A flexible payment scheme and its role-based access control. IEEE Trans. Knowl. Data Eng. **17**(3), 425–436 (2005)
94. Wang, H., Cao, J., Zhang, Y.: Delegating revocations and authorizations in collaborative business environments. Inf. Syst. Front. **11**(3), 293 (2008)
95. Wang, H., Cao, J., Zhang, Y.: Delegating revocations and authorizations in collaborative business environments. Inf. Syst. Front. **11**(3), 293 (2008)
96. Wang, H., Cao, J., Zhang, Y.: A flexible payment scheme and its role based access control. IEEE Trans. Knowl. Data Eng. **17**(3), 425–436 (2005)
97. Wang, H., et al.: Authorization algorithms for the mobility of user-role relationship. In: Proceedings of the Twenty-eighth Australasian Conference on Computer Science - Volume 38, ACSC'05, pp. 69–77. Australian Computer Society, Darlinghurst (2005)
98. Wang, H., et al.: A framework for role-based group deligation in distributed environments. In: Proceedings of the 29th Australasian Computer Science Conference, vol. 48, pp. 321–328 (2006)
99. Wang, H., et al.: Authorization approaches for advanced permission-role assignments. In: 2008 12th International Conference on Computer Supported Cooperative Work in Design, pp. 277–282 (2008)
100. Wang, H., et al.: Editorial: special issue on security and privacy in network computing. World Wide Web. **23**, 951–957 (2020)

101. Wang, H., Sun, L., Varadharajan, V.: Purpose-based access control policies and conflicting analysis. In: Security and Privacy – Silver Linings in the Cloud, Berlin, pp. 217–228. Springer, Berlin (2010)
102. Wang, H., Zhang, Y., Cao, J.: Ubiquitous computing environments and its usage access control. In: Proceedings of the 1st International Conference on Scalable Information Systems, InfoScale'06, New York. ACM, New York (2006)
103. Wang, H., Zhang, Y., Cao, J., Varadharajan, V.: Achieving secure and flexible m-services through tickets. IEEE Trans. Syst. Man Cybern. A Syst. Hum. **33**, 697–708 (2003)
104. Wang, H., Zhang, Z., Taleb, T.: Editorial: Special issue on security and privacy of IoT. World Wide Web **21**(1), 1–6 (2018)
105. Wang, Y., et al.: MTMR: Ensuring mapreduce computation integrity with merkle tree-based verifications. IEEE Trans. Big Data **4**(3), 418–431 (2018)
106. Wang, Z., Zhan, Z., Lin, Y., Yu, W., Wang, H., Kwong, S., Zhang, J.: Automatic niching differential evolution with contour prediction approach for multimodal optimization problems. IEEE Trans. Evol. Comput. **24**, 114–128 (2019)
107. Weippl, E.: Security in E-Learning. Springer, New York (2005)
108. Weippl, E., Quirchmayr, G.: Revisiting mandatory access control: improving the security of e-learning systems. In: Proceedings of International Conference on Communication and Computer Networks, pp. 118–126 (2004)
109. White, G.: The changing landsacpe: E-learning in schools. In: Technical report at education.au limited (2003). www.education.edu.au/papers/changing_landscape_gw.pdf
110. Xiao, Y., Jia, Y., Liu, C., Cheng, X., Yu, J., Lv, W.: Edge computing security: state of the art and challenges. Proc. IEEE **107**(8), 1608–1631 (2019)
111. Yacobi, Y.: Efficient electronic money. In: Advances in Cryptology–Asiacrypt'94. Lectures Notes in Computer Science, vol. 917, pp. 153–163. Springer, Berlin (1995)
112. Yao, W., Moody, K., Bacon, J.: A model of OASIS role-based access control and its support for active security. In: Proceedings of ACM Symposium on Access Control Models and Technologies (SACMAT), Chantilly, pp. 171–181 (2001)
113. Zhang, F., Wang, Y., Wang, H.: Gradient correlation: are ensemble classifiers more robust against evasion attacks in practical settings? In: Web Information Systems Engineering – WISE 2018, Cham, pp. 96–110. Springer, Cham (2018)
114. Zhang, L., Ahn, G., Chu, B.: A rule-based framework for role-based delegation. In: Proceedings of ACM Symposium on Access Control Models and Technologies (SACMAT 2001), Chantilly, pp. 153–162 (2001)
115. Zhang, L., Ahn, G., Chu, B.: A role-based delegation framework for healthcare information systems. In: Proceedings of ACM Symposium on Access Control Models and Technologies (SACMAT 2002), Monterey, pp. 125–134 (2002)
116. Zhang, L., Ahn, G., Chu, B.: A rule-based framework for role-based delegation and revocation. ACM Trans. Inf. Syst. Secur. **6**(3), 404–441 (2003)
117. Zhang, Y., Jia, X.: Transaction processing. Wiley Encyclopedia of Electrical and Electronics Engineering **22**, 298–311 (1999)
118. Zhang, Y., Gong, Y., Gao, Y., Wang, H., Zhang, J.: Parameter-free voronoi neighborhood for evolutionary multimodal optimization. IEEE Trans. Evol. Comput. **24**, 335–349 (2020)
119. Zhang, Y., Shen, Y., Wang, H., Zhang, Y., Jiang, X.: On secure wireless communications for service oriented computing. IEEE Trans. Serv. Comput. **11**(2), 318–328 (2018)
120. Zheng, H., He, J., Huang, G., Zhang, Y., Wang, H. Dynamic optimisation based fuzzy association rule mining method. Int. J. Mach. Learn. Cybern. **10**(8), 2187–2198 (2019)

Chapter 13
Distributed Access Control Through Blockchain Technology

This chapter lists the contributions of this book and introduces future work. The contributions of this book are presented in the first section while the second section includes Access control methods and Blockchain technology. The third section discusses Blockchain Based Access Control and the fourth section describes Blockchain-based access control framework for the Internet of Things. The last section explains the future research work.

13.1 Introduction

A blockchain, as defined in [64], is a distributed, always available, irreversible, and tamper-resistant public database. A set of peers or notes manages data access and evolutions. Blockchain technology itself does not require trusted relationships between users. A distributed consensus algorithm is applied to ask users to agree on an append-only operation as an obligation without interactions with a trusted third party [1, 45, 95]. The processing structure of Blockchain is simplified without a trusted third party, the algorithm is implicitly included in a joining process.

Access control systems are used to limit the access to critical or valuable resources. Several access control models including the rules expressing access rights to resources, have been discussed [18, 29, 37, 79, 124, 131]. The rules have to be satisfied by subjects or roles accordingly in order for access rights to be granted. The rules may include pre-conditions, post-condition and obligations [8, 10, 11, 14, 42, 85]. A well-known policy language to express access control algorithms is the eXtensible Access Control Markup Language (XACML) [7, 12, 13, 119].

As an important feature of Blockchain, there is no needs for a trusted third party [16, 17, 23, 24]. As a result, a blockchain-based access control policy can be evaluated by any party, even not trusted. For instance, the party that evaluates the policy and enforces the result could maliciously force the system to deny an access

© Springer Nature Switzerland AG 2020

H. Wang et al., *Access Control Management in Cloud Environments*,
https://doi.org/10.1007/978-3-030-31729-4_13

although the policy would have granted it. The design of Blockchain technology can be exploited to fix this problem. In Blockchain technology, both access rules and attributes are available and open access for any users, users know policies for access requests and related contexts. This public availability allows distributed auditability, detecting parties that fraudulently alter access rights.

13.2   Access Control Methods and Blockchain Technology

13.2.1   Access Control Methods

Software technology, including access scheme, payment, and access control management for e-commerce, is an important dimension in e-commerce [74, 137]. Although the importance of electronic-payment in e-commerce has been recognized for a long time, it has not received much attention in research literature while role based access control has been discussed. There are three enhancements in this book [111, 120–123]. The first enhancement is a ticket-based access scheme for mobile and non-mobile users. The second is a scalable anonymity payment scheme and the third is formal authorization approaches for role based access control.

13.2.2   Enhancements on Ticket-Based Access Control Scheme for Mobile User

We have proposed a ticket-based access control model for mobile users [52, 110]. The model supports efficient authentication of users and service providers over different domains and can also be used by wired terminal users [53, 84, 99, 144]. Tickets are used to verify correctness of the requested service as well as to direct billing information to the appropriate user. The service providers can avoid roaming to multiple service domains, only contacting a Credential Centre to certify the user's ticket since tickets carry all authorization information needed for the requested services. The user can preserve anonymity and read a clear record of charges in the Credential Centre at anytime. Furthermore, the identity of misbehaving users can be revealed by a Trusted Centre [21, 34, 41, 62]. Other related work either has the weakness of not providing anonymity to users or solving only for particular mobile access problems [19, 20, 113, 115, 118].

13.2.3   Enhancements on Anonymity Payment Scheme

A secure, scalable, anonymous, and practical payment protocol for Internet purchases has been presented. The protocol uses electronic cash for payment transactions [108, 111, 112, 116, 117]. From the viewpoint of banks, this new protocol allows users are worried about disclosure of their identities to maintain anonymity. An agent provides a higher anonymous certificate and improves the security of the consumers. The agent certifies re-encrypted data after verifying the validity of the content from consumers, without requiring the private information of the consumers. With this new method, each consumer can get required anonymity level, depending on the available time, computation, and cost [26, 36, 145].

We also analyze how to prevent a consumer from spending a coin more than once and how to use the proposed protocol for Internet purchases. After comparing with another scheme and discussing the properties of the new payment protocol, the new method has been proven more efficient, and can effectively prevent from eavesdropping, tampering, and "perfect crime". It is promising for electronic trades through the Internet [63, 126, 129, 135].

13.2.4   Enhancements on Formal Authorization Approaches for Role Based Access Control

We have developed formal authorization allocation algorithms for role-based access control (RBAC) [89, 114, 127, 133]. The formal approaches are based on relational structure, and relational algebra and operations. The processes of user-role assignments and permission-role assignments are two important issues in RBAC because they may modify the authorization level or imply high-level confidential information to be derived while users change positions and request different roles and permissions [49, 86, 88, 96]. There are two types of problems which may arise in user-role assignment. One is related to authorization granting process. When a role is granted to a user, this role may conflict with other roles of the user or together with this role; the user may have or derive a high level of authority. The other is related to authorization revocation. When a role is revoked from a user, the user may still have the role from other roles. Similarly, there are two types of problems that may arise in permission-role assignments. One is related to authorization granting process. Conflicting permissions may be granted to a role, and as a result, users with the role may have or derive a high level of authority [55, 109, 125]. The other is related to authorization revocation. When permission is revoked from a role, the role may still have the permission from other roles [58, 59, 93, 128].

To solve these problems, authorization granting algorithms, and weak revocation and strong revocation algorithms that are based on relational algebra for user-role assignments and permission-role assignments have been presented [87, 98, 134]. The algorithms can automatically check conflicts when granting more than one role (permission) to a user (a role) in a system [51, 100, 132]. They can prevent users from accessing unauthorized use of facilities when users change position within the organization and demand the modification of security rights. The roles and permissions can be allocated without compromising the security in RBAC and provide secure management for systems. The complexities of the algorithms are also analyzed. Furthermore, the extensions of the algorithms are deeply analyzed that include the mobility of user-role and permission-role relationships. As shown in this book, the mobility of users and permissions are very significant and therefore some users with roles and some roles with permissions can be further assigned while some cannot. We have discussed how to use the algorithms for the electronic payment scheme. It gives ideas for using role-based access control to manage electronic payment system. The algorithms can be applied in system management which uses RBAC [60, 61, 102, 125].

13.2.5 Blockchain Technology

A blockchain, originally block chain, is a growing list of records, called blocks, that are linked using cryptography. Each block contains a cryptographic hash of the previous block, a timestamp, and transaction data [72]. A blockchain is not permitted to modify the data in a block. Blockchain is an open, distributed system with capabilities of efficiently recording transactions between two parties in a verifiable and permanent way [43].

Open blockchains are more user-friendly than traditional ownership records, which, while open to the public, still require physical access to view. Blockchain is a new technology with lots of arguments. One of them is whether a private system with verifiers tasked and authorized by a central authority should be considered a blockchain. Private chains, on the other side, argue that the term "blockchain" may be applied to any data structure that batches data into time-stamped blocks [76, 107]. These blockchains serve as a distributed version of multiversion concurrency control (MVCC) in databases. MVCC prevents two transactions from concurrently modifying a single object in a database, blockchains prevent two transactions from spending the same single output in a blockchain.

The great advantage to an open, permissionless, or public, blockchain network is that guarding against bad actors is not required and no access control is needed. This means that applications can be added to the network without the approval or trust of others, using the blockchain as a transport layer [3, 32, 33].

Permissioned blockchains use an access control layer to govern who has access to the network [28, 50, 136, 146]. In contrast to public blockchain networks, private blockchain networks are verified by network owners. They do not rely on anonymous nodes to validate transactions nor do they benefit from the network effect [65]. Permissioned blockchains can also go by the name of 'consortium' blockchains.

13.3 Blockchain Based Access Control

Four major types of blockchain networks are introduced in applications. They are public blockchains, private blockchains, consortium blockchains and hybrid blockchains.

Public Blockchains

A public blockchain has absolutely no access restrictions. Anyone with an Internet connection can send transactions to it as well as become a validator. Users are involving in the execution of a consensus protocol. Public blockchain networks offer economic incentives to users who secure and utilize some type of a Proof of Stake or Proof of Work algorithm. The world famous public blockchains are the bitcoin blockchain and the Ethereum blockchain.

Private Blockchains

A private blockchain is limited to join under an invitation from its network administrators. In other word, it is restricted for participant and validator [25, 38, 65]. Private blockchains are normally applied by companies that are interested in the application technology of blockchain but not like to be used as public networks without any limitations. The companies prefer to incorporate blockchain technology into systems with record-keeping procedures and do not sacrifice autonomy and reduce the risk of disclose sensitive data to a public internet.

Consortium Blockchains

Consortium blockchains differ to both public blockchains and private blockchains. Users in Consortium blockchains are permissioned with conditions to be granted access to consortium blockchains. Consortium blockchains can be described as semi-decentralized because the access to a consortium blockchain is granted to a group of individuals, not a single user. Instead of allowing anyone to participate blockchains in public blockchains, users of a consortium blockchain are to be a group of pre-approved entities. Therefore, consortium blockchains have security features inherent in private blockchains, while users in the group have a greater degree of access permissions [66, 97, 105].

Hybrid Blockchains

A hybrid blockchain is a combination of but with different characteristics of both public and private blockchains. It has two fields of private and public for protected information and unprotected information [5, 31, 35, 54]. Decentralization in a hybrid blockchain is a significant process in relation to centralized private blockchains. Transactions do not need to keep inside of its own network, a hash function result can be posted on completely decentralized networks such as bitcoin. By submitting hash results of transactions on public blockchains like bitcoin or Ethereum, privacy or sensitive data concerns are resolved, since personal information is hided and cannot access in a public blockchain.

Blockchain technology employs a distributed consensus algorithm to allow the users to agree on immutable and auditable append-only operation without requiring interaction with a trusted third party. Access control systems are meant to regulate the access to critical or valuable resources. Several access control models have been discussed in this book by defining various rules expressing the access rights of subjects to resources. It is in infant stage for the research work with both blockchain and access control.

13.4 Blockchain-Based Access Control for the Internet of Things

Access control mechanisms provide users' capabilities for centralized authorities in governments or companies [47, 91, 92, 101]. On the other hand, service providers are able to collect and analyze user's data. As a result, it causes ethical and privacy problems. For example, Fitbits, makes small devices to track customers for their fitness activities. The system broadcasts the activity of a group of users. Fitbits make the gathered data public. Unfortunately, the collected data shared with third parties, it straight away loses access control and ownership. From customers' point view, they do not know how to control their data if they stop to use a service. From service providers' side, they do not know what the data shared to a third part will be. That is, the data is out of control and kept in other systems without any control [2, 39, 67, 78].

The Internet of things (IoT) is the extension of Internet connectivity into physical devices and everyday objects. Embedded with electronics, Internet connectivity, and other forms of hardware (such as sensors), these devices can communicate and interact with others over the Internet, and they can be remotely monitored and controlled [75, 130, 137, 142].

The definition of the Internet of things has evolved due to the convergence of multiple technologies, real-time analytic, machine learning, commodity sensors, and embedded systems. Traditional fields of embedded systems, wireless sensor networks, control systems, automation (including home and building automation), and others all contribute to enabling the Internet of things [40, 81, 83, 135]. In the consumer market, IoT technology is most synonymous with products pertaining to the concept of the "smart home", covering devices and appliances (such as lighting fixtures, thermostats, home security systems and cameras, and other home appliances) that support one or more common ecosystems, and can be controlled via devices associated with that ecosystem, such as smartphones and smart speakers [48, 90, 106].

Ouaddah et al. [67] designed a new FairAccess framework that breaks this custom and gives people what fairly belongs to them. Actually, they believe that IoT needs a new access control framework that satisfies its specific requirements and characteristics, where users are able to control and master their own privacy. This "shift" will require rethinking access control technologies and building new solution with IoT privacy and security requirement in mind.

Numerous efforts have been emerged in adapting traditional access control models to meet new IoT security requirements. In other hand, across the industry, many companies implement their own proprietary authorization software based on the OAuth protocol [69, 82, 138], in which they serve as centralized trusted authorities.

Traditional security and access control standards today are built around the notion of trust where a centralized trusted entity is always introduced, which harm user transparency and privacy [11, 44, 56, 68]. In addition, they are built around a single logical server and multiple clients. As a consequence, access control is often carried out within the server side application, once the client has been authenticated. IoT reverses this paradigm by having many devices serving as servers and possibly many clients, taking part in the same application [9, 10, 52, 131]. More importantly, servers are significantly resource-constrained, which results in the minimization of the server side functionality. Subsequently, access control becomes a distributed problem. Blockchain is a technology breakthrough that has fundamentally changed the notions of centralized authority [15, 46, 67, 71, 139].

13.5   Future Work

Based on the research work in this book, we propose the following future research directions and issues.

13.5.1   Improvement of the Payment Scheme

We have built a consumer scalable anonymity payment protocol that provides different requirements of anonymity for users [94, 103, 104, 143]. When a system with the payment protocol has many users such as hundreds of millions, the data of consumers and coins increase very quickly. The bank and the AP agent need to keep the data of consumers and coins that are used to verify and solve problems between consumers and shops, this may cause a bottleneck problem. In the future, we plan to develop a distributed payment solution to address the bottleneck issue.

13.5.2   Extension of Formal Authorization Approaches for Role Based Access Control

In this book we presented formal authorization approaches for user-role assignment and permission-role assignment which can be used to automatically check conflicts when granting roles (permission) to a user (a role) and revoking roles (permission) from a user (a role) in a system. The roles and permissions can be allocated without compromising the security in RBAC [6, 22, 57]. In the future, we would like to extend formal authorization approaches, investigating formal authorization approaches for user-user assignment. We must also determine how these algorithms can be used to enforce an RBAC management system.

13.5.3 Electronic Commerce with RBAC

There are several examples of role based access control for payment scheme [70, 73, 77, 140, 141]. These examples provide a way to use RBAC to manage electronic payment schemes. However, the use of RBAC for generic electronic commerce systems is still far from being achieved. We like to analyze how RBAC management can be used in generic electronic payment systems and implement the system to prove its practicality. Then we will extend the results to generic electronic commerce systems.

13.5.4 Implementation Issues

We would like to build tools that can check the syntax and the semantics of the ticket based access control system, consumer anonymity scalable payment scheme, and formal authorization approaches for role based access control [4, 27, 30, 80]. The tools might provide visual support for the payment scheme and authorization approaches to make them more efficient. The visual tool of formal authorization approaches, for example, would display all of the components such as role and permissions that can be used in database. In addition, it shows what components are used and are available for the authorization approaches. Furthermore, using the visualization tool, system administrators can easily check the current status of components in systems.

References

1. Alqhatani, A., Lipford, H.: "There is nothing that i need to keep secret": Sharing practices and concerns of wearable fitness data. In: Fifteenth Symposium on Usable Privacy and Security (SOUPS 2019), Santa Clara, CA, August 2019. USENIX Association
2. Andreoli, J., Pacull, F., Pagani, D., Pareschi, R.: Multiparty negotiation of dynamic distributed object services. Journal of Science of Computer Programming (1998)
3. Antonopoulos, A.: Bitcoin Security Model: Trust by Computation. Radar. O'Reilly (2014)
4. Barkley, J.F., Beznosov, K., Uppal, J.: Supporting relationships in access control using role based access control. In: Third ACM Workshop on Role Based Access Control, pp. 55–65 (October 1999)

5. Beam, C., Segev, A.: Electronic Catalogs and Negotiations. CITM Working Paper 96-WP-1016, August 1996
6. Ben-Shaul, I., Gidron, Y., Holder, O. (eds.): A Negotiation Model for Dynamic Composition of Distributed Applications. Institute of Electrical and Electronics Engineers (1998)
7. Bertino, E., Bettini, C., Ferrari, E., Samarati, P.: An access control model supporting periodicity constraints and temporal reasoning. ACM Trans. Database Syst. **23**(3), 231–285 (1998)
8. Bertino, E., Ferrari, E.: Secure and selective dissemination of xml documents. ACM Trans. Inf. Syst. Secur. **5**(3), 290–331 (2002)
9. Bertino, E., Bonatti, P., Ferrari, E.: Trbac: a temporal role-based access control model. In: Proceedings of the fifth ACM Workshop on Role-Based Access Control, pp. 21–30. ACM Press (2000)
10. Bertino, E., Bonatti, P., Ferrari, E.: Trbac: A temporal role-based access control model. ACM Trans. Inf. Syst. Secur. **4**(3), 191–233 (2001)
11. Bertino, E., Byun, J., Li, N.: Privacy-Preserving Database Systems, pp. 178–206. Springer, Berlin, Heidelberg (2005)
12. Bertino, E., Castano, S., Ferrari, E.: Securing xml documents: the author-x project demonstration. In: Proceedings of the 2001 ACM SIGMOD International Conference on Management of Data, p. 605. ACM Press (2001)
13. Bertino, E., Castano, S., Ferrari, E., Mesiti, M.: Specifying and enforcing access control policies for XML document sources. World Wide Web **3**, 139–151 (2000)
14. Bertino, E.,Castano, S., Ferrari, E., Mesiti, M.: Controlled access and dissemination of xml documents. In: Proceedings of the Second International Workshop on Web Information and Data Management, pp. 22–27. ACM Press (1999)
15. Byun, J., Bertino, E., Li, N.: Purpose based access control of complex data for privacy protection. In: Proceedings of the Tenth ACM Symposium on Access Control Models and Technologies, SACMAT '05, pp. 102–110. Association for Computing Machinery, New York, NY, USA (2005)
16. Canetti, R., Goldreich, O., Halevi, S.: The random oracle methodology. In: Proceedings of the 30th ACM STOC '98, pp. 209–218. IEEE (1998)
17. Canetti, R., Micciancio, D., Reingold, O.: Perfectly one-way probabilistic Hash functions. In: Proceedings of the 30th ACM STOC '98. IEEE (1998)
18. Cao, J., et al.: Towards secure xml document with usage control. In: Web Technologies Research and Development - APWeb 2005, pp. 296–307. Springer, Berlin, Heidelberg (2005)
19. Chan, A., Frankel, Y., Tsiounis, Y.: An efficient off-line electronic cash scheme as secure as RSA. Research report nu-ccs-96-03, Northeastern University, Boston, MA, 1995
20. Chaum, D.: Blind signature for untraceable payments. In: Advances in Cryptology - Crypto 82, pp. 199–203. Plenum Press, NY (1983)
21. Chaum, D.: An Introduction to e-cash. DigiCash, http://www.digicash.com (1995)
22. Chen, Z., Lee, M., Cheung, C.: A framework for mobile commerce. In: Proc. Americas Conference on Information Systems 2001, E-Commerce: Wireless/Mobile. AISeL (2001)
23. Chenthara, S., et al.: Security and privacy-preserving challenges of e-health solutions in cloud computing. IEEE Access **7**, 74361–74382 (2019)
24. Chenthara, S., Wang, H., Ahmed, K.: Security and Privacy in Big Data Environment, pp. 1–9. Springer International Publishing, Cham (2018)
25. Dogac, A.: Survey of the current state-of-the-art in electronic commerce and research issues in enabling technologies. In: Proceeding of uro-Med Net 98 Conference, Electronic Commerce Track, March 1998
26. Du, J., et al.: Feature selection for helpfulness prediction of online product reviews: An empirical study. PLOS ONE **14**, e0226902 (2019)
27. ElGamal, T.: A public key cryptosystem and a signature scheme based on discrete logarithms. IEEE Trans. Inform. Theory **IT-31**(4), 469–472 (1985)
28. Feinstein, H.L.: Final report: Nist small business innovative research (sbir) grant: role based access control: phase 1. technical report. In: SETA Corp. (1995)

29. Ferraiolo, D.F., Kuhn, D.R.: Role based access control. In: 15th National Computer Security Conference, pp. 554–563. ferraiolo92rolebased.html, 1992

30. Ferraiolo, D.F., Barkley, J.F., Kuhn, D.R.: Role-based access control model and reference implementation within a corporate intranet. In: TISSEC, vol. 2, pp. 34–64 (1999)

31. Ford, W., Baum, M.: Secure Electronic Commerce: Building the Infrastructure for Digital Signatures & Encryption. Prentice Hall PTR (1997)

32. Frankel, Y., Yiannis, T., Yung, M.: Indirect discourse proofs: achieving fair off-line electronic cash. In: Advances in Cryptology–Asiacrypt'96, vol. 1163 of Lectures Notes in Computer Science, pp. 286–300. Springer (1996)

33. Franklin, M., Yung, M.: Secure and efficient off-line digital money. In: Proceedings of the Twentieth International Colloquium on Automata, Languages and Programming, vol. 700 of Lectures Notes in Computer Science, pp. 265–276. Springer (1993)

34. Gabber, E., Silberschatz, A.: Agora: A minimal distributed protocol for electronic commerce. In: The 2rd USENIX Workshop on Electronic Commerce, Oakland, CA, 1996

35. Garfinkel, S., Spafford, G.: Web Security & Commerce Risks, Technologies, and Strategies. O'Reilly & Associates, Inc. (1997)

36. Ge, Y., et al.: A benefit-driven genetic algorithm for balancing privacy and utility in database fragmentation. In: Proceedings of the Genetic and Evolutionary Computation Conference, pp. 771–776. Association for Computing Machinery, New York, NY, USA (2019)

37. Goldschlag, D., Reed, M., Syverson, P.: Onion routing for anonymous and private Internet connections. Commun. ACM **24**(2), 39–41 (1999)

38. Green, S., et al.: Software Agents: A review. Tcd-cs-1997-06. Trinity College Dublin and Broadcom Eireann Research Ltd., Ireland (May 1997)

39. Guttman, R.H., Maes, P.: Cooperative vs. competitive multi-agent negotiations in retail electronic commerce. In: Proceedings of the Second International Workshop on Cooperative information Agents (CIA'98), Paris, France, July 1998

40. He, J., et al.: D-ecg: A dynamic framework for cardiac arrhythmia detection from iot-based ecgs. In: Web Information Systems Engineering – WISE 2018, pp. 85–99. Springer International Publishing, Cham (2018)

41. Herzberg, A., Yochai, H.: Mini-Pay: Charging per Click on the Web. http://www.ibm.net.il, 1996.

42. Hsu, C., Lin, J.: An empirical examination of consumer adoption of internet of things services: Network externalities and concern for information privacy perspectives. Comput. Hum. Behav. **62**, 516–527 (2016)

43. Iansiti, M., Karim, R.: The truth about blockchain. Harv. Bus. Rev. **95**(1), 118–127 (2017)

44. Jansen, W., etc.: Security policy management for handheld devices. In: Proceedings of the 2003 International Conference on Security and Management (SAM'03), 2003

45. Jordi, P., et al.: Distributed access control with blockchain. CoRR, abs/1901.03568, 2019

46. Juels, A., Luby, M., Ostrovsky, R.: Security of blind digital signatures. In: Advances in Cryptology - Crypto 97, vol. 1294 of Lectures Notes in Computer Science, pp. 150–164. Springer (1997)

47. Kabir, E., Wang, H.: Conditional purpose based access control model for privacy protection. In: Proceedings of the Twentieth Australasian Conference on Australasian Database - Volume 92, ADC '09, pp. 135–142. Australian Computer Society (2009)

48. Kabir, E., et al.: Microaggregation sorting framework for k-anonymity statistical disclosure control in cloud computing. IEEE Trans. Cloud Comput., 1–1 (2018)

49. Kabir, M., Wang, H.: Microdata protection method through microaggregation: A median-based approach. Inf. Secur. J. Global Perspect. **20**, 1–8 (2011)

50. Kabir, M., et al.: A novel statistical technique for intrusion detection systems. Futur. Gener. Comput. Syst. **79**, 303–318 (2018)

51. Kabir, M., Wang, H., Bertino, E.: A conditional purpose-based access control model with dynamic roles. Expert Syst. Appl. **38**(3), 1482–1489 (2011)

52. Kabir, M., Wang, H., Bertino, E.: A conditional role-involved purpose-based access control model. J. Org. Comput. E. Commerce **21**(01), 71–91 (2011)

53. Kabir, M., Wang, H., Bertino, E.: Efficient systematic clustering method for k-anonymization. Acta Informatica **48**(1), 51–66 (2011)
54. Ketchpel, S.P., Garcia-Molina, H.: Making trust explicit in distributed commerce transactions. In: IEEE Proceedings of the 16th ICDCS, pp. 270–281 (1996)
55. Khalil, F., Li, J., Wang, H.: Integrating recommendation models for improved web page prediction accuracy. In: Proceedings of the Thirty-first Australasian Conference on Computer Science - Volume 74, ACSC '08, pp. 91–100. Australian Computer Society, Inc., Darlinghurst, Australia (2008)
56. Klasnja, P., et al.: Exploring privacy concerns about personal sensing. In: Pervasive Computing, pp. 176–183. Springer, Berlin, Heidelberg (2009)
57. Klusch, M.: Intelligent Information Agents: Agent-Based Information Discovery and Management on the Internet. Springer (1998)
58. Li, M., Wang, H.: Abdm: An extended flexible delegation model in rbac. In: 2008 8th IEEE International Conference on Computer and Information Technology, pp. 390–395 (July 2008)
59. Li, M., et al.: Advanced permission-role relationship in role-based access control. In: Information Security and Privacy, pp. 391–403. Springer, Berlin, Heidelberg (2008)
60. Li, M., et al.: Optimal privacy-aware path in hippocratic databases. In: Database Systems for Advanced Applications, pp. 441–455. Springer, Berlin, Heidelberg (2009)
61. Li, M., Wang, H., Plank, A.: Privacy-aware access control with generalization boundaries. In: Proceedings of the Thirty-Second Australasian Conference on Computer Science - Volume 91, ACSC '09, pp. 105–112. Australian Computer Society, Inc., Darlinghurst, Australia (2009)
62. Loudon, D., Della, B.: Consumer Behavior: Concepts and Applications Fourth Edition. McGraw-Hill, Inc. (1993)
63. Lynn, B., Xun, Y.: Off-line digital cash schemes providing untraceability, anonymity and change. Electron. Commer. Res. (2018)
64. Maesa, D., Mori, P., Ricci, L.: Blockchain based access control. In: 17th IFIP International Conference on Distributed Applications and Interoperable Systems (DAIS), pp. 206–220 (2017)
65. Marvin, B.: Blockchain: The Invisible Technology That's Changing the World. PCMAG Australia. ZiffDavis, LLC., (30 August 2017)
66. Neubert, R., et al.: Virtual enterprises – challenges from a database persperctive. In: Proceedings of ADC'01. IEEE, GoldCoast, Australia (2001)
67. Ouaddah, A., Kalam, A., Ouahman, A.: Fairaccess: a new blockchain-based access control framework for the internet of things. Secur. Commun. Netw. **9**, 5943–5964 (2016)
68. Papazoglou, M., Tsalgatidou, A.: Special issue on information systems support for electronic commerce. Information Systems **24**(6), 425–427 (1999)
69. Peng, M., et al.: Pattern filtering attention for distant supervised relation extraction via online clustering. In: Web Information Systems Engineering – WISE 2019, pp. 310–325. Springer International Publishing, Cham (2019)
70. Pointcheval, D.: Self-scrambling anonymizers. In: Proceedings of Financial Cryptography. Springer, Anguilla, British West Indies (2000)
71. Pointcheval, D., Stern, J.: Security arguments for digital signatures and blind signatures. J. Cryptol. **13**(3), 361–396 (2000)
72. Popper, N.: A Venture Fund With Plenty of Virtual Capital, But No Capitalist. The New York Times (2016)
73. Poutanen, T., Hinton, H., Stumm, M.: Netcents: A lightweight protocol for secure micropayments. In: The 3rd USENIX Workshop on Electronic Commerce, Boston, Massachusetts, August, 1998
74. Rasool, R., et al.: Cyberpulse: A machine learning based link flooding attack mitigation system for software defined networks. IEEE Access **7**, 34885–34899 (2019)
75. Rasool, R., et al.: A novel json based regular expression language for pattern matching in the internet of things. J. Ambient Intell. Humaniz. Comput. **10**(4), 1463–1481 (2019)

76. Reutzel, B.: A Very Public Conflict Over Private Blockchains. PaymentsSource. SourceMedia, Inc., New York, NY (2015)
77. Rivest, R.T.: The MD5 message digest algorithm. Internet RFC 1321 (April 1992)
78. Rohm, A.W., Pernul, G.: COPS: A Model and Infrastructure for Secure and Fair Electronic Markets. In: Proc. 32nd Hawaii International Conference on System Sciences (HICSS-32). IEEE Computer Society Press, Hawaii (1999)
79. Sandhu, R.: Role activation hierarchies. In: Third ACM Workshop on Role Based Access Control, pp. 33–40. ACM Press (1998)
80. Schnorr, C.P.: Efficient signature generation by smart cards. J. Cryptol. **4**(3), 161–174 (1991)
81. Shen, Y., et al.: Microthings: A generic iot architecture for flexible data aggregation and scalable service cooperation. IEEE Commun. Mag. **55**(9), 86–93 (2017)
82. Shenoy, J., et al.: Jive: Spatially-constrained encryption key sharing using visible light communication. In: Proceedings of the 16th EAI International Conference on Mobile and Ubiquitous Systems: Computing, Networking and Services (2019)
83. Shu, J., et al.: Privacy-preserving task recommendation services for crowdsourcing. IEEE Trans. Serv. Comput. 1–1 (2018)
84. Spegel, N., Rogers, B., Buckley, R.: Negotiation Theory and Techniques. Skills Series. Butterworths (1998)
85. Sun, L., Wang, H.: A purpose based usage access control model. Int. J. Comput. Inf. Eng. **4**(01), 44–51 (2010)
86. Sun, L., Wang, H.: Access control and authorization for protecting disseminative information in e-learning workflow. Concurrency Comput. Pract. Exp. **23**, 2034–2042 (2011)
87. Sun, L., Wang, H.: A purpose-based access control in native xml databases. Concurrency Comput. Pract. Exp. **24**(10), 1154–1166 (2012)
88. Sun, L., et al.: Purpose based access control for privacy protection in e-healthcare services. JSW **7**, 2443–2449 (2012)
89. Sun, L., Li, Y., Wang, H.: M-service and its framework. In: 2005 Asia-Pacific Conference on Communications, pp. 837–841, Oct 2005
90. Sun, L., Wang, H., Yong, J.: Authorization algorithms for permission-role assignments. J. Univ. Comput. Sci. **15**, 1782–1798 (2009)
91. Sun, X., et al.: An efficient hash-based algorithm for minimal k-anonymity. In: Proceedings of the Thirty-first Australasian Conference on Computer Science - Volume 74, ACSC '08, pp. 101–107. Australian Computer Society, Inc., Darlinghurst, Australia (2008)
92. Sun, X., et al.: Enhanced p-sensitive k-anonymity models for privacy preserving data publishing. Trans. Data Privacy **1**(2), 53–66 (2008)
93. Sun, X., et al.: (p+, α)-sensitive k-anonymity: A new enhanced privacy protection model. In: 2008 8th IEEE International Conference on Computer and Information Technology, pp. 59–64 (2008)
94. Sun, X., et al.: Injecting purpose and trust into data anonymisation. Comput. Secur. **30**(07), 332–345 (2011)
95. Sun, X., et al.: Privacy-aware access control with trust management in web service. World Wide Web **14**(4), 407–430 (2011)
96. Sun, X., et al.: Publishing anonymous survey rating data. Data Min. Knowl. Disc. **23**(3), 379–406 (2011)
97. Sun, X., et al.: An approximate microaggregation approach for microdata protection. Expert Syst. Appl. **39**(2), 2211–2219 (2012)
98. Sun, X., et al.: Satisfying privacy requirements before data anonymization. Comput. J. **55**(4), 422–437 (2012)
99. Sun, X., Li, M., Wang, H.: A family of enhanced (l, α)-diversity models for privacy preserving data publishing. Future Gener. Comput. Syst. **27**(3), 348–356 (2011)
100. Sun, X., Sun, L., Wang, H.: Extended k-anonymity models against sensitive attribute disclosure. Comput. Commun. **34**(4), 526–535 (2011). Special issue: Building Secure Parallel and Distributed Networks and Systems

101. Sun, X., Wang, H., Li, J.: Priority driven k-anonymisation for privacy protection. In: Proceedings of the 7th Australasian Data Mining Conference, vol. 87, pp. 73–78, 2008
102. Sun, X., Wang, H., Li, J.: Microdata protection through approximate microaggregation. In: Proceedings of the Thirty-Second Australasian Conference on Computer Science - Volume 91, ACSC '09, pp. 161–168. Australian Computer Society, Inc. (2009)
103. Sun, X., Wang, H., Li, J.: Satisfying privacy requirements: One step before anonymization. In: Advances in Knowledge Discovery and Data Mining, pp. 181–188. Springer, Berlin, Heidelberg (2010)
104. Sun, X., Wang, H., Sun, L.: Extended k-anonymity models against attribute disclosure. In: 2009 Third International Conference on Network and System Security, pp. 130–136 (Oct 2009)
105. Timmers, P.: Global and local in electronic commerce. In: Proceedings of EC-Web, vol. 1875 of Lectures Notes in Computer Science. Springer, London (2000)
106. Vimalachandran, P., et al.: Preserving patient-centred controls in electronic health record systems: A reliance-based model implication. In: 2017 International Conference on Orange Technologies (ICOT), pp. 37–44 (Dec 2017)
107. Voorhees, E.: It's All About the Blockchain. Money and State (30 October 2015)
108. Wang, H., Duan, T.: A signature scheme for security of e-commerce. Comput. Eng. **25**, 79–80 (1999)
109. Wang, H., Li, Q.: Secure and efficient information sharing in multi-university e-learning environments. In: Advances in Web Based Learning – ICWL 2007, pp. 542–553. Springer, Berlin, Heidelberg (2008)
110. Wang, H., Sun, L.: Trust-involved access control in collaborative open social networks. In: 2010 Fourth International Conference on Network and System Security, pp. 239–246 (Sep. 2010)
111. Wang, H., Zhang, Y.: A protocol for untraceable electronic cash. In: Lu, H., Zhou, A. (eds.) Proceedings of the First International Conference on Web-Age Information Management, vol. 1846 of Lectures Notes in Computer Science, pp. 189–197. Springer, Shanghai, China (2000)
112. Wang, H., Zhang, Y.: Untraceable off-line electronic cash flow in e-commerce. In: Proceedings of the 24th Australian Computer Science Conference ACSC2001, pp. 191–198. IEEE Computer Society, Gold Coast, Australia (2001)
113. Wang, H., Cao, J., Kambayashi, Y.: Building a consumer anonymity scalable payment protocol for the internet purchases. In: 12th International Workshop on Research Issues on Data Engineering: Engineering E-Commerce/E-Business Systems, San Jose, USA (Feb. 25–26, 2002)
114. Wang, H., Cao, J., Ross, D.: Role-based delegation with negative authorization. In: Frontiers of WWW Research and Development - APWeb 2006, pp. 307–318. Springer, Berlin, Heidelberg (2006)
115. Wang, H., Cao, J., Zhang, Y.: A consumer anonymity scalable payment scheme with role based access control. In: 2nd International Conference on Web Information Systems Engineering (WISE01), pp. 53–62, Kyoto, Japan (December 2001)
116. Wang, H., Cao, J., Zhang, Y.: A flexible payment scheme and its role-based user-role assignment. In: Proceedings of the second International Workshop on Cooperative Internet Computing (CIC2002), pp. 58–68, Hong Kong, China (2002)
117. Wang, H., Cao, J., Zhang, Y.: A flexible payment scheme and its user-role assignment. In: Chan, A., et al. (eds.), Cooperative Internet Computing, pp. 107–128. Kluwer Academic Publisher (2002)
118. Wang, H., Cao, J., Zhang, Y.: Formal authorization allocation approaches for role-based access control based on relational algebra operations. In: 3nd International Conference on Web Information Systems Engineering (WISE02), pp. 301–312, Singapore (December 2002)
119. Wang, H., Cao, J., Zhang, Y.: Ticket-based service access scheme for mobile users. In: Proceedings of the Twenty-fifth Australasian Conference on Computer Science - Volume 4, ACSC '02, pp. 285–292. Australian Computer Society, Inc., Darlinghurst, Australia (2002)

120. Wang, H., Cao, J., Zhang, Y.: Ticket-based service access scheme for mobile users. In: Twenty-Fifth Australasian Computer Science Conference (ACSC2002), Monash University, Melbourne, Victoria, Australia (Jan. 28–Feb. 02, 2002)
121. Wang, H., Cao, J., Zhang, Y.: A flexible payment scheme and its permission-role assignment. In: Proceedings of the Twenty-Sixth Australasian Computer Science Conference (ACSC2003), pp. 189–198, Adelaide, Australia (2003)
122. Wang, H., Cao, J., Zhang, Y.: Formal authorization allocation approaches for permission-role assignments using relational algebra operations. In: Proceedings of the 14th Australian Database Conference ADC2003, Adelaide, Australia (2003)
123. Wang, H., Cao, J., Zhang, Y.: An electronic payment scheme and its RBAC management. Concurrent Eng. Res. Appl. **12**(3), 247–275 (2004)
124. Wang, H., Cao, J., Zhang, Y.: A flexible payment scheme and its role-based access control. IEEE Trans. Knowl. Data Eng. **17**(3), 425–436 (2005)
125. Wang, H., Cao, J., Zhang, Y.: Delegating revocations and authorizations in collaborative business environments. Inf. Syst. Front. **11**(3), 293 (2008)
126. Wang, H., et al.: Authorization algorithms for the mobility of user-role relationship. In: Proceedings of the Twenty-Eighth Australasian Conference on Computer Science - Volume 38, ACSC '05, pp. 69–77. Australian Computer Society, Inc. (2005)
127. Wang, H., et al.: A framework for role-based group deligation in distributed environments. In: Proceedings of the 29th Australasian Computer Science Conference, vol. 48, pp. 321–328 (2006)
128. Wang, H., et al.: Authorization approaches for advanced permission-role assignments. In: 2008 12th International Conference on Computer Supported Cooperative Work in Design, pp. 277–282 (2008)
129. Wang, H., et al.: Protecting outsourced data in cloud computing through access management. Concurrency Comput. Pract. Exp. **28**(3), 600–615 (2016)
130. Wang, H., et al.: Editorial: Special issue on security and privacy in network computing. World Wide Web (2019)
131. Wang, H., Sun, L., Bertino, E.: Building access control policy model for privacy preserving and testing policy conflicting problems. J. Comput. Syst. Sci. **80**(8), 1493–1503 (2014)
132. Wang, H., Sun, L., Varadharajan, V.: Purpose-based access control policies and conflicting analysis. In: Security and Privacy – Silver Linings in the Cloud, pp. 217–228. Springer, Berlin, Heidelberg (2010)
133. Wang, H., Zhang, Y., Cao, J.: Ubiquitous computing environments and its usage access control. In: Proceedings of the 1st International Conference on Scalable Information Systems, InfoScale '06. ACM, New York, NY, USA (2006)
134. Wang, H., Zhang, Y., Cao, J., Varadharajan, V.: Achieving secure and flexible m-services through tickets. IEEE Trans. Syst. Man Cybern. A Spec. Iissue M-Services, 697–708 (2003)
135. Wang, H., Zhang, Z., Taleb, T.: Editorial: Special issue on security and privacy of IoT. World Wide Web **21**(1), 1–6 (2018)
136. Wang, Y., et al.: Mtmr: Ensuring mapreduce computation integrity with merkle tree-based verifications. IEEE Trans. Big Data **4**(3), 418–431 (2018)
137. Wang, Z., Zhan, Z., Lin, Y., Yu, W., Wang, H., Kwong, S., Zhang, J.: Automatic niching differential evolution with contour prediction approach for multimodal optimization problems. IEEE Trans. Evol. Comput., 1–1 (2019)
138. Xiao, Y., Jia, Y., Liu, C., Cheng, X., Yu, J., Lv, W.: Edge computing security: State of the art and challenges. Proc. IEEE **107**(8), 1608–1631 (2019)
139. Yacobi, Y.: Efficient electronic money. In: Advances in Cryptology–Asiacrypt'94, vol. 917 of Lectures Notes in Computer Science, pp. 153–163. Springer (1995)
140. Yiannis, T.: Fair off-line cash made easy. In: Advances in Cryptology–Asiacrypt'98, vol. 1346 of Lectures Notes in Computer Science, pp. 240–252. Springer (1998)
141. Yiannis, T., Yung, M.: On the security of ElGamal-based encryption. In: International Workshop on Practice and Theory in Public Key Cryptography (PKC '98), vol. 1346 of Lectures Notes in Computer Science. Springer, Yokohama, Japan (1998)

142. Zhang, F., Wang, Y., Wang, H.: Gradient correlation: Are ensemble classifiers more robust against evasion attacks in practical settings? In: Web Information Systems Engineering – WISE 2018, pp. 96–110. Springer International Publishing, Cham (2018)

143. Zhang, J., et al.: Detecting anomalies from high-dimensional wireless network data streams: a case study. Soft Comput. **15**(6), 1195–1215 (2011)

144. Zhang, Y., Jia, X.: Transaction processing. Wiley Encyclopedia Electr. Electron. Eng. **22**, 298–311 (1999)

145. Zhang, Y., Gong, Y., Gao, Y., Wang, H., Zhang, J.: Parameter-free voronoi neighborhood for evolutionary multimodal optimization. IEEE Trans. Evol. Comput. 1–1 (2019)

146. Zhang, Y., Shen, Y., Wang, H., Zhang, Y., Jiang, X.: On secure wireless communications for service oriented computing. IEEE Trans. Serv. Comput. **11**(2), 318–328 (2018)

Index

© Springer Nature Switzerland AG 2020   299
H. Wang et al., *Access Control Management in Cloud Environments*,
https://doi.org/10.1007/978-3-030-31729-4

Printed in the United States
by Baker & Taylor Publisher Services